SPORTS, INC.

SPORTS, INC.

100 YEARS OF SPORTS BUSINESS

Event Evolution • Global Properties • Sponsorship • Franchise Relocation
Radio and Television • Stadium Issues • Endorsements

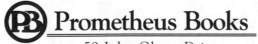

PHIL SCHAAF

Prometheus Books

59 John Glenn Drive
Amherst, New York 14228-2197

Published 2004 by Prometheus Books

Inquiries should be addressed to
Prometheus
59 John Glenn Drive
Amherst, New York 14228–2197
VOICE: 716–691–0133, ext. 207
FAX: 716–564–2711

08 07 06 05 04   5 4 3 2 1

Library of Congress Cataloging-in-Publication Data

Schaaf, Phil, 1964–
    Sports, Inc. : 100 years of sports business / by Phil Schaaf.
        p. cm.
    Includes bibliographical references and index.
    ISBN 1–59102–112–X (cloth : alk. paper)
    1. Sports—Economic aspects. 2. Sports—Marketing. I. Title.
GV716.S315 2003
338.4'7796—dc21

2003010191

Printed in the United States of America on acid-free paper

To Allison

CONTENTS

ACKNOWLEDGMENTS

Colton Dirksen, Joe Barrow Jr., Heather Bell, John Carthum, Andy Dolich, Tom Farrey, Mike Finn, Rob Grady, Jeff Harmet, Jennifer Hastings, Tracy Huber, Jeff Idelson, Julie Krisor, Sherrie Lee, Sieg Lindstom, Dave Lombard, Clay Luraschi, Art Morley, Marc Morley, Scot Mondore, Renaldo Nehemiah, Alice Newton, Rick Oleshak, Larry Pegg, Robert Reed, Tom Shepard, Mike Sherman, Damon Skyta, Patrick Spreng, Jennifer Stansbury, Pat Toomay, Robyn Trani, Kirsten Van Sickle, and David Young.

Dwight Bandak, Mike Barnes, Buddy Benz, Dennis Cardoso, Mary Carroll, Katja Dahl, Fernanda Erlanger, Brian Ford, Doreen Ford, Kaleigh Ford, Ann Larson, Jim Larson, Mark Longstaff, Paul Mangiantini, Mike O'Donnell, Hazel O'Keeffe, Pat O'Keeffe, Jason Pearson, Torri Randall, Chase Schaaf, Hank Schaaf, Janice Schaaf, Jean Schaaf, Joe Schaaf, Ray Schaaf, Reed Schaaf, RJ Schaaf, Sis Schaaf, Trey Schaaf, Amy St. Clair, Rob Simonds, Rob Ulveling, Jackie Yau, and Nick Zaharias.

Special thanks to the Prometheus staff for patience, guidance, and professionalism.

TW, TF, TA, MS, GWL, MB, PS, JW (PSU from above!)

INTRODUCTION

During the 1912 Summer Olympics in Stockholm, American Jim Thorpe easily won the Pentathlon and the Decathlon, a remarkable achievement in any era. Impressed, host King Gustav said to Thorpe, "You, sir, are the greatest athlete in the world!"

Thorpe's response?

"Thanks, King."[1]

Centuries before Thorpe, the first known sports champion was a Greek cook named Coroebus. In 776 B.C.E., he won the "Stade," a race of approximately two hundred yards held at the original Olympic site. While his winning time is not known today, Coroebus ran in front of thousands of spectators. Coroebus did not compete in Nike, Asics, or Adidas track spikes. In fact, he didn't wear anything at all. Fittingly, the first recorded sports champion ran naked, a true solo performance.

But even twenty-eight hundred years ago, society wanted more sporting events, so the Games expanded to meet the demand. By 708 B.C.E., two more foot races, wrestling, and the pentathlon, complemented the Stade. Twenty years later, boxing formally became an Olympic sport,* and in 680 B.C.E., the featured event was the newly added four-horse chariot race. Less than one hundred years after Coroebus dashed to glory, the Games had already undergone considerable progression, a metamorphosis. Some of the athletes were even clothed.

---

*Boxing actually dates back five thousand years. However, no champions or formal event names are known from that time. Stone carvings indicate that the sport originated in Sumeria (Iraq).

Those original Games honored Zeus, the supreme deity of the ancient Greek people. An Olympiad even meant the suspension of all war activities, a supremely difficult task to achieve. Rival nation states clearly took great pride in their champions and their devotion to Zeus. But by the fifth century B.C., Zeus's abstract appeal diminished, and the competition dissolved into the simple achievement of records. In 393 C.E., after staging over three hundred separate Olympiad, the Games were deemed entirely pagan and Emperor Theodosius outlawed them.

The Olympic Games lay dormant for 1,503 years before resuming again in Athens in 1896. It is here that the modern sports era establishes the foundation for the multibillion-dollar industry that we know today.

***

Sports, Inc. is a two-part book. Part 1, or "The First Phase of the Modern Era," is defined as the time between the resumption of the 1896 Athens Olympic Games and Peter Seitz's landmark 1975 ruling that granted free agency to baseball players Dave McNally and Andy Messersmith. Organized sporting events certainly existed prior to 1896—most notably baseball leagues—but the Athens Olympics galvanized disparate entities behind the concept of athletics and helped sketch the blueprint for large-scale sporting events. Sports marketing programs even helped defray the actual costs of staging those "resumption" Games.

The First Phase covers some of the compelling economic, industrial, technological, and sociological movements that contributed to the power, wealth, and popularity of sports entertainment. *Sports, Inc.* will not take a precise chronological approach to the industry's growth, but a contextual one that highlights the forces which gave it legitimacy and financial stability. Specifically, it will help identify how fan bases, reliable revenue streams, and beloved traditions got their start.

Part 1 will also establish that the popular sports leagues and events that we cherish today arose from ambitious people whose efforts laid the foundation for the sports industry. Furthermore, successful sports enterprises have a shared past of humble origins. Even something as grand as the National Football League (NFL) started small, found its niche, and mushroomed to sustainable profitability as external forces encouraged its success.

One progressive adhesive in the industry's evolution has been the lucrative integration of inventions such as radio, television, air travel, and later, the Internet. These developments helped sports evolve from a simple afternoon pastime to a booming enterprise that employs millions of people and generates billions of dollars in business. Most important, the mechanism of sponsorship began to evolve as companies like Anheuser-Busch, IBM, and Gillette discovered ways to leverage sporting events to promote their products and services successfully within the context of a competition's presentation.

Part 2 of *Sports, Inc.* covers the time from 1976 to today. It begins with the onset of free agency and the rise of the industry's revenue generation mechanisms. Part 2 will analyze the income sources of modern sports entertainment, including broadcasting, stadium revenues, and integrated sponsorship platforms. It will discuss how multinational companies such as Visa, FedEx, Clorox, and Nike invest millions into marketing rights created from sports properties and describe how they prosper from the association. Lastly, *Sports, Inc.* hopes to further the understanding of the sports industry through the logical discussion of the many applications of proven sports marketing techniques as it impacts the presentation of global sports entertainment.

NOTE

1. Gerry Brown, "Thorpe Speed," infoplease.com [online], www.infoplease.com/spot/mm_thorpe.html [December 3, 2002].

PART 1

FIRST PHASE OF THE MODERN SPORTS ERA

CHAPTER I

TIMELINE OF THE MODERN ERA

"I'm out to get the money, and I don't care who knows it. Furthermore, my advice to everybody is to get to the gate while the getting's good."[1]

—Harold "Red" Grange

In November 1925, Red Grange played his last college football game for the University of Illinois. He immediately signed with the Chicago Bears of the fledgling NFL and suited up before a record crowd of thirty-six thousand curious fans the next week. The Bears and their marquee player then barnstormed the nation, playing exhibitions wherever his legend would sell tickets. Grange was truly ahead of his time as he sold trinkets bearing his likeness, starred in a movie, and traveled with his agent, C. C. Pyle. In a career of firsts, it seems that Grange had the very first entourage! In 2003, high school basketball phenom LeBron James played a national schedule before thousands of fans in person and millions more on ESPN. He even drove a swank Hummer to school. When James used up his last bit of high school eligibility, he entered the NBA draft and was selected with the first pick by the Cleveland Cavaliers. And before he played one second of professional basketball, James signed a $90 million endorsement contract with Nike.

Red Grange did not play for a televised audience, drive a Hummer, fly first class to facilities, or sign an endorsement deal with an athletic shoe company, but he and James have a lot in common. Their exploits, though separated by decades, provided the kind of great sports entertainment that enthuses fans, attracts media, and stimulates economic activity. The only difference for James and other twenty-first-century athletes is that many more millions, and sometimes billions, of both fans and dollars, are involved.

But jumping from Red Grange to LeBron James requires some review of the events and eras that impacted their respective careers. In short, to understand the financial dimensions of the sports industry today, one needs to go back and look at some of the forces that developed its past.

1896–1915

The early foundation of the modern sports industry began with the reinstatement of the Olympic Games as a recognized international event. A wealthy, aristocratic Frenchman, Pierre de Coubertin, had sublime intentions for the Games. He felt that the individual, as a world citizen, needed to better develop himself in order to be a responsible contributor to any enduring Republic. Having witnessed tumultuous times in his own country, Coubertin felt that athletics, not politics, offered the common man his best hope. He tirelessly pushed this premise and succeeded in bringing the modern Games back to Athens in 1896. He did it without telephones, high profile public-relations assistants, or the Internet. His efforts were herculean in scope, and even greater in effect. The fact that the Games persist and thrive today is a testament to his vision.

The first "resumption" Games were not executed like the Games of the twenty-first century. Many athletes paid their own way. Some were simply tourists in Greece who represented their countries. The dominant theme was simple sportsmanship, and the event succeeded and endured due to the spectacle of competition and athletic valor. Coubertin's vision was quickly embraced as nations and athletes supported the concept of the Games.

In late-nineteenth-century America, professional baseball had begun to establish itself, and vied with boxing and horse racing in terms of recognition, spectacle, and revenues. College football had developed into a reliable attraction, but became characterized by violence and injuries.[3] After seventy-one high school and college players died between

1900 and 1905 (eighteen in 1905 alone), President Teddy Roosevelt intervened to standardize the game with rules. That organization formed would later become the NCAA.

The first African American champion, boxer Jack Johnson, was barely tolerated, and certainly not embraced by segregated America. On December 26, 1908, Johnson defeated Tommy Burns in Melbourne, Australia, to become the first black heavyweight champion. Though Johnson's victories would evoke controversy and even rioting, he was still the first black American champion. Ultimately harassed by the police and convicted of a crime,[4] Johnson paid the price for being a superior athlete in a prejudiced society.

In 1904 the Fédération Internationale de Football Association (FIFA) was founded in Paris. It would take several years for the World Cup tournament format to succeed, but FIFA persisted through the will of the Europeans committed to international sport. In the United States, football as we now know it was treated with ambivalence in the early days of the twentieth century. It would take decades for it to capture the imagination of Americans.

Sponsorship was nothing more than limited advertising at facilities, and advertising in newspapers. The only form of media was the newspaper. In those days, the athletes needed the press more than the press needed them, because written accounts were the only ways in which teams and athletes could spread word of the compelling action. Sports stories took a backseat to international events like the sinking of *Titanic* (1912) and the beginning of World War I (1914), but they began to find a niche.

Leagues had no financial clout with bankers and there were no outside subsidies like the broadcast contracts of today. Events depended solely on attendance and limited concession revenues. The trappings were modest and the pay was poor, but it was a start.

Some notable facts: The Yankees averaged over three hundred thouosand fans per season in the years 1903–1915. And commemorative Olympic stamps were a fundraising mechanism for the Games. Baseball cards also became a staple, but were not enclosed with bubble gum, which had not been invented yet. Baseball cards got their start with tobacco (more on that later).

1916–1935

The first Golden Age of sports emerged after the conclusion of World War I, when America was looking for heroes in the boom years of the 1920s. The sports industry happily obliged as champions like Jack Dempsey, Walter Hagen, Bill Tilden, Johnny Weismuller, and Bobby Jones were deified for their individual exploits.

The storied history of the New York Yankees really began after the team purchased Babe Ruth from the Red Sox in 1919. There are two competing theories for the sale. The first version comes from writer Fred Lieb, who wrote what was supposed to be the first authoritative history of the Boston Red Sox in 1946. Lieb's version claims that Red Sox owner Harry Frazee needed the money in order to stage a Broadway play, *No, No Nanette*, which featured his girlfriend in the lead role.[5]

Lieb's account has led to the famous myth of the "Curse of the Bambino," which is said to haunt the Red Sox to this day. The "curse" implies that trading Ruth has hexed the franchise and keeps them from winning the World Series. The second account does not have the same sex appeal. It merely states that Frazee owed the prior Red Sox owner, Joe Lannin, money on his purchase of the club and Frazee sold Ruth to pay off the debt.[6] Regardless of the actual motivation, the decision to sell Ruth still haunts Red Sox fans to this day. Ruth became the most important athlete in the history of team sports (at that time), and the Yankees, in 1920, his first season there, became the first Major League Baseball team to attract over a million fans (1,289,422) in one season.

This era reflected the great optimism that immediately followed the end of the first World War. Jack Dempsey fought in the first million-dollar sporting event (a heavyweight title bout in New York vs. Georges Carpentier in 1921) and the first $2 million sporting event (a 1927 loss to Gene Tunney in Chicago). Boxing was so big that its own publication, *Ring Magazine*, debuted in 1922. Sportswriters were idol makers and savvy athletes courted the print media, the *only* source of public relations.

An American Olympian, Gertrude Ederle, became the first female to swim the English Channel in 1926. Mildred "Babe" Didrikson entered a track meet as a one-person team for the Employers Casuality Company of Dallas, Texas, in 1932, and won the meet! She later went on to win three Olympic medals in the 1932 Los Angeles Olympic Games.[7]

Professional football, hockey, and motor sports got their legitimate, focused starts and began to produce personalities like Ernie Nevers (NFL), Busher Jackson (NHL), and Wilbur Shaw (motor racing). Athletes like this are barely remembered today in the dusty annals of their sports, but they played a critical role in developing fan bases and the modern structure of competitive team sports.

African Americans still lived behind the intractable wall of segregation, so high-profile professional sports were primarily played by white people and watched by white people.[8] The first baseball game aired on radio in 1921, but it wasn't until 1935 that a team, the Chicago Cubs, broadcasted all of its games. Teams actually prohibited radio broadcasts of games until the mid 1930s, meaning that newspapers and sportswriters still maintained a powerful hold over the development of sports celebrities and basic promotion of the industry.

More notable facts: Ruth also got the first exclusive media endorsement deal in sports when he was paid five dollars to describe each home run he hit in a written exclusive to United Press International. In 1920, the American Professional Football Association began. It would become the NFL in 1922. Yankee Stadium opened in 1923 The 1932 L.A. Olympics were the first Games to have an Olympic Village and to play the national anthems for the gold medalists during the respective medal ceremonies. In 1933, baseball cards and bubble gum discovered one another.

1936–1957

This was the most important twenty-year interval in the business of sports. It saw developments that changed the financial and social architecture of the industry. Undefeated heavyweight Joe Louis lost to German Max Schmeling in 1936, only to avenge his loss in a thrilling, one-round fight at Yankee Stadium two years later. Occurring at the height of American anxiety over German nationalism, Louis struck an everlasting blow for both American pride and African Americans in less than two minutes of actual boxing.

The 1936 Olympics also served as the international coming-out party for the despotic Adolph Hitler. Hosting both the Summer and Winter Games, Germany blatantly leveraged the Games as a political statement. Hitler's choreographed pageantry stunned the world with both its powerful display and dangerous message.

The times validated sports as a sociological metaphor for fans, and that only increased the stakes for competitors as varied as Sachel Paige, Joe DiMaggio, and Byron Nelson.

In 1938, as America struggled to emerge from the economic doldrums of the Great Depression, an overlooked horse named Seabiscuit captured the nation's fancy and became the story of the year. This was no small feat, given that the vast majority of the nation lived much closer to the media capitol, New York, than San Francisco, where Seabiscuit was based.

The mass media emerged as well. Not only did the business of radio fully embrace the sports industry; the sports industry embraced it back. It presaged the advent of television in the late 1940s and early 1950s, when sponsorship started to move into the national broadcasting of sporting events. In 1946, in a formula that would ultimately get a lot of use, NBC and Gillette presented Joe Louis versus Billy Conn from Yankee Stadium. It was considered a huge success; 150,000 viewers watched from an estimated 5,000 TV sets. It was the first time many had ever seen a TV, much less an event on TV. The first edition of *Sports Illustrated*, the most successful nationally focused weekly sports magazine,[9] hit the newsstands on August 16, 1954.

The end of the World War II gave enterprising entrepreneurs the idea that GIs coming home might mean that new sports leagues could start up, since the supply of both fans and players would increase. The All-America Football Conference (AAFC) established teams in New York, California, Florida, and Missouri, and signed a huge charter airline deal with United Airlines to facilitate the ambitious goals of competition between the teams while promoting the new concept of commercial air service. In 1949, Cleveland, San Francisco, and Baltimore joined in the NFL. The AAFC would serve as the template for the AFL in the 1960s.

The end of the war did bring people back to the ballparks as the exuberant GIs flocked to the baseball games in record numbers. The (baseball) New York Giants had their first season of one million in attendance in 1945. The Boston Red Sox, Cleveland Indians, Philadelphia Phillies, Washington Senators, and St. Louis Cardinals all crossed the one million mark in attendance for the first time in 1946. The Pittsburgh Pirates and Boston Braves followed suit in 1947. Prior to 1946, only four teams, the Yankees, Cubs, Dodgers, and Tigers, had ever sold over a million tickets in a given season. The fact that eight new teams realized the attendance milestone in a three-year span speaks to the cultural euphoria over baseball in post-war America.

Most significant, baseball, the national pastime, finally integrated in 1947. Branch Rickey, general manager of the Brooklyn Dodgers, signed Jackie Robinson, and black America finally had its second nationally recognized hero after Joe Louis. Bill Veeck, owner of the Cleveland Indians, quickly followed suit and signed Larry Doby. Now whites would finally pay to see a black man play the national sport.

Robinson's presence on the Dodgers, and Doby's on the Indians, meant that an African American would be on the radio and in the papers almost every day for six months of the year. The integration of baseball also signaled the beginning of the end of the Negro Leagues, since the best players were all vying for Major League Baseball opportunities, even if it meant toiling in the minor leagues. The Detroit Tigers sold for $5.5 million in 1956, proving that concepts like sports brand values and reliable revenue streams were acknowledged in ownership acquisitions, if not used as terms to describe the motivation in buying a team.

Lastly, the Brooklyn Dodgers and New York Giants moved to California after the 1957 season. The post-war economic boom and the integration of commercial air travel now opened up the entire nation to the possibility of professional sports. Other baseball teams, the Athletics and Browns, had also relocated just a few years earlier, but the two-team exodus from New York to California had repercussions still felt today. The Giants and Dodgers might have broken hearts in New York, but as pioneers in the West, they opened up a whole new market for the sports industry.

More notable facts: The Olympics were suspended during World War II. Women played professional baseball and started a golf tour. Rocky Marciano retired as heavyweight champion in 1956 with a perfect 49–0 record. His trainer, Charlie Goldman, said about Marciano, "He must be good. He always beats the other fellow." Althea Gibson, a black woman, integrated women's tennis in 1950. She endured heavy resistance from the tennis establishment, but later won Wimbledon and the U.S. Open in both 1957 and 1958.

1958–1975

Armed with technological advancements that integrated into society, the business of sports became as high profile as the actual outcome of the competitions. This era featured landmark legal cases in both baseball and football where players fought the systems that conscripted their services. NFL commissioner Pete Rozelle even got federal legislation passed (1961) to allow sports leagues to negotiate collectively on broadcast contracts. Some parts of the event supply side of the sports industry, namely, the NFL, figured out how to work with television to market the sport, instead of worrying about it taking away paying customers at the gate.

In terms of actual competition, milestones had great meaning, as events produced a historical context for achievement and performance. In 1958, Roger Bannister broke the magic four-minute-mile barrier (3:59.4), and it was significant because people had been trying to do it for sixty years. Both Roger Maris and Hank Aaron chased and caught two different Babe Ruth home run records, which had seemed an impossibility during the Babe's career.

Rights fees in both television and radio became reliable revenue streams for sports property owners. Another first, *Monday Night Football*, teed it up and kicked off for the first time in 1970. It would ultimately become the longest running prime-time show in the history of television. At the time, neither the NFL nor ABC had any premonition of its eventual success. It was entirely experimental.

Muhammad Ali fought the government, not other boxers, after his suspension from boxing for resisting the draft to the Vietnam War. He ultimately won his legal battle, but lost three years during the prime of his career. Jackie Robinson retired, and a young golfer named Arnold Palmer charged out of Latrobe, Pennsylvania, and made golf relevant to those who had never even played it. He even revived interest in the British Open, an event American players, sponsors, and fans had steadily ignored since Bobby Jones's dramatic overseas victories. Palmer also did something of great consequence off the course. He modernized sports marketing techniques with the help of the original superagent, Mark McCormack of I.M.G.

In 1968, professional tennis entered the "Open" era, allowing prize money for its major events. The first prize money pool at the 1968 U.S. Open in Forest Hills, New York, was $100,000 total for the field of 96 men and 63 women competing in singles and doubles that year. Today, the prize money pool for the more-than-600-person field is in excess of $16 million. In 1968, barely 97,000 people attended the event that approximately 640,000 saw in 2001. Times do change.

Joe Namath brought flair to the sports world and envy to his colleagues when he signed a contract for more than $427,000 out of college with the upstart AFL. Namath would later lead his team to victory in Super Bowl III and become a star, endorsing products as diverse as panty hose and shaving cream, and he even acted in films. Baltimore Colts tight end John Mackey became the first president of the NFL Players Association and successfully sued the league over the contractual rights of a team.

Julius Erving (Dr. J) brought a sense of style to sports by being acrobatic, not just taller and stronger. His style of play was as important as its quality, and both were unparalleled in his day. Billie Jean King defeated Bobby Riggs in a celebrated "Battle of the Sexes" tennis exhibition in the Houston Astrodome. The 1973 match was watched by 48 million people in the United States and 90 million worldwide. King easily dispatched Riggs and helped put women's sports on the front page of America's conscious for a brief but lasting moment. The Boston Marathon allowed its first official woman entrant in 1972, the same year that Title IX federally mandated that women's sports get funding.

Rival leagues in basketball (ABA), hockey (WHA), and football (AFL, WFL, and USFL) all tried to share in the success of the established sports industry. Their successes and failures still resonate today as some teams merged into their established competitive leagues and others are nothing more than answers to trivia questions posed by sports buffs. In

1975, the first African American (Frank Robinson) got a managerial position in baseball, fulfilling one of Jackie Robinson's final wishes. (Robinson died in 1972). The Super Bowl truly became "super" and George Steinbrenner was just getting ready to restore the Yankees to a dominant level of play.

More notable facts: Dodger Stadium is built and privately financed. There would be no more privately financed baseball parks until Pacific Bell Park in 2000. *Monday Night Football's* halftime highlights, and Howard Cosell, presage *SportsCenter*. Catfish Hunter was actually baseball's first free agent after the 1974 season, but not because of a courtroom victory over the Reserve Clause. Hunter, instead, correctly argued that the owner of his team, Charles O. Finley, had not honored a clause in his contract, thereby voiding it.

Spencer Haywood, in 1970, defeated the NBA in court, winning the right to play professionally without going to college, or having to wait for four years after high school. In 1975, Peter Seitz ruled that Dave McNally and Andy Messersmith would be free agents, finally cracking baseball's Reserve Clause system that unfairly restricted players' choices and movement. And something that will probably never be seen again, but should never be forgotten: Ethiopian Abebe Bikila won the gold medal for the marathon in both 1960 and 1964. He ran the 1960 Rome marathon in his bare feet!

1976–TODAY

It is in this time period (which will be covered extensively in part 2) that the sports industry truly profited from the extensive business layers it had built since the end of the nineteenth century. The games that used to be reported on by a solitary print reporter now had multiple print, radio, TV, and Internet newspeople covering the action in multiple languages and for multiple outlets. Game action went from being called "highlights" or "game action" to "content." Content comes via all of those traditional sources in newsprint, radio and TV and a few new ones: computer, cell phone, and pager!

The Olympics went from the tension of a U.S. boycott in Moscow

(1980) to the incredible commercialism of the Los Angeles Games—
boycotted by the Russians—under Peter Ueberroth's direction just four
years later. Team values soared from tens of millions to hundreds of millions of dollars and broadcasting rights fees went up concomitantly.
Mega-stars like Michael Jordan, Tiger Woods, and Wayne Gretzky
became more significant than the sports that gave them their fame. The
acronym ESPN begins to define sports culture.

The second football icon to follow Joe Namath and become an
actor/personality, O. J. Simpson, spiraled to infamy when he was accused
of double murder. Exposed as a wife beater, Simpson was ultimately
acquitted in the matter of *State of California* v. *Simpson*,[10] but ruined as a
public figure. His trial and the public's obsession with it showed the
merging interests of sports and celebrity. It also gave Americans an
opportunity to reflect, albeit briefly, upon the merits of deification.

Technology became even more important as the cable and com-
puting infrastructures made sports information more accessible to the
world. In the short history of the Internet, sports sites consistently rank
among the leaders in terms of traffic and commercial activity.

The actual competitive nature of the events has changed very little.
Baseball might have added a designated hitter and odd statistics called
"hold" and "defensive indifference," but Jason Giambi swings at the same
right field fence that Babe Ruth swung at. In football, they moved the hash-
marks in, but Marshall Faulk eludes defenders just like Red Grange did.

Joe Louis's second fight with Max Schmeling was the first international broadcast (radio) and it filled Yankee Stadium with fight fans. The
gate soared to over $1 million, no easy feat in the Depression. A full 50
percent of the advanced tickets were sold to people from different states,
a staggering figure in an era where orders were taken via mail. The bout
brought over $3 million of economic activity to the New York City area.
In a fight that lasted less than two minutes, it provided income and tax
receipts that carried some businesses for two months.

Sixty-four years later, in the midst of a minor economic malaise,
Mike Tyson and Lennox Lewis squared off in Tennessee in a highly anticipated heavyweight bout. The ring was still four corners, and the pugilists
each had two fists and one chin. Fans came from all over the country and
the fight was decided by a decisive knockout. The only differences were

the number of zeroes before the decimal point for all of the participants. It became the highest grossing Pay-Per-View event in the history of boxing, grossing $103 million on 1.8 million fight fans who paid an average of $57.22 for the cable hookup.[11] The economic impact in Memphis itself added up to $30 million.

That championship boxing grew from a $1 million event to a $100 million event demonstrates the enormous growth of sports' financial dimensions. This book will trace the development and implementation of the funding sources of the sports industry while revealing the marketing motivations of the companies that sponsor sports and subsidize its growth.

Whether it's Yale against Princeton at Palmer Stadium, or the Columbus Blue Jackets against the San Jose Sharks at the HP Pavilion, the focus on the action has direct and residual financial ramifications. Sports may be too commercialized for some people's tastes, but the financial dimensions perpetuate its growth.

Commercialization creates more sports programming, more sports content, more sports talk radio stations, and even more sports trinkets in your cereal boxes. This book will show how the confluence of innovation, consumer marketing, and simple demand has built a multibillion-dollar industry that continues to expand into every corner of the world.

NOTES

1. Benjamin Rader, Sports Trivia [online], www.sports-trivia.net/red-grange.html [September 15, 2003].

2. James, from Ohio, played in Los Angles, California, and Greensboro, North Carolina, among other places.

3. Author Andrew Zimbalist reports in *Unpaid Professionals: Commercialism and Conflict in Big-time College Sports* (Princeton: Princeton University Press, 2001) that as early as the 1880s, the Yale-Princeton football game was attracting crowds of forty thousand fans and $25,000 in gate receipts.

4. Johnson was convicted of violating the Mann Act in 1913. The Mann Act banned the transportation of women across state lines for immoral purposes. Once convicted, Johnson tried to appeal his sentence, and ultimately fled the country.

5. Noted in the text on Fred Lieb.

6. Glenn Stout and Richard Johnson, *Red Sox Century* (New York: Houghton Mifflin, 2000).

7. A talented basketball player, Didrikson was hired by the Employers Casualty Company of Dallas in 1930 to lead the company's semiprofessional women's basketball team, the Golden Cyclones. After the Olympics, she went back to the Cyclones but the Amateur Athletic Union disqualified her because her name was used in an automobile advertisement.

8. The Negro Leagues (baseball) had a very passionate following, but the heavy hand of segregation impinged on the integration of sports. The city of Pittsburgh even built a separate ballpark for Negro League baseball.

9. *The Sporting News* was considered the backbone of baseball, but it was more of a newsprint publication than a magazine. *Ring Magazine* was specific to boxing, while *SI* pandemic was in orientation.

10. Simpson would lose the civil trial two years later.

11. "Sports Business Timeline (2002)," *SBJ* (January 12, 2003): 17.

CHAPTER 2

VISIONARIES SHAPE THE INDUSTRY

I've tried not to exaggerate the glory of athletes. I'd rather, if I could, preserve a sense of proportion, to write about them as excellent ball players, first-rate players. But I'm sure I have contributed to false values.

—Red Smith

R ed Smith forged a famous career as one of the earliest of the influ-ential sports writers. He both wrote about legends and he created them. Today, athletes do not need a reporter to make them famous. The industry guarantees them, and the events that make them famous, daily coverage and exposure.

If you open up the modern sports section of a newspaper, you will find a calendar of events depicting the sports offerings of the day and where you can watch, listen, or find the action. You will see local, national, and, where appropriate, global events posted. You can get the same information on the Internet or via sports-specific radio and televi-sion stations. Essentially, the collision of mass media and the sports entertainment industry filters over many layers of the fan's life, so it can then be scheduled into his or her chosen activities.

Athletes, teams, and the games they play have attained a permanent position in the background of our everyday lives. Frequently, when the significance of the action or the moment dictates, the events come to the forefront of our society.

But it wasn't always this way. The very first modern sporting events of the early twentieth century were more of a curiosity than part of the cultural fabric. In those days, organized sporting events were either

extremely exclusive, or simply small of scale. Baseball, the national pastime, was only played in a handful of states and before small crowds. Professional football, by far the most popular sport in America today, was
dwarfed by college football in its first thirty years of existence. In fact, the
NFL found its original following in small industrial towns like Canton,
Ohio, and Decatur, Illinois, before migrating to larger, more industrial-
ized cities.

Basketball? The first real organized teams were named after tire companies and quickly forgotten. Golf and tennis both had loyal followings,
but they were really small-scale attractions with narrowly defined niches of
fans. Auto racing might have been the most successful integrated business
enterprise, because the auto manufacturers had a tangible product to bring
to market that the event showcased. Henry Ford, Ferdinand Porsche, and
their contemporaries all furthered their manufacturing and distribution
aims through the spectacle of racing. The first American car race took
place in 1895. Six cars raced from Chicago to Evanston, Illinois, and back
in the *Chicago Times-Herald* race. Only two cars finished and the winning
time for the fifty-four-mile distance was nine hours. Proving that sporting
events and advertising go together, 1895 was also the same year that the
first automobile advertisement appeared, in *The Horseless Carriage*.

Events did not have the structure that we associate with them today.
Exhibitions and barnstorming happened in conjunction with fairs and
festivals. Promotional outlets were newspapers, town squares, and word
of mouth. Companies and promoters had no fixed-position advertising
opportunities on network or cable television. Advertising agencies did
not assist brand managers and marketing strategists to leverage sports-
promotion vehicles. Populations were not conditioned to expect football
on Sundays, wrestling on cable, and baseball on the radio.

The most glamorous sports in the early twentieth century were
boxing and horse racing. They attracted the most money and, perhaps
more important, the most hype. If Babe Ruth hadn't started hitting base-
balls over fences in bunches, it might have delayed baseball's ascension
as the dominant American sport of the twentieth century. And Ruth's
exploits and baseball's rise in popularity were helped by geography, too.
Had Ruth played in Cincinnati, as opposed to New York, he might not
have gotten the same attention he garnered in Gotham.

In Babe Ruth's day, there was no *Baseball Tonight* with Karl Ravech, Peter Gammons, and the rest of the capable ESPN crew. Babe Ruth made his legend happen with the writers of his day and an enterprising agent named Christy Walsh, who nurtured the press.

The sports industry grew slowly and deliberately as the layers of media, sponsorship, and commercial enterprise grew from the actual games and events. As time went on, and a degree of routine and permanence became attached to the events, the sports industry developed the infrastructure that would become the multibillion-dollar platform of today.

DEVELOPING NECESSARY INFRASTRUCTURE

The global sports industry started in a very simple fashion, without traditions, revenue streams, or a dedicated place in our culture. As the infrastructure of communication, transportation, and commerce nurtured its growth, its business scope expanded.

The advent of integrated rail travel made intra-city competition possible. As soon as air travel became reasonable, new markets opened up for sports franchises in the western and southern portions of America. The invention and application of the radio and television industries also impacted the way sporting events were presented and merchandised.

The main revenue streams for the Yankees in Babe Ruth's hey-day were simply tickets and concessions. Today the primary sources are tickets, national television contracts, local television contracts, cable television packages, radio rights, premium seating options, concessions, parking, licensing revenue, team sponsorships, global marketing agreements, and online revenue. The team has intricate contracts with companies, partners, broadcasters, publishers, and licensees on both a regional and national level. They even have partnerships with foreign sports franchises like Manchester United and the Yomiuri Giants to assist in "global branding" matters.

The business of the Yankees has grown tremendously in the last eighty years, but the game that is played in Yankee Stadium has not really changed that much. The dimensions of the park and the rules that govern the competition are essentially the same today as they were for the Yankee legends like Ruth, Gehrig, Mantle, and Berra. As soon as Derek Jeter, Bernie Williams, and Jason Giambi step off the field, however, everything is different.

In the early days of professional sports, the games and athletes had to stimulate demand for their performance. The test of their marketing muscle always came on game day or the day of the match. The only way to make more money was to get more fans to your event. Today, the sports industry enjoys stable fan demand as it looks to new lands for new legions of fans.

Today, since teams are essentially public goods in terms of civic stature, but very private commodities when it comes to revenue division, they enjoy a unique way of doing business. How else could the Los Angeles Rams leave southern California and the nation's second-largest media market (15.8 million people), for St. Louis, the eighteenth-largest media market (12.6 million people) and make more money? They did it by making a better deal for the team in their new city.

Football fans who watched Red Grange score four touchdowns in twelve minutes against the University of Michigan had to see it in person or read about it in the newspapers, via the few, select writers who covered the sport. Today, Ricky Williams's fans can get information on him and his brethren via national newspapers, regional newspapers, football specific publications, TV, radio, or the Internet. Williams's high public profile is built on the legacy and foundation of his predecessors. More tellingly, the contributions that Williams's makes to his team's value, both in terms of wins and financial value, build the brand of the Dolphins, the NFL, and its promotional partners.

The key to understanding the sports landscape of today rests in acknowledging the limited resources of the first pioneers, who charged money for tickets, sold soda, hired the athlete performers, and sold the first sponsorships. Imagine the guts it took to knock on a company's door and ask the boss for sponsorship money when sponsorship had scarcely been invented.

The pieces slowly gathered around the simple concept of a captive audience and a continuous storyline of athletes competing and aspiring to be champions. That strong relationship between the excitement of the action and the curiosity of the fan remains the heartbeat of sports entertainment.

A MATCH MADE IN HEAVEN

What the sports industry needed was a customer base, and a big one. So promoters, owners, and operators of sporting events courted the press. Before *SportsCenter* was on the air six times a day and everyone bookmarked sports information sites on their computers, people relied on word of mouth and tales of greatness extolled by the capable, if not entirely factual, sportswriter.

In fact, in the early days of boxing, it was a known aspect of handling a fighter to get key members of the press to report favorably on the pugilist. Boxers, and their agents, needed a big gate to have a decent payday. They needed hype to sell tickets. So legends of boxers like Jack Dempsey and Gene Tunney grew as tales of their exploits found their way to the eyes and ears of the common man through newsprint.

The news media learned early that the common man might be more interested in affairs of sport than affairs of the state. On July 1, 1921, the U.S. Senate passed a peace resolution with Germany. This was big news with global implications. But the biggest headline in the *New York Tribune* that day involved heavyweight boxing champ, Jack Dempsey: "Dempsey and Georges (Carpentier) Fit for Battle Today. Gate nears $1,500,000."[1]

Dempsey was the first boxer to court the press, and it paid off, literally. His first championship bout netted him $27,500 in 1919, but his last in 1927 saw him split a purse of $2.6 million with Gene Tunney. Dempsey knew the press made his fortune. He once told famed sportswriter Roger Kahn: "I had great writers covering me. Ring Lardner. Grantland Rice. Heywood Broun. I was lucky they came along the same time I did."[2]

More important, people bought newspapers featuring stories on the athletes and their events. The press became such a distraction during the training of Seabiscuit, that the horse's trainer, Tom Smith, used a look-alike horse for the laborious task of accommodating the news demands!

The fans of the day were used to the exhibition nature, or spectacle, of sporting events. Players would barnstorm; fighters would train in different cities, and horses would have whistle stops where locals could come in and look at them. In many respects, the only organization in sports focused on choreographed media opportunities and the games themselves. The loosely based system was a network of writers and editors who needed to create stories that retained interest, so sports figures served a purpose.

The formula of sports and the newspaper industry served dual purposes globally. The Tour de France, in fact, originated out of a quest to increase a paper's circulation or market share. In 1903, *L'Auto's* editor Henri Desgrange devised the race through France as a publicity stunt. It worked, as the novel race instanced spiked *L'Auto's* circulation and it distanced itself from its main competitor, *Le Petit Journal*. *L'Auto*, today, is now *L'Equipe*, France's top sports newspaper.

Start Small . . . and Get to the Garlic Fries Later

Peanuts and sodas were not served on the Wright Brothers' first flight in Kitty Hawk, and old stadiums did not have luxury suites, elevators, and garlic fries at the concession stand. The staging of the events and the external components have grown from a simple and uncluttered past. More important, the sports marketing industry has allowed events to flourish and evolve in a deliberate fashion, resulting in everything from loge seats to those garlic fries and premium specialty beers.

As soon as television became a reliable industry, where the audience was verifiable through services like Nielsen Research, advertising could develop some structure where brands would pay for the privilege of commercial interruption. This took two to three decades for the infrastructure of the advertiser-broadcaster-advertising agency-entertainment property to blossom. Once this occurred, then the industry could reliably smooth out their broadcast advertising revenues and support year-round staff and maximum promotion for the events.

For instance, the resumption of the Olympic Games relied upon the issuance of coins and stamps in order to raise the necessary funds for subsidy, since ticket sales income would not be final until the events were being staged. Two local philatelists suggested issuing commemorative stamps, with a part of the proceeds going to finance the facilities. Coubertin and the Greek organizers needed money, so there was little debate. They made the stamps and the program carried the day.

The very first international sports licensing deal was a Greek

Olympic stamp and it helped, literally, build the foundation of the modern Games. Today, the sophisticated Olympic partnership Visa enjoys has its roots in that original Olympic stamp. What makes the story most remarkable is that the idea originated from a stamp collector and enthusiast, not a marketing maven or high priced consultancy. The industry was able to try experimental concepts with little risk and no ego. It must have been very refreshing. By contrast, the modern twenty-first-century Olympic marketing revenue breakdown is as follows:

Percentage	Source
50	Broadcast
40	Sponsorship
8	Ticket sales
2	Licensing

Source: International Olympic Committee

Clearly, the 90 percent portion represented by the sponsorship and broadcasting components is a departure from the 1896 model!

TRIAL AND ERROR

Try to imagine what it was like when cars had no headlights, no gas stations for refueling, and no established traffic rules to follow. Then imagine what it was like without defined roads, streetlights, or wary pedestrians. It is a scary thought.

Sports, like any other institution, needed to establish itself first and then branch out. The industry did not emerge overnight, or even as quickly as the computer became an office staple. Instead, it took shape over time as it integrated the entertainment demands of contemporary society, technological innovation, cultural twists, and most important, the pursuit of money.

For all of its successes, there are also failures and excesses. Does anyone really remember the WFL, or even the XFL? How about the USFL? How about sports-focused Internet companies like Athlete Direct, or Ultimatebid.com? These are failures from the last twenty-five years of the twentieth century; the first twenty-five years had too many failed sports enterprises to mention.

So much of what the sports fan takes for granted has simply evolved slowly over time. Dr. Naismith invented basketball with peach baskets and its first steps into the mainstream were awkward. As in football, the college hoops game caught the fans' attention first. With a built-in fan base and the infrastructure to support a team from an administrative end, the college game did not need multimillion, or billion-dollar broadcast deals. Maybe the best, and most important, aspect was that they did not have to pay the players. All of these factors allowed the sport to develop and maintain an enthusiastic fan base.

Metropolitan arena facilities, in the mid-twentieth century were used for cattle auctions, rodeos, boxing, circus events, and college basketball. Given the competition for available dates, the professional game had to migrate to smaller cities like Rochester, Syracuse, Ft. Wayne, and Minneapolis. Booking Madison Square Garden, Chicago Stadium, and the Boston Garden was difficult for the Basketball Association of America (the East Coast pro league) and the National Basketball League (its Midwestern rival).

Since crowds expected two college games at forty minutes apiece, promoters of the original pro game made one game forty-eight minutes in length to give the appearance of greater value to the fans. It took the 1951 City College of New York point-shaving scandal to rock college basketball and drive the college game out of the city centers, especially New York City and its arenas. This sent the game back to the campuses, which allowed professional basketball to set down roots, grow, and finally flourish.

Who remembers names like the Akron Firestone Non Skids? What about the Toledo Jim White Chevrolets? These cognomens all belonged to National Basketball League teams in the late 1940s. The Fort Wayne General Electrics paid their players five dollars per game.

Even though corporate subsidy was an early solution for these leagues, companies could not really do much from a sponsorship standpoint because the teams were not prestigious . . . yet. In fact, teams were assembled to boost corporate morale and provide a diversion to manufacturing needs. Companies did not get involved in order to market their products.

Companies had close affinities to the towns and felt compelled to sponsor these efforts, almost like Little League teams get support today. By paying for uniforms, equipment, and modest salaries, it was a type of community goodwill with a sporting touch. The club teams in basketball were doomed to fail in that form because tire companies wanted to manufacture and sell tires, not promote a basketball team. But it demonstrates that corporate interests and sports properties were destined to coexist.

Owning a team was a personal choice, not a civic good. You couldn't expect the city to help with construction expenses, easements, and practice facilities. Owning or working for a team meant thin margins. The sports industry did not have the revenue streams it now enjoys. No licensing, broadcast, luxury suites, or expansion stripends. These profitable layers had not yet been added to the business base.

CHARISMA MAKES A DIFFERENCE

The early phase of the sports industry was characterized by ambition and chutzpah. Select individuals saw a great future in sports events, and they pursued and perfected the early stages of commercial enterprise related to the industry.

In 1949 an enterprising lawyer turned resort operator, Alex Cushing, opened up the Squaw Valley resort, a remote outpost in the Lake Tahoe, California, area. Six years later, Cushing was in Paris, France, presenting his case to the IOC (International Olympic Committee) for his resort to host the 1960 Olympic Games. Cushing had beaten out Anchorage, Alaska and Reno, Nevada for the USOC's (United States Olympic Committee) nomination. The now-famous quote from IOC President Avery Brundage to Cushing was, "The USOC has obviously taken leave of their senses."[3] The resort was barely a couple of rope tows, a chair lift, and a small lodge at the time of the bid proposal. Cushing had a model of the Olympic Village that was too big to bring into the IOC building, so he had it displayed at the U.S. Embassy. He spent $30,000 on his bid proposal and focused his efforts on persuasion and presentation.[4] It worked. The IOC, by a 32–30 vote awarded the Games to Squaw Valley.

Cushing had single handedly convinced the most prestigious sports body to stage the Winter Games at his resort. Because of his model's size, he had to display it at a separate site necessitating a fifteen-minute walk for committee members, a time Cushing used wisely to lobby on Squaw's behalf. The combination of that valuable time alone, and Cushing's vision brought the Olympics to the remote resort.

In 1955, one man's charisma could pull off the task. When Cushing made his presentation, he did not have a Powerpoint presentation projecting against a screen on the wall. He did not have flow charts and graphs showing where sponsors could sell merchandise and schmooze clients. Instead, Cushing convinced the committee that a brand new mountain resort, featuring thirty feet of pristine snow, could be a spectacular and worthy Olympic venue. The committee, more keen on competition than sponsorship, broadcasters, and logistics, agreed.

At the time of his pitch, there was no broadcast contract in hand, no licensing deals already signed. When the 750 athletes from thirty-four countries showed up for the Games, Squaw Valley had grown from a 4,000-acre site that cost Cushing $400,000 to an international sports destination that would change the Olympics forever.

The 1960 Games were significant on many levels. They were the first that were televised, and the first aided by computer-generated results, compliments of IBM. The computer building was as much a destination site as many of the competitions. As Vice President Richard M. Nixon officially opened the Games, the Walt Disney Co. had organized a ceremony resulting in 2,000 doves being released into the sky.

The significance of the television broadcast, Disney choreography, and computer integration cannot be underestimated, for it was a demonstration of the way sports entertainment and technology would ever after be linked. Just as air travel allowed the Giants and Dodgers to move west for the 1958 season, IBM's computers meant that results and statistics were now available in a fast and formatted fashion. More important, Disney's pageantry and CBS's successful broadcast meant that the luge, ice skating, hockey, and skiing had commercial viability and the Olympic property grew in stature and value. CBS's bold experiment with the Olympics was not done casually. The network sent Walter Cronkite, its venerable reporting presence, to the Games. Cronkite's participation indicated that CBS didn't look at the event as merely an amusing sports spectacle. It was a reporting job on a world event, and Cronkite gave it instant legitimacy. CBS paid a paltry $50,000 to broadcast from Squaw.[5] The good old days, indeed!

At the outset of the Games, anxious discussion of the finances prompted Vice President Richard Nixon to say; "I have an attitude about Squaw Valley which some may not share. I've read that the Olympics here won't take in as much at the gate or return as much in TV fees as was expected. Those stressing this completely miss the Olympic spirit. We should feel it a privilege to be able to pay for the contribution we are making toward international goodwill. Some think goodwill is not a good substitute for policy, but in the long run we must realize you can't settle grave differences between nations without goodwill. It is absolutely essential to bring people together. The Olympics is but one event, but is a vitally important one, even if it lasts only 11 days."[6]

The 1960 Games drew over 240,000 spectators, 15,000 for the opening ceremonies and a record 47,000 on one day, a record for a winter sports program at the time. The Games cost the state of California $8,990,000 and returned a value of $10,604,000 in addition to the exposure and goodwill earned from the media scrutiny and reporting. The Organizing Committee reported that revenues from the ticket sales, TV, licensing, and all other sources topped out at $2.7 million.[7]

These Games, though, meant much more than attracting tourists and business. They merged the progressive elements of television, television personalities, political figures, and sponsor products into sports entertainment. The blend of corporate and public interests created a new model of event execution based on sports competition. The free market of consumer brands and broadcasters would now bid on the Olympics and other properties. Moreover, they would merchandise it according to the value it brought to their brand and bottom line.

The 1960 Winter Games were charmed in another way that would impact the sports industry. A young CBS executive got the assignment of a lifetime when he convinced his management to make a large production out of the Winter Games. The original plan was to do simple updates on newscasts, not emphasize the action and pageantry in prime-time coverage. CBS even tried to push the Olympics off onto ABC, but it rejected the concept. Ultimately, the young executive got the job. He also got his way and ended up influencing the presentation of sports to this day.

The ambitious executive decided to treat the Games like a political convention by setting up a main news desk as the anchor position of the broadcast. He hired "name" experts in certain fields to provide trenchant commentary on the action. During the previous summer he had the necessary cables imbedded for special angles, so that winter weather would not set back the production timeline. One hundred people spent parts of two years on the project to supply a total of eighteen hours of broadcast coverage to the nation. The effort was a smash hit, but it would be the visionary's last Olympics. After Squaw Valley, Tex Schramm went to work marketing the Dallas Cowboys and helped turn the franchise into America's Team, and professional football into the most popular sport in America.[8]

Schramm's groundbreaking ideas did not end when he left CBS. He started a fan publication, the *Dallas Cowboys Newsweekly*, and it quickly became a huge success. He created the famed Dallas Cowboy Cheerleaders and built the first network of radio stations to carry one team. By 1979, Cowboys games were broadcast on 225 stations in 19 different states. He also had the team's games broadcast in Spanish and that network grew to 16 stations in seven different states and Mexico.

Schramm was the point man for integrating IBM into the 1960 Games. Likewise, the Cowboys quickly became the first pro franchise to make use of computer data in analyzing its business. He worked behind the scenes on the merger with the AFL and helped introduce such accepted practices as the Wild Card playoff entry. He contributed many other ideas to the league, like putting a microphone on the referees and the thirty-second clock between plays.

Sports needed innovators like Alex Cushing and Tex Schramm. The industry had little definition, and certainly no marketing experts. It was fertile ground for anyone who had a little bit of vision and the gift of persuasion.

DECISIONS BASED UPON WHIMSY

Spring training is now a very big business. Arizona and Florida rake in millions of tourist dollars derived directly from the spring-training activities of Major League Baseball. Towns compete for the privilege of hosting a team and, in many ways, it is a microcosm of the larger big league sports drama that goes on today. Towns know that being the six-week host to a big league team can mean tens of millions of dollars for local merchants and the city's coffers.

The key is to offer dedicated facilities for the entire organization. If the town can come up with the land and the necessary fields, clubhouses, and training requirements, they might just have a deal. Today, towns make coordinated presentations and invest significant resources to attract teams. Often, areas will attempt to attract multiple teams so that there is enough competition in the local area to ensure that the teams are prepared for the regular season. In short, a lot of preparation and effort goes into the process.

The concept of attracting a big league team for civic benefit has been around for decades. The Tampa Bay Devil Rays play their spring training games at Al Lang Field in Tampa. Al Lang was an individual who saw that sports might be a good investment. Lang persuaded Branch Rickey to bring the St. Louis Browns into St. Petersburg to prepare for the season. In those days, St. Pete was a sleepy place in even its most crazed moments, but the townspeople loved baseball. Unfortunately for Lang, the team left after one year because the players complained loudly about the town's conservative night life.

But that did not deter Lang, who convinced the Phillies to take the Browns' place. Soon after, the Yankees and Red Sox arrived, making central Florida a major destination for spring training. Many teams have come to the Sunshine State since then, making tens of thousands of dollars in the 1920s and millions in the 1990s and beyond. But it all started with one guy, Al Lang, who fixated on bringing baseball to central Florida.

Spring training locations have long been a sports marketing proving ground. The Chicago Cubs, for example, have had many sites, and for different reasons.

Chicago Cubs Spring Training Sites Since 1900

Location	Years
Selma, AL	1900
Champaign, IL	1901–1902
Los Angeles, CA	1903–1904
Santa Monica, CA	1905
West Baden, IN	1906–1908
Shreveport, LA	1909
West Baden, IN	1910–1911
New Orleans, LA	1912
Tampa, FL	1913–1916
Pasadena, CA	1917–1920
Catalina Island, CA	1921–1941
French Lick, IN	1942–1945
Catalina Island, CA	1946–1947
Los Angeles, CA	1948–1949
Catalina Island, CA	1950–1951
Mesa, AZ	1952–1965
Long Beach, CA	1966
Scottsdale, AZ	1967–1978
Mesa, AZ	1979–present

Sources: mlb.com and baseball almanac.com

Originally, the decision was basic. The team had to prepare for the season under blue skies and on grassy, not snowy, fields. So training in Chicago was not viable. Also, it offered the opportunity to do small-scale barnstorming and promote the team. In the case of an eccentric owner like the Cubs' William Wrigley, it gave him a chance to market an obscure island. It would never happen in 2003, but in 1921, it all made sense.

William Wrigley originally sold soap door-to-door and gave away chewing gum as a premium incentive to buy the soap. After a while, Wrigley learned that his customers liked the chewing gum more than the soap and he dropped soap from his product list. By the time he perfected the chewing gum business, Wrigley was one of the richest people in America and he began to spend his money on hobbies, starting with the Cubs. Wrigley bought a stake in the team in 1916 and by 1921, owned it outright.

In 1919 he bought Santa Catalina Island, a beautiful island twenty-five miles off the coast of California. Wrigley had never even seen the place, but he paid $3 million for it. He immediately started building infrastructure like roads, plumbing, and telegraph lines. In 1921, he merged his two projects: the Cubs and Catalina. The team would train there for many years, in one of the more impractical arrangements in the history of sports. Wrigley, a benevolent, beloved owner, could watch the team from his mansion on Catalina and thousands came over to see the team train on the beautiful island.

The Cubs' West Coast presence had other effects besides bringing baseball to a once-deserted island. Ronald Reagan came with the team to California because he was announcing Cubs games. While there, he decided to do a screen test in nearby Los Angeles, his first foray into film.

Wrigley didn't want to inspire future politicians, he wanted to encourage tourism on Catalina, and having the team train there certainly attracted fans and curiosity seekers. In those days of rail and steamship travel, a baseball team on a desolate island almost made sense. Wrigley did not really seem to mind that it might mean the players did not have the best preparation for competition. The team was a piece of his total empire, not one that he needed to generate certain revenues, or have meet performance guidelines. Today, the only remnants of the Cubs on Catalina are found in photographs, but for more than twenty glorious years, the team made the island its spring training home.

SOMETIMES REACH EXCEEDS GRASP

Not everyone succeeds like Tex Schramm, William Wrigley, or even Al Lang. For each success story like Schramm, Wrigley, or Lang, there is a Loy Molumby. Molumby was a Montana oil man who wanted to bring the promise of sports and its riches to Shelby, Montana. Instead of earning riches and plaudits however, Shelby became the site of one of the worse sports-finance fiascos in a municipality's history.

Shelby had experienced some success in the oil business in the 1920s and the visible signs of prosperity sprang up around the town: banks, hotels, and a modern train station. America's economy boomed from coast to coast as industry, invention, and the pursuit of prosperity swept the nation. With growth, the need for spectacle and validation arose, something that sports entertainmen began to deliver for host cities.

Local Shelby businessmen, led by the star-crossed Molumby, wanted the town to host a championship prize-fight, with the idea that Shelby might one day become a boxing Mecca. The plan looked great on paper: build a first-class facility and then host the biggest name in the sport, Jack "The Manassa Mauler" Dempsey. Just like every football play drawn on a chalkboard looks like a touchdown, the Shelby plan seemed bullet-proof. At least it seemed that way to Molumby's and Shelby's cognoscenti.

Shelby didn't wade into boxing slowly, it went in hard and fast and right to the biggest name in the sport. Just like towns today pursue sports franchises to put themselves on the map, a boxing match featuring Jack Dempsey could have propelled Shelby to great heights in 1923. Shelby would be in the papers from coast to coast and on the tips of the tongues of legislators in Washington, D.C., or at least that's what the folks in charge of Shelby's sports foray thought.

Shelby dispatched Molumby to track down Dempsey's manager, Doc Kearns. Kearns, suspicious of the stranger, told Molumby that he would meet him in Chicago. Kearns promptly forgot about the appointment and left for New York. The persistent Molumby went to Chicago only to learn that Kearns had left for New York. Unfortunately he did not realize this was an omen.

The determined Molumby tracked Kearns down in New York City. Predictably, Kearns told Molumby that he would need big money to get the champ's attention. Molumby showed him $100,000 in cash and then committed the cardinal sin of event promotion. He handed the money over to Kearns, thereby giving all control over the event to Dempsey and Kearns. Had Molumby put a reasonable percentage in an escrow account, Dempsey's camp would have had the incentive to make sure the fight was a success. Instead, Molumby now had to put pressure on his group to ensure that Dempsey would show up.

Doc Kearns was not done dealing with Molumby once he got the $100,000. He insisted on a deal for $300,000, to be paid in three $100,000 installments prior to the fight. Furthermore, if the Shelby promoters did not make a required payment, then Dempsey had no obligation to return any portion of it, much less fight. The opponent, Tommy Gibbons, would get his share only once certain attendance and revenue milestones were met. Kearns knew the meaning of leverage and he wielded it to both Gibbons's and Shelby's disadvantage.

The fight was cursed from the beginning. In the 1920s, fights were famous for not actually happening, and having unscrupulous promoters run off with the money prior to the bout. Hence the press always investigated whether the fight was nothing more than an apocryphal fantasy. Unfortunately for Molumby, the word from the press was that the fight wouldn't happen.

In actuality, Dempsey wanted to fight. He hadn't fought an official fight, just several exhibitions, since his million-dollar bout versus Georges Carpentier two years previously. He wanted to shed the ring rust and earn some money. He just didn't particularly care about going to Montana to do it.

Unfortunately, the press kept reporting trouble with the fight's financing. So before even one ticket had been sold, the general attitude toward fight was skepticism, not anticipation. Had Dempsey's money been sitting in escrow, he and Kearns would have been on the pulpit, talking up Shelby, his tricky opponent, and how much he loved Montana. Instead, Dempsey was quietly training and Doc Kearns wasn't doing much to help the situation.

Dempsey and Kearns were skeptical of the Shelby braintrust. When it came time for the second installment of $100,000, the promoters had only sold $1,800 in tickets. They proposed giving sheep, or cattle, in lieu of cash, but Kearns only wanted the greenbacks.[9] So Molumby and the other Shelby promoters did the irresponsible thing: they borrowed the money from the people of Montana through the local banks, without telling the depositors.

By this time, ticket sales should have soared, but everything was falling apart. The railroad had decided that the reports were true and the fight wouldn't happen. They therefore cancelled the special trains that were part of the original plan to transport fight fans to Shelby. That meant that the only way to get there was via automobile, but most people in the 1920s didn't own a car. When people inquired about fight trains, the rail representatives could only say that they had no plans for any, further discouraging patronage.

Also complicating matters was the fact that the road to Shelby was difficult to navigate. The West in 1923 did not feature many amenities with respect to roadways, and scheduling an event in the middle of next to nowhere made the fight a tough sell and the logistics even tougher. At the time, large successful fights that attracted press and visitors were all staged in modern city centers, or near them. New York, Chicago, and Jersey City all had the necessities to accommodate a large flow of people. Shelby, Montana, did not.

Rumors and the lack of adequate preparation killed the potential gate. With skepticism running rampant, fans would not buy tickets in advance. Further complicating matters was that tickets were priced at $25 and $50. This was steep for a small outpost like Shelby. Potential patrons felt that the promoters would take their ticket money and run. It was a vicious circle of negativity, and it had heavy consequences.

Dempsey never got his third $100,000 payment. But seeing that Gibbons got nothing, Dempsey fared pretty well. Up to the very last minute, the bout was in question. But the combatants did fight, and Dempsey won the fight on a decision in front of barely 7,200 fans. The total gate was just over $80,000.[10] The angry mob that witnessed the bout paid an average of $11 per ticket, not the $25 to $50 that the promoters originally asked for. Doc Kearns, Dempsey's manager, had to bribe a station engineer with $500 to get him out of town via rail the night of the fight. Kearns knew the aftermath would not be pretty, but he could never have predicted what did happen.

The very next week, the Stanton Trust & Savings Bank went under. The following day, First State Bank of Shelby closed its doors. The day after that, First State Bank shuttered its doors.[11] In three days, three banks went out of business. They couldn't handle withdrawals on their accounts because the money had gone to pay Jack Dempsey. Since there was no F.D.I.C. in those days, every bank customer lost his or her entire savings. Just one month after the triple header of bank closures, the First

National Bank of Shelby followed suit. One fight and four closed banks added up to an epic disaster for Shelby and its citizenry.

Lessons of the Shelby Disaster

It should be noted that the disaster was not Jack Dempsey's fault. He took the fight based on his manager's negotiations and even went through with the bout when it was clear that his payment conditions were not going to be met. He could have done more to promote the fight and worked with the press to assuage the public's fears, but in Dempsey's defense, he took a pay cut from his last championship bout, was working in a foreign place, trained well outside of Shelby, and had no real forum for doing a massive PR campaign.

What really went wrong started with the Shelby promoters. Shelby was not a major city and did not have the infrastructure to accommodate the audience required for an event of this magnitude. They built the facility and felt that would suffice. They should have tried to assemble a fight card of lesser stakes to build up to the championship scale, to learn how to deal with the unexpected, the obvious transportation issues, and especially, to establish credibility with the fight community and the press who would cover the bout.

Shelby's representatives gave in to Kearns and the Dempsey camp way too early. That gave Kearns no incentive to promote the fight, put on the best public relations front, and work with the media to attract interest in the bout. The negotiations were finalized with no checks and balances in place. Kearns merely wanted to make sure that he got his money. He had no motivation to help the Shelby promoters generate interest in the bout, much less make money. The promoters never expected the negative press. They were not prepared to respond to the rumors and bad publicity that went with the skeptical reaction to the bout. They should have bought an inside reporter, but such are the oversights of novice promoters.

Shelby looked at Dempsey's last million-dollar fight against Carpentier in Jersey City, and wanted to emulate its success. But Montana was not the eastern seaboard, and Gibbons did not have the matinee idol charm of Carpentier. Furthermore, major sports promotion, even in

1923, required experience and savvy. With only one publicity outlet, the newspapers, they needed more experience and insider access to manage the medium. Molumby could have paid off key writers, but he did not think of it. The Shelby promoters felt that bringing in Dempsey would be enough. They thought the press corps would be impressed by their perspicacity. Sadly, the event only brought skeptical criticism, not praise for ingenuity.

Shelby had great intentions and almost all of the necessary ingredients to stage a successful event. In theory, it all seemed very simple: build a venue, schedule a glamor event, and count the money. Unfortunately, the reality for Loy Molumby and the rest of Shelby did not follow this script.

But Molumby shared a vision and a belief that sports could change the fortunes of his town. He just did not expect the direction the change took. Today, visitors to Shelby go to the Marias Museum of History and Art, where they can see a replica arena and artifacts from the bout.

NOTES

1. Roger Kahn, A *Flame of Pure Fire: Jack Dempsey and the Roaring Twenties* (New York: Harcourt, 1999), p. 236.

2. International Olympic Committee, "Marketing Revenue" [online], www.olympic.org/uk/organisation/facts/revenue/index_uk.asp [October 13, 2002].

3. Squaw Valley archives.

4. T. Gardner, *Ski Magazine*, October 2002.

5. Rudy Martzke, "NBC Keeps Rights for Olympic Broadcasts through 2012," *USA Today* [online], www.usatoday.com/sports/olympics/2003-06-06-nbc_x.htm [September 15, 2003].

6. Squaw Valley Archives

7. Ibid.

8. Schramm got his start in sports working for the L.A. Rams as a publicist. He left the Rams and went to work for CBS in 1957.

9. R. Kahn, *Flame of Pure Fire* (New York: Harcourt, 1999), p. 318.

10. Marias Museum of History and Art.

11. Ibid.

CHAPTER 3

LAYING A FOUNDATION
OWNERSHIP AND ADMINISTRATION

I never thought anything of racing, but the public refused to consider the automobile in any light other than as a fast toy. Therefore later we had to race. The industry was held back by this initial racing slant, for the attention of the makers was diverted to making fast rather than good cars . . . [but it] . . . brought advertising of the only kind that people cared to read.

—Henry Ford, 1902

Sports entertainment offers much more than simple amusement. From the first time that a promoter put up a ticket booth and a fence around a ball field, ring, or court, he has not only attempted to amuse and entertain, but to profit. As the industry has absorbed the inventions of modern man, from radio, commercial air travel, television, and luxury suites in domed, airconditioned stadiums, sports promoters and agents have always tied the notion of revenues and profits to the concept of a performance. When one looks at the current contracts signed by players, the staggering fees associated with team ownership, or even owning the rights to broadcast a team, the forces associated with those investments lie in sports' bedrock or foundation, in the early twentieth century.

Sporting events create jobs, subindustries, and billions in global wealth. Sports has proven to be the preferred medium for many demographics, as it consistently draws large audiences and top-dollar commitments from partners, investors, and sponsors. Perhaps most important, the industry has evolved to have the administrative layers necessary for streamlining its myriad business activities. It has reliable media and publicity outlets, distribution centers at events, and retail partners. Ticketing, legal, marketing, and event production staff work year round.

As sports has organized according to its business objectives, the infrastructure from an administrative side nurtures and perpetuates each existing revenue stream. In the early part of the twentieth century, if fans wanted to see Ty Cobb, they would have to go to the ballpark and see him with their own eyes. Maybe they could read about him in the newspaper, but daily deliveries across the entire American landscape weren't certainties. Word of mouth, and old-fashioned story telling, helped galvanize crowds before the media grew up around sports.

When the radio had built a sustainable industry, which was no small feat, then sports could travel great distances in real time. Regional personalities could become national stories in an instant. Exploits could enthrall the masses. Gerald Ford, later the thirty-eighth president of the United States, recalls being a Joe Louis fan as a youth. "We had listened to that fight [Schmeling-Louis, 1936] on the radio. It was shocking and it was sad because, by that time, I had gotten enthusiastic about this young man who was doing so well. It was beyond my comprehension that Schmeling could defeat him."[1]

Radio drew increased attention to all sports, expanding their market and increasing the demand for more sporting events and more sports heroes. It became an opportunity for property rights holders to manage and nurture.

The business layers of sports entertainment originated from the competition. Like a sapling grows branches, the game grew into an industry, and the growth was nurtured by owners and promoters.

THE FRONT OFFICE

In the old days, when the gate was the main revenue source, expenses were closely watched. The teams were run on tight margins. They didn't have weight rooms, strength and conditioning coaches, or team psychologists. They had players, coaches, and a trainer.

The situation was similar in the front office. Owners did not invest in corporate sales agents, sponsorship directors, media sales representatives, public relations staff, or even in a large ticket sales force. The finances of baseball did not warrant that type of staff, nor could they financially support it. Clubs were lean on the field and lean in the front office. The 1959 Chicago Cubs media guide shows the following front office directory for the team:

Philip K. Wrigley, club president
John Holland, vice president
Clarence Rowland, vice president
Charles J. Grimm, vice president
William Heyman, secretary-treasurer
Robert C. Lewis, traveling secretary
Gene Lawing, secretary of affiliated clubs
George Doyle, ticket manager
E. R. Saltwel, concessions manager
Stanton West, club statistician
Peter Marcantomo, grounds superintendent

The Cubs did not have positions in public relations, community relations, media services, director of new media, corporate liaison, or even business development. In 1959, the prevailing thought held that newspapers would tell fans when the games started, the radio would let people know if rain was expected, and the Cubs' front office trusted that fans could find the intersection of West Addison, Clark, and Waveland all on their own. At that time, newspaper and radio were the media for communicating with the team's fans, especially in a newspaper-friendly town like Chicago, where writers and columnists loomed as large as the athletes.

Eleven people listed on their executive masthead! Eleven! It boggles the mind to think that they could have put on a full season of entertaining, major league baseball, but they did. The relationship between management, fans, and players was very simple. Players were bound to the team via collusive and monopolistic legal precedents and the fans were game-to-game customers. Corporations operated very conservatively and advertised primarily in print or on radio via relationships managed by the broadcaster, not the club. There were fewer facets, outlets, or places to optimize the confluence of fan, sponsor, and property. The logistical requirements for games were met with fewer staff, and they did it quite well. No on who saw Ernie Banks play complained about download times for his statistics.

The Cubs' primary business was presenting the team to the public. Concessions offered a secondary revenue stream. Today, the job of concessions manager encompasses more responsibilities and even more products. In the early days at Wrigley Field, it was merely a matter of boiling the hot dogs and tapping the kegs.

If any schmoozing went on in the stands, it was between fans, because the Cubs didn't invite corporate clients to the game to demonstrate the ways Cubs Baseball could help them sell cars, soda, beer, typewriters, financial services, and other products and services of the day. The Cubs certainly were not crafting need-based marketing plans that allowed companies to leverage their logo with retail partners and use their mailing list for business-to-business purposes. These things all had to wait until the 1980s.

Two thousand miles west, the 1961 Los Angeles Dodgers media guide read like this:

E. J. Bavasi, executive vice president
L. Fresco Thompson, VP and director minor league operations
Richard B. Walsh, VP and director stadium operations
E. John Burns, assistant treasurer and comptroller
Joe Ziegler, executive assistant
Arthur E. Patterson, director of promotions and PR
Harold Parrott, director of ticket sales
Al Campanis, director of scouting
Danny Goodman, advertising director
William P. Scweppe, assistant director minor league operations
Robert Schenz, director of transportation
Lee Scott, traveling secretary
Allan Roth, statistician
George "Tick" Stainback, group ticket sales and Knothole Club

Perhaps the proximity of Hollywood encouraged the mild foray into an expanded front office (14 people!), but the team still did not emphasize corporate deal making or sponsorship subsidy. In fact, no team did, nor could they. At the time, the business base was not nearly as broad. The explosion of consumer products and choices had not taken off. Television was still a three-channel industry. The telecommunications industry consisted of one national company. No Snapple, bottled water, or sports beverages quenched anyone's thirst, much less sponsored any events. The high-tech industry was represented by radios, television sets, some power tools, and precious little else compared to today. No Dell, HP, Apple, Microsoft, Intel, or Gateway to approach about advertising with the team.

The entire delivery industry was also a federal agency called the U.S. Postal Service. The Cubs, Dodgers, Yankees, Tigers, and other teams of that time couldn't call on DHL, FedEx, UPS, AirBorne, or Emery. Simply put, the selling side of sports did not need to employ a staff to sell to companies that did not exist yet. By the time the Dodgers decided to leave Brooklyn, almost 70 percent of the team's revenue came from ticket sales, so the emphasis on the administrative side clearly had few obligations beyond getting people into the stands. It is not as if a team could have tried to sell personal seat licenses (PSLs), luxury suites, facility entitlement zones, and club seats. There would have been no takers.

Because the Dodgers relocated from Brooklyn, the new concept of commercial air travel brought an added layer to their administration. Hence the position, director of transportation. Mr. Robert Schenz had the task of getting the Dodgers to their necessary destinations. He did not benefit from large charter companies offering full service amenities, but as sports grew, the infrastructure from both an administrative and service side grew concomitantly around the game.

In those days, Coca-Cola, Anheuser-Busch, and the auto industry were focused on manufacturing, distribution, and marketing to their trade business and print media, not integrated sponsorships. If a company were to involve itself in a sports promotion, it would likely be with a broadcaster, not with the team itself. Sports was seen as separate to a company's business, not as a potential agent of the company's business. The Cubs, Reds, and other teams were in the business of entertaining fans and selling tickets to fans, not nurturing corporate clientele.

Ford and Chevrolet did not see sports entertainment as a way to sell cars. In many ways, the corporate advertising people were learning the nuances of their industry as well. The concepts of channel marketing and utilizing specialty agencies did not exist at this point. Teams had not yet figured out that their venues, trademarks, and mass appeal had great value to emerging brands.

One man who knew otherwise was Gussie Busch, the influential owner of the St. Louis Cardinals and the chairman of Anheuser-Busch. Busch, the proud brewer of Budweiser, used his personal relationships with other owners to get his beer sold at their stadiums. He knew that the Cardinals baseball team was the leading arrow in marketing Budweiser in more stadiums. He also knew that thirsty baseball fans drink beer when they're not at the ballpark, too. To Busch, Cardinals baseball marketed Budweiser to both trade customers and end-user consumers.

Busch did not have to negotiate for the "pouring rights" at each venue. He lobbied behind the scenes to get his product in front of the fans, and it was a much more informal arrangement than the complex and binding agreements that exist today.

Today, lawyers and marketing executives negotiate for weeks, months, or years over these deals. The early days of sports could not have supported the administrative layers that are now on teams' payrolls. These layers require that large amounts of business be cultivated, nurtured, and executed around sporting events.

Owners did not have the leeway to invest in manufacturing sweatshirts, caps, and big foam fingers. They relied upon fans to show up and watch the game. Even if they had a team of savvy, progressive corporate sales executives, the other side of the industry, the promotional buyers, simply weren't ready to listen to their slick sales pitches and leaf through their custom presentations of glossy photographs and tiered sponsorships. Those days were looming, though.

OLD-TIME MANAGEMENT

Buying a team in the early days of sports used to make for a fairly simple storyline in newsprint. There would be a paragraph of the man, whose reputation was probably already known. The writer would acknowledge his social standing and attribute a quote to him, saying something along the lines of, "ever since I was a little boy, I always wanted to own a baseball team."

Every now and then, a real maverick like Bill Veeck came into the mix, but normally it was someone who would give the Citizen Kane "Rosebud" speech publicly and then do everything in his powers to keep the players' negotiating power diminished and his profits secure.

Despite their tight-fisted ways, sports fans should look understandably on these pioneering owners. Their circumstances were difficult when teams only enjoyed one reliable revenue stream, ticket sales. Compounding that was the nagging paranoia that the entire system was truly corrupt and that the government might revoke the empowering Reserve Clause, which bound players to teams.

Reserve Clause in a Nutshell

Baseball's Reserve Clause is the historical reason baseball's labor supply was restricted from seeking competitive employment offers for the majority of the 1900s. The owners loved it, because it secured the valuable labor pool on their penurious terms.

In August 1913, the Federal League had existed as a minor league with intentions to challenge the establishment of Major League Baseball. To accomplish that goal, it raided the rosters of existing Major League players. In 1915 the Federal League even sued Major League Baseball, claiming restraint of trade. Illinois U.S. District Judge Landis (later baseball's first commissioner) said, "I am shocked because you call playing baseball labor."[2]

Landis ultimately encouraged a settlement between the two leagues, which transpired in November 1915. The pesky Baltimore franchise, the Terrapins, did not accept the terms. Instead, they filed an antitrust suit in 1916 and won. The victory was short-lived when that decision was later reversed in the District of Columbia. The ruling stated, among other things, "the fact that the owners produce baseball games as a source of profit . . . cannot change the character of the games. They are still sport, not trade."[3] Those words haunted players for a long time. It gave the existing major leagues an effective monopoly on baseball.

The ruling was upheld in the Supreme Court in 1922. The owners claimed that the clause gave them the option of renewing the player's contract for one year in perpetuity, tying the player to an organization for as long as the team wanted his services. On the open market, Babe Ruth's rights were sold to the Yankees for $125,000 in 1919, but he earned a salary that was less than 10 percent of his purchase price that very next year. If the Babe's rights were worth $125,000, then how could management pay him less than 10 percent of that figure? One simple answer: the Reserve Clause. Ruth and his colleagues were bound to the team, not potentially available to the highest bidder. In 1970 Curt Flood sued baseball over his rights as a player, protesting his trade to Philadelphia. And in 1972, fifty years after the first Supreme Court ruling, the decision was upheld yet again, thereby reinforcing the team's right to renew a player's contract on their terms and thus dictate his place of employment.

The Flood decision meant that collective bargaining was the only real solution for the players to effect change, so they went out on strike for almost two weeks in 1972 and have engaged in multiple work stoppages since then in order to gain and protect their basic freedoms.

Under the leadership of Marvin Miller, the Player's Association negotiated the right to salary arbitration. This milestone slowly turned the leverage over to the players, who finally turned back the perpetuity interpretation of the Reserve Clause via a ruling by independent arbitrator Peter Seitz. Seitz ruled that Dave McNally and Andy Messersmith, by not signing their 1975 contracts, had played out their option obligation. The Reserve Clause had finally been neutralized.

Old-Time Ownership

Most old-time owners liked the notoriety and high profile associated with baseball, though maintaining the safe distance of their patrician lives. The basic concept was fairly simple: hold down labor costs, quash competitors, and keep business matters a private affair.

But the owners knew they had a good product, and they succeeded for seventy years by treating their teams with a combination of whimsy and autocratic behavior that would never be accepted today. Looking back, one must consider that the owners were the negotiators for sport. They alone navigated the uncharted territory of broadcast contracts, broadcast implications, labor disputes, and the basic concepts of promotion and sponsorship.

And to the owners, it wasn't always a clear-cut, antiseptic analysis to build the prestige of the sport, or the brand of the team. In 1919, Harry Frazee needed money, so he sold Babe Ruth. After the 1946 season, Walter Briggs, owner of the Detroit Tigers, saw a photo of his star slugger, Hank Greenberg, wearing a Yankees jersey. So perturbed was he at the sight of his MVP in the arch-enemy's uniform, he sold Greenberg's contract to the lowly Pittsburgh Pirates of the National League. Briggs did not want to see a picture of his player in another team's uniform, especially one in the same league! As a matter of fact, the photo was ultimately traced to Greenberg's stint in the Army. He had put it on for an exhibition abroad, because it was the only one that would fit his 6'4" frame. His fate had been determined by simple pettiness, even after an exceptional career for the Tigers.

Briggs, though, had nothing on Charles Comiskey. Comiskey had been a player himself in the late nineteenth century, and had revolutionized play at first base. Prior to Comiskey, all first basemen played the position with one foot on the bag. He was the first to roam away from it while the pitcher wound up and threw to the plate, only returning to make the out or hold the runner on. But despite his playing past, Comiskey was not compassionate to labor once he became an owner. He underpaid his dominant team, the Chicago White Sox. In 1917, he promised the players a bonus for winning the World Series. When they won, the bonus came in the form of a case of cheap champagne. He paid 25 percent less than other teams in meal money for players on the road and he lowered salaries even when attendance went up!

Comiskey promised star pitcher Eddie Cicotte a $10,000 bonus if he won thirty games in a season. As Cicotte got close to the magical thirty-game goal, Comiskey had him benched for almost a month to keep him from earning the bonus.[4] Comiskey's miserly treatment ultimately ended up hitting him where it hurt the most, in the wallet, because his players were ripe for a bribe. Eight players went in on a fix of the 1919 World Series and were thrown out of baseball with lifetime bans by Commissioner Kenesaw Mountain Landis. Not only did the White Sox lose the World Series, Comiskey lost eight great players and his team sank in the standings. Comiskey, empowered by the Reserve Clause, felt that he could dictate all of the terms to the players, but they made it a very personal mission to fight back. All parties lost, especially White Sox fans.

Comiskey did, ultimately, do something for his unlucky employees. The players, it turned out, couldn't afford their legal fees. Comiskey quietly paid them. Maybe the old player did have a heart after all.

ONE TEAM'S EVOLUTION IN OWNERSHIP

Universally recognized as the premier franchise in North American team sports, the New York Yankees had humble beginnings. In 1903, two gentlemen named Frank Farrell and Bill Devery bought the defunct, original Baltimore Orioles team for $18,000 and moved it to New York City. Called the Highlanders, the team toiled for ten years at Hilltop Park, located in Manhattan at Broadway and 168th Street.[5] In 1913, they moved to the Polo Grounds (the Giants were their landlord) and were renamed the Yankees.

Farrell and Devery were financially squeezed, though, and had to sell the team. Not only did banks not loan money to operating baseball teams, the owners had no revenue-source partners like broadcasters, concession companies, or corporations buying expensive sponsorships. At the time, the notion was as far-fetched as space travel.

Farrell and Devery did enjoy significant asset appreciation, however, when they sold the club for $460,000 to Tillinghast Huston and Jacob Ruppert, a beer meister. Ruppert wanted to change the name of the team to "Knickerbockers" after his beer brand, but the proposed change brought about a major outcry from the fans and Ruppert relented.

On December 26, 1919, Ruppert and Huston consummated the deal for Babe Ruth. They were immediately rewarded when the team drew over 1.2 million fans to see the Babe and the rest of Miller Huggins's Yankees during Ruth's first season. In May of 1922, Ruppert bought out Huston for $1.5 million, and the next year Yankee Stadium opened.

In 1945, the Yankees were sold again. This time, Dan Topping, Del Webb, and Larry MacPhail bought the team from the estate of the late Col. Jacob Ruppert for $2.8 million. The troika didn't keep the team for perpetuity, but for profit. In 1964, the Yankees changed hands again when CBS bought 80 percent of the team for an eye popping $11.2 million. CBS later purchased the remaining 20 percent and became the sole owners before selling the team to a limited partnership headed by shipping magnate George Steinbrenner in 1973 for $10 million.

Today, the Yankees might be worth a billion dollars, which raises the question, "how could the marquee team in all of sports sell for so little in 1973?" When you dig a little bit deeper, things get even stranger. The Cleveland Indians sold for $10.3 million in 1972 and the San Diego Padres sold for $12 million in 1974. Did the open marketplace really value each baseball team so similarly? Was there no distinction over market size, ballpark leases, local media rights, much less tradition in these transactions? The San Diego Padres, a six-year-old franchise, with no record of success or tradition, sold for $2 million more in 1974 than the Yankees did one year prior. To think that a team with no history was valued higher than such a historically rich team in the nation's largest media market boggles the mind. Maybe George Steinbrenner is an even better negotiator than people think.

Ownership Was More Casual

The Baltimore Colts had actually been a failed franchise. Originally a member of the All America Football Conference, the team disbanded after the 1950 season. In 1953, the Colts received their second chance. NFL Commissioner Bert Bell wanted the city of Baltimore to show that they could support a team and asked that 15,000 season tickets be sold in a six-week period. The fans snatched up the ducats with two weeks to spare. And they were rewarded when the Colts became one of the best franchises in all of professional sports, winning the 1958, 1959, and 1968 NFL championships and then Super Bowl V. The team had a marching band and the fans formed booster clubs called the Colts Corral. Players became legends and the team defined the town.

And then in 1972, team owner Carroll Rosenbloom traded his franchise for the Los Angles Rams. The straight swap with Robert Irsay went unchallenged. It was hard to tell if Rosenbloom wanted out of Baltimore or into Los Angeles. Thirty years later, when the owner of the Montreal Expos became owner of the Florida Marlins and the Marlins owner became controlling partner of the BoSox, the motive was obvious: to upgrade their ownership profile by getting into better markets. Though the moves were personally motivated, they contrasted with the Rosenbloom-Irsay swap because they took place more in public than in private.

Ownership in the first era of the modern sports industry focused on the basics. There really weren't too many broad visionaries who saw billions in broadcasting, facility entitlement, and synergies with other teams, cable operators, and licensors. Nor was there anyone who wanted to change the closed way most operations were run.

But there was one unique guy who really did dare to be different.

BREAKING THE MOLD: BILL VEECK

Bill Veeck had a spark of genius; he loved baseball and entertaining fans and he made a career out of doing it differently than just about anyone else. Veeck put the ivy on the outfield walls at Wrigley, and placed names on the backs of players' uniforms. He invented the concept of fireworks after a home run and he even sent a midget to the plate.

The son of the president of the Chicago Cubs, Veeck truly grew up around Major League Baseball. His first job, in fact, was selling hot dogs and peanuts at Wrigley Field. Veeck also spoke candidly. He once said of Babe Ruth: "A man of gigantic appetites. He ate more, drank more, chased more girls . . . caught more too."[6]

Some Veeck Highlights

- He contracted the first African American, Larry Doby, to play in the American League.
- He set the all-time attendance record (at the time) of 2.6 million fans as owner of the Indians in 1948.
- He testified for Curt Flood in his case against Major League Baseball owners.
- He despised his fellow owners, once referring to them as the "forward-looking fossils who run the game."
- He once ran a promotion where the fans could determine the strategy on the field by holding up signs from the stands.

- He was a war veteran who ultimately lost part of his leg due to a wound.
- Veeck marched in civil rights demonstrations.

Veeck always wanted to make the game more progressive and more entertaining. He wanted to bring two-way radios into his ballpark to increase communication capacity, and he really did get a midget into a Major League Baseball game. In 1951, Veeck owned the St. Louis Browns, a disastrous squad that had trouble attracting fans. With a long, hot, losing summer ahead, Veeck knew he needed to get some help to promote the team and, being a progressive owner, he looked to his corporate partners.

As he said in his autobiography, *Veeck-as in Wreck*, "the best bet seemed to be to call upon the resources of our radio sponsors, Falstaff Brewery. For although Falstaff only broadcast our games locally, they had distributors and dealers all over the state."[7]

Veeck truly was a visionary. He saw, in his sponsors, resources to help promote his team, not just a revenue stream. He also knew the benefit of stretching the truth. Veeck knew that 1951 was the fiftieth anniversary of the American League. Veeck wanted to throw a birthday party for the American League and for the brewery. As Veeck noted, "Nobody at Falstaff's seemed to know exactly when their birthday was, but that was no great problem. If we couldn't prove it fell on the day we chose, neither could anyone prove that it didn't."[8]

The "birthday party" was to be held on August 19, 1951 during a double header with the lowly Detroit Tigers. Veeck promised the Falstaff executives that he would generate mass amounts of press that would capture all of baseball's attention. Veeck personally sold the concept to Falstaff and assured the brewery that he would deliver on his promise. At the time of his sales pitch, Veeck had no idea what he was going to do, but by the time he interviewed 3'7" Eddie Gaedel, Veeck knew that he had found his stunt. Veeck signed Gaedel to an official contract and wired the league on the Saturday night before the game so that no one would question the validity of the move since the office was not open on Sunday. He instructed his manager about making the substitution and gave him a copy of the official contract in case the umpire questioned the substitution.

Eighteen thousand fans were at the park that day, and there was a giveaway of a can of beer and a hot dog to make the occasion that much more festive. Between the games, Gaedel jumped out of the cake and the Falstaff brass thought that was Veeck's stunt. They had no idea of the planned substitution in the first inning of the second game.

Wearing number 1/8, Gaedel entered the game and took four pitches for a walk. Immediately substituted by a pinch runner, Gaedel's at bat would place him and Veeck in baseball immortality. Everyone in the stands howled. The umpire and other players shared in the laugh as well. When Gaedel walked off the field, he took his sweet time and savored his part in one of sports' most outrageous promotions.

Different Sport, Another Influential Owner

One football legend actually got his start in baseball. George S. Halas, who would later be known as "Papa Bear," had been a star outfielder in addition to playing wide receiver at the University of Illinois. And the New York Yankees took notice. Halas went to spring training and made the team in 1919, but he hurt his hip, was released, and went back to Illinois to pursue a traditional career. Halas then played on weekend semipro football teams and was recruited to work at A. E. Staley, a Decatur, Illinois, company, in 1920. At Staley, Halas had a regular job, played baseball, and organized the company's football program.

When he took the job, he negotiated that all football recruits would get jobs with the company and could practice, with pay, during company hours. Mr. Staley might have been the first CEO who loved sports, because he let young Halas dictate the terms. In 1920, recruiting football players by offering full-time jobs gave Halas a distinct advantage. To schedule games, Halas decided that pooling resources made sense. The previous year, a team in Ohio, the Canton Bulldogs, had tried in vain to get a league formalized. Halas felt that his Decatur team could help galvanize the league and the two teams spearheaded an eleven-team league. The Staleys shut out their first opponent, the Moline Tractors, and they were off to a 10–2–1 record in their first year.

Halas paid his guys well, maybe too well. The company took a $14,000 net loss on the venture. For the 1921 season, the team moved to Chicago and still went by the name Chicago Staley's, when the shrewd

Halas got Mr. Staley to pay him $5,000 to keep the Staley name. The next year, the team became the Bears and in 1925, they signed collegiate sensation Red Grange to a $100,000 contract right after his season at the University of Illinois ended. Together, Grange the whippet halfback, and Halas, the baseball player turned football maverick, went on the first successful football barnstorming tour of the United States.

Halas was not a promoter by trade, but Grange's manager, C. C. Pyle, certainly was. The tour gathered momentum and set attendance records whenever they played. The Bears, hyped by the mystique of Grange, played nineteen games in less than ten weeks. The first game that Grange played with the Bears (in Chicago) attracted 36,000 paying customers, or 28,500 more than the week before his arrival. Some reports say that Halas cried when he counted the game receipts.

St. Louis, Philadelphia, New York, Washington, Boston, Pittsburgh, and Detroit were the first stops. Then Grange and the Bears headed out West where they smashed their previous attendance record of 73,000 fans (New York) by attracting 75,000 fans and curiosity seekers to see them take on the Los Angeles Tigers in the Coliseum.

Grange's influence drew fans *and* sportswriters to the sport. That was what Halas, and all of pro football, sought. Sportswriters in the 1920s were like John Madden, Chris Berman, and Bob Costas all rolled into one: the gatekeepers to the audience. And that might be an understatement. After the game in New York's Polo Grounds, sports writer Allison Danzig wrote, "to call these 70,000 spectators football followers needs correction. There were thousands in that tremendous assemblage who probably never saw a game before, who did not have the slightest idea of what the proceedings were all about."[9] Another writer of the same era, Damon Runyon said of Grange, "On the field, he is equal of three men and a horse."[10]

The most important writer of the era, Grantland Rice, scripted the most famous reference to Grange when he called him the "Galloping Ghost of the Gridiron." To get Grantland Rice's approval meant that the personality, and his sport, had arrived.

But success had its price, even in the nascent days of the 1920s. The next year, Pyle demanded that Grange receive an ownership stake and Halas refused, ending a brief but glorious association. Grange later came back and played with the Bears in 1929, but his timely arrival four years earlier had made football viable in those critical years of fragility, and cemented Halas's legacy as the true father of professional football.

If someone had told the skinny outfielder with a bad hip that he would alter the landscape of professional football as he left the Yankees in 1919, he might not have believed the messenger. But George Halas, with timely help from Red Grange and other pigskin visionaries, made it happen.

Buildup to the First Really Big Game

Tim Mara, a bookmaker with no college education, bought the New York Giants in 1925 for $500, but it would be thirty-three years before the team would capture the imagination of its city. The football Giants had long competed with neighboring baseball teams such as the Yankees, Dodgers, and Giants, which made it rough on the gridiron pros. College basketball, boxing, and horse racing also consistently relegated the Giants to the back of the sports section. And when Sid Luckman starred at quarterback for Columbia, the gridiron Giants took a backseat again. They were practically the Rodney Dangerfield of the New York sports scene, they got so little respect in the early days of the franchise. But Mara kept at it and the Giants slowly became a fixture on the New York sports scene. When the Dodgers and baseball Giants left for California after the 1957 season, the stage was set for the football Giants to ascend to the top of the New York sports scene.

Nationally, the NFL had been a challenging sell prior to 1958. The league only had twelve teams—the Baltimore Colts, Chicago Bears, Chicago Cardinals, Cleveland Browns, Detroit Lions, Green Bay Packers, Los Angeles Rams, New York Giants, Philadelphia Eagles, Pittsburgh Steelers, San Francisco 49ers, and Washington Redskins—largely concentrated in the Midwest and Northeast. The Redskins were the southernmost franchise, and the Rams and 49ers were the only two West of the Mississippi. So the league was very small, not nationally identified with one event, like the Super Bowl, or aligned with a focused broadcast/promotional effort.

Football fans were loyal to the college game, because it served both social and nostalgic purposes. The college game had a lot of advantages:

built-in facilities, traditions such as homecoming, and personal connections between the fans and the academic institutions. Last but not least, the big colleges packaged and delivered several thousand new, enthusiastic fans each year in the form of the freshman class, so it was naturally building the fan base.

College games were also played one day before the pro game, giving them a head start there as well. For fans, attending one game per weekend was enough and the Saturday games posed fewer conflicts with respect to religious observances. Furthermore, just as the weather assists the TV ratings today, it hurt the NFL in its earlier years. Looking back at the old films and seeing players dash through the mud and snow sure presents a romantic vision of the game, but it did not attract hordes of new people to the stands. With the twelve teams largely located in cold-weather cities, those November and December games had some built-in barriers, like inclement weather, that inhibited the fan base from growing. And when the college season ended in late November, many fans had had enough football and were content to wait for spring training to commence.

In spite of those impediments, the NFL forged ahead, crafting its image and entertainment. Once they got a boost from the emerging TV industry, success soon followed. The DuMont Network waded into the NFL first, paying $75,000 to broadcast the title game in 1951 and NBC paid $100,000 for the privilege in 1954. By 1958, the expanded media coverage helped fans appreciate the gridiron exploits of its star players. And it was the championship game for that season, between the Colts and the Giants, that would vault the NFL into the limelight, though no one realized it at the time.

Playing before 64,000 fans in Yankee Stadium three days after Christmas, a tough Giants defense went up against a diverse and dangerous Colts offense, led by Johnny Unitas. The Colts were Unitas's third pro team. The first team, the Pittsburgh Steelers, cut him. The second, a semiprofessional team called the Bloomfield Rams, paid him six dollars a game before the reformed Baltimore franchise gave him another chance. The Colts would be where Unitas made history, and it galvanized that day.

The reports vary, but anywhere from 30 to 50 million people tuned in their TV sets and watched the 1958 Championship Game that the

Colts won in overtime on a one-yard TD plunge by Alan Ameche. Unitas's star was rising so fast that the network people offered him $750 to stay and conduct postgame interviews and to be available to the press the following day. The consummate team player, Unitas turned down the money and returned to Baltimore with his teammates.

How historic was this game? The Giants' *assistant* coaches were two guys named Vince Lombardi and Tom Landry. Kyle Rote, a star player for the Giants, later commented on the game, "Everything came together then for the greatness of pro football. New York is the heartbeat of the media—including Madison Avenue, where the commercial dollar is. Those ad men were young guys—young and sharp—and suddenly they happened to tie into pro football, just when television advertising was hitting its peak."[11]

The NFL had truly arrived. No longer the sport that came after baseball, football proved so alluring that when the AFL, a rival league, began play in 1960, they secured a broadcast deal with ABC at $2 million per year. This was a league with no track record and no brand equity. It was merely a business based on the NFL model.

In 1961, NBC signed the now-established NFL to a two-year contract for radio and television rights to the championship game for $1,230,000. Later that year, at the behest of the NFL, Congress passed a bill allowing single network contracts for sports leagues. The single network contract legislation meant that teams couldn't negotiate independently; it was the perfect blend of socialism and capitalism and it ensured their mutual interests. Simply put, this meant that broadcast income would rise dramatically as leagues negotiated national, not regional, deals.

In 1962, CBS paid $4.65 million annually for two-year broadcasting rights to NFL regular season games, more than double what the AFL earned from ABC. The next year, they formed NFL Properties to handle all licensing matters. It didn't matter that sports licensing hadn't really been perfected yet; the league saw it coming. In 1964, CBS added two more years to its deal at $14.1 million per annum and $1.8 million for the championship games. Meanwhile, the AFL cemented a five-year, $36 million deal with NBC in 1965 and the Jets signed Joe Namath to an astronomical, at the time, $427,000 contract. Something else of note happened as well that year. A Harris Survey poll indicated that Americans preferred football (41 percent) over baseball (38 percent).[12]

After toiling in dusty towns like Canton and Decatur and enduring failed leagues and franchises, professional football had finally risen to the top through persistence, endurance, and a little bit of luck. Most important, the product stayed fresh and it allowed the fans to acclimate themselves to the action without jeopardizing its health. In other words, the things that work for most successful businesses worked for the NFL.

Power: In Retrospect and in Play Today

Pete Rozelle saw the potential of television as the medium to bring football to the masses and he rightfully gets credit for cementing the relationship between football and television. But Bert Bell was the commissioner when the league broadcasted its first championship games, including the 1958 Baltimore Colts-New York Giants classic that still stirs emotions today.

When the NFL finally realigned in 2002 along sensible geographic borders, it was only thirty years overdue. For thirty-one years, the NFC West featured Atlanta, San Francisco, New Orleans, Los Angeles/St. Louis, and later, Carolina. Anyone who looked at a map knew that this had to change. What most people did not know was that the divisional alignments had been determined in 1970 by Pete Rozelle's secretary pulling various scenarios out of a hat.

Some of the richest and most influential people in all of America resorted to random chance to determine the fate of their teams' gridiron matchups. The resulting divisions were not suggested by a high-priced consultant, or determined via a sophisticated computer program. The various formats were written on small slips of paper and put into a hat and drawn by an observer. Today the league has a special committee to cover everything from rules and competition, to issues like realignment, development and broadcast partnerships. To think that they might resolve a serious matter like realignment via drawing slips of paper out of a hat demonstrates that the times do indeed change.

Today, the NFL makes so much money in so many different categories that they even legislate nostalgia. No exceptions allowed. Peyton

Manning wanted to wear high-top cleats to honor Johnny Unitas on the Sunday following his passing in 2002, but the league publicly warned that such action would be met with heavy fines.[13] Virtually no one could believe the league's position on the matter; even broadcast partners took exception to the intransigence of the NFL's brass. But the league was merely protecting the sanctity of its uniform rules and contractual obligations to its licensees. They did not want attention diverted from their choreographed efforts at image presentation. The NFL's uniform policy is exhaustive and covers details like the color of tape on the player's shoes (it has to match the color of the shoe). It also extends to those popular towels you see dangling out of players' pants; they can be a maximum of six inches wide by eight inches long.

With respect to Manning's attempt to honor the former Colt, league policy states, "Items to celebrate anniversaries or memorable events, or to honor or commemorate individuals, such as helmet decals and arm bands and jersey patches on players uniforms, are prohibited unless approved in advance by the league office."[14] And Manning did not get approval for the high-tops.

The business of the NFL has evolved from meeting in an automobile showroom and pulling slips of paper out of a hat to monitoring the dress code of its star players. The league has over seventy-five years of history: games, moments, personalities, and accumulated fans. It all comes at a price, with no discount for sentimentality.

Since the currency of the league is contractual reciprocity, it protects the uniform companies, the beverage companies, and all of their licensees as long as they are under contract. With a tradition-laden foundation, the NFL today enjoys selling a brand built by circumstances almost as compelling as the games themselves.

A Quick Comparison: Looking at Two Different Eras

One of the best things about baseball is daydreaming about matchups, and the endless possibilities between your favorite players of today and the best of yesterday. For example, how would you like to see Bob Feller pitching against someone like Jim Thome. A power hitter against a power arm, righty versus lefty, it would be a great matchup.

Though not nearly as fun as the Thome-Feller confrontation, another comparison worth thinking about is the top eight salaries of the 1927 Yankees versus the top eight salaries of the 2002 Yankees. Seventy-five years from now, what will the top eight Yankees earn?

1927		2002	
Babe Ruth	$70,000	Derek Jeter	$14,600,000
Herb Pennock	$17,500	Bernie Williams	$12,357,143
Bob Meusel	$13,000	Mike Mussina	$11,000,000
Joe Dugan	$12,000	Jason Giambi	$10,428,571
Waite Hoyt	$12,000	Roger Clemens	$10,300,000
Earle Combs	$10,000	Andy Pettitte	$ 9,500,000
Lou Gehrig	$8,000	Mariano Rivera	$ 9,450,000
Tony Lazzeri	$8,000	Robin Ventura	$ 8,500,000

NOTES

1. Quoted in Munder Barrow, *50 Years an American Hero* (New York: McGraw Hill, 1998), p. 68.

2. Andrew Zimbalist, *Baseball and Billions* (New York: Basic Books, 1994), p. 9.

3. Ibid., p. 10

4. However, after a third pennant and second world championship in 1917, Comiskey donated 10 percent of the team's 1918 gross receipts to the American Red Cross.

5. Quirk and Fort, Pay Dirt (Cambridge: Princeton University Press, 1992), p. 405.

6. Christian Walsh, "Sports Heroes" [online], http://myhero.com/hero. asp?hero=billveeck [September 15, 2003].

7. Bill Veeck, *Veeck-as in Wreck* (Chicago: University of Chicago Press, 1962), p. 18.

8. Ed Linn and Bill Veeck, "Veeck—as in Wreck" [online], http://www.baseballlibrary.com/baseballlibrary/excerpts/veeck_as_in_wreck.stm [September 15, 2003].

9. John Carroll, "The Impact of Red Grange on Football in 1925," Professional Football Researchers Association [online], www.footballresearch.com/articles/frpage.cfm?topic=redpro [December 18, 2002].

10. Ibid.

11. D. Phillips, "Epilogue," *The Turning Point* [online], www.ravensnests.com/1958game/trngpt8.htm [January 1, 2003].

12. "Record and Fact Book," NFL [online], www.nfl.com/randf/chron70.html/ [December 18, 2002].

13. The Baltimore Ravens' quarterback, Chris Redman, defied the rule and wore high-tops in honor of Unitas. He was fined.

14. NFL rules state that teams designate whether they are a "black shoe" team or "white shoe" team prior to the season. The Colts and the Ravens (Redman's team) both chose white shoes. Had they voted for the black shoes, both could have worn the black high-tops that Unitas was famous for wearing without incurring a fine.

CHAPTER 4

FROM SIMPLE AMBITION TO SPORTS INSTITUTION

John J. McDermott of the Pastime Athletic Club of New York won the distance run, and he was given an ovation as he went around the Irvington oval track finishing a record-breaking performance. He made the distance, 25 miles, in 2h 55m 10s, which puts in the shade the performance made by the Greek peasant, Spiros Louces, from Marathon to Athens, last season, by about 30 seconds.[1]
—Boston Globe coverage of the first Boston Marathon
April 20, 1897

That first Boston Marathon field consisted of fifteen runners. The Boston *Globe* reported that "hundreds" of spectators took trains to the starting line to see the beginning of the race at 12:19 P.M. The starter, Tom Burke, simply said the word, "go." And the runners were off, beating the path of what would become one of the most important running events in the world. The competitors did not have water stations carefully placed along the course, or large timing mechanisms to chart their progress over the course. The runners in the original Boston Marathon ran out of curiosity and daring, not for the spectacle of being in the most important marathon in America.

Things are a bit different in the twenty-first century. Modern day Boston Marathon fans don't take the same train to Ashland to see the start, and race organizers have had to establish qualifying guidelines to limit the field. The Boston *Globe* is no longer the only major media outlet that reports on the race. The 2002 Boston Marathon issued credentials to three hundred media outlets and thirteen hundred journalists who wanted to cover the event. In fact, next to the Super Bowl, it is the largest one-day media event in North American sports.

Clearly, everything about the race has changed except for the sweat, grit, and determination of the runners who still enthrall and inspire race fans. The Boston Marathon, like virtually every other valuable sports property, has gone from being a simple ambition to an international institution. Tracing its steps, and those of other events and traditions, provides a valuable context for understanding what formulas work in the modern sports industry.

Central to a successful sports venture is a committed group with resources, either financial, or functional, or both. The caretakers of the property, or idea, allow the event or application of the idea (radio, TV) to filter to the fans, sponsors, and partnering organizations. Trends that become traditions (tradition is covered in greater detail in chapter 5) were subjected to the same syndrome of trial, error, and constant revision. And many of the lessons learned along the way had an impact on the way sports is packaged and priced today.

The Boston Marathon attracted enough runners and organizers to give the event a chance to succeed and weave itself into the sports fabric of Boston, the Northeast, and ultimately, the world. The first era of the modern sports industry nurtured ideas, competitions, and event structures that set the stage for the sponsors of today.

RUNNING DOWN A DREAM

The fictional brothers Randolph and Mortimer Duke once made a famous $1 bet on the age-old question of "nature versus nurture," and it could have applied to the marathon. Easily one of the most challenging and impressive events in all of sports, it has found an important niche in both athletic and sponsor circles. Today, the New York Marathon, Boston Marathon, Chicago Marathon, and Marine Corps Marathon are premier track and field events, with lucrative cash prizes and long-term sponsor commitments. The only thing these races have in common, aside from a preponderance of Kenyans, is the common distance of 26.2 miles and thousands of competitors. It was not always that way.

In 490 B.C.E., a Greek soldier named Pheidippides started the Marathon legend.[2] He ran the twenty-five miles from Marathon to Athens to inform the Athenians of the outcome of their victorious battle with the invading Persians. Traversing hills and obstacles without any shoes or sandals, Pheidippides arrived in Athens exhausted and with severely bleeding feet. After delivering his message of victory, the legend goes, he collapsed and died.

At the first modern Olympic Games in Athens (1896), marathoners commemorated Pheidippides's legendary effort by approximating the same course that he ran 2,300 years earlier. For the first official marathon, the seventeen-man field consisted of thirteen Greeks and four international runners, Edwin Flack of Australia, Arthur Blake of the United States, Albin Lermusiaux of France, and Hungary's Gyula Kellner. Flack, Blake, and Lermusiaux finished first, second, and third in the 1,500 meter run, but the marathon field obviously favored the home country. On that inaugural race day, a Greek peasant named Spiros Louces ran through 100,000 cheering countrymen to victory. Once across the finish line, he was immediately summoned to the King's box, establishing a long-held Olympic tradition of royal acknowledgment of great champions.

Organizers repeated the event at the 1900 and 1904 Games, but with varying distances. At the 1908 Games, due to a royal family request, the marathon began at Windsor Castle. This would have a lasting effect, since the distance from Windsor Castle to the Olympic Stadium finishing line was 42,195 meters (or 26 miles and 385 yards). In 1921 the International Association of Athletics Federations (IAAF) adopted this as the standardized length of a marathon. At the time, the race was only for men, and there were very few competitors specializing in the discipline. But the mystery and majesty of an individual willing to run for 26.2 miles had taken root. It would be years before event operators would start making money on the marathon, but its evolution as an important event and lifestyle had begun. How, then, did it take root from such improbable beginnings?

After the 1896 Athens Games marathon, the American press pounced on the story of Louces, the peasant turned national hero. So dramatic and persuasive was the collective prose that it galvanized

enough support among the prestigious Knickerbocker Athletic Club
(New York City) membership to hold their own marathon, from Connecticut to the Bronx, New York, so just six months after the Athens
Games, America crowned its first marathon champion, John J. McDermott, who won the New York race in just under three hours, twenty-six
minutes.

In those days, people didn't jog down the roads and streets of their
neighborhoods to get a "cardio" workout in before meeting friends for
Happy Hour. A marathon was a radical concept, not just logistically, but
also in terms of finding capable runners. To think that so few individuals
could stage a meaningful, twenty-five-mile race is astounding.

The idea was not the Knickerbocker's alone. Bostonians had also
decided to stage their own marathon, and were going to use their own
resident club, the Boston Athletic Association (BAA), to do it. The
BAA was an established athletic club, and had sent the majority of the
first American Olympic team to the Athens Games. John Graham, the
team manager, helped lead the BAA members to six gold medals at those
inaugural Games, and he came back with an idea.

Graham wanted to stage a marathon at the conclusion of the club's
own BAA games and he, along with businessman Herbert Holton, convinced the rest of the members to include the challenging event. In
1897, they called it the "American Marathon." Little did anyone know
at the time, but it was the start of a sporting institution.

Four years later, Canadian J. J. Caffrey won the 1901 Boston
Marathon in 2h 29m 23s in front of twenty-five thousand cheering fans.
Competing with thirty-seven other runners, twenty-three more than ran
in the first marathon in 1897, Caffrey beat the existing marathon record
by a full ten minutes. By 1907, the tenth year of the "tradition," the race
consisted of a 124-man field, many more thousands of fans, and a new
record by Thomas Longboat of 2h 24m 24s.

Perhaps the most important development, besides the addition of
fans, smashing of records, and widespread civic interest, was the validation that the BAA could pull off an event that the media and public both
acknowledged and supported. Clearly, the race earned its credibility, and
the reward became the stewardship of the most important long-distance
race in the country, and perhaps the world. The BAA was not selling

water-pouring rights at drink stations, or official, energy-bar category status, but they were assembling the pieces to one day pursue those opportunities, even if that wasn't the goal at the time.

Imitation Is Indeed the Highest Form of Flattery

Ironically, when the BAA formed in 1887, it wanted to emulate the New York Athletic Club's success. But when the New York Marathon began in 1970, they strove to mimic the BAA. The first New York Marathon featured a field of 127 runners (only 55 finished) running just over four laps in and around Central Park. Today, the race of 30,000-plus runners covers all five New York City boroughs and is watched by 2 million people[3] in person and seen by 347 million people in 150 countries on TV.

Marathons today are a way of life for the runners and a full-time business for many event organizers. According to Hickock Sports, American runners can find an average of six marathons each weekend during the spring and fall marathon seasons. In 1999 alone, 435,000 runners finished at least one marathon.

Modern marathons use updated methods of event promotion, selling integrated sponsorships and product placement to consumer product companies around the globe. Sponsors, in turn, improve the events by lending resources to pay for the staff that supervises and shepherds the event through its logistical requirements. Simply imagine what it takes to stage a 30,000-person race through New York's five boroughs, crossing bridges, parks, and traffic arteries, and you can appreciate the efforts of the organizing staff.

The events work with sponsors as well. For example, the Boston Marathon has changed its finish line twice to accommodate sponsoring companies. In 1965, when Prudential Insurance Company became the top sponsor, the race ended at the base of that building. When John Hancock supplanted Prudential in 1986, the finish line moved toward its landmark building. These simple, subtle changes demonstrate how events can flex to meet their financial needs.

Furthermore, tracing the marathon back through time reveals the adaptive nature of sports, its promoters, fans, and media. All of the groups assembled slowly, almost deliberately, for the purpose of staging an event and identifying a champion. The millions of dollars in corporate relationships were not the focus. Today, interests like shoe, clothing, and energy food manufacturers all owe a great deal to the largely apocryphal legend of a Greek war correspondent.

REGULATION SETS UP SUCCESS

Boxing has a sordid history of violence, abuse, and scandal. And that only describes the Don King era! The sport actually dates back over five thousand years and ultimately manifested itself in England, where bare-knuckle fights drew crowds, heavy wagering, and a brutal reputation. A gentleman named James Figg introduced the first phase of modern boxing in the early eighteenth century, with some modest rules. He opened his own school and taught boxing as well as competing himself.[4] Figgs's rules, though, weren't very civil. There were no rest periods, so no "rounds," no protection, and certainly no ten-point must system.

In 1743, another Englishman named Jack Broughton introduced the concept that a fight ended if one competitor could not continue after being down for thirty seconds. The fights were still continuous, and the new regulations were referred to as "The London Prize Ring Rules."[5]

Boxing stayed unchanged until the Marquess of Queensbury sponsored "The Queensbury Rules of 1872," a code of twelve rules that still exists in boxing today. The main upgrades were the introduction of gloves, and three-minute rounds interrupted by sixty seconds of rest. The fighter is also protected if he is driven to one knee, and if knocked down, he has ten seconds to rise before the fight is declared over. What the Queensbury Rules did was bring a tolerable structure to an activity that had existed on the fringes of society for centuries. By bringing in a civil structure, it allowed an industry, albeit one with problems, to grow. City governments, police, and the populace would allow boxing under these circumstances, but not the boxing of Jack Broughton's day.

Most important, these standards allowed boxers to develop public careers. By leaving the garishness of its past, the mainstream media could bring it to the front pages of its newspapers and give it a promotional push, effectively making it a mass-market activity. It is no coincidence that forty-nine years after the Queensbury Rules were adopted, boxing inspired sports' first million-dollar event, and its first two-million-dollar event six years later. The roots of those financial rewards lie in the establishment of the Marquess's Rules. Without the structure, boxing never would have left the sordid squalor of society's margins and those million-dollar prize fights would have been fought for a few thousand dollars behind some dank warehouse.

Culturally, boxing defined the early-twentieth-century American sports scene. Champion prize fighters lived like kings and the public lionized them. Jack Dempsey passed the torch to Joe Louis, who then passed it to Rocky Marciano, Sugar Ray Robinson, Jake LaMotta, and the other great American fighters of the mid twentieth century. Without the Queensbury Rules, we wouldn't have seen those great fighters, or others like Muhammad Ali, Joe Frazier, and Thomas Hearns.

We probably wouldn't know how fabulous bacon tastes when cooked on a George Foreman Grill, either. But that is a topic for another chapter.

WHAT'S IN A CARD?

As baseball evolved from a late nineteenth-century club sport into a mainstream commercial venture, it spawned the very first enduring auxiliary industry, the baseball card. Originating as a promotional incentive, the industry today sells almost half a billion dollars' worth of cards annually as a stand-alone product.[6] The evolution of baseball cards, in fact, mirrors the sports industry. Cards found a consumer identity and then developed their own viability over time as the layers of the sports industry and society supported them.

In the late 1800s, baseball's ticket buyers were men. There were no Kid Zones at the ballpark and parents couldn't find changing tables in the bathrooms. Baseball was not marketed as a family activity. Children stayed at home with their mothers and the men attended games, talking and smoking various tobacco products. Tobacco was one of the first high-traffic items sold at retail, and baseball cards were included in various tobacco products for two reasons: to help sell product to men and to stiffen the packaging for optimal merchandising.

Goodwin & Company developed the first card "brand." It placed a small baseball card into packs of its Old Judge brand tobacco. Hence, the name "Old Judge" cards still exists today. Competitors like May & Company followed suit and put cards into their tobacco packs as well. Tobacco customers loved the gimmick and almost two thousand different player images were ultimately used with various tobacco products. Goodwin & Company even had the idea to enclose special coupons in addition to the cards. Once a person collected enough coupons, they could be redeemed for bigger and better cards. And just like that, the first sports-marketing affinity program was born!

The card industry got an unlikely boost just after the turn of the century when the government broke up the American Tobacco Company. The split of American Tobacco's interests encouraged heightened competition for the tobacco consumer and resulted in some of the most popular cards ever, including the production of the undisputed king of baseball cards, the T206 Honus Wagner.[7]

But the tight link between tobacco and baseball would soon start to loosen. Kids started to play baseball and attend the games as well. As America transitioned from an agrarian to an industrial society, children stayed in school longer instead of working the family farm. This meant that high school teams began to emerge and the game now had a supply of fresh young players. Bringing kids into the game, both as players and fans, meant that candy companies started to take notice. Cracker Jack put cards in its snack boxes as early as 1914 and that tipped the scales away from tobacco and adults to a new combination of candy and kids. The American Caramel Company also made use of baseball cards as customer incentives in its candy, and had a successful run into the 1930s. What the cards sought was the perfect partner product, a logical consumer retail extension. Just like chocolate discovered peanut butter, baseball cards needed to find that complementary confection. By the 1930s, the relationship with bubble gum had begun. It would ultimately propel card sales like a hot day sells ice cream.

Charting the Collision Course of Gum and Baseball Cards

1870: First gum developed. "Black Jack" is still sold today.

1891: Wrigley Company founded. Starts selling gum the following year.

1893: Wrigley introduces Juicy Fruit and Wrigley's Spearmint.

1928: Bubble gum is created. Supposedly, the color was chosen because pink was the only available coloring agent in the lab at the time of the discovery.

1933: Goudey Gum Company bundles cards and gum together.

1938: Topps gum manufactured in Brooklyn, New York. Topps is sold as a "change maker": instead of taking a few cents change, the customer could take a few pieces of gum.

1941: World War II creates a paper shortage and suspends card production.

1948: Bowman Gum Company bundles cards and gum.

1951: Topps puts out a fifty-two-card set, but not as a comprehensive set.

1952: Topps's first full set modern cards, designed by Topps executive Sy Berger. First card in the set was of Andy Pafko (Dodgers). The design and style became the standard for all cards.

1956: Topps bought Bowman Gum Company and ruled the card market into the 1980s, when aggressive competitors appeared.

Topps became the Microsoft of baseball cards. And it ruled for many reasons. The cards had a simple design that resonated with early hobbyists and collectors. Topps beat Bowman, its only serious competitor, by offering players $25 more to sign with them, or $125 total to each player. More important, Topps's cards brought professional baseball players to life and made them human.

As Topps spokesperson Clay Luraschi stated, "for most baseball fans in the early 1950s, these players lived as names in black and white in a regulation-sized box score in the local newspaper. When kids opened up the packs for the first time, the color, artwork, and detailed information must have been overwhelming. Baseball cards put a face to the names, and it brought the players into the kids' homes that couldn't get games on the radio. It also gave fans a way to increase their participation through collecting and trading with their friends."[8] Topps also benefited from having the cards follow another Topps brand, Bazooka gum, into retailers. Topps had a relatively strong distribution network in place and a strong identity with the retailers who handled their merchandise.

Conclusions

Baseball cards went through the same copycat cycle decades apart. Just like Goodwin Tobacco attracted May & Company, the Goudey Gum cards of the 1930s ultimately brought rivals like the Delong Gum Company and the National Chicle Company into the card mix.

Entering the card wars in order to sell tobacco or gum shows that baseball had equity in auxiliary markets, something that costs licensees dearly today. These early sports-marketing pioneers did not realize it, but they created a new revenue stream for all of sports, and a new way to value sports properties. By the time Topps bought the Bowman Gum Company, the concept of production, distribution, and licensing was slowly coming together, and it was only a matter of time before other forms of licensed merchandise would hit the shelves and start selling. In fact, just seven years after the Bowman buyout, NFL Properties formed.

But to this day, the card industry stands as a success story of sports spin-offs. Companies even create marketing programs featuring prizes of classic cards. Wal-Mart recently gave away the prized T206 Wagner card through a promotion and the winner sold it for $640,500. And Topps, in a stroke of promotional genius, conducted its own fifty-year anniversary promotion, where it gave away vintage cards from its first 1952 set. Hundreds of media outlets carried the story of Topps's fiftieth anniversary. It was a public relations jackpot as collectors from all eras shared their passion. Ironically, all of the fifty-year-old cards given away for the promotion had to be bought off the collector's market at a cost of $250,000. Topps hadn't saved any inventory from 1952. The cards that it had left over were thrown out years before to the bottom of the Atlantic Ocean.

TUNING IN PROFITS

America, prior to the advent of radio, had been a strong newspaper society. In 1920, one year before the first sports radio broadcast, there were 2,042 newspapers and a total circulation of 27.8 million. During the Depression, many papers either went out of business or had to merge due to economic necessity. Still, the existing 1,888 papers in 1939 had even stronger circulation figures of 39.7 million.[9] The newspaper was the primary method of news retrieval for Americans.

Furthermore, the relationship between the writer and the sports personality had solidified. Both sides were comfortable with each another and were familiar with the others' purposes, even if individuals did not always get along. Athletes knew that the press could make or break them. Gamesmanship had as much to do with maneuvering the media as your opponent. Moreover, companies and merchants felt comfortable with placing advertisements in the newspapers. The results were tangible, and seeing their name in print had a reassuring effect on the ad buyers.

The radio, like anything else, took some getting used to. More important, it took buyers. A signal transmitted, but not received, is of no value. But Americans wanted the device. They knew it would be a welcome source of information and entertainment. And it brought immediacy to Depression-era America at a time when domestic news was very important. It also helped galvanize interest in international affairs, specifically the military escalation of the Third Reich. Providing free programming certainly didn't hurt its appeal, either.

According to the Institute of Electrical and Electronics Engineers, radio really got its public start in Pittsburgh at KDKA, broadcasting the Harding versus Cox presidential election returns on November 2, 1920. Less than a year later, KDKA broadcast Davis Cup tennis and Pirates baseball. They weren't running listener incentive programs, but they knew they were on to something. Predictably, the established business side of the media had their doubts. Since many of the first pioneers of radio came from the news business, print people had to fight for the experimental medium. One early radio convert, a circulation manager named Harold Hough (*Ft. Worth Star-Telegram*) asked his boss, Amon Carter, for the $300 necessary to start a radio station, WBAP, in 1922.

Carter approved the expenditure, but not before saying, "when that $300 is gone, we're out of the radio business." Hough acted as the engineer, announcer, and program director when the station signed on in May of 1922. WBAP is still on the air today.

Sports were a logical programming extension because the events were dynamic in nature and they soaked up a lot of air time, something that radio station program managers needed to do. The advertising mechanism was slow to take hold, but broadcasters knew that they had a winner if they could just keep their costs down.

Sports Radio: An Early Timeline

Nov. 25, 1920: WTAW went on the air from College Station, Texas with the first college football broadcast. Texas University versus the Agricultural and Mechanical College of Texas at College Station. Operating under an "experimental" license, WTAW went by the call letters 5XB via a spark transmitter.

July 2, 1921: Jack Dempsey vs. Georges Carpentier first live boxing broadcast (from New Jersey).

Aug. 4, 1921: KDKA in Pittsburgh broadcasts Davis Cup tennis, Britain vs. Australia, being played in Pittsburgh.

Aug. 5, 1921: KDKA is on a roll. They become the first station to broadcast a baseball game featuring the Pirates and the Phillies (Pirates, 8-3). Harold Arlin was at the mike.

Aug. 25, 1922: The Queensboro Corporation paid $100 for a ten-minute commercial. There is some disagreement over this fact, but it is widely considered to be the first commercial ever on radio. Later that year, Secretary of Commerce Herbert Hoover stated, "It is inconceivable that we should allow so great a possibility for service, for news, for entertainment, for education, and for vital commercial purposes, to be drowned in advertising chatter."[10]

Oct. 4, 1922: The World Series is broadcast in its entirety. WJZ "repeats" the signal to WGY.

Jan 1, 1923: First regional broadcast of what is now the Rose

Bowl by KHJ in Los Angeles. The first national broadcast was four years later on NBC.

Oct. 10, 1923: The first World Series heard on a nationwide radio network.

1928: Columbia Broadcast System (CBS) has forty-seven affiliate stations. Executive William Paley brokered the deal where the affiliates received free programming in exchange for advertising time that CBS could sell to national advertisers. This was a landmark development for all marketing, not just sports marketing.

1935: NBC founded its radio recording division, establishing an archive of broadcasts, and advertisements. Radio is not only viable, but it is deemed necessary to business interests in order to reach their customers. The Chicago Cubs become the first team to allow all games to be broadcast.

1937: Adams Hats becomes first sponsor to subsidize a series of boxing events, or a season package, "18 Weeks from the NY Hippodrome."

1938: The Louis-Schmeling rematch is the first international radio broadcast of a live sporting event.

1939: All Major League Baseball teams now broadcast their games on radio. World Series rights sold for $400,000.[11]

1940: Bears vs. Redskins NFL championship game broadcast for the first time. Mutual Broadcast System paid $2,500 for the rights to carry the signal out to 120 stations.[12] Red Barber called the action.

The origins of the industry reflected the times. The Roaring Twenties were known for excesses and great ambition. Radio represented an enormous leap of faith when it first came onto the national scene. Electricity wasn't in every home yet—electrical current intended for domestic residencies only standardized in 1920—but no one could deny the promise of broadcasting. Except sports teams it seemed. Team owners lived in a paranoid state of rival leagues, betting scandals, and fan desertion. Of course, there was not much fan dissension, much less desertion. Even the Depression couldn't totally keep fans away and kill the sports industry.[13] But the

owners resisted broadcast partnerships. The owners only had one significant revenue stream, attendance, but several prominent expenses: salaries,
travel, equipment, scouting, and administration.

Anything that could threaten the gate was anathema to the sports
owners. For fifteen years, radio generated more wariness than excitement. Once owners determined that it wouldn't kill the live gate, they
embraced it as a revenue stream and marketing tool. It also paved the
way for the introduction and transition to television in the 1950s.

TRANSITION TO THE MAINSTREAM: SWITCHING TO EVENT SUBSIDY

Professional tennis had an awkward transition from amateur to professional status. The big tournaments were all amateur events until 1968.
The powers that ruled tennis did not necessarily want to make the sport
professional, but the players had different ideas, and for good reason. But
making the switch meant changing the way everything had been done in
previous years. How do you ask a company for prize money when there
was no tradition for awarding prize money? Athletes had always shown
up and played without prize money, so how do you reconcile the change
of heart? It takes a super salesman and tennis had one: Donald Dell.

Soliciting money is very hard work. The first professional tennis
tournament in Washington, D.C., was one such event that sought outside money. Organizer Donald Dell found business leaders to donate
$5,000 each, with the idea that he would stop at $25,000. In the event
one title sponsor would step forward, then the individual contributions
would be returned. So much for second tier sponsorships. It was all or
nothing in the early days and Dell got the *Washington Star* to be the title
sponsor. Dell had some built-in advantages. First and foremost, Dell's
most important position was heading the U.S. Davis Cup team. This
meant that he had tremendous access to the top players, and he secured
Arthur Ashe and Stan Smith for the first year of the professional tourney.

Ashe grew up in Virginia and wanted the event held in an integrated
neighborhood. As reigning U.S. Open champ, he carried a lot of influence, and Dell readily agreed to Ashe's suggestion. The Park Service had

a good location downtown, so that was the target area. Temporary bleachers went up around some clay courts and just like that, a professional tournament had its beginning. Players stayed with local families and changed in tents adjacent to the makeshift stadium. But it was legitimate and very real. In the gritty times of urban America in the late 1960s, it was a perfect setting for top-notch tennis, even if the water came from simple outdoor spigots instead of Evian, Perrier, or Aquafina bottles.

In the early days of professional tennis, the amateur side struggled to maintain power over the ambitious professionals. They simply did not want to lose their influence over the sport and its tournaments, but the sport needed to modernize. Wimbledon had a strong following, drawing over 200,000 fans. But attendance for the French, Australian, and U.S. Opens all struggled in the low to mid-five figures. Joseph Cullman became tournament director of the U.S. Open and instantly went about commercializing the sport. He got a five-year, $100,000 contract with CBS to broadcast the event and then started selling boxes for $900 apiece. Today boxes sell for $50,000, with suites costing up to $100,000 each.[14]

Dell ultimately started the landmark sports marketing agency ProServ and became one of the most respected voices in the industry.

BROADCAST TV'S AWKWARD FIRST STEPS: THE DuMONT NETWORK

In post–World War II America, most TV stations were independently owned, but affiliated with one of the radio networks, ABC, NBC, or CBS. The radio networks had a natural platform to extend into the new medium from both a marketing and technological standpoint.

Their idea was to sign up regional TV stations as affiliates, or to get existing radio affiliates to start up their own VHF-TV stations in desirable markets. The plan was an informal franchising, without the associated start-up fees. The parent station would provide programming, the local stations would provide reach, and overnight they could attain a national network without incurring exorbitant capital expenditures. In short, the established businesses at NBC, CBS, and ABC radio provided a stable base for television, a developing, speculative business. Radio financed the early days of the industry that supplanted it.

One company not financed by radio was DuMont Laboratories, a manufacturer of high end TV sets and components. DuMont had developed, among other processes, the use of cathode-ray tubes as TV screens, a cathode-ray radio tuning indicator, and the kinescope process. NBC's first broadcast at the 1939 World's Fair was, in fact, on DuMont TV sets. DuMont decided to get into the broadcast business and it had initial success, having a 99 percent penetration into available TV homes in 1949. Of course, in 1949, only 11.5 percent of homes owned a television set. In 1951, DuMont had the vision to broadcast the first NFL championship game between the Cleveland Browns and Los Angeles Rams, paying $75,000 for the rights.[15] DuMont owned two eastern TV stations outright and had affiliates through two Paramount controlled station in the West. DuMont hoped that it would soon have a national TV network comprised almost entirely of regional affiliates looking to cash in on the new broadcast medium. So what happened?

DuMont had one major problem to overcome. The radio-backed companies could rely on programming from their radio business to transfer over to the fledgling TV business. DuMont had no such luxury of accessible, affordable programming. DuMont was TV only, and it was too far ahead of its time. DuMont also had the misfortune of being on the wrong end of a key FCC ruling. The FCC decided that they needed to standardize elements like UHF transmission and colorization in 1948. This essentially put a moratorium on the licensing and development of new stations, which froze the DuMont distribution network. It would take four years for the FCC to process the issues of UHF standardization and the amount of VHF licenses granted to each market. To DuMont's dismay, the FCC decided only three VHF stations would be granted in each market.

DuMont, at that time, had two hopes to succeed: Bob Hope and no hope, and Bob Hope was an NBC man all the way. NBC and CBS had spent the years between 1948 and 1952 cementing significant affiliate relationships and ABC had forged its own deals leaving it as the third largest network. DuMont was left to the no-man's-land of UHF[16] as NBC and CBS dominated the early VHF marketplace and ABC held on to its third-place VHF status.

DuMont tried to make the UHF strategy work, but could not compete with the VHF businesses. Had the installed base of today's cable or satellite television markets existed in 1952, DuMont might have been the original ESPN or TNT but it was limited by the scope and capacity of technology, regulations, and market resources (advertising funds, affiliate revenues and available programming) of the era.

Complicating matters, the FCC also categorized the Paramount Studio stations as DuMont-owned, which hurt DuMont's efforts to get more stations. DuMont suffered the same fate that would cripple Internet companies fifty years later, being underfunded in an immature market. Everyone knew that TV would be a great place to find content and to market products to customers; DuMont just did not have the resources to wait for the advertising model to grow up around it.

But DuMont saw something in sports television and committed broadcast resources to football and boxing. They knew that sports on TV would be a success, but didn't stick around long enough to do it themselves. Fittingly, DuMont went off the air with sports in 1956, televising *Boxing from St. Nicholas Arena*, where the host was a young Chris Schenkel, who later went on to fame as a long-time ABC sportscaster.[17]

DuMont's legacy shows many accomplishments, chief of which was broadcasting the first live NFL games. They also produced the first children's show, first daytime programming, and first soap opera. Roone Arledge, who later created *Monday Night Football* for ABC in 1970, briefly worked at DuMont.

BIG LEAGUE DREAMS

Can you name the league responsible for these teams?[18]

Chicago Majors	Los Angeles Jets
Cleveland Pipers	Pittsburgh Rens
Hawaii Chiefs	San Francisco Saints
Kansas City Steers	Washington Tapers

How about the league that spawned these franchises?[19]

Birmingham Americans	Jacksonville Sharks
Chicago Fire	Memphis Southmen
Detroit Wheels	New York Stars
Florida Blazers	Philadelphia Bell
Hawaiians	Portland Storm
Houston Texans	Southern California Sun

Extra credit for anyone who can identify the league for these franchises:[20]

Philadelphia Freedoms	Detroit Loves
Boston Lobsters	Pittsburgh Triangles
Baltimore Banners	Cleveland Nets
New York Sets	Buffalo-Toronto Royals
Minnesota Buckskins	Denver Racquets
Houston E-Z Riders	San Francisco Golden Gaters
Florida Flamingos	Los Angeles Strings
Chicago Aces	Hawaii Leis

A few more teams with an illustrious past:[21]

Anaheim Amigos	Minnesota Muskies
Dallas Chaparrals	New Jersey Americans
Denver Rockets	New Orleans Buccaneers
Houston Mavericks	Oakland Oaks
Indiana Pacers	Pittsburgh Pipers
Kentucky Colonels	

All of the above franchises had dreams of being big league teams, with staying power, community clout, happy sponsors, and multimillion-dollar values. Many of them saw the boom in sports entertainment, knew that there was more money to be earned, more concessions to be sold, more licenses to peddle, and TV networks to leverage. They all pursued a variation of two strategies:

1. Keep costs low, build a fan base, and establish the league.
2. Sign as many high profile stars and merge with a larger league.

All new leagues say they will follow strategy number 1. They swear they know the evils of fiscal imprudence, and are as interested in their fellow owners succeeding as themselves. This remains true until they need to sell tickets, of course. At that point, they go to the formula: "hype = fans = money = stability," where strategy number 1 is forgotten and ignored, and they proceed directly to strategy number 2.

The Namath Principle

New league owners all know that when the New York Jets' owner Sonny Werblin signed Joe Namath to a $427,000 contract out of college, the Jets were excoriated for being imprudent. They also know that the AFL soon merged with the NFL after Namath signed and lived prosperously ever after. They just know it will happen again. Except for a handful of ABA teams that migrated to the NBA, it never has.

Namath was tremendously important to the AFL, football in general, and the times. He wore full-length mink coats, appeared in panty-hose commercials, and brashly predicted victory in Super Bowl III even though the Jets were eighteen-point underdogs. Most important, he pulled it all off with a smile. When people think of starting professional sports leagues, they read about how signing Joe Namath catapulted the AFL onto the same plateau as the NFL and augured the merger.

That is true. What is false is the notion that another Namath will come along again, and have the same effect. It won't happen. Broadway Joe Namath played the role of 1960s antihero as well as he played quarterback. In the macho world of pro football, he could wear mink coats, stay out late, and be uninhibited in his bachelorhood.

The Csonka, Kiick, and Warfield Principle

In early 1975 Larry Csonka, Jim Kiick, and Paul Warfield were three offensive stars for the back-to-back Super Bowl Champion Miami Dolphins. Csonka had just won the Super Bowl MVP and the Dolphins were undeniably the league's best team, and one of the best ever. The NFL had soared in popularity and there was room to grow, or so felt the people that started the World Football League (WFL).

The WFL looked good on paper. Hoping to emulate the success of the AFL, the league raided the NFL for talent, and the Dolphins' trio represented the best the NFL had to offer. By getting established stars, the league hoped to grab headlines, sell tickets, and secure a long-term broadcasting contract.

John Bassett, the owner of the Memphis Southmen, where the three players were headed, ponied up $3 million plus cars and an apartment to land the three stars.[22] The players were all making less than $100,000 in the NFL. The decision did not take long to make.

The key to the "Namath Principle" was recognizing the time and the person. Namath could admire his friend's wife and get away with it. More important, he backed it up on the field with great play. He was the only NFL player to throw for more than 4,000 yards in a fourteen-game season. The other component was that he played in New York in the late 1960s. His easygoing style and party image fit the New York scene perfectly during that time. Csonka, Kiick, and Warfield were nothing like Namath, and Memphis was nothing like New York. And the WFL certainly was nothing like the NFL.

The ex-Dolphins never even finished their only season in the WFL, just playing in seven games. They were great football players. But great football players toiling in the shadow of Graceland could not inject life and viability into a rival league in the mid-1970s. The owners of the WFL, WTT, and ABL franchises all saw the bright lights of Yankee Stadium and Soldier Field and wanted to participate in that level of success. Though their desire was understandable, those wannabe owners forgot that the original Yankees played at Hilltop Park, a single-deck facility that took six weeks to construct. They also forgot that the Bears played in Decatur in front of sparse crowds, or that Shelby, Montana, failed to be a prize-fight destination. In short, they overlooked the humble beginnings of established, successful sports teams. They wanted to get to the penthouse without taking the stairs or even waiting for an elevator. In sports, as in life, it rarely happens.

Swing and a Miss

Match each the following teams with its competitive professional league that either failed outright, or achieved limited penetration into a larger, more established league. (Answers on page 97.)

1995–96, IHL; 2000, XFL; 1984, USFL; 1976, NASL.

Philadelphia Stars	Houston Gamblers
New Jersey Generals	Michigan Panthers
Pittsburgh Maulers	San Antonio Gunslingers
Washington Federals	Oklahoma Outlaws
Birmingham Stallions	Chicago Blitz
Tampa Bay Bandits	Los Angeles Express
New Orleans Breakers	Arizona Wranglers[1]
Memphis Showboats	Denver Gold
Jacksonville Bulls	Oakland Invaders

NY/NJ Hitmen	Las Vegas Outlaws
Chicago Enforcers	Orlando Rage
Memphis Maniax	Birmingham Bolts
LA Xtreme	San Francisco Demons[2]

Atlanta Knights	Houston Aeros	Milwaukee Admirals
Chicago Wolves	Indianapolis Ice	Minnesota Moose
Cincinnati Cyclones	KC Blades	Orlando Solar Bears
Cleveland Lumberjacks	Las Vegas Thunder	Peoria Rivermen
Detroit Vipers	LA Ice Dogs	Phoenix Roadrunners
Fort Wayne Komets	Michigan K-Wings	SF Spiders
		Utah Grizzlies[3]

Chicago Sting	Washington Diplomats	St. Louis Stars
Toronto Metros-Croatia	Philadelphia Atoms	San Jose Earthquakes
Rochester Lancers	Miami Toros	Dallas Tornado
Hartford Bicentennials	Minnesota Kicks	Los Angeles Aztecs
Boston Minutemen	Seattle Sounders	San AntonioThunder
Tampa Bay Rowdies	Vancouver Whitecaps	San Diego Jaws
New York Cosmos	Portland Timbers[4]	

NOTES

1. Sources conflict as to the exact spelling of Louces's name—some spell it Spiridon Louys. For the purposes of conformity, this book will use the version printed in the 1897 Boston Globe.

2. This is a much disputed and contested legend. Not too many people dispute that it was a war messenger running from Marathon to Athens after victorious battle with the Persians, but the identity of the runner and whether or not he died has been contested and debated and remains undetermined.

3. Steinfeld, *Welcome. NYC Marathon*, event program, 2002, p. 15. C. Roche and J. Chiat, "Mayor Giuliani Hosts Reception for the 29th Running of the NYC Marathon," NYC Sports Commission, press release, April 20, 2001.

4. B. Sugar, "Boxing," *World Book*, Online Americas ed. [online], www.owingsmillsboxingclub.com/boxing.htm [August 12, 2001].

5. Ibid.

6. Associated Press, "Baseball's Labor Pains Damage Trading and Industry," CNNSI, August 29, 2002. This is down from a high of almost one billion in annual sales prior to the strike of 1994. Some analysts blame the strike, others point to the expense of the average card and the emphasis on selling premium cards by the manufacturers.

7. Wagner didn't like the tobacco association, and requested the removal of his card, resulting in only fifty being distributed. Currently, a mint version of the T206 sells for more than $600,000.

8. Interview with Clay Lureschi, Topps spokesperson, November 27, 2002.

9. Victor Bondi, *American Decades 1930–1939* (Detroit: Gale Research Inc., 1995), p. 345.

10. L. Genco, "First Commercial Introduced on Radio Broadcast," Old Time Radio [online], www.old-time.com/commercials/1stcommercial.html [December 4, 2002].

11. Andrew Zimbalist, *Baseball and Billions* (New York: Basic Books, 1994), p. 149.

12. "History Chronology," *NFL* [online], http://www.nfl-football1.com/ nfl_history_30s.html [December 20, 2002]. Just seven years after the Bowman buy out, NFL Properties formed.

13. The Depression certainly hurt sports. Baseball leaguewide attendance hit a a low of 6.3 million fans and even Babe Ruth took a salary cut. Players ultimately barnstormed to try and make up the wage losses.

14. Bruce Goldman, "Open Minded," *Cigar Aficiando* [online], www.ciga-

raficionado.com/Cigar/CA_Archives/CA_Show_Article/0,2322,519,00.html [November 14, 2002].

15. Peter King et al., *75 Seasons* (Atlanta: Turner Publishing, 1994), p. 104.

16. VHF frequencies were strong enough to work over vast spaces, connecting cities and other large areas. UHF, in many cases, could not cover a large city.

17. Clark Ingram, "The DuMont Television Network" [online], http://members.aol.com/cingram/television/dumonta3.htm [September 15, 2003].

18. American Basketball League, circa 1961.

19. World Football League, circa 1974.

20. World Team Tennis, circa 1974.

21. American Basketball Association, circa 1967.

22. The team intended to play in Toronto and be called the Northmen, but the Canadian government ruled that they couldn't compete with the CFL, so they relocated to Memphis and became the Southmen.

Answers to "Swing and a Miss"
1. 1984, USFL
2. 2000, XFL
3. 1995–96, IHL
4. 1976, NASL

CHAPTER 5

SPORTS STEW
SOCIETY, POLITICS, AND TRADITIONS INFLUENCING THE GAMES

The other day Willie Mays hit his five hundred and twenty-second home run. He has gone past me, and he's pushing, and I say to him, "go get 'em Willie." Baseball gives every American boy a chance to excel. Not just to be as good as anybody else, but to be better. This is the nature of man and the name of the game. I hope some day Satchel Paige and Josh Gibson will be voted into the Hall of Fame as symbols of the great Negro players who are not here only because they weren't given the chance. As time goes on I'll be thinking baseball, teaching baseball, and arguing for baseball to keep it right on top of American sports, just as it is in Japan, Mexico, Venezuela, and other Latin American and South American countries . . . So in closing, I am grateful and know how lucky I was to have been born an American and had the chance to play the game I love, the greatest game.

—Ted Williams, July 25, 1966
Hall of Fame Induction Speech
Cooperstown, New York

Ted Williams served in the military and flew missions with future astronaut and congressman John Glenn. He hit a home run in his last at bat in a Red Sox uniform.

On induction day, Williams could have taken out the cliché jar and shaken a few them onto his speech sheet. He could have opted for a simple list of "thank-yous" to teammates and coaches. He could have said nothing at all and it would have still been a remarkable and special occasion. But with the civil rights movement boiling and Vietnam War protests polarizing communities throughout the United States, Williams's poignant, pointed message stood out like a beacon.

Williams did not have the easiest upbringing in San Diego, California. He could have easily been left on the wrong side of society's blurred margins, but baseball gave him focus and purpose at a young age. Williams knew better than anyone how baseball had given him a chance.

So when he had the ear of the nation, Ted Williams wanted to convey a message about access to opportunity. For all of his great deeds on the diamond, and for all of his selflessness on behalf of his country, Williams's best moment arguably came on this day. It is hard to fathom today, but in Williams's day, the political and cultural influences of the era severely impacted sports for both the competitors and the audience.

MISSED CHANCES

Today, sports images bombard people from all angles, and color, creed, or nationality have almost no bearing. Pepsi runs advertisements with Sammy Sosa and Ken Griffey Jr. Tiger Woods, in his twenties, is the most appealing pitch man in the world. Michael Jordan, the most important endorser prior to Woods, ruled spokesman territory for almost a dozen years. George Foreman signed the largest contract in the history of sports marketing when he sold the rights of his name to Salton for the George Foreman Grill.

It wasn't always this way. Jackie Robinson, Ollie Matson, Nat "Sweetwater" Clifton, and many other great African Americans did not get national endorsement deals while they played. The great Roberto Clemente was called "Bobby" Clemente by the Pittsburgh Pirates announcers in order to Americanize him to the fans. Clemente, from Puerto Rico, hated being called Bobby, but he had little leverage in the matter.

Jesse Owens won four gold medals in the 1936 Berlin Summer Olympic Games, where German Reichschancellor Adolf Hitler snubbed him. Owens returned home, supposedly to a hero's welcome stateside, where a party was thrown for him at the upscale Waldorf Astoria in New York. But Owens probably did not feel like too much of a hero when he was told that he had to ride the freight elevator to get to the party. Owens's post Olympic glory did not include endorsements, speaker tours, and exorbitant appearance fees. He was reduced to racing in exhibitions to make ends meet. Sometimes he had to race dogs and horses. "I won four gold medals," he said. "You can't eat four gold medals." Owens would lace up his spikes, head to the track, receive cheers while running, and then have to duck from the scorn of some parts of society.

Twenty-four years after Jesse Owens rode a freight elevator to his own party, Wilma Rudolph won three gold medals, running for the United States in the Rome Olympic Games. Rudolph beat both cultural and physical odds to become one of the most important sprinters in American history. The twentieth of twenty-two children, Rudolph had polio as a child and battled pneumonia as well. Her illnesses resulted in her wearing a leg brace from the age of five to eleven. At one point, there was doubt whether she would ever be able to walk normally, much less run.

But Rudolph was determined to do much more than walk, and she ultimately earned a place on both the 1956 and 1960 Olympic teams. After the triumphant 1960 Games, her hometown (Clarksville, Tennessee) wanted to celebrate her achievements with a parade. Tennessee was segregated, like much of the South. Rudolph refused to cooperate if the parade was segregated, and the mayor of Clarksville relented. It was the first integrated event in the city's history. Rudolph had overcome much bigger obstacles than simple ignorance. Her intransigence on the parade demonstrated a championship spirit away from the track as well.

Prejudice was not exclusive to people of color. Hank Greenberg, the Hall of Fame slugger, faced years of anti-Semitism, even after he became an established star. Greenberg won two MVP awards, was the first ballplayer to enlist in the Army for World War II, and gave the first credible chase to Babe Ruth's home run record of sixty, finishing with fifty-eight in 1938. But that did not matter to a very vocal group of society. Greenberg endured the humiliation of derision from strangers, simply because of his religion. Ironically, Greenberg did not even prioritize religion in his life, yet he was taunted relentlessly throughout his career.

The dignified Greenberg ended his career in the National League after the 1947 season. Playing for the lowly Pirates that season, he had a chance to meet, and befriend, Jackie Robinson, competing in his first season. "As rough as I had it," Greenberg observed, "it wasn't even close to what Jackie went through."

Sociologists will debate the circumstances and consequences of bigotry forever and they might not ever be able to determine the costs, impact and misunderstandings. From a sports business standpoint, analysis raises some interesting points. Opening up athletics to all competitors does three essential things:

1. Determines more fairly who really is the best athlete, team or performer(s).
2. Dilutes the polarization of cultures.
3. Creates and expands new markets.

The third result might be the most significant. Restricting people from athletics means that less people will identify with the athletes and events, which means they will spend money elsewhere. Lady Footlocker began only after women's sports had a chance to take hold. Women were not even allowed to run the Boston Marathon until 1972, or have their own marathon in the Olympics until 1984. If foolish rules had continued to prohibit their inclusion from these events, maybe Lady Footlocker would never have evolved.

Similarly, it is no surprise that Fernando Valenzulea's games in his Dodgers heyday were a tough ticket. The Latin community in Los Angeles embraced the Mexican-born pitcher and flocked to Dodger Stadium to support him. And the Dodgers profited tremendously from his popularity.

Ironically, the culture of fear that held back the integration of sports only held back the development of business prospects for the game. Joe Louis had gate appeal. Bill Veeck's 1948 Cleveland Indians team set a Major League Baseball attendance record after he hired two blacks, Larry Doby and Satchel Paige, to play for the Indians. It's no surprise that the attendance corresponded to their championship play, either. Doby and Paige were instrumental contributors to the team. Indians fans came out for the team because they were winning. Black players helped them win. It was a very simple equation, really.

Perhaps the most telltale sign is that in 1946, the year before Jackie

Robinson joined the Dodgers, they drew 1,796,000 fans to Ebbets Field. In 1947, Robinson's first year, they drew 1,807,000 fans. In fact, the Dodgers 1947 attendance figure would be the highest in franchise history until 1958, the franchise's first year in Los Angeles. If Jackie Robinson's presence had hurt the Dodgers' gate appeal, it would have been reflected via boycott in 1947, his first season, the year they posted their best attendance figure. The fact that the fans had their best turnout in franchise history indicates that rooting for an African American as part of a team could easily be done.

Jackie Robinson Helped Keep Dodger Attendance above the Major League Average

Year	Dodger season	MLB average
1947	1.8 million	1.3 million
1948	1.4 million	1.2 million
1949	1.6 million	1.2 million
1950	1.2 million	1.05 million
1951	1.3 million	900,000

Source: baseball-almanac.com

More telling, the Dodgers kept adding African Americans such as Roy Campanella and Don Newcombe to their roster. Not only did the players help the Dodgers stay near the top of the standings (they won the 1955 World Series), but they also kept the team's attendance ahead of Major League Baseball's average every year except 1957. Of course, 1957 was their last year in New York, when fans had every reason to be turned off by a front-office decision to move to Los Angeles.

Clearly, Jackie Robinson, Larry Doby, and other early African American professionals only helped Major League Baseball in a business sense. Integration expanded their pool of talent, broadened their fan base, and effectively scuttled the competition of the Negro leagues.

Baseball and Robinson get the most publicity, because baseball was the most popular sport in America and Robinson the first man to cross the color barrier. But other leagues had to have their "firsts" as well. In 1950, Nat "Sweetwater" Clifton (Knicks), Chuck Cooper (Celtics), and

Earl Lloyd (Syracuse) all broke into the NBA and had to suffer their own share of indignities. Today, the NBA is the most international sports league in the world, and the most integrated.

The NFL began a twelve-year hiatus in allowing blacks to play, when they mysteriously cleared the league's rosters of African Americans in 1933. Ray Kemp (Pittsburgh) and Joe Lillard (Chicago) were the last African Americans to suit up in the NFL before the Rams signed Kenny Washington in 1946. Many theories abound, the primary one being that the Depression was so difficult on everyone that the thought of a black holding a high profile job as an athlete would have been too much for the developing (mostly white) audience to tolerate. Whatever the motivation, blacks were excluded from all sports just like they were excluded from restaurants, hotels, bathrooms, and schools. The shame of racism was shared by all sectors of American society, even the sports industry.

The reality behind all of the segregation is that it had one source, ignorance. The small-minded caretakers of sports felt that their leagues' fragile, delicate balance could be tipped by the perception of social equality. Most teams simply went along with the prevailing mentality that having prominent black athletes was simply too risky at the time. Segregation took its toll on virtually every sector of the sports industry. Not only were fans deprived of the best competitive entertainment, they were also denied the business rewards of a larger talent pool and audience.

History books often mention Josh Gibson, DeHart Hubbard, Harry Wills, and other great African American athletes, but they seem to overlook people like Dr. George Grant. Dr. Grant, an African American dentist from Massachusetts, invented the golf tee. Grant filed the very first patent on the tee in 1899, but never got credit for his invention. Nor did Dr. Grant get any profits. Industry ignored the African American as an entrepreneur, so Grant had no chance to make his invention a widespread addition to the game. The inventive dentist gave them out to his acquaintances instead. Twenty-five years after Grant filed for his patent, another dentist, William Lowell filed a similar patent claim and received a patent on the product. From 1924 until 1991, the United States Golf Association (USGA) recognized Lowell as the inventor. In 1991, they finally corrected their mistake and acknowledged Grant as the original inventor. Golf must have been a very tough place for an African American in 1899.[1] The fact that Grant even filed for a patent must have taken courage and moxie. Of course, the patent application probably did not ask his ethnic background under the product description.

ONE LAST THOUGHT ON SEGREGATION IN SPORTS

You will often hear athletes say, "even if the money wasn't so great, I'd still play for the love of the game." A common story is about an athlete returning for the enjoyment of sport. Michael Jordan, coming back to play for the Wizards, donated his salary to the 9/11 relief effort and truly was playing for the love of the game. The fact that he was a part owner made him play for Washington, but he would have found his way to the professional hardwood even if he hadn't taken a management role. Jordan, in fact, even had a "love of the game" clause in his Bulls contracts during his heyday, stipulating that he could play basketball whenever he wanted.

Jordan was lucky to have been born in the 1960s. Had he been born in 1900, he would not have had the stage, the audience, or even the opportunity. No manufacturer would have wanted to use him in an endorsement, much less shake his hand on the golf course. He wouldn't even have been invited.

John Henry Lloyd is a name that means very little today, though he was a magical baseball player in the early twentieth century. No less an authority than Hall of Fame Manager John McGraw said, "if we could just bleach this Lloyd boy, we would show the National League a new phenomenon."[2] Lloyd loved the game and displayed his gifts on the diamond, but not as a major leaguer against other major leaguers. He was denied the opportunity that Ted Williams talked about in his Hall of Fame induction speech. Lloyd truly did play for the love of the game, even if only part of the game could love him in return.

POLITICS

As soon as politicians saw the big audiences that were captivated by athletic competition, they recognized a perfect opportunity for self-promotion.
Furthermore, the idea that fans would pay to see their heroes perform
meant that they were passionate about the medium, and the politicians
sought the positive association. The sports power brokers realized that
political allies could be useful and would later lean on them for favorable
federal legislation regarding labor and broadcasting, and taxation on a
regional level for facility construction and improvements.

But early on in the development of the sports industry, political symbolism trumped the importance of political dealings behind the scenes.

The most politically significant sporting event of all time is the
second bout between Max Schmeling and Joe Louis in 1938. Schmeling,
a German, had defeated Louis in their first bout in 1936. The twelfth-
round knockout by the older German stunned Louis and boxing
observers. Schmeling had been a gifted pugilist, but he was not considered to be Joe Louis's toughest challenger, or even one of the top heavy-
weights of the day. Yet on the night of their first meeting, Schmeling
walked out of the ring a victor.

Up to that fight, Louis had seemed invincible, completely unlike any
other boxer. He moved with great purpose, economy, and force in the
ring. Louis was poised, skilled, and powerful and he disposed of his opponents with startling efficiency. Louis also fought cleanly and did not
involve himself with the seamy side of boxing. He ascended to the top of
the boxing world and held the position with great dignity. The fact that
he was an African American during the Depression made such a status
all the more improbable. And America could not have been luckier than
to have found this hero in the 1930s.

In July of 1938, the time of the second Louis-Schmeling bout,
America was not a very good deal for its minorities. The country was also
in the grip of the worst financial crisis of its short history. The rematch,
as a matter of sport, and politics, was highly anticipated. The fight as a
symbol of the free world versus Hitler's treacherous dogma made it the
first great international professional sporting spectacle, and an international radio broadcast guaranteed a rapt audience. Louis predicted vic-

tory before the second bout, but the pressure was unbelievable. Weeks before the fight, President Roosevelt told Louis during a White House visit, "Joe, we need muscles like yours to beat Germany." Talk about a prefight pep talk!

The mood and feeling in Yankee Stadium was electric, and a Louis victory would symbolize that the looming threat of the Nazis was not insurmountable. Americans needed to know that the madman acting as German Chancellor was crazy, not correct. Louis carried more than simple athletic hopes as he climbed through the ropes that night.

Schmeling was an athlete, not a Nazi. He fought Louis as a sportsman, not as a racist. He did not preach Nazi propaganda, nor did he embrace its ignorance. He even had a Jewish-American manager, Joe Jacobs. But despite his best intentions and prior victory, he was no match for Joe Louis that night as Louis knocked out Schmeling in the first round. Financially, the fight was also a smash to the New York City coffers, bringing $3 million in business activity to the city in less than two minutes of actual boxing.

Louis later joined the military and donated boxing purses to the national cause in World War II. America needed a man of action, and in Joe Louis, they got one. As a member of the Army, Louis fought over 100 exhibitions, traveled more than 70,000 miles, and spent $100,000 of his own money on the troops.

Joe Louis was not the only boxer who raised funds for the cause, just the most famous and most dedicated to the cause. Beau Jack and Bob Montgomery were two fighters who participated in the War Bond Fight on August 4, 1944. Instead of buying a ticket to gain admission, fans bought a War Bond. And buy they did, purchasing 15,822 bonds to raise a total of $35.9 million.[3]

The Jack-Montgomery bout was not the first U.S. War Bond effort, either. The Boston Marathon of 1918 was altered to feature a relay of the various service organizations running 2.5-mile intervals over the course in full uniform. The batons bore the inscription; "We will fight to the limit. We expect you to buy to the limit." Politics and sport have long been linked.

Military Conflict Influences Sport in Other Lands

War and its insidious effects motivated some to pursue athletic ventures as a national tonic. In fact, it kick-started the Olympic movement of the 1890s. Reeling from the Franco-Prussian War and a succession of failed Republics and monarchies in France, Pierre de Coubertin truly felt that society had a weakness of character where the individual could not develop a sense of purpose or esteem. "The foundation of real human morality lies in mutual respect," he said. "And to respect one another it is necessary to know one another."[4]

Coubertin had seen enough of base human behavior on his continent and he felt that sports offered a solution. Specifically, he felt that the heuristics of athletic competition could teach the individual the key lessons of life. "Peace could only be the product of a better world. A better world could only be brought about by better individuals; and better individuals could be developed only by the give and take, the buffeting and battering, the stress and strain of fierce competition."[5]

Fifty years later and thousands of miles away, another entrepreneur had a similar idea about the impact of sports upon his people in a postwar society. In Japan, Kihachiro Onitsuka felt that sports would be a good pursuit for a country reeling from the Second World War. He founded a shoe company and set out to make athletic shoes. Facing an uphill battle, he enlisted the endorsement of high school coaches and players to persuade wholesalers and retailers to carry his line. He ultimately succeeded and introduced a basketball shoe and then a blister-friendly running shoe. He then persuaded Ethiopian marathoner Abebe Bikila, who won Olympic gold in 1956 while running barefoot, to run in his shoes. Onitsuka also distributed 70 percent of the company's stock to employees and enfranchised them in the business. This company would go on to be one of the top five shoes companies in the world: ASICS Tiger, founded on principles by a man seeking an emboldened spirit from the ashes of war.

Global Political Upheaval

Strife, racism, and political tension in sport were not unique to twentieth-century America. Germany in particular had a tumultuous century.

The nation's role in two World Wars precipitated a chain of events that led to an ever changing complexion of Germanic identity in international competition. Berlin was originally chosen as the host of the 1916 Games, but they never took place because Europe was literally a field of trenches. The First World War ended in 1918, but lingering resentments ultimately kept Germany out of the 1920 and 1924 Games. Fortunes began to change for Germany on the athletic front when the nation was allowed back into the Olympic Games as a competing nation in 1928. The IOC even awarded the Winter and Summer Games in 1936 to Berlin and Garmisch, respectively.

Adolf Hitler and his Nazi party assumed official, state-controlling power in 1933. At the 1936 Games, he displayed his Aryan vision to the world and it was captured by renowned film maker Leni Riefenstahl.[6] The facilities were excellent, even if the politics were horrendous. In 1939, despite the blatant militancy and egregious dogma of the regime, the Germans were granted the 1940 Winter Games again. However, they never really got beyond the planning stages because Germany invaded Poland on September 1, 1939, and the Second World War commenced. No Olympic Games occurred in 1944 and the Germans were not invited to participate in the 1948 Games.

The political split brokered between the victorious Allies created East and West Germany following World War II. In spite of the deep political divide, the Germans competed as one team from 1952 until 1968, when they first competed as two separate teams in Mexico City. Munich was the site for the 1972 Summer Games, and the West Germans had high hopes to present a positive face to the world. Sadly, the Israeli delegation was victimized by a militant extremist group, and eleven Israelis were killed. The legacy of these games was terrorism, not the healing of national identity and Mark Spitz's seven gold medals. The West Germans did not compete in the Moscow Games of 1980 due to the Soviet invasion of Afghanistan. And the East Germans returned the favor by not coming to Los Angeles (neither did the Soviets) in 1984. When the Berlin Wall fell in November 1989, the stage was set for a common German team to once again walk into an Olympic venue, truly united, in every sense of the word, for the first time since 1936. In 1992, in Albertville, it finally happened.

Any mention of twentieth-century German sports culture would be incomplete without mentioning the legacy of the Soviet-influenced East German athletic system. East Germany made sports one of its main national pursuits during the Cold War era. And while the efforts produced many gold medals and world class athletes, they came at a steep price. Revelations since the reunification have confirmed what many suspected all along: East German sports administrators fed their athletes a steady stream of illegal substances to enhance training and performance. *Der Spiegel*, a popular German magazine, estimated that "up to 10,000 athletes may have passed through the drug program." The East Germans even developed athletes institutionally, going as far as separating children from their families once their athletic prowess had been identified.

WOMEN IN THE EARLY DAYS OF SPORTS

Long before Annika Sorenstam played in the Bank of America Colonial in 2003, women fought stereotypes in order to compete. Women couldn't participate in the original Olympics, or run in an Olympic Marathon until 1984! Yes, 1984! They couldn't even officially run in the Boston Marathon until 1972. In 1966 Roberta Gibb was told that women weren't physically capable of running a marathon and she was denied entry to the race. Not only was Gibb fit enough, she beat many in the field as she entered the race after hiding behind a bush. She ran "unofficially" in 3:21:15, an excellent time, considering the obstacles. The next year, Gibb ran again, but race officials escorted her off the course just before she was able to finish.

One runner they didn't escort off the course in 1967 was K. V. Switzer of Syracuse, New York. When race officials discovered, a few miles into the race, that K. V. was a she, they tried to remove her from the course. But Ms. Switzer pulled a page out of Vince Lombardi's arsenal and had blockers for the race. She ultimately finished, but required subterfuge to pull it off.

What Could They Play?

Women trickled into athletics. In 1884 tennis offered women their first real break. That landmark year, the first Women's Wimbledon Championship was played. The U.S. Open followed suit in 1887, and the French Open in 1897 included women. Women could not vote in the United States, but they could play major tennis events.

The times gave women few choices. They were locked into the home and not considered as athletes, much less as an important demographic for sponsorship. By the 1890s women were finally depicted outside the home in a few bicycle advertisements. In 1900, women competed in three Olympic events, and even by 1992, women still competed in seventy-three fewer Olympic events than men during the Summer Games. Thirty-four countries had no female athletes at all at those Games.

Baseball

In late 1942 Chicago Cubs owner Philip Wrigley wanted to make up for the lack of minor league baseball and the drain the war was taking on the supply of male athletes. He decided to front half the costs for a women's baseball league (the host cities would assume the other half), and any extra costs that came up. They determined the league would have four teams based in Rockford, Illinois; South Bend, Indiana; Racine, Wisconsin; and Kenosha, Wisconsin. Along with baseball skill, the players would have strict moral codes to abide by and a chaperone would be present at all times. Wrigley also placed a priority on femininity and designed fashionable uniforms and provided beauty tips to the players. And just like that, the All-American Girls Professional Baseball League was born.

The first year was a huge success, drawing more than 176,000 fans to the small, four-team league over a 108-game schedule.[7] People wanted the distraction during the war, and the women played exciting ball. The women liked it too and earned an average of $60 plus a week. In 1944 the league added two teams that would play in Milwaukee and Minnesota, and the four original cities financed their own franchises. Wrigley, however, soon lost interest in the league and left it to those who had been running it. Milwaukee and Minnesota drew poorly, but overall league attendance grew in 1944 and hit 450,000 in 1945. The league expanded and the combination of athletic women in small-town America struck a chord.

The league peaked in 1948 when the ten teams drew over 900,000 fans, but the decline began as teams started having problems finding players. The transition to a peace-time economy coincided with an increasing birth rate and caused a diminishment in women's baseball. The league attempted to change with the times in the early 1950s, but ultimately disbanded after the 1954 season, leaving an impressive legacy. It inspired the movie *A League of Their Own* and continues to live in women's softball and baseball to this day.

Other Efforts

Women could compete in some Olympic events, but matriculated to no real professional athletic career once the Games ended. That didn't mean they would stop trying. In 1944, Betty Hicks, Ellen Griffin, and other ambitious women golfers established the Women's Professional Golf Association. Seeing that the men's game was largely comprised of exhibitions and a few select tournaments, this was a bold move. That inaugural year, the women played fourteen sanctioned events for $50,000 in total prize money, good pay in those days. The twenty-first-century LPGA tour has grown to over $36 million in prize money and its competitors represent many nations.

Today women compete in basketball, soccer, hockey, rugby, golf, cycling, tennis, skiing, skating, running, softball, baseball, rowing, and extreme sports. They report on the events and make decisions on sponsorships. They are a force as consumers, participants, spectators, and industry decision makers. But they, too, had to fight ignorance and prejudice to get their chance.

THREADING THE PAST TO THE PRESENT

One component of the sports culture that has been a particularly valuable asset to the industry is tradition. Tradition has great value, not only in building the brands of our global sports icons, but in galvanizing and representing the simple joy of being a fan or enthusiast. To promoters, property rights holders, and licensors, the celebration of sports traditions also means money.

People reference sports traditions in conversation as easily as they exchange pleasantries. Just as people know that "Gotham" refers to New York City, or "The Windy City" is Chicago, people understand that the "Fall Classic" is the World Series, and that "Super Sunday" doesn't refer to Easter, but to the Super Bowl. Here are some other word/sport associations:

Yellow Jersey: Tour de France
Azaleas, Dogwood: The Masters
The Granddaddy of Them All: Rose Bowl
Medalist: Olympics
Sport of Kings: Horse racing
Air: Michael Jordan

"Ruthian" evolved from Babe Ruth's otherworldly exploits and the incredible impact he had upon 1920s society. Charles Lindbergh was a hero from the same era, but there is no word "Lindberghian," for daredevil overachievers. Furthermore, though Lindbergh was an incredibly important icon of his time, his legend has not endured to the extent of Babe Ruth's. Lindbergh's achievements were indeed great, but aviation does not share the same status with the media and populace in modern America, as a home run hitter whose name still ranks high in several statistical categories.

Traditions manifest via perceptions and the delivery of expectations. Fans develop affinities for their teams, personalities, and icons due to the quality and consistency of their user experience. Sitting at Wrigley Field, gazing at the ivy on the outfield walls, watching the Green Bay Packers leap into the Lambeau Field stands after scoring touchdowns, or even watching Tiger Woods slip on another green jacket are all comforting images and honor cherished traditions in the sports culture.

Red Sox fans cannot bear to think of watching baseball anywhere but Fenway Park on Yawkey Way, even if it means a paucity of rest rooms, cramped seats, and some blocked site lines. For a true Red Sox fan, eating an Italian sausage outside the park and strolling in and staring at the Green Monster out in left field has as much significance as the Boston Tea Party or the Battle of Bunker Hill.

The Indy 500 winner drinks from a milk jug. Winning coaches in big football games get a Gatorade bucket bath. If the victory is really important, like a Super Bowl or college championship, they get carried off the field. Frenzied college football fans tear down goal posts. The Williams College football team walks through town and stops at a local establishment, in uniform, to sing songs and swap stories with locals after the last home game. Why? It's a tradition.

Tradition and nostalgia are also two critical elements of sports promotion. Baseball has long held Old Timer's Day as a way to connect their past to their present (and to sell tickets). All leagues have had special "retro" promotions where the players wear old uniform designs. Sometimes the league mandates it, sometimes the individual teams decide to do it. In some cases, it serves to remind fans why they buy the tickets. In all cases, there is a financial motive, since they can sell nostalgic merchandise to commemorate the occasion. The Celtics left the Boston Garden, but duplicated the parquet floor at the Fleet Center. The parquet floor is the only remaining vestige from their days at the Garden, but it is as much a critical link to their past as Red Auerbach's cigar, or Bill Russell's number "6" jersey. The opening of the Baltimore Orioles' Camden Yards demonstrated that "retro" was, indeed, a hit with fans, and it reinforced the concept that tradition is one of the hot spots of sports marketing, resonating with fans and with their wallets. Not only did the success of Camden Yards touch off a $15 billion spending spree that reconfigured sports facilities across North America, it also empowered legislatures to implement tax increases and attempt urban redevelopment with sports franchises as the centerpiece.

Seat licenses and facility names are not considered sports traditions. Not yet, anyway. Let's examine just a few of sports' cherished traditions and look at their humble, almost accidental origins.

Green Jacket

The Masters champion dons a green jacket after winning the first major tournament of the competitive golf year. Originally instituted in 1937, club members wore the visible jacket to help spectators identify them at the early Masters Tournaments, in the event the ticket-buying guest needed assistance. It ultimately evolved into a symbol of enormous privilege; the jacket can only be worn at the club and for official club events. The Green Jacket ceremony held in Butler Cabin on Augusta National's grounds remains arguably the most unique victory tradition in golf.

Frozen Octopi

Since 1952, Detroit hockey fans throw, hurl, chuck, and heave octopi onto the ice after significant Red Wings victories. Two brothers, Pete and Jerry Cusimano, owned a Detroit area fish shop, and they began the tradition when the Red Wings were on their way to the 1952 Stanley Cup. Given the recent success of the Red Wings in the Yzerman era, the tradition thrives to this day. The team even sells merchandise based on the celebratory octopus theme. When an identity becomes commercial, no further proof is necessary of its importance to team tradition.

Got Milk?

Whoever wants to challenge the power of a single image must not be a racing fan. Louis Meyer, winner of the 1936 Indianapolis 500, was photographed drinking from a bottle of buttermilk after his victory. It turns out that his mother had recommended the buttermilk to him. An enterprising and opportunistic Milk Foundation seized the opportunity and has supplied a bottle to the victor in the winner's circle ever since. Today it might be impossible to establish such a tradition, given the financial requirements of product placement in athletic events, especially elite events.[8] But since it's considered "tradition," it stays.

Twelfth Man

In 1922, Texas A&M, playing in the Dixie Classic, suffered a slew of first-half injuries, so many that the head coach, Dana Bible, went into the stands and asked E. King Gill to suit up. Gill had played football, but left the sport to concentrate on basketball. Heeding coach Bible's request, Gill donned pads and took to the bench for the second half. Gill never took the field, but by the end of the game (an A&M victory), he was the only one left on the bench. The symbolism of coming out of the stands to help the team inspires a unique feeling in the Aggies. It is serious business, too. Texas A&M has trademarked the terms "Twelfth Man," "12th man," and "12th mania" to protect their interests in this tradition, which persists today and will for perpetuity.

Wrigley Ivy

Bought and planted by Bill Veeck at the request of William Wrigley, the team's owner, the ivy's presence was the fulfillment of a promise made by Wrigley to minority owners. Veeck had to act quickly, because the request came from Wrigley while the team was on the road. Since 1937, the ivy has come to symbolize Wrigley Field as much as the old-fashioned scoreboard, seventh inning stretch, and roof-top seats from outside the park. The brick behind the ivy is unforgiving to the players, but the ivy will never be cut.

Day baseball was once as much of a tradition as the ivy at Wrigley Field, but that tradition gave way to financial interests in 1988. The economics of baseball mandate maximizing the broadcast revenue stream, especially for a media conglomerate owner like the Tribune Company. Exclusive day baseball had to end at Wrigley so that the team could optimize its audience for itself and its opponents.

One of the reasons why they had to add lights was for the event of postseason play, something Cubs fans usually only dreamed about. The year after adding the lights, the Cubs made the playoffs and played night baseball at Wrigley, but lost to the San Francisco Giants in a thrilling playoff series.

Ryder Cup

In 1927, a rich Brit, Samuel Ryder, donated a gold cup to be awarded to the winning team in a round of friendly golf matches between Britain and the United States. Ryder had no particular golfing pedigree, but he was certainly a businessman of distinction. It is unfathomable to think that a modestly wealthy person today could bequeath an enduring international symbol of sport. There is only one Ryder Cup. No duplicates exist. It is literally priceless. Awarded every two years, its value and significance only increases as it adds to international tradition of competitive golf between Europe and the United States.

The significance of the Ryder Cup, or the Indy buttermilk ceremony, at their points of origin is that there was no financial mechanism that interjected into the event. These two happenings occurred randomly and without financial, or contractual, mandates. The fact that they persevered shows that the events, their organizers, and competitors emphasized the competition and experience more than the inherent business elements in the evolution of the "tradition."

"Take Me Out to the Ballgame"

Neither the composer nor the lyricist of "Take Me Out to the Ballgame," written in 1908, had been to a game before penning the song. In fact, they didn't attend a game for years afterward. Jack Norworth wrote the words while riding the New York subway and Albert Von Tilzer later supplied the music. Norworth did not go to a game until the Dodgers honored him in 1940, thirty-two years after he wrote the song! Von Tilzer had been to a game about ten years previously. The classic song has been recorded more than one hundred times and in 1971 was further popularized by Harry Caray as the song sung during the seventh inning stretch. "Take Me Out to The Ballgame" is sung more often than any song in America, except for the National Anthem.

FIGHTING IRISH:
DUE TO A VISIONARY, NOT A PUGILIST

The University of Notre Dame presents the perfect example of a thriving sports tradition. Today, it receives over $9 million in annual television rights fees from NBC and enjoys a national following. It was, in fact, the first college team to sign an independent deal with a national network, and it has, arguably, the most loyal national following in all of college football. How did a small school located in South Bend, Indiana, capture the nation's interest and become an enduring property of great emotional and financial value?

The University really owes it all to one person, who may be the most remarkable man in college football history, Knute Rockne: Rockne's teams and ideas about promoting them gave hope to the millions of Irish-Catholic immigrants who came to America to discover its promise. The University acquired fans and buoyed their hopes with its gridiron exploits, becoming a mass-media hit before just about anybody else.

Not only was Rockne a great coach, but he was a master of just about everything. He taught chemistry and was the athletic director, ticket manager, and equipment manager. He answered his own fan mail, wrote several books, worked for Studebaker, and did some film work in his spare time. This is a guy who didn't need a lot of sleep. He was a master promoter, realized the power of the media, and would make time for virtually any member of the media, regardless of the outlet represented.

But the significance of Notre Dame was the connection between heritage, institution, and sport, and all from a sleepy little town in Indiana. To think that one man could bring all of those elements together, craft a powerhouse that has endured for decades, and still be a relevant name so many years after his death demonstrates that society yearned for the tradition that he masterfully created.

Yellow Jersey—"Le Maillet Jaune"

In 1903, French newspaper editor Henri Desgrange put some distance between his paper, *L'Auto*, and its rival, *Le Petit Journal*. His brainchild was the Tour de France, a 1,500-mile race staged over nineteen days. The race helped circulation double. Today, the 2,130-mile race is one of the biggest events in the world and the signature event in cycling.

The now famous Yellow Jersey, which is worn by the leader, was instituted in 1919 to help the press and spectators spot the leader. *L'Auto* had been printed on yellow newsprint, so the colorful marker was a natural fit and a link to the race's original sponsor. On July 18, 1919, Eugene Christopher became the first competitor to wear the coveted jersey now recognized as one of the greatest symbols in sport.

IN THEIR OWN WORDS: WHERE TRADITION THRIVES

Jeff Idelson is the Vice President, Communications and Education at the National Baseball Hall of Fame and Museum. The Hall of Fame has many duties as one of America's most cherished History Museums. Not only is the Hall the caretaker of all things baseball in America, but it connects the past to the present and will weave it to the future.

The Hall has exhibits, stages elaborate educational outreach programs, and, of course, features the images, names, and moments of the players, coaches, broadcasters, and personalities that make the National Pastime the greatest game of all.

Mr. Idelson discusses the philosophy, goals, and business of the Hall of Fame, and demonstrates how the game of baseball has relevancy way beyond the confines of a boxscore.[9]

Philosophy

"Our philosophy can be summed up by six words: 'Honor excellence. Connect generations. Preserve history.' We are a nonprofit history museum, responsible to present the history of baseball in an educational, accurate manner.

"The Hall's business, historically, has been as caretakers. At one point that was the only mission, but now it is just a portion of the mission.

"Babe Ruth's bat is still here, but so is the history of blacks in baseball from the Civil War to the present. And our women's baseball exhibit is one of the most popular and important exhibits in the history of the Hall. In many respects, baseball is simply the medium for one historical perspective on America.

"Our best promotional outlet is to collaborate with MLB and the 30 teams. They give us distribution through stadium broadcast opportunities, like the scoreboard, and actual game broadcast partners to run Public Service Announcements (PSA's). We only started the PSA's in the mid 1990's, but they are a great way to talk to the baseball audience and get them exposed to our programs.

"We also promote educational efforts via our website and in lectures to appropriate groups, whether it be academic classes, groups like the National Press Club, or foundations that serve causes such as ALS (Lou Gehrig's Disease). The Hall of Fame represents and reflects history. We at the Hall never want to stray from that understanding, so our approach will always be to pursue only the appropriate audience.

"We also have a traveling show, 'Baseball's America,' that brings Cooperstown to the people. Through our web site and the traveling exhibit, we can market ourselves, and the rich history of baseball more readily to a greater audience. And that is our job, to promote the history of the game, and its significance, in as many ways as possible.

"We recently were part of a joint venture between Project View, a Federal Grant administered by Schenectady School District program, and Ball State University during Black History Month. We had Jackie Robinson's daughter, Roberto Clemente's son, and others to broadcast their thoughts to 20 million kids via the Internet and PBS. It was a tremendous success and a good example of how the Hall can live up to that six word philosophy."

Timing

"Perhaps our best recent endeavor happened in 1998 when Mark McGwire and Sammy Sosa were simultaneously chasing Roger Maris' Home Run record. We noticed that McGwire, in particular, was getting a little emotional when talking about Roger Maris. He lamented the fact that he never got to know him and he wanted the Maris family present when he broke the record.

"On a hunch, we took the Maris bat, the one he used to break the record, to St. Louis, where the Cubs were playing the Cardinals at the time the record breaking moment was coming up. This is sacrilegious; to remove an artifact, especially one like this. But we just had a feeling that it was appropriate, and maybe it would result in a nice photo op with McGwire and Sosa.

"As soon as I got to St. Louis, where both teams were playing (Labor Day Weekend), I realized that the bat was more than just a curiosity. It had great meaning to both players.

"I saw Sammy first and when he handled Maris's bat and swung it in the clubhouse, he immediately gave us the bat he used to break Hack Wilson's franchise Home Run record, saying 'this bat belongs in the Hall, too.' When I showed it to McGwire, he rubbed it against his chest and said, 'Roger, you will be with me tonight.'

"That night, he hit #62 to break Maris's record.

"After the game, McGwire gave the Hall of Fame everything for display: his uniform, helmet, bat and ball. His son was Bat Boy that night and I asked for that, too. Since the Hall is about connecting generations, it would enhance the exhibit to display his son's uniform. Sammy Sosa, too, presented his mementos for the Hall a week later.

"At the press conference, both bats were there and it generated an unbelievable amount of publicity for us, and for baseball. The Hall had enormous crowds in October, November, and December. There was so much curiosity around the objects and the record.

"Americans love history. Malcom Gladwell wrote a book called *The Tipping Point*, which talks about the manner one event, or one moment in time, can generate tremendous interest in something. And that bat, and the Home Run record display became our 'Tipping Point,' and it brought 100,000 people back to the Hall."

Impact on Attendance

"We had a record number of visitors in 1993, 407,000, and were on a pace to break the record in 1994, but the strike brought our numbers down to 345,000, and things declined from there.

1995	326,000
1996	303,000
1997	284,000
1998	331,000
1999	384,000

The 1997 figure represents the first year since 1987 that we had less than 300,000 people visit the Hall. But due to the great interest in the McGwire-Sosa achievements, we were able to get back 100,000 visitors."

Today

"For years, the only outreach program was the Induction ceremony. Now, we have 300 separate events, including multi media presentations, movie series, interactive trivia games for families, book signings (25 authors come every Summer) and traditional exhibits. We do a Legends Series and oral histories where anyone who has a compelling story to share can participate. We got a great reaction when we had a Yankee Bat Boy from 1958–1962 come and talk.

"Our goal is to keep people connected to the Hall, not just as a one time destination. Our quarterly publication used to be a 4 page, 2 color production. Now, it is 30 pages of 4 color information. We have gone from 4,000 to 13,000 members.

"We have an aggressive and strong development effort to build a substantial endowment. We target individuals and corporations, but we are not interested in selling entitlement to an exhibit. Commercialization is not even a temptation. Our museum has a gold label reputation and we would never sell the name of a wing, or exhibit. It is not the right fit for us, or for companies. We will always find the most dignified way to grow and to involve those who are the right partners.

"We license our image to select commercial productions, Wal-Mart and Alamo are two family oriented companies that featured the Hall prominently in commercials and it was a privilege to associate with them. We were part of a unique Wheaties box when Dave Winfield and Kirby Puckett were inducted into the Hall. It was the first time Wheaties developed two separate 'fronts' for the same box series, one with each inductee. The Hall of Fame logo was right there next to the pictures of Winfield and Puckett.

"There is no extra burden on controversy at the Hall of Fame. We have representation of Shoeless Joe Jackson, Pete Rose and some stories that are decidedly not warm and fuzzy. Our job is to display and tell the definitive story of baseball history. We present the facts and let people make up their own minds."

One Particular Inspiration

"One person impacted by our exhibits was Penny Marshall, the actress/director. In November 1988, we unveiled our 'Women in Baseball' exhibit. This was four years prior to *A League of Their Own*. Penny Marshall came up to meet and to interview some of the former players and hear their stories. She was so moved that she decided to do the movie.

"We did another educational effort in March of 2003 on 'Women in Baseball' where the broadcast emanated from Wrigley Field, because Phil Wrigley was a proponent of the successful All America Girls Professional Baseball League.

"In the case of the women's exhibit, it shows how the evolution of the Hall continues. We started with one display, then the movie created more demand for information and now we are doing this outreach program. So we add to our past successes through partnerships and technology to educate people about the cultural significance of baseball. In that process we honor excellence, connect generations and preserve history."

NOTES

1. The issue of discrimination in golf has had moments of irony. In a 2002 interview with *Golf Digest*, golfer Gary Player remarked, "Protesters of South Africa's apartheid policy gave me grief for a couple of years. . . . I struggled through it . . . It was a tough two years. But Nelson Mandela, who spent over 20 years in prison, had it a whole lot worse."

2. J. Lopez, "These Are My Heroes," *Houston Chronicle* [online], www.chron.com/content/chronicle/sports/special/barriers/before.html [December 18, 2002].

McGraw saw him play in Cuba, the only acceptable place at the time for a figure of McGraw's stature to see integrated baseball.

3. Ed Maloney, *"Beau Jack W 10 Bob Montgomery,"* CBS Sportsline, August 4, 1944.

4. "History of the Olympic Games Starting with 776 B.C.," U.S. Swimming [online], www.usswiming.org/media_services/template.pl?opt=news+pubid=216 [December 18, 2002].

5. Ibid.

6. Her film of the 1936 Games, *Olympia*, is still a sports masterpiece. In it, she invented or perfected many techniques, such as: slow motion, underwater diving shots, extremely high and low shooting angles (from towers and pits), panoramic aerial shots, and tracking systems for following fast action.

7. J. Lesko, "AAGPBL League History," All American Girls Professional Baseball League [online], www.aagpbl.org/history/History_1.html [December 28, 2002].

8. This tradition has its detractors, chiefly PETA. The organization states that it is a "beverage born out of cruelty to baby calves." Time will tell if they persuade race organizers to share their opinion.

9. Personal interview with the author.

PART 2

SECOND PHASE OF THE MODERN ERA

1976–TODAY

The layers of the sports industry first took a significant turn after the 1974 baseball season when an arbitrator, Peter Seitz, ruled that Jim "Catfish" Hunter was a free agent. Hunter's owner, Charlie Finley, had violated the terms of his contract and Seitz ruled that Hunter should be available to the open market. Hunter, later elected to the Hall of Fame, became the first prime-time free agent in baseball. Other athletes in different sports had jumped leagues to earn more money, but none had so clearly broken away into the open market of his own league for the purposes of unrestricted, hot-blooded bidding.

Hunter, in a move that proved to be a harbinger for the times ahead, signed a multiyear guaranteed contract with the Yankees. One year later, Seitz ruled on another player-contract case involving two other pitchers, Andy Messersmith and Dave McNally. These two pitchers were dissatisfied with the terms of their contracts and refused to sign a contract for the 1975 season. Their owners automatically signed them to a one-year deal (their contract option under the restrictive, court-supported Reserve Clause meant that their contract could be automatically renewed at the previous year's salary), but the players never signed, and were granted free agency through Seitz's ruling at the conclusion of the season. "The difference between winning and losing was billions and billions of dollars, maybe tens of billions of dollars," said Dick Moss, the lawyer who argued the case for the Players' Association. Seitz ended up losing his job, but he left an indelible print upon the sports landscape.

The floodgates opened; free agency arrived and professional baseball would never be the same. Quickly players in all sports leagues bargained for and won the rights that Curt Flood had pursued in the courts, and salaries started to climb throughout the industry.

Year	Average MLB Salary (rounded)	Average NBA Salary	Average NFL Salary
1975	$45,000	N/A	(1976) $78,000
1980	$144,000	$170,000	$117,000
1985	$371,000	$370,000	(1986) $288,000
1990	$598,000	$823,000	$430,000
1995	$1,100,000	$636,000	$752,000
2002	$2,300,000	$4,500,000	$1,100,000

Sources: NBA 2001; NFL 2002, P. Dukcevich, "Super Bowl Stars are Underpaid," *Forbes* [online], www.forbes.com/2003/01/24/cx_dd0124 players.html [June 8, 2003]. MLB 2002, "Average Baseball Salaries," *Sporting News* [online], www.sportingnews.com/baseball/articles/20021217/445909.html [June 8, 2003]. NBA 1990, 1995; NFL 1975, 1980, 1985, 1990, 1995; MLB 1975, 1980, 1985, 1990, 1995, "Average Salaries by Sport," *Slam!Baseball* [online], www.canoe.ca/ BaseballMoneyMatters/salaries_by_sport.html [June 7, 2003]. NBA 1985, P. Bender, "1985–86 NBA Salaries" [online], www.dfw.net/ ~patricia/misc/salaries86.txt [June 7, 2003].

The increase in salaries can be attributed to four things:

1. Increased legal mobility.
2. Player agents.
3. Greater revenues and more sources of revenues.
4. More media covering, carrying, promoting, and profiting from, sports.

In 1956, the players' share of total baseball revenue was less than 13 percent, but players got more than 60 percent of 1999 revenues of $2.7 billion.

By the end of the twentieth century, the average major team sport professional athlete was earning more than $1.4 million annually, thirty-five times the $41,000 they were making in 1974.[1]

The events of the first seventy-five years of the twentieth-century sports industry yielded significant development. In that time, we saw the formation of leagues, racial integration of competition, technological advancements like radio, television, and commercial air travel. The confluence of the competition, the media, and the need for companies to market themselves blew the roof off of sports, turning it, over the next twenty-five years, into the twenty-second largest industry in the world.[2]

More important, we can look back and see how ruthlessly Darwinian sports leagues were. The teams and leagues fended off competitors, kept the labor supply at a disadvantage, and developed the infrastructure that provided reliable, sustainable revenue streams. Penny-pinching ownership and ruthless contractual dealings allowed the major sporting events to contain their costs and allow the games to persist, build fan bases, and imbed themselves into the fabric of the culture first and the fabric of multinational companies second.

Once the ancillary cash flows became established and endogenous parts of the professional sports landscape, then the athletes' compensation rose to the astronomical levels that they enjoy today. Mickey Mantle had been the greatest player on the biggest stage for many years, but ownership avoided paying him like the marquee players of today. If the Yankees had had one hundred luxury suites, the rich cable package, and diversified sponsor portfolio that they now enjoy, Mantle would have made a lot more money. Joe DiMaggio, when asked what he would have asked for contractually in the modern era, simply replied, "Mr. Steinbrenner, we're going to be partners."

The fact that players' pay rose at the same time as owners' revenues is partly causal. Once the players got an idea of the types of revenues the owners were making and had legal maneuverability, they finally had a basis point for negotiation. And they had someone to do it for them, the player agent. More important, they had an entity to protect them, their labor union. As soon as athletes gained a measure of freedom, they needed representation in order to maximize their opportunity. And the agents have obliged; some think that they have been too effective. But the players were not the only ones to make out. As the layers of modern sports entertainment matured, and the cash flows became both apparent and reliable, owners began to realize tremendous franchise appreciation:

Team	Year of Sale	Purchase Price
Seattle Mariners		
	1981	$13 million
	1988	$89.5 million
	1992	$106 million
Baltimore Orioles		
	1979	$12 million
	1989	$70 million
	1993	$173 million
Texas Rangers		
	1971	$10 million
	1989	$86 million
	1998	$250 million

Sources: J. Quirk and R. Fort, *Pay Dirt* (Princeton, N.J.: Princeton University Press, 1992), pp. 400, 407–408; and C. Lewis, "Bush's Deal for the Texas Rangers," Tom Paine.common sense [online], www.tompaine.com/feature2.cfm/ID/2675 [December 3, 2002].

Things only seem to get crazier in the twenty-first century. The Washington Redskins sold for $800 million and the Boston Celtics for $360 million. Franchises command these prices because of brand equity and the lucrative rights to physical and broadcast territories. Most important, teams have great value because they have loyal customers (fans) and sponsor-friendly, cash rich mechanisms such as broadcasts that enable companies to market products and services to fans.

BRANDS LEVERAGE SPORTS ENTERTAINMENT

Brand specialists need to break through the clutter. They need to give their product an edge at the impulse moment of point of purchase. When kids in the 1960s went to buy baseball cards, they bought Topps. And Topps was just as interested in selling its Bazooka gum along with the cards, either in packs, panel boxes, or alongside the cards in single servings. Today, kids have to wade through a sea of choices for both products. In the gum world, there is sugarless, fruit-flavored, chewing gum, bubble gum, breath-freshening gum, teeth-whitening gum, and gimmick gum like Big League Chew. And that is just the first rack at the store. If the same customer looks for cards, Topps, Upper Deck, Fleer, Don Russ, and Pinnacle all have at least two types of cards, some even more.

The point is that there is a lot to choose from. Anyone who has tried to rent a video or buy a new golf club can empathize with the simultaneous good fortune and difficulty of wading through so many choices.

Manufacturers seek an advantage when it comes time for consumers to open their wallets and make purchases. This has made the relationship with teams, leagues, and athletes very popular with corporate marketing executives. Gatorade, for example, sponsors events, sports leagues, individuals, and teams. Most of their containers on the sidelines just hold water, but having them there sure seems to work with customers; they hold 82 percent of the American market share in the sports-drink category. Not only do they rule the marketplace, but the product line and brand appeal were so strong that beverage giant Pepsi felt compelled to buy Quaker Oats, the former parent company of Gatorade.

That is the ultimate compliment in any corporate world: to so thoroughly dominate your competition that they have to buy you out. Pepsi wants even more out of the brand, so it is pushing Gatorade into the energy bar category to go up against PowerBar, which was recently bought by Nestle. Pepsi is no stranger to trench warfare with a deep-pocket competitor, having battled Coca-Cola in global supermarkets and fountains for many years. Trying to wedge the Gatorade name onto a different shelf seems like an easy task, but it takes time, patience, and resources. The fact that Pepsi is going up against Nestle means that the struggle for the energy-bar category could get very interesting as resources are deployed to promote the brands.

Moving into the second phase of modern sports entertainment, the individual sports properties and their partners affect one another's bottom line. The amount that CBS pays to the NFL influences how

much it can pay the PGA for golf broadcast rights. The amount of money
that Chicago sports fans had to commit to their Bulls tickets might affect
their incentive to buy Cubs or Bears ducats. Furthermore, IBM, General
Motors, and Pepsi can only sponsor so many events. At some point, they
need to determine which events bring them the best mix of channel marketing exposure, leverage, and promotional access to target markets.

Part 2 of *Sports, Inc.* will discuss how television, global markets, and the
industry's uncanny ability to sell, sell, sell have created a platform that
makes sports entertainment a financial and cultural juggernaut around
the world. Specifically, it will look at the financial optimization of the
layers that evolved between 1896 and 1975. Since 1976, issues such as
stadium revenues, high profile endorsements, satellite broadcasting,
long-term sponsorships, and the Internet have become front-page stories
and multibillion-dollar revenue streams that intersect and affect all
aspects of the industry.

NOTES

1. Craig Lamber, "The Dow of Professional Sports," *Harvard Magazine*
[online], http://harvard-magazine.com/on-line/09014.html [September 15,
2003].
2. Jay Abraham, "Sports Careers National Conference," *Sports Careers*
(September 1992): 7.

CHAPTER 6

TV IS KING

What Pete Rozelle did with television receipts probably saved football in Green Bay.
—Vince Lombardi
Coach, Green Bay Packers

More than fifty years after the DuMont Network broadcast the first NFL game (1951), TV has truly perfected capturing and packaging the frenetic pace of the game. In fact, it delivers the action like a perfect Montana to Rice spiral.

Professional football has gone from a Sunday-only event on two networks in the 1960s to being featured on three major broadcast networks and a cable station, and dissected on every airwave possible seven days a week in the twenty-first century. HBO does not have a broadcast contract with the NFL, but they have an analysis show. The fruitful relationship between the NFL and its broadcast partners has helped make the draft, preparation for the draft, and even spring minicamps part of the sports news of the day. In 2002, the league experimented with a new season-opening concept: a Thursday night game on ESPN. The game between the 49ers and Giants was well received by fans, sponsors, and broadcasters. The season "opener" is certain to become a long-term fixture. Americans truly love their pigskin.

The NFL is only the tip of the TV iceberg. The Olympics, golf, basketball, and wrestling all enjoy the gold rush of television. NBC recently made a profit of $75 million on the 2002 Winter Olympics (on sales of approximately $720 million in advertisements) in spite of a very soft economy and tightened advertising budgets. Golf's most recent contract represents a 46 percent increase over the last broadcast fees, primarily due to Tiger Woods's celebrity. The NBA, signed a significantly enhanced contract with two media companies, Disney and AOL Time Warner, at the exact time that they were attempting to sell their sports franchises (Braves, Angels, Mighty Ducks, Hawks, and Thrashers) in order to get out of pro sports ownership. To Disney and AOL Time Warner, "airing" not "owning" became the goal.

Fox's parent company, News Corp, took an $809 million charge on its balance sheet in 2002, citing extended sports commitments. This prompted News Corp president Peter Chernin to comment; "You would have to say, we've overpaid." Regardless, of Chernin's sober assessment, the commitment from TV to the sports industry keeps increasing.

Total National Broadcasting Revenue in Major League Baseball

1950	$1.2 million
1960	$3.3 million
1970	$16.6 million
1980	$47.5 million
1990	$365 million
2000	$570 million

Source: Kris Vaillancourt, "The Relationship of Sports and Broadcasting in Society" [online], http://web.bryant.edu~history/h364proj/fall01/vaillancourt/television.htm [September 15, 2003]; Howard Fendrich, "Fox Lands Exclusive TV Rights to Postseason Baseball," *SouthCoast Today* [online], http://www.s-t.com/daily/09-00/09-28-00/b05sp082.htm [September 15, 2003].

It's the same story for virtually every sports property you see on television. And despite the competition for the fans' attention, sports still attracts viewers and delivers reliable numbers of a specific composition of audience. As long as that happens, TV and sports will maintain this multibillion-dollar relationship.

Industry statistics back it up. In the twenty-first century, and especially in North America, there is no disputing that TV is king. Television provides America with most of its information and entertainment, and

TV sets are found in almost 99 percent of American households. A look at the top ten TV shows in U.S. history demonstrates three general points about our television culture.

Top 10 TV Shows in U.S. History

SHOW	Date	Rating	Share	#Households
M*A*S*H* (final episode)	2/83	60.2	77	50.1 million
Dallas ("Who Shot JR?")	11/80	53.3	76	41.4 million
Roots (Part 8)	1/77	51.1	71	36.38 million
Super Bowl XVI	1/82	49.1	73	40 million
Super Bowl XVII	1/83	48.6	69	40.48 million
XVII Winter Olympics (Harding-Kerrigan skating)	2/94	48.5	64	45.69 million
Super Bowl XX	1/86	48.3	70	41.49 million
Gone with the Wind (I)	11/76	47.7	65	33.9 million
Gone with the Wind (II)	11/76	47.4	64	33.7 million
Super Bowl XII	1/78	47.2	67	34.4 million

Source: Associated Press, "All-time Top TV Shows Listed," Shawnee [online], http://www.news-star.com/stories/082500/ent_toptv.shtml [September 15, 2003].

Three conclusions:

1. Five of the ten events are sporting events.
2. All of the events happen during months of inclement weather.
3. TV is the medium that can, and does, interconnect America.

TV plays a role beyond simple delivery mechanism. TV's pervasive power has spawned trends, made heroes out of anonymous souls, and generated billions of dollars. ESPN was once the struggling idea of an enterprising sports fan. But today, it takes the pulse and sets the tone for the global sports industry.

The sporting events in the table are all championship-type contests. This shows that the basic premise of athletic competition, that is, winning and losing at the highest level, appeals to the vast demographics of

American culture. To say Americans respond to the drama of championship competition is like saying, "gee, submarines are cramped." But it demonstrates why leagues emphasize the pinnacle of performance and build brand identity into inanimate object like trophies and postseason success. The Stanley Cup is the single biggest marketing tool for the NHL. It stands for excellence and symbolizes the best in NHL action. And the teams and networks promote it. The Super Bowl awards the Lombardi trophy, the most coveted item in football. The league and its sponsors put premiums on marketing the Super Bowl, and it is restricted to its most select sponsors and partners. Furthermore, titles and glory always make good promotional copy. In the absence of a compelling plot, determining who is best is always a safe script to follow.

Second, all of these events happen in November, January, and February, when there is relatively less competition for the attention of Americans. The weather is so bad that people want to stay indoors, hence the largest audiences aggregate. Most people welcome indoor events when it is too cold to go on a camping trip! Furthermore, none of the top ten events happen in December, when virtually all of the holiday parties take place. It is no coincidence that the ten most-watched shows of all time occur in November, January, and February. Perhaps most important, no other sport really can compete against the NFL, or the Winter Olympics, during this time. The NBA, NHL, and NCAA basketball seasons are in midseason swing, but they do not offer the drama of the football playoffs or Olympic glory.

The beauty of sports is that there are very few mysteries. Michael Jordan, Tiger Woods, Muhammad Ali, Larry Bird, and Wayne Gretzky were all superior performers. There are no minimum intelligence requirements for recognizing that. The same holds true for many of the successful business principles of sport. If a group, promoter, or property rights holder stages a highly desirable event of public interest and makes it accessible, then the spectators will attend: in person, or by watching TV.

With respect to the Olympic figure-skating inclusion on the list, it shows how the confluence of hype, scandal, and competition can impact a popular televised event. Forever known as the Tonya Harding and Nancy Kerrigan affair, this was not a head-to-head match. Instead, the skating competition took place in the wake of the assault on Kerrigan by

Harding camp flunkies. The unbelievable absurdity of the attack was only exceeded by the press coverage that followed. Women's figure skating has long been an audience magnet, but with the attack as a backdrop, the record ratings were virtually guaranteed.

More than 106 million American households are wired for TV. The proliferation of channels and various forms of content continues to evolve. The industry continually upgrades the equipment for viewing and creates new ways to get the signal. Regardless of whether you receive your broadcast transmission from a cable, a dish, or a rabbit-ear antennae, America is wired for televised entertainment.

Lastly, the amounts that networks pay for the broadcast rights shows that sports works with their consumers—the viewers and the advertisers. Despite complaints of the dilution of product, the attenuation of the audience and competitive ad markets, rights fees keep climbing. It is hard to believe that sports, as a business franchise, are in a decline when the main revenue source keeps increasing its investment in the property.

Major Rights Fees

League	Network	Contract length (in years)	Last year	Amount
MLB	Fox	6	2006	$2.5 billion
	ESPN	6	2005	$875 million*
NBA	ABC/ESPN	6	2008	$2.4 billion
	AOL	6	2008	$2.2 billion
NFL	ABC	8	2006	$4.4 billion
	CBS	8	2006	$4 billion
	Fox	8	2006	$4.4 billion
	ESPN	8	2006	$4.8 billion
NHL	ABC/ESPN	5	2004	$600 million
NCAA Men's	CBS	11	2013	$6 billion

NCAA				
Women	ESPN	11	2013	$200 million
NCAA BCS	ABC	8	2006	$930 million
NASCAR	NBC/AOL	6	2006	$1.2 billion
	Fox	8	2008	$1.6 billion
Olympics	NBC	13	2008	$3.5 billion†
PGA	ABC/ESPN	4	2006	$850 million‡
	CBS/USA	4	2006	
	NBC	4	2006	
	Golf Channel	4	2006	

Source: K. Downey, "Sports TV Gets Pricier and Pricier. Here's Why," *Media Life* [online], www.medialifemagazine.com/news2001/ aprD1/aprog/ 04_thurs/news/thursday.html [December 28, 2002].

* Not reported, but various outlets peg the fees between $140 and $175 million annually.

† NBC owned the Olympic broadcast from 1996 to 2008, with only CBS airing the 1998 Winter Games.

‡ This figure reprensents a total package including all broadcast partners.

This chart has several meanings:

- Sports are a proven property.
- It took them almost fifty years to mature to this point.
- Networks clearly have confidence that it will still be the definitive medium of content delivery in the near future.

Compare the current national revenues for the three major sports to two previous years:

Sport	1970 revenue	1985 revenue
NFL	$50,000,000	$450,000,000
NBA	$ 2,000,000	$ 45,000,000
MLB	$18,000,000	$ 16,600,000

The networks' current contractual commitments exceed $40 billion. The NFL alone divides over $1 billion annually among its teams, more than all three major sports leagues earned in 1985 and 1970 combined!

The $40 billion does not represent the broadcasters' real expenses, either. Dick Ebersol, the long time head of NBC Sports, noted that each Olympics broadcast costs over $100 million to produce. Other sports have similar requirements. Sending reporters and camera personnel to games and having them file reports from the road costs money that is not visible in the rights fees, but shows up in the broadcaster's accounting department. Therefore, the sports rights fee system places a great strain upon itself. The layers of ad specialists, agencies, and creative contributors need to continue to blend persuasive images with the action in order to maintain and subsidize the mechanism of sports broadcasing.

And TV does deliver real value. Public companies like Ford, Nike, and Visa would not pour money and labor resources into TV campaigns if they did not translate into positive consumer response.

MEASUREMENT MATTERS

The very first TV ad aired in 1941 and cost nine dollars for a ten-second spot. That figure was arbitrarily determined. The pricing structure has progressed significantly since then, and spots on *Monday Night Football*, playoff baseball, and even an end-of-the-season game all have prices justified by audience size, merchandise concerns, and overall media delivered. The fundamental premise is that TV exposure has value and that the medium capably delivers an audience. More important, the industry of buyers and sellers has developed a structure where consumer brands and services have reliably leveraged the medium to market their products and services for their benefit. This unshakeable truth helps television retain its viselike grip on the advertising industry. With so many competitive promotional outlets for companies, whether it be online, print, outdoor, radio, venue oriented, direct mail, email, couponing, or simple event promotion, television still reigns supreme, and for many reasons.

First of all, it works. Companies and agencies that promote television media strategies get results. Furthermore, the increase in overall programming reflects that sports works for broadcasters and advertisers. In 1960, ABC, CBS, and NBC broadcast approximately 750 hours of sports programming. That had doubled by 1985. And by 1994, according to BJK&E Media Group, Americans watched an average of 179 hours of sports annually. As the costs and stakes for marketing efforts rise, all participants need to prove their worth and justify their fees. Television gets ratings and ratings translate into brand awareness and consumer action.

Second, the infrastructure is in place. Brand managers, advertising agencies, and even analyst agencies such as Joyce Julius, help funnel creative marketing efforts toward a television broadcast solution. As the advertiser target gets more defined along certain demographic lines, the composition of the audience is as important as its actual size. Joyce Julius, for example, told Adidas that Nebraska's 2002 Rose Bowl appearance gave the shoe company $11 million in exposure. That level of evaluation helps Adidas decision makers in many phases of their business, from product development (how big to design the logo of a shoe used in high-profile games), to forecasting how future similar events might impact brand visibility and relevant sales.

Third, the relationship between broadcasters, sponsors, and events is symbiotic. They all have separate objectives that are served by one another, and they work well toward their individual objectives through one another's medium.

With the advent of the Internet, on-demand media, and even the wireless serving of content, decision makers who purchase these opportunities need verifiable proof of their decisions. They literally cannot afford to just make "a good buy." They need to back it up with data. And the industry obliges. Just as the New York Yankees compete with the Nets, Islanders, Knicks, Giants, Jets, Rangers, the U.S. Open (tennis),

St. Johns, the NIT, and other New York City sports institutions, television competes with their own set of sponsor seekers: radio, ESPN.com, print outlets, concert tours, theme parks, movies, and many other ad vehicles.

Television also gives precision data about its audience. For example, Monday, October 14, 2002, had significant meaning for San Francisco Bay Area sports fans. Their beloved 49ers were playing the Seattle Seahawks on *Monday Night Football* while the San Francisco Giants hosted the St. Louis Cardinals in what turned out to be deciding game of the National League Championship Series. Normally, *Monday Night Football* dwarfs local baseball coverage, but the tense Giants-Cardinals playoff series proved a formidable, alluring alternative.

How formidable? The Giants' Fox broadcast had a 27.1 rating/43 share in the local (Bay Area) overnight ratings, while the ABC *Monday Night Football* contest had a 15 rating/22 share. The Giants versus Cardinals game was a low-scoring, one-run affair but in the game's final hour, ratings steadily climbed.

For this playoff game, when David Bell slid home with the winning run in the bottom of the ninth inning, the Giants' broadcast had a whopping 40.7 rating/55 share for the fifteen-minute interval between 8:15 and 8:30 P.M. in its local San Francisco–area market.[1] Those figures are Super Bowl–type returns.

As the Giants' drama unfolded, the 49ers' viewing figures in the Bay Area were a 11.9 rating/16 share between 8:15 and 8:30 P.M. But as soon as Bell scored the winning run, the 49ers and Seahawks' ratings started to climb. The 8:30 to 8:45 quarter hour yielded a 23.6 rating/32 share, and the next fifteen-minute interval, from 8:45 to 9:00 P.M., when Terrell Owens was about to bust out his Sharpie and autograph a touchdown catch, ABC's telecast had a 27.3 rating/37 share, a healthy audience.

Nationally, *Monday Night Football* outflanked the deciding game of the National League Championship Series (NLCS), where pigskin had 14.3 million viewers and the rawhide gathered 10.3 million viewers. But in the critical Bay Area market, baseball came out on top in terms of audience size, and the broadcaster has proof!

Sports compete with one another, sitcoms, news magazines, and made-for-TV-movies. It needs to respond to emerging developments.

When *Monday Night Football* started in 1970, it was truly a novelty. ABC executive Roone Arledge and NFL commissioner Pete Rozelle gave it a shot, but the risk was very low. Monday night had traditionally been a weak programming night. Networks developed prime programming for later in the week and on weekends. Monday night on television was like Palm Springs in the middle of summer—an "off" season. But it has proven to be an incredible addition for ABC, the longest running series in prime-time history.

Monday Night Football vs. Average of all NFL Broadcasts

Year	ABC ~ MNF	ABC, CBS & Fox (averaged)
2000	12.6	10.7
1999	13.7	11.4
1998	13.9	11.3
1997	15.0	11.8
1996	16.2	12.3

Source: http://www.medialifemagazine.com/news2001/apr01/apr09/ 4_thurs/news1thursday.html

As the comparative chart above shows, ABC's *Monday Night Football* (MNF) yields superior ratings when compared to the NFL's national network average. MNF has the distinct advantage of airing both AFC and NFC games (Fox has the NFC rights and CBS the AFC rights), but what it really has is exclusivity in its time slot. Monday nights only feature professional football on one network. And only one network has live sports action. ABC made the Monday night time slot its own and the results plainly speak for themselves, consistently outperforming the Sunday afternoon NFL broadcasts.

The sociological forces (church, perhaps) behind these facts can be debated and dissected by advertising buying experts. But the precision of the feedback to advertisers has a significant impact on future commercial purchases.

The level of detail that the networks, sports leagues, sponsors, and ad agencies use to analyze the resulting consumer behavior validates the medium. Local and national broadcasters can determine which audience segment tunes in and which tunes out. This information gives quantifiable proof to those involved in decision making and allows them to justify future investments in similar, or even contrasting, opportunities. No brand executive, or advertising agency representative, will place his or her job on the line by diminishing a commitment to television until a more effective medium proves itself.

RATING POINTS

Ratings points measure the number of homes with televisions that are tuned to a particular show. One national ratings point equals 1 percent of the estimated TV homes in the United States, or 1,067,000 households (there are 106.7 million homes with TVs). The "share" is determined by the percentage of households watching a specific show from the total number of TVs in use at that particular time.

The ratings and share determinations have significant value in the advertising and sponsorship world. By delivering certain results, buyers validate their decisions. It is also one basis for paying "promotional debt." If certain target ratings are not met, then the networks will offer "make goods" or advertising inventory on other programs in order to deliver the desired number of eyeballs to the commercial sponsor.

It might not be a perfect science, but it works for industry buyers and sellers. For national ratings, Nielsen Media uses a sample of five thousand–plus households, which comprises an audience sample-size greater than thirteen thousand people. Nielsen places meters on TVs, VCRs and any cable connection in order to accurately track a household's viewing pattern. Household residents then push a button when they start and stop watching a specific program. And ratings are to advertisers what point spreads are to gamblers.

Super Bowl XXXV Ratings

Time Interval	Household Rating	Adults 18–49 Rating	Men 18–34
6:00–6:30 P.M.	36.7	30.0	32.3
6:30–7:00 P.M.	39.0	32.6	35.1
7:00–7:30 P.M.	41.1	34.9	37.6
7:30–8:00 P.M.	42.3	36.7	39.6
8:00–8:30 P.M.	40.2	36.9	37.6
8:30–9:00 P.M.	41.9	37.6	39.3
9:00–9:30 P.M.	40.5	37.5	39.3
9:30–10:00 P.M.	37.7	35.1	37.4
Total Ratings	**40.4**	**35.8**	**37.9**

Super Bowl XXXV Big Spenders (Nielsen)

Company	Time	Investment
Anheuser-Busch	4 minutes	$17.6 million
Pepsi	3.5 minutes	$15.4 million
Accenture	2 minutes	$8.8 million
Volkswagen	2 minutes	$8.8 million
Verizon	1.5 minutes	$6.6 million

Source: 2001 MediaVest based on Nielsen data.

Simply put, communicating with the Super Bowl audience for one thirty-second interval is an expensive effort. In 1972, a thirty-second Super Bowl ad cost $86,000. That investment bought the sponsor an audience of almost 57 million people. Twenty-nine years later, a 2001 Super Bowl commercial cost $2.1 million to reach nearly 88.5 million people. And today buyers have a better idea of actual audience composition with respect to age and gender.

Everything has gone up in price: the price of the commercial slot, and especially production expenses. The average cost to produce a thirty-second spot is $343,000. Since the Super Bowl is to commercial production what the Oscars are to diva fashion statements, the average cost for a company, after agency and production expenses, can exceed $3 million per spot for the Super Bowl.

PAY-PER-VIEW . . . AND CABLE/SATELLITE

If you want to get literal, most of television is pretty much pay-per-view nowadays. Over 70 percent of Americans receive cable, and nineteen million more have satellite-dish systems in their homes. Subscribers literally pay for cable and satellite. Pay-Per-View (PPV) television, though, commonly refers to added, single-feature events.

Pay-Per-View has primarily piggybacked on the boxing industry to become a viable form of entertainment distribution for both the supply and demand side of the industry. Without question, the boxing matches of Mike Tyson, George Foreman, Evander Holyfield, Oscar de la Hoya, and their opponents have been the biggest draws for PPV.

Pay-Per-View in the Recent Past

Year	Revenues
1997	$232 million
1998	$40 million
1999	$219 million
2000	$116 million
2001	$93 million

The much anticipated Mike Tyson versus Lennox Lewis heavyweight bout took place in 2002. It was slated to move to the top of the Pay-Per-View heap, and it did. Over 1.8 million people ordered the fight and watched Lewis defeat Tyson. The record haul of $103 million was shared between Showtime and HBO, two premium cable channels. The Associated Press reported that 19,185 fans crammed into the Pyramid in Memphis, Tennessee, to watch the bout in person, resulting in a gate of $23,026,042. But it was the PPV crowd at home that really lined the pockets of the promoters, fighters, agents, and lawyers who have perpetually feasted on the high-profile events of the sport.

Tyson-Lewis was so big that De La Hoya-Vargas at 900,000 buys and $46 million pales in comparison. The PPV industry should pay Tyson some kind of reward. During the one year he was suspended from boxing, 1998, total PPV revenues slid to $40 million. Iron Mike is clearly the greatest global drawing card in the history of boxing, financially speaking.

Another permutation of Pay-Per-View is the enhanced premium package option added to your base cable or satellite system. Currently, the satellite systems, like DirecTV, offer more capacity, that is, channels, for the consumer to get total sports coverage. It has proved to be quite popular and an incentive to buy a "dish."

During his bye week in the 2002 season, NFL coach Dave McGinnis got a chance to watch all of his competition from one seat. "That DirecTV, that's something. When you start watching it as a fan, and you remove the immediate impact of winning and losing, I can see where that's some fun stuff. It was just nice to not have my mortgage on the line for once. But I can see why people flock to the stadiums to watch it all. I can see why this league is the 10,000-pound monster it is. It was that good. It was that compelling."[2]

DirecTV readily agrees, especially because NFL Sunday Ticket is exclusive to DirecTV satellite service; no cable system carries the package. Satellite television is cable's only competitor and its flexibility might be even greater since it can offer more stations with less bureaucracy than cable systems. DirecTV has 11.5 million subscribers, and that means an attractive revenue stream that can subsidize rights fees to sports leagues. The NFL, for example, nets $400 million annually on the DirecTV deal.

In an industry move, EchoStar and DirecTV, the top two satellite providers, attempted to merge in 2002 in order to take on the cable operators. But that move got blocked by the Department of Justice (DOJ). The DOJ felt that the combined company would then have a monopoly power, even though it would only have a little over 20 percent of the 92 million paying customers for television (cable plus satellite).

In the coming years, the cable versus satellite battle will really take off. Consumers hope that the competition will result in lower prices and better services, but that remains to be seen. As of July 2002, according to the National Cable and Communications Association, cable had 73.6 million subscribers. Its counterpart, the Satellite Broadcasting and Communications Association, tallied 19.3 million satellite or dish subscribers. With dish prices, including promotional incentives, becoming lower than cable, the competition for the viewer will get very aggressive.

IN-HOUSE OPERATIONS AND
REGIONAL SPORTS NETWORKS

The old model was that teams sold cable rights to regional broadcasters whose broadcasts were carried by cable system operators in the region. For the cable industry, it was yet another way to make easy money from fans and sponsors. In the twenty-plus years since cable access became widespread, teams have become part of regional sports networks that can monopolize broadcast access to a team.

The New York Yankees, New Jersey Nets, and New Jersey Devils are broadcast by the Yankee Entertainment and Sports Network, or YES. YES is 60 percent owned by YankeeNets, the owners of the three teams. By controlling 60 percent of the broadcasting arm of these three teams, the YES Network demonstrates how the synergies of modern-day management can consolidate the viewing of the old box known as a TV set.

This is a tremendous development if you are an owner of an appealing team. What it does for the competitive balance of the teams in their respective leagues is debatable. Just as Vince Lombardi sung the praises of Pete Rozelle for smoothing broadcast revenues, the Kansas City Royals might not experience the Yankees' cable successes. Furthermore, a struggling team on its own network might not get distribution on the relevant cable systems in order to maximize profitability.

The Yankees made a reported $57 million in regional broadcasting fees before YES. Those revenues equaled Milwaukee, Pittsburgh, Kansas City, Cincinnati, Oakland, Anaheim, and Minnesota combined! Some analysts think that the team will double that under YES in the not so distant future.

It used to be that the YES teams sold their rights to a local broadcaster on both "free" and cable TV, and then let them worry about selling the ad inventory. Now the teams have figured that if they own it, why not profit from it? They can approach cable operators, advertisers, and the agencies and offer multiplatform opportunities year-round with access to the NHL, NBA, and Major League Baseball. By selling all three properties to the same core companies, agencies, and ad buyers, YES will maintain close ties to primary financial sources through sports.[3]

But YES and the other cable networks are all doing a little of the same thing: finding more ways to sell even more profitable packages to the same buyers. In essence, by owning the network, teams can take the sales administration of some of their TV broadcasts "in-house." In other words, they assume the risk, responsibility, and potential rewards.

In-house advertising sales is expanding in all of sports. The Los Angeles Dodgers took their Spanish language radio sales efforts in-house and realized dividends from the decision instantly. They had previously worked by the old model, where they sold their radio rights to a Spanish language station and left the selling of the ad inventory to them. This resulted in the Spanish language marketplace being an afterthought, even though the Dodgers have a strong Latino following.

But once the team began managing the process internally and committed the necessary resources to the task, its fortunes changed. The Dodgers soon inked deals with Anheuser-Busch, Toyota, and long-time English language radio sponsor, Farmer John (sausage). The Dodgers lost the lump-sum up-front money of the rights sale, but they will gain a profitable business in an emerging market in the long run. They anticipate that the revenue stream might approach $10 million in the next five years.

Perhaps more important, as the Dodgers get closer to the Latin American advertising marketplace, the Dodgers expand their business to include both Latin sponsors and fans. The early era of modern sports marketing did not afford teams the opportunity to assume a couple years of losses in an endeavor. They had to take the conservative route. But with money from so many different sources stabilizing the operation of a team, franchises and other properties can assume the enterprise themselves and reap the higher margins once the channel matures. Other teams are experiencing similar results. The Arizona Diamondbacks are adding Spanish language games slowly into their mix and currently sell about $4,000 worth of ads per game in that marketplace.

If the Dodgers feel they can make $10 million in Spanish language radio in five years by independently handling the accounts, then the Yankees will definitely be able to reap great riches from their new deal with YES. And the real, invisible reward is the relationship ownership they will achieve. By getting closer to the money sources, the Yankees, Nets, and Devils remove the excess administrative layers that supported other people's broadcast interests. This only means that the Yankees,

Nets, Devils, Dodgers, Diamondbacks, and other teams with in-house sales efforts in more broadcast markets, will earn more money to put into their teams.

Red Sox Nation? More Like Red Sox Area . . .

When the Red Sox were sold in 2002, part of the sale included a piece of the New England Sports Network (NESN), a valuable commodity. Red Sox Nation represents more than the folks in Beacon Hill, Cape Cod, Chestnut Hill, and Cambridge. The Red Sox are New England's team. The football Patriots took the moniker "New England" but it really applies to the Red Sox, and the most immediate method of interconnectivity is the broadcast network. Not only does it link the fans to the team, it links the team to advertisers who want to connect with the fans.

If you want to follow the Red Sox and can't make it to Fenway, you need their broadcast partner. The cable industry was deregulated in 1984 and moves in ways that benefit the cable companies, not necessarily the fans. In the time since deregulation, consolidation has limited fans' choices. Either you pay the cable company or satellite broadcaster for their services, or you do not receive the sports programming.

If you live outside the boundaries of the New England Sports Network and want the Red Sox, or Bruins games, then you have to buy MLB Extra Innings, or NHL Center Ice from DirecTV. NESN only controls the broadcasts within its territory. Therefore, the consumers' choices are governed by the deals that the clubs and the pay television industry formulate within the context of baseball's territorial divisions.

This practice is great for a team, but not necessarily great for a fan, who might be interested in more than just the local team. As the Internet and reliable delivery of content via broadband becomes more common, look for this situation to change. Major League Baseball already has an online business set up for selective game viewing. This will one day be their primary source of broadcasting revenue since they will be able to charge fans directly for each game viewed, not indirectly charging fans through broadcasters who are looking to profit from the same exercise.

The exception exists for cable broadcasts carried on national systems, like the Atlanta Braves on TBS. Teams that broadcast on a "super station" make a payment to Major League Baseball based on the number of homes that carry the channel and the number of games that the station airs. The Braves, for example, paid $10 million to the fund in 1991 for those superstation privileges.

THE COMPETITION FOR TV'S AD DOLLARS

Just like sporting events, teams and properties compete with one another for the ad budgets of companies, TV ad sellers are swimming in a sea of competition as well. As the advertising layers have grown, companies are now finding new media and places to put their dollars. And there are many more proposals than ad dollars to go around. Television has been so successful in attracting and retaining audiences that it is difficult to think of all the other relevant outlets. TVs are in almost 99 percent of all households, and television is a great way to visually and audibly approach a customer. Given its facile measurement characteristics and its long-standing success in working with sports properties, it is the medium of choice for many advertisers. To appreciate what television offers a sponsor, one should also understand what other advertising opportunities offer marketers. In 2002, for example, $249 billion was spent on advertising. Where else do ad dollars get placed?

Competitors for TV Ad Dollars

Newspapers

As of the year 2000, almost 1,500 daily newspapers existed. Altogether, they had circulation figures of 47 million on weekdays and almost 60 million on weekends. The top five newspapers are: USA Today, the Wall Street Journal, the New York Times, the Los Angeles Times, and the Washington Post. In the nineteenth century, newspapers and external signage such as postings, signs, and billboards accounted for virtually 100 percent of advertising expenditures, since there were no electronic media opportunities.

Advertising takes different forms in newspapers. Companies can

either take out line-item ads (classifieds), or full-page color advertisements. A full-page, weekday ad in *USA Today* costs $110,000 and for the
weekend edition, it is $132,000. A full-page ad in a regional metropol-
itan newspaper can cost between $20,000 and $50,000, depending on the
size of the area it serves. Today, newsprint advertising is still robust and
accounts for 21.7 percent of all ad expenditures.

Internet

The Internet is the only true interactive ad medium. To advertisers,
"point and click" means that Internet ads can lead to a sale, subscription,
or to people revealing valuable marketing data about themselves. Television is essentially a passive environment, even though many TV ads
encourage specific online behavior, a concept known as convergence.
And while most sports properties (and sponsors) do promote their Web
sites as part of any broadcast advertising relationship, only an online ad
seen by an online user can result in an immediate transaction, something
that Internet advertising sales people reinforce in their sales pitches.

Sports is, predictably, one of the most popular subject matters pursued on the Web. TV networks, most notably ESPN and CBS, have promoted their sites to the very top of their category in terms of popularity.
However, people like the couch and TV environment. "Appointment"
Internet activities will never fully replace the television model, but as
more parts of the world acclimate themselves to being online, it will draw
people from "Must See" TV. Clearly, marketing experts know the World
Wide Web needs to be addressed with both marketing strategy and dollars. Even though the Internet seems to have been around forever, it is
not even ten years old in the form we're familiar with, meaning the
industry can expect great change in the near future. Yet despite its relative youth, it still accounted for almost $229.9 million in sports-related
ad spending in 2001 out of $4 billion in total online ad spending.[4]

Radio

There are more than 400 million radios that transmit signals from over
10,000 radio stations in the United States. Each station sells ad schedules

that broadcast over those 400 million radios in cars, cubicles, and homes across the country. Sports action, sports talk, and analysis comprise an important category in virtually every market in the nation. Over $2.3 billion is spent on sports radio advertising annually.[5] It is a promotional staple.

Magazines

Foote Cone and Belding research unearthed this statistic: a company would need to invest $6.1 million to run a thirty-second TV commercial in each of the top twenty-five prime-time shows to target the 18–49 adult marketplace. To target the same group with a four-color print ad in the top twenty-five magazines would cost $3.9 million, over a 36 percent savings. These are the kind of stats that magazine sales representatives bring with them when they talk with buyers, and the kind of data that TV sales people need to refute to make their own sales pitch the superior plan for the brand in question.

A full-page, four-color "bleed" in *Sports Illustrated's* national edition (over 3.1 million in circulation) costs $247,000.[6] The magazine can offer content-specific opportunities around a certain sport and it has its specials, like the swimsuit edition.

The magazine industry has its own auditing bureau, like the Nielsen Media group, called the Audit Bureau of Circulation and they conduct surveys that confirm the reach and geographic dispersal of the magazine. Again, the reliability of the advertising vehicle helps convince buyers to invest in the opportunity.

Direct Mail

Companies expect a 2 to 3 percent return on all direct-mail campaigns (similar to coupon distribution programs); not a high return, but when you consider the forest that would still be standing if you didn't get all of that junk mail, the process is profitable for the manufacturers that subsidize it.

Outdoor Advertising

Outdoor advertising commonly refers to billboards, road signs, event venues and car/bus wraps. Outdoor offerings are usually done by media conglomerates such as Clear Channel, or even by municipalities, who own the freeways and signs posted at high profile venues. Outdoor advertising is just like radio, TV, online, and print. The property holder packages it and presents it to interested parties. With respect to sports, the complexes, buildings, and facilities are clearly dynamic places since opponents and events change with the seasons, ensuring more variety to those passing by and/or patronizing one of the teams.

The Oakland/Alameda County Complex, including the New Arena and the Network Associates Stadium, hosts the Oakland A's, the Raiders, and the Golden State Warriors. The facilities also host special events like the circus and premier concerts. Most important, the facilities are located directly on Interstate 880, a major thoroughfare. The events draw over 3.6 million fans annually to the facilities, and the highway traffic adds another 70 million eyeballs according to advertising analysts. To enhance the opportunity, architects have erected twenty-five structures to carry advertising. The structures vary from ten-story-high billboards to special kiosks and gateways. The property estimates that it can bring in $60 million over the next twenty years.[7] The revenue will be divided between the teams, the city, and the county.

Nissan, Starbucks, Infiniti, and Warner Brothers all stepped up and bought inventory prior to construction. Advertisers get unique placements in spaces that had been devoid of commercial messaging and along routes that historically have not been tapped. The landlord and teams get another revenue stream, and the companies get yet another way to tie into sports entertainment via the facility.

Wireless

This is an emerging category, especially as cell phones, PDAs, and global communication infrastructure increases. Buffalo Bills fans, through a promotion with Verizon, can get updates and late-breaking news stories delivered on their phones. Pretty soon, a Budweiser logo might also stream across the phone's message space. The medium has yet to be fully exploited, but it does exist. As video-game play on cell phones takes hold globally, then the phone will become a ripe target for commercial interruption.

Video Games?

All of those video games in all of those hands. Over and over and over and over the gamers play. Talk about frequency, demographics, and product positioning! You have access to the desired customer in the comfort of his or her home. The only lack of realism in a game like *John Madden Football* is the lack of commercial presence. Some manufacturers and brands are beginning to make use of the medium. Very soon it could be as competitive and hot as the video-game business itself. It has a huge installed base of loyal repeat customers, a high degree of engagement, and an attractive audience. It is only a matter of time before brands heavily advertise in the medium.

The important conclusion is that all of these other avenues have their strengths and shortcomings. Radio is only audible, and most people hear it while in the car, so they can't easily write down where the sale is, or how to participate in a promotion. Newspaper ads are visually less impressive than alternative forms of advertising. Newsprint quality limits the options, and the ad has a short life span. They wear out their relevancy in twenty-four hours. The Internet still does not have the total trust of the user, nor the established industry infrastructure to place dollars effectively within its marketing engine, and Internet users do resent too much interruption.

Magazines, on the other hand, have long lead times with respect to the printing requirements, they have poor frequency, and lack a certain energy in a dynamic world. An ad lying on a page, interrupting a story, does not clamor for attention. It is difficult to ask a reader to interrupt his or her train of thought on a specific issue to give legitimate, absorbed thought to a product pitch. In short, all of TV's competitors complement advertising on television; they don't replace it.

FROM PASTIME TO PRIME TIME

The most valuable inventory of time is always for the playoffs and championship phase of any competition: the Sunday round at the Masters, the seventh game of any playoff, and the Super Bowl or finals of the NCAA championship. In 2002, for Super Bowl XXXVI, Fox sold over nine and-one-half hours of game-related advertising for a staggering $200 million. Not only is it the most sought-after time for an advertiser, it presents the best opportunity for the sport to market itself to all of its fans. It also gives the broadcast partner a chance to promote its own series, shows, and personalities. When CBS televises a Bowl game, you might just see someone from *Everybody Loves Raymond* on the sidelines, but you won't see anyone from *Friends* because it's on a different network.

PRIME TIME MEANS PRIME DOLLARS

2002 NFL season playoff schedule (games played in 2003):

Saturday, January 4, 2003
4:30 PM ET
  Wild Card Playoff (ABC)

8:00 PM ET
  Wild Card Playoff (ABC)

Sunday, January 5, 2003
1:00 PM ET
  AFC Wild Card Playoff (CBS)

4:30 PM ET—
  NFC Wild Card Playoff (Fox)

Saturday, January 11, 2003
4:30 PM ET
  AFC Divisional Playoff (CBS)

8:00 PM ET—
  NFC Divisional Playoff (Fox)

Sunday, January 12, 2003
1:00 PM ET
  NFC Divisional Playoff (Fox)

4:30 PM ET—
  AFC Divisional Playoff (CBS)

Sunday, January 19, 2003
3:00 PM ET
  NFC Championship Game (Fox)

6:30 PM ET
  AFC Championship Game (CBS)

Sports properties are always interested in increasing the value of their TV package. By pushing their events to later hours like the NFL did to their 2002 playoff schedule (see table above), it ensures that their product can reap the maximum ad dollars. Major League Baseball has not played a World Series "day" game in years because it would mean less broadcast money.

It may seem subtle, but it means millions of dollars for the networks. "Our primetime Saturday playoff games were well-received last year," said Commissioner Paul Tagliabue. "The changes put in place for this season will further expand our potential audience for the playoffs."[8]

Commissioner Tagliabue can say that with certainty, since the 2001 playoff games in prime time yielded record results. The Jets-Raiders game, broadcast on Saturday, January 12, had 22 million viewers. The following week's Tuck Rule game, featuring the Raiders and the Patriots on January 19, drew almost 29 million viewers. This was a 47 percent increase in ratings over the previous year's divisional playoff and ABC's highest-rated Saturday evening prime-time telecast in seven years.

Furthermore, the NFL knows that creating attractive, stand-alone franchise events pays off. Nothing substantiates that more than the Super Bowl advertising rates:

Super Bowl	Year	Network	30 second spot
XXX	1996	NBC	$1,085,000
XXXI	1997	Fox	$1,200,000
XXXII	1998	NBC	$1,291,100
XXXIII	1999	Fox	$1,600,000
XXXIV	2000	ABC	$2,100,000
XXXV	2001	CBS	$2,200,000

Source: "Super Bowl Ad Rates," Super Bowl-ads.com [online], www.superbowl-ads.com/articles_2000/html-files/Super.Bowl.Ad. Rates. html [January 11, 2003].

The NFL does not expect similar results for all of its playoff games, but they want to approximate the conditions to maximize the opportunity. A quick look at the 2002 playoff schedule (on the previous page) shows that all of the games were played in January, 2003. Conveniently, the NFL playoffs began after the distraction and competition of the Christmas and New Year parties ended. Furthermore, the competition and distraction of the College Bowl situation subsided after January 3.

Jan. 1	Rose Bowl	5:00 PM ET Pasadena, CA	Oklahoma vs. Washington St.
Jan. 1	Sugar Bowl	8:30 PM ET New Orleans, LA	Georgia vs. Florida St.
Jan. 2	Orange Bowl	8:00 PM ET Miami, FL	USC vs. Iowa
Jan. 3	Fiesta Bowl	8:00 PM ET Tempe, Ariz.	Miami vs. Ohio State University

Therefore, the only remaining football story to watch, discuss, and enjoy is the NFL. The league wouldn't have it any other way. As time moves forward, they will persist in building this new format of playoff action in January, and their ad rates will do nothing but climb. Furthermore, by pushing their playoff action into January, they can theoretically get companies to spend from their "new" budgets, as it will be first quarter of the new year, as opposed to the last weeks of the prior year when budget has already been spent, stretched, and tapped. The first "great" NFL championship game in 1958 occurred in late December. Forty-five years later, the Super Bowl was played on the last Sunday in January.

Other big games and large events enjoy the best buyer response. The 2002 World Series, for example, sold its first five games of ad inventory before the teams had even been identified. Advertising agencies for big brands like Budweiser, Chevrolet, Coors, Nike, and FedEx can all make last-minute spending decisions for special events like the World Series.

Fox, the broadcaster, sold its thirty-second spots for approximately $325,000 each and raked in almost $20 million per game.[9] Having invested over $400 million per year into Major League Baseball, Fox can recoup 25 percent of its investment in just five games. They can also promote their fall and winter lineup to the millions tuning in and gearing up for the cold winter, a very important advantage.

If the teams cooperate, everyone wins. The 2001 World Series certainly exceeded expectations for dramatic baseball. The New York Yankees and their star-studded lineup met up at full force with the Arizona Diamondbacks' twin towers on the mound, Randy Johnson and Curt Schilling. By the time the teams had battled through five games, America took notice. The sixth game drew 22.6 million viewers, and the thrilling game 7 tallied 39 million.

A DEVELOPING STORY

The big night for TV and its advertisers has become Thursday. It is the last night that people are at home and in their routines before the weekend. Come Friday, people leave for the weekend, or go out and start consuming. The advertisers would rather plant their messages about soda, beer, autos, movies, credit cards, and fast food on Thursday than on Monday. NBC did a masterful job of turning Thursday night into "Must See" TV, and they did it without sports programming. CBS has countered with *Survivor*, its biggest new programming franchise in many years.

In a move to pull away some of the crowd, TNT has planned an NBA doubleheader. If TNT can develop a loyal core, then the composition, or demographic profile, of that audience might just make it a profitable evening for them. TNT obviously feels that there are some disenfranchised males on Thursday night who don't care about *Friends*, or who get voted out of some make-believe "tribe." They have six years on their contract and exclusivity on Thursday nights. They are starting their broadcasts at 7:30, giving their double header a full half hour head start on the competition. Their performance bears watching. It could be the start of a whole new effort to make Thursday night a sports night as well.

Sample Rates

Everyone knows that thirty-second Super Bowl ads now run for $2 million. The very first Super Bowl ad was $42,500 on CBS and $37,500 on NBC. Both broadcasted Super Bowl I, but charged different rates. Ticket prices for the first Super Bowl, which was really more of a challenge match between leagues, were set at $12, $10, and $6. The game did not sell out, but that, like the prices charged for tickets and ad inventory, changed drastically as time went on.

Most ad buys are not single item purchases. That is, buyers usually do not simply buy one ad at a time. They buy a schedule which covers more than one time slot. If an advertiser has a relationship with Fox during the season, then they will get first crack at playoff and premium advertising in the postseason. But they do get broken down into single units as a basis for evaluation.

Sample 2002 30-Second Ad Rates
*SportsCenter:**	$11,000
U.S. Open Finals	$175,000
Monday Night Football	$325,000

Major League Baseball
Division Series	$90,000
League Championship	$175,000
World Series	$300,000

Source: These figures come from industry sources and ad agencies.

Some Other Ad Rates† on a Global Basis

Reader's Digest	$530,907
Time	$343,852
Elle	$310,000
National Geographic	$233,310
The Wall Street Journal	$205,661
CNN International	$6,000
Cartoon Network	$5,000

Sources: "What Do Global Ad Buys Cost," *Advertising Age* (February 8, 1999).

*The popular ESPN show airs at many different times in the day. The prime-time show, obviously, carries a higher value than the early morning editions.

†Print rates are for one-time, four-color full-page ads; TV rates are for thirty-second spots.

Regardless of the medium, or subject matter, advertising is costly. Many of the same brands that advertise in sports media leverage the above outlets for branding purposes as well.

Rights Fees for One Premium Winter Event

The Winter Olympics are an established franchise for networks and their advertisers. Their escalating fees demonstrate their success in attracting viewers and sponsors.

Year	Site	Fees	Network
1960	Squaw Valley	$50,000	CBS
1964	Innsbruck	$594,000	ABC
1968	Grenoble	$2.7 million	ABC
1972	Sapporo	$6.4 million	NBC
1976	Innsbruck	$10 million	ABC
1980	Lake Placid	$15.5 million	ABC
1984	Sarajevo	$91.5 million	ABC
1988	Calgary	$309 million	ABC
1992	Albertville	$243 million	CBS
1994	Lillehammer	$300 million	CBS

1998	Nagano	$375 million	CBS
2002	Salt Lake City	$555 million	NBC
2006	Torino	$613 million	NBC

Source: M. Hiestand and R. Martzke, "Bidding for Olympics on TV," *USA Today* [online], www.USatoday.com/sports/Olympics/2003=04=21=tv= rights_x.htm [April 21, 2003].

The rights fees increased dramatically in forty-two years. The Squaw Valley Olympic Games were the first Winter Olympiad broadcast in America and drew the best ratings in the history of the Winter Games prior to the Salt Lake City Games. The first Olympics enjoyed that magical combination of newness and the patriotic feeling of hosting the Games. Given the fact that there were only two other channels operating, those Olympic Games historically benefited from the lack of programming competition, the climate and the magic that is athletic competition.

Today, most important to the IOC, NBC, and the sponsors, is the fact that people who are watching TV are tuned into their event. For example, the opening ceremony of the 2002 Winter Games set a ratings record with 72 million viewers and a 25.5 rating/42 share. Other channels also had to answer to advertisers for their programming selections sharing the same time slot.

Competitors' Ratings during the 2002 Opening Ceremony

CBS

JAG	5.2/8
First Monday	5.3/8
48 Hours	5.8/8

ABC

America's Funniest Home Videos	2.5/7

Fox

That 70's Show	3.7/6
Malcolm in the Middle	3.3/5

UPN

Space Jam (Michael Jordan)	2.8/4

Source: J. Grossberg, "NBC Puts Olympic Rivals on Ice," Eonline (February 11, 2002).

Not only did NBC and the Olympic advertisers get a huge audience, but they crushed the competition, something which is very important in the broadcast advertising world. The trend may be that the audience divides with the proliferation of channels and choices, but when the property and timing align, sports can still rule the TV domain. Furthermore, the networks and the propery owners want to make the Opening Ceremony a reliable ratings bonanza, even if there is not one second of athletic competition, just many hours of anticipation.

Year	Site	Hours*	Network	Opening Ceremony Rating
1960	Squaw Valley	15	CBS	24.2/37
1964	Innsbruck	18	ABC	12.3/25
1968	Grenoble	27	ABC	2.9/20
1972	Sapporo	37	NBC	19.1/33
1976	Innsbruck	44	ABC	23.2/37
1980	Lake Placid	54	ABC	10.2/31
1984	Sarajevo	63	ABC	17.2/27
1988	Calgary	95	ABC	17.1/29
1992	Albertville	116	CBS	14.5/24
1994	Lillehammer	119	CBS	20.9/34
1998	Nagano	128	CBS	17.1/29
2002	Salt Lake City	375.5	NBC	25.5/42

Source: B. Horn, "A Golden Start for NBC," *Dallas Morning News* [online], olympics.belointeractive.com/otherstories/0210olytvrating.baa76.html [January 15, 2003].

*In 1992, 1994, and 1998, CBS allowed broadcast partner TNT to air fifty hours of each Olympiad. TNT paid for the privilege. The 2002 hours for NBC combine the times the Olympics aired on NBC, CNBC, MSNBC, and NBColympics.com.

TV: TO MAKE OR BREAK

A TV contract is the IPO for sports properties. It generates millions without significant additional incremental costs. The property is already suiting up and playing the game. The stadium has been swept and the administrators compensated for their time. Bringing in the cameras is like bringing in a bag of money. And money goes a long way toward building and maintaining both a brand and a great asset. As soon as the NFL, PGA, NBA, and other sports started to rake in broadcast money, the scope of their business expanded to meet the audience watching at home.

In no place is this more true than college football. Notre Dame has signed fifteen-years worth of exclusive contracts with NBC that would make Knute Rockne proud. Not only does the money go back into the program, but the games act as infomercials for the football program, its players, and coaches. At first, other schools had some understandable issues with Notre Dame's progressiveness, but the smart ones organized along conference lines and pursued TV contracts themselves.

The Southeast Conference[10] does not feature prime markets like Los Angeles, New York, and Chicago, yet teams in the SEC rake in more money than most colleges from those larger media markets. And they do it primarily through TV, though their game receipts are also extremely healthy. The Big 10, Big 12, and Atlantic Coast Conference (ACC) all make about $84 million per year, primarily from football-related broadcast contracts and Bowl appearances. By comparison, the SEC makes almost $100 million from their TV and Bowl business.[11]

The conference has football in its blood and its leadership saw that TV could provide the revenue stream to increase both exposure and the bottom line. The extra revenue goes to fund all athletic programs, not just football, and ensures the health of the SEC in the long run. The exposure also means that potential recruits are more familiar with SEC football and its teams, which helps perpetuate the business.

On the other hand, TV money lured the University of Texas, Texas A&M, Texas Tech, and Baylor out of the established Southwest Conference and into the Big 12, thus devastating the Southwest Conference and bringing over $17 million a year from ABC to the newly formed Big 12. In 2003, the Big East lost Virginia Tech and Miami to the ACC, so consolidation is a true threat to almost any non-"superconference."

The SEC's success shows that excellent management of a great product can make a difference in a sports property's stability. Just as the lack of a national TV contract hurt rival pro leagues like the WFL and USFL, the presence of a strong partnership between TV and a sports property can propel it to success. Of course, fans of the eighty-year-old Southwest Conference, or the schools left out of the Big 12 ABC gold rush, may feel cheated by the system. TV truly giveth and taketh away life support in sports entertainment.

WHAT TV DID TO SPORTS

TV has had many influences. Some obvious, others not so apparent. Much has been written about the size of the audience, the billions aggregating to the Olympics, Super Bowl, NCAA tournament, and any golf tournament that Tiger Woods is leading! It has also had some other, more subtle, influences. TV gave the games mandatory time-outs to air commercials. Baseball has a change every half-inning, but football's changes of possession are not as predictable. Hence, the TV time out. Once the concept was scoffed at, but now no one complains.

TV also inspired names on jerseys, instant replays, and the elimination of day World Series games. The TV people build up the climax of a season, and they pay handsomely for the privilege to broadcast championship events or series, so they want to start the games when the audience is at home, not at work or school.

TV makes stars and leverages them to become even more integrated into the cultural fabric. The cameras trained their eyes on a young golfer named Tiger Woods, and by his fifth season as a pro, he had revolutionized the ratings for golf fans and reaped enormous riches for the PGA Tour and his fellow pros.

Tiger's star power is so bright that the PGA negotiated a 46 percent increase in rights fees for the PGA events in 2003–2006. The $850 million that the PGA negotiated will subsidize their tournaments, foment more fervent fan support, and build the audience of golf for their next round of contract negotiations.

TV is the reason that football is the most popular sport in America. It's also the reason for *Monday Night Football* and those insufferably long, but impossible to turn off, Super Bowl preview shows. It's the reason the O. J. Simpson trial replaced the Richard Bruno Hauptman Lindbergh kidnapping case as the definitive trial of the century.

In college football, it has changed the Bowl system, and many say not for the better, at least not yet. The Rose Bowl no longer features the best of the Pac 10 versus the best of the Big 10. Instead, the Rose Bowl has become one fourth of the complicated Bowl Championship Series, an attempt to determine college football's best team.[12] The system is not an elimination tournament, but ranks the year's top teams and then matches them accordingly.

TV is also the reason that Howard Cosell's half-time highlights helped define a reporter and an era of America's sporting history. Those highlights, complete with Cosell's inimitable narration and interpretation, were the precursor to the wildly popular *SportsCenter*, perhaps the definitive sports-viewing experience and icon in North America. *SportsCenter* has spawned its own industry: its personalities write books, host radio shows, write columns, and even appear in ads that define our times. Television has made celebrities out of other journalists as well. Chris Berman, Curt Gowdy, Chris Schenkel, Bob Costas, Jim McKay, and Al Michaels represent the evolution of Grantland Rice and Red Smith from yesteryear. John Madden retired as one of the best coaches in NFL history, compiling one of the best records of any coach in any sport. He won a Super Bowl and left the sport after having influenced it greatly. He then proceeded to become one of the most important announcers in the history of television. When he retires, he will be remembered more for his announcing than coaching, an improbability when he was hoisted onto his players shoulders after winning the Super Bowl. Television has helped create brands and has inspired innovations like infomercials, slick thirty-minute product pitches that sell golf swing devices, George Foreman Grills, and in-home exercise machines. In short, TV has become, and will forever be, the critical medium for the modern sports fan.

IF TV IS KING, THEN ESPN IS ITS PRINCE

As of 2002, ESPN had a worldwide distribution of 140 countries or territories worldwide, including 76 million American homes. In 1998, ESPN created a reported $356 million in cash flow on revenues exceeding $1 billion.[13] Not bad for an entity whose first broadcast was slow-pitch softball. The Entertainment Sports Programming Network started in 1978 with these fateful words: "If you're a fan, what you'll see in the next minutes, hours and days may convince you you've gone to sports Heaven."

How big is ESPN? In 1992, even before it created its own branded events like the ESPYs, or was owned by Disney, the small, Bristol-based business out-earned its parent company, ABC. Over four million homes watch *SportsCenter* at least once a day.

ESPN is a marketing machine that brings relevancy and urgency to its promotions. To compete in the print arena, it launched a magazine, *ESPN The Magazine*, in 1998. Circulation opened at 350,000. With a year of clever promotion, circulation more than doubled to 850,000. They launched a Web site and it now resides near the top in traffic and user loyalty. ESPN also pursues its own projects, recently venturing into dramatic productions on Bobby Knight and Bear Bryant. The network frequently reports on challenging issues in *Outside the Lines* and never cheats its loyal fans on any worthwhile sports highlight or bit of trivia. In a world of conflicting opinions and never-ending arguments, all sports fans agree that ESPN is a truly necessary and appreciated pleasure in their lives.

ESPN has become the most powerful brand in all of sports. In just over twenty years time, it has become intertwined with all that is relevant in the world of sports. ESPN has kept the approach fresh, yet mindful of tradition. It has spawned some imitators, but no equals. A brief look at some of its international expansion shows how it, like the sports industry, spreads slowly and certainly throughout the globe.

ESPN Timeline

1978: Goes on Air

1983: ESPN starts to syndicate programs internationally.

1984: It acquires a part of The Sports Network in Canada.

1988: ESPN International becomes an official division.

1989: ESPN Latin America launches, and ESPN buys a part of the French language Canadian sports broadcaster.

1990: ESPN partners with Japan Sports Channel and they launch ESPN New Zealand.

1992: ESPN Asia debuts.

1994–95: ESPN is now available in North Africa, the Middle East, Brazil, India, and Australia.

1996: ESPN2 moves into Latin America.

1998: ESPN Taiwan debut.

2000: ESPN Israel debut.

2001: ESPN Classic Canada debut.

2002: ESPN Classic Sport in France and Italy debut.

NOTES

1. S. Kroner, "Giants Top 49ers in Ratings," *San Francisco Chronicle*, October 16, 2002, p. C2.

2. Banks, "McGinnis invigorated by up-and-coming Cardinals," CNNSI, October 12, 2002.

3. YES instantly became embroiled in a sticky legal dispute with Cablevision, the former owner of Yankee cable rights. Cablevision wanted YES to be a premium channel and YES wanted to be a part of basic cable. The dispute ended up depriving millions of Yankees fans of cable access and costing YES millions in earnings. As of this book's printing, the dispute had not been legally resolved. Cablevision lost 39,400 subscribers between January 1 and October 1, but only 1,300 once the season ended.

4. "By the Numbers 2003," *Sports Business Journal* (December 30, 2002): 152.

5. Ibid., p. 151.

6. "Bleed" refers to color going all the way out to the edge of the page. A non-"bleed" ad means a reduction in price by 15 percent, so image has its price!

7. "O-town takes a cut of new arena outdoor ad revenue," *Media Week*, November 18, 2002.

8. "New Times Announced for NFL Playoff Games," NFL [online], http://www.nfl.com/news/story/5849166 [September 15, 2002].

9. George Raine, "Advertisers Hope Series Is Wild—Through Game 7," *San Francisco Chronicle*, October 22, 2002, p. B12.

10. Alabama, Arkansas, Auburn, Florida, Georgia, Kentucky, LSU, Mississippi State, Ole Miss, South Carolina, Tennessee, and Vanderbilt.

11. David Markiewicz, "How the SEC Made it Big," *Atlanta Journal-Constitution*, August 19, 2002, p. B4.

12. BCS consists of Rose Bowl, Nokia Sugar Bowl, FedEx Orange Bowl, and the Tostitos Fiesta Bowl.

13. Michael Freeman, *ESPN: The Uncensored History* (Dallas: Taylor Publishing, 2002), p.6.

CHAPTER 7

SPONSORSHIP
DEVELOPING A MARKETING PLATFORM

S ponsorship, simply put, is the mechanism that supports and sustains the sports entertainment industry. Due to the effective implementation and analysis of sponsorship, the sports industry has risen to its current financial state. To appreciate sponsorship, one needs to consider the context of the overall advertising market. Today, industry analysts calculate ad spending at more than $249 billion per year, or approximately 2.5 percent of the Gross Domestic Product.[1] In the United States, over $2.35 is spent every day advertising some product or service to each American man, woman, and child. And messaging comes in a variety of forms and via many delivery mechanisms. People get bombarded listening to the radio, watching TV, surfing the Internet, driving down a highway, reading the paper, or walking into a sports facility.

Marketers have devised ways to mix persuasive images for their products with movies, music, education, amusement parks, and the entire gamut of the sports industry. From Little League to the four major leagues, virtually every team seeks some sort of corporate subsidy, selling everything from the team's audience to their logo and likeness.

IEG Sponsorship Report, a leading authority that tracks sponsorship investment, states that sponsorship has grown at more than twice the rate of traditional advertising and sales promotion. Total sponsorship spending (sports, entertainment, arts, etc.) in 2001 was $23.6 billion globally and $9.3 billion in the United States. Approximately $6.4 billion, or 69 percent, is invested into sports marketing opportunities.[2]

Considering that teams, leagues, and event promoters did not have dedicated sponsorship departments until the 1980s, this development is a recent phenomenon. Companies succeed in sponsoring myriad events, but in a sports-obsessed culture, sports marketing applications dominate the landscape.

Sponsorship validates the fact that the revenue-generating layers of the sports industry are both proven and effective. Not only do they earn money for the properties, but they deliver marketing value for the participating companies. Teams did not accidentally dream up entitlement zones, retail licensing privileges, and fixed-position in-game advertising spots. Diverse concepts like named facilities, co-branded features, and category exclusivity were created by innovative individuals solely to use the sports property as an advertising, or sales, vehicle, to generate revenue for the team or event. The fact that it successfully markets products and services perpetuates its evolution.

Sponsorship means two things for the two separate forces that shape it: first, it provides marketing platforms for buyers; second, it creates, augments, and fortifies revenue streams for sellers.

THE SELLER

The seller has built up the advertising and promotional commodities of his. property over time and looks to merchandise them to brands, or any entity with a promotional budget, for the purpose of revenue generation.[3] Simply put, selling the sports property means offering access, identification, and the opportunity to build relationships with a consumer segment and your own business channels through the entertainment of the sporting event, team, or personality. Furthermore, all promotional inventory featured in sponsorship packages are commodities that have a vibrant market, and it must be positioned that way; otherwise, its value will never be returned.

As mentioned in the discussion of the first phase of the sports industry, ticket sales represented the primary revenue stream for the sports industry. In fact, the property rights holders had such suspicion for anything that might threaten their physically captive audience that they resisted the integration of radio broadcasts for almost fifteen full years. Just think how many more kids would have loved to hear about Babe Ruth!

But as soon as they accepted radio and developed it into a reliable promotional and financial component to their business model, the owners discovered the beauty of developing new revenue streams. Today, virtually every form of sponsorship aims to service one particular revenue stream of a property and it props up and solidifies the base of the sports industries multiple platforms.

SPONSORSHIP BENEFITS

The seller's task is to identify the pieces of his event that have commercial value, attach a price, and then allow the corporate customer to exploit them for their own purposes, yet within the guidelines of the property. For the buyers, they receive a marketing platform that they can use to create programs, brand identity, consumer focus, and team spirit among their employees.

Potential goals for a sponsor:

- Reach an event's audience at the event and through the available media. Whether it is a national broadcast or regional event, the audience has value.
- Build brand identity with on-site visibility and naming rights. Fans will not remember that Coca-Cola sponsors the team unless Coke does its best to place its identity within the action and personality of the event. Fans attend for entertainment and excitement, not memory exercises. Coke needs to position its logo and messaging to create the lasting connection.
- Sample your product or service. By providing a positive user experience for new customers, you can convert them. Signing up a fan for a credit card at the facility and giving them a licensed hat is better than sending a nondescript piece of direct mail to the person's home.
- Reward employees and create incentive programs involving the property. By having an internal marketing tool like a relationship

with a sports property, companies have a convenient method to extend their business to a more informal setting.

- Create their own programs within the event. Someone came up with the idea for the half-court shot at half time and the "fan of the game" concept. By putting their own signature on an event, companies create franchises that resonate with fans once they leave the facility. In the case of Taco Bell, when they give out free Chalupas when the home team scores a certain amount of points in a game, they get fans chanting "Chalupa." Thousands of people chanting for your product doesn't happen at the symphony!

- Lightning in a bottle. If something tremendous happens, that can be a flash-point for your brand or product. Jerry Rice wore the CNS nasal strip (an antisnoring device) on *Monday Night Football*. The announcers talked about it all game. The next day, the stock of the company went up 11 percent. Eight years later, another San Francisco 49ers receiver, Terrell Owens, created a Monday night stir. Owens pulled a Sharpie pen out of his sock to sign an autograph after scoring a touchdown, and gave the ball to a friend in the stands. The Sharpie brand received millions of dollars worth of exposure in the ensuing months. They even created an advertising campaign around the incident.

- Build partnerships with other sponsors. Coke and Budweiser sell products with many retail partners. A sporting event offers an opportunity to direct fans and consumers to specific retailers or points of sale, or through specific actions such as visiting a Web site.

- Integrate your product into the event. Wilson is the official football of the NFL. Gatorade pays to supply teams with jugs, product cups, and towels. Coca-Cola pays for pouring rights at facilities, and the list extends into all aspects of a team's administration and competitive presentation.

- Leverage special mailing or customer lists. The best consumers are often season-ticket holders. Not only are they individuals with disposable income, but they have influence where budgets get allocated. Direct access to loyal fans can be significant business for brands. Fans use long distance, buy shoes, and have checking accounts, too.

- Sell your product at the event via concession access privileges. Get your product into the fans' hands and their money into your coffers.

Since staging events have significant expenses, from renting facilities to hiring talent and administrators, pursuing sponsors spreads the cost of managing a sports property to somebody other than the owner and direct consumer of the events.

The seller needs to know enough about the prospective customer to highlight the features of the property that the buyer will deem most valuable to their strategic interests. Furthermore, the seller cannot think that he or she knows the sponsors' business better than they do. The true job for the seller is not simply to close the deal and cash a check. The seller wants the buyer thinking about ways the property can make their business more effective in both the near and long term. Once the buyer believes the sports property will be a catalyst for their goals, then the seller's job becomes executing the sponsor's goals and the property can gain a long-time corporate ally.

Seller's Mantra

Before an effective sponsorship salesperson can sell his opportunity, he should think about how the property can benefit a partner.

"Our event, team, or property offers integrated partnership opportunities that cater to each corporate partner's marketing goals. Our philosophy emphasizes total integration of partner brands with our event, team, property. This means that brands can be featured at our venue, on all messaging, on communications with our fans, and in our local market, leveraging the rights and assets that you attain through this category-exclusive opportunity. Our promotions will drive traffic to specific retail locations, create new revenue streams, and build customer and brand loyalty throughout your entire sales channel."

Sellers can never lose sight of their needs as an organization. Responsible, savvy sports sponsorship sellers know the dimensions, limits, and value of their event. The International Olympic Committee is one organization that knows the context of its sponsorship sales goals, and what it needs from its corporate partners in order to succeed. In 1948, there were 17 sports, 136 events, and 4,092 athletes at the London Olympic Games. Fifty-two years later, after the Sydney Games, the IOC decided that they needed to set limits of 28 sports, 300 events, and 10,500 athletes. The Study Commission determined that one extra Olympian costs $30,000. Since sponsorship and broadcast fees subsidize the Games, the IOC needed to achieve a knowledge of specific incremental costs. Only then will their total sponsorship sales strategy make sense.

For the IOC, their highest priority is to sustain the Games and maintain their integrity. Sponsorship will allow them to fulfill those twin objectives. By limiting the number of events and participants, they can make budgets and meet them. The IOC's job has grown dramatically since Pierre de Coubertin convinced the world to resume the Olympics, and sponsorship allows the IOC to manage the Games for the world's participation. Most important, sponsorship will allow them to continue to subsidize the participation of poorer nations. By setting the contextual limits of the Games, the IOC can responsibly value the opportunities for their many sponsors. By creating categories and specific rights and access to opportunities, the IOC has created an environment that fosters sponsor success.

Buyer's Edict

On the other side of the equation is the lucky buyer, the entity with the budget to invest in sports marketing opportunities. Smart sponsorship buyers do not go where their personal interests lie, but where their customers and business partners exist. The buyer needs to tell himself: "Investing in the property gives our brand the opportunity to communicate with a specific audience. It also presents the right to use the property within the framework of our own business structure to grow our customer base, galvanize internal operatives and learn more about our consumer. The primary objective of our sponsorship will be to learn the best ways to feature our products and services in the relevant markets."

Once the buyer and seller determine to work together, they need to identify what specific rights, privileges, and programs they want to pursue. Six popular implementations, or applications, of sponsorship are the following:

- Retail marketing program execution
- To generate media traffic
- Devise internal sales tool
- Create on-site marketing and event programs
- Product placement and technological integration
- Endorsements

RETAIL EXECUTION

Walk into any supermarket. Go up and down the aisles and look for sports identification. You will see it everywhere. You will find images of teams and athletes on labels of Campbell's Chunky Soup, twelve-packs of Coca-Cola, and on Nestle's Crunch wrappers. The structure of a retail promotion normally follows a formula. The manufacturer uses an image of a team or person to help sell a specific product or products. The company usually has a contest or premium item associated with the display or point of sale. The display signifies that the store or retail location has been persuaded to buy more product and to allow its valuable space to be used specifically for this program. Normally, the manufacturer then dedicates money to invest in awareness campaigns to drive traffic to the specific store. Often you will hear commercials saying something like, "To win your chance to go to the Super Bowl, go to your participating retailer and look for the Coca-Cola display." That ad means that the participating retailer, whether it be Kroger, Target, or 7-11, has entered into an agreement with Coca-Cola to promote one another over a specific, negotiated, promotional period.

One of the best retail programs is Anheuser-Busch's "Bud Bowl." The Bud Bowl started in 1989 with one purpose: to sell more Budweiser products. Budweiser, and their major competitor, Miller, both had NFL marketing rights in 1989, with Miller owning exclusive Super Bowl trademark marketing privileges. This gave them the right to use the term "Super Bowl" and its logo in any marketing communication materials they developed. Miller chose not to advertise on the broadcast that year and Anheuser-Busch pounced on the opportunity. They made a heavy investment in the NBC broadcast, enjoyed category exclusivity, and created the Bud Bowl to counter their chief rival's own Super Bowl plans. More important, Anheuser-Busch took the program to its retail partners. They set up elaborate store displays featuring Budweiser and Bud Light, gave away $1 million, and involved everyone in their sales and distribution network in this program.

Anheuser-Busch also enlisted well-known personalities like Joe Namath and Chris Berman at various points in the program to increase the campaign's visibility. In the first year of the program, January brewery sales rose 17 percent over the previous year.[4] It takes a philosophical commitment, and an investment of resources and planning, to make a retail program successful. Anheuser-Busch's Bud Bowl is a textbook case.

Twelve years later, the Bud Bowl still worked as a Super Bowl anchor. In fact, the long-term investment in it gave the term "Bud Bowl" a life of its own. In Tampa, for Super Bowl XXXV, the Ybor city district, a night life destination, became the place to be for Super Bowl–related festivities. Creating a Bud Bowl in Ybor city helped generate publicity and sales around the event. EventSavvy, a promotional operator in the Tampa Area, estimates that beer sales increased by 20 percent in the Tampa/Orlando area during the Super Bowl period. Also, seventy-five separate media events originated from Ybor City's Bud Bowl.

The Budweiser brand has developed a long-term platform off its original Bud Bowl investment and cemented its ties with football fans through their retailers. The Bud Bowl persists because it is a successful program. And Anheuser-Busch has developed a successful and fun promotional franchise. The feedback that they have received has only helped it to evolve and improve.

Anheuser-Busch is not the only beer company, nor the only beverage company, executing retail programs. According to *Beverage World* magazine, almost 20 percent of all supermarket revenue comes through some type of beverage purchase. Anheuser-Busch spends the most on sports advertising, investing in the neighborhood of $220 million annually. Pepsi spends almost $200 million annually on sports, and Coca-Cola in the $135 million range. That is a lot of marketing muscle, but with one in five dollars at stake, the rewards are enticing.

But every retail product and each category of retailer, whether it be auto parts, paint, stereo equipment, or food and beverages, conducts sports programs designed to get sports fans into their stores to spend money. The lesson is always that the right mix of product and promotion works with sports fans as consumers.

TO GENERATE MEDIA TRAFFIC AND AWARENESS

Several forms of sponsorship manifest in media impressions, and across many different forms of media such as radio, television, and outdoor billboards and print. There are direct purchases of time and opportunities where exposure and the impressions are reliable and priced accordingly. A second pursuit has residual media consequences. Buying a Super Bowl spot, for example, has spun off an auxiliary industry all its own. Each ad gets rated and written up across America. USA Today devotes entire articles to the companies that create ads for the broadcast, and the discussion of the Super Bowl ad sweepstakes takes on a life of its own. Anheuser-Busch, in the "Whassup" campaign, generated positive buzz that followed the airing of the ads for weeks after its debut, even spawning a satiric response from Heineken.

Media traffic used to be a linear issue, where commercial buys were separate expenses handled by different personnel. The Olympics still operate in that fashion. But many properties have begun to integrate their sponsorships and include many forms of media along with other privileges.

Some say that presents a problem, that with so many entitlement components and sponsor-driven features, the media exposure blurs right into the competition. Commonly referred to as advertising "clutter," brands do not like getting lost amid many forms of commercial interruption. But the prevailing thought is simply that companies like to see their name and logo wherever they can generate an impression.

The Staples Center in Los Angeles is a good example. Why would an office supply chain, especially one based in Massachusetts, want to put its name on an arena in Los Angeles? Simply put, the Staples Center investment helps establish Staples as a national brand and heightens its profile with all categories of customers, especially those in southern California.

That might sound like nothing but buzzword gobbledygook, but it is an understatement of what the venue association has meant. The Staples

Center is the premier arena in the western United States, maybe in all of the United States It hosts the Clippers, Kings, Lakers, Sparks, and many concerts and prime events. Sporting events anchor the facility and keep the Staples name in the spotlight in the second largest media center in the nation. Staples pays $5 million for the privilege, but goes coast to coast with their various events on ESPN, Fox, ABC, and all of the accepted media outlets.

It used to be that sponsors would simply pay for the name of the broadcast and a couple of spots during the telecast, like *Shell's Wonderful World of Golf* series. The current model moves toward an integration of the sponsor with the event. For example, when a baseball team changes pitchers, they will often have a segment where they take the opportunity to make a play on words: "when it's time for a change, take your car to Jiffy Lube for their fourteen-point inspection." Both the property and sponsor look for ways to tie companies to the action and create brand exposure within a sports environment. ESPN's *SportsCenter* has created entitlement features like the Budweiser Hot Seat, just like Visa, Dockers, and other companies became sponsors of Fox's halftime show. As media expands into the Internet, cable, satellite, and wireless, the methods that companies use to gain access to eyeballs will evolve, but the intent of generating impressions will not.

INTERNAL MARKETING TOOL

In many ways, one of sports marketing's first, and most important, applications came through informal incentives like giving away tickets to star employees and their clients, customers, and friends. Taking a valuable commodity and rewarding an employee for a job well done only reinforces the idea that sports merchandise and entertainment has great value in the corporate world. Over time, the concept of the boss dropping two ducats off at your desk has evolved into significant incentive programs, and is a key selling tool of sports property owners.

The John Hancock Insurance Company, for example, bought sponsorships in the 1994 and 1996 Olympics. They had several plans for the relationship, and one in particular was for their employees. They awarded special trips to top producers in the company. By dangling an attractive carrot in front of company employees, Hancock saw revenues related to the contest increase by $50 million.[5] Furthermore, two out of every three employees participated in some type of Olympic promotion and 95 percent attended some form of Olympic event. Hancock employees also started buying corporate merchandise in droves once the coveted rings adorned them. Merchandise sales went up 450 percent!

This type of feedback says that employees like the identification with institutions such as the Olympics. They might downplay it externally, but deep down there is real pride in these types of associations. To Hancock's decision makers, the Olympic participation figures showed that employees took ownership of the Olympic sponsorship. And that might be the most important aspect of the investment. Motivating a work force can be tricky. The forces that influence output are not always constant. Sometimes, something like an internal promotion around a landmark activity, so much larger than any one individual, has an impact on an organization.

CREATE ON-SITE MARKETING AND EVENT PROMOTIONS

Old-time sports promotion still thrives. "Beanie Babies," "Bobbleheads," and old standards such as "Bat Day," are all programs that hark back to the past of the sports industry, devised to lure both fans and companies to the park. Beanie Babies and Bobbleheads even became their own cottage industries, trading on eBay at astronomical prices. Some people credit eBay's initial spark of celebrity to the Beanie Baby trading craze.

Throwing out the first pitch, signing up for licensed credit cards in the concourse, being selected as the "fan of the game," the "Punt, Pass, and Kick" contest, or the half-court shots on goal are all prime inventory for sponsors. These in-game opportunities offer companies the ability to work with the sports property on a special feature to perform multiple functions: highlight their brand, showcase their product, or work within their own sales channel to offer a premium incentive.

When MBNA purchases the license of Major League Baseball teams and the privilege of doing on-site promotions, it can increase its credit card issuance figures. MBNA will set up tables at the various ballparks where fans can sign up for their team's image on a credit card and MBNA gives away a shirt, hat, or some other team-specific premium. If the fan gets the card and uses it, then MBNA has paid a very small price to acquire a customer. MBNA buys brand loyalists—to the team, that is— when it goes into stadiums and arenas to sign up subscribers for its product. If it can turn the sports brand loyalist into a customer through a combination of the licensed image of the franchise, a small premium incentive, and the timing of making the offer, then it has maximized the environment, image, and loyalty of the fan.

On-site sweepstakes and giveaways will never go away. They make the games fun for the fans and offer sponsors and advertisers a logical way to associate with the team. The next time you get a free poster, calendar, or team magnet for your refrigerator, you enjoy one of the oldest and most persistent forms of sports marketing.

Companies and teams are getting creative in other areas as well. The San Francisco Giants sold a ten-year, $15 million sponsorship to Catholic Healthcare West, a major Health Care provider.[6] They have even set up facilities at Pacific Bell Park. Now that is capitalizing on an association. Catholic Healthcare provides first aid at games, and services to Major League Baseball players. The park also features public access to automated external defibrillators.[7] The on-site partnership between the team and the health care provider is the first of its kind in pro sports. The health care company gets the validation of a MLB team in the marquee edifice in the city of San Francisco, and the Giants continue to build on its platform of marketing partnerships. If the platform included cars, soda, tobacco, and beer companies in the 1960s and has progressed to include health care, Internet, wireless, and office supply chains, then sports still has room to accommodate even more categories in the future.

PRODUCT PLACEMENT AND TECHNOLOGICAL INTEGRATION

There are many forms of product placement and usage including the health care example mentioned above. Uniforms, balls, sideline bever-

ages, and even those headsets that football coaches wear all have manufacturers who are corporate sponsors or partners. Motorola creates great
exposure during NFL games when the cameras pan the tense sideline
scene and the team's coach is shown observing the action. What
Motorola, Nike, Wilson, and Gatorade all want to show is that products
serve a purpose in the competition.

IBM, by creating the first on-site computer center at the 1960
Winter Olympics, showcased their technology as a useful, necessary piece
of equipment to assist in staging the Games. IBM has maintained a similar philosophy to this day, both designing, hosting, and maintaining
sports Web sites like tennis's U.S. Open. To IBM, being in the game as a
piece of equipment, or a reliable service provider, confirms that its technology, or product, meets the highest competitive standards.

NHL commissioner Gary Bettman, in a speech to the Economic
Club of Detroit, said, "Our fan base is deep and passionate about the
game and has an insatiable appetite for coverage and stats. And in the
partnership with Sun (Microsystems)—using their industrial strength
hardware and software in the market—we are taking NHL content to the
next level. New technology is not a free-standing, separate revenue gen-
erator. It is integral to who we are and how we function as a business. For
example, in a B to C relationship, fans will be close to the game."[8]

Kenesaw Mt. Landis, Bowie Kuhn, Fay Vincent, Pete Rozelle, Larry
O'Brien and other past commissioners of major sports leagues probably
never made a "B to C" reference while presiding over their sport.
Bettman not only promotes Sun, he does it in their language. The only
reason that Bettman would even know about a company like Sun is that
they are in an emerging sponsorship category, and an important one for
both financial support and as purveyors of technological infrastructure to
further engage hockey fans.

A world away, another technology company takes the same principle
and puts it to practice over more than 1,100 miles of rough terrain. GCI,
a telecommunications provider and presenting sponsor to the Iditarod
Sled Dog Race, has the perfect product line to enhance and accentuate
this Alaskan sports institution. GCI does many things:

- Underwrites the long distance, local, and fax needs of the race.
- Outfits checkpoints and all official race stations with Internet connections.
- Installs Webcams at race points, including the finishing line, so that the world can follow the action.
- Staffs and outfits the halfway point of the race. GCI presents the Dorothy G. Page Halfway Prize to the first musher reaching that destination, including $3,000 worth of gold. The second musher gets $2,000 worth of gold and the third-place prize is $1,000 worth of gold.
- GCI has five full-time people at the halfway point, which alternates between the cities of Cripple, Alaska, and Iditarod, Alaska. GCI workers do everything at the halfway point, including all physical chores associated with maintaining the station for the execution of the race.

In total, GCI spends $250,000 in cash and services on its sponsorship. In many ways, the Iditarod, one of the most regionally specific events in all of sports, brings technology to all of the race outposts that wouldn't get it otherwise.

The Iditarod perfectly fits many of GCI's marketing needs. It would seem inconceivable that a sled dog race could help a telecommunications company, but it truly is a great match between sports event property and sponsor. The Iditarod truly represents the state, the people, and its heritage, the customer that GCI needs to identify with. Furthermore, telecommunications companies don't have traditional brands that can be marketed along the lines of a packaged good. To stand out against the competition, GCI needs to resonate with Alaskans, and Alaskans only.

When people think of Alaska, they might think of Denali State Park or Secretary of State Seward, or some place that Dick Cheney wants to send an oil rig, but it is a very remote, isolated, and vast expanse of beautiful land. Cities are not connected by multiple interstates and modern rail lines. Nome, Anchorage, Sitka, and other cities are connected by ice and snow and the brute force of nature. In the twenty-first century, it presents marketing challenges that do not exist in the "lower 48."

By leveraging the state's most famous and prestigious event, GCI makes it a more positive experience, and helps distance itself from its competitors, AT&T and ACS. In 1995, GCI installed phone and fax lines along the trail and at key points for race administration. It was the first time in race history that it had that level of technology or infrastructure. When it upgraded the system to include the Internet, GCI kept current with the technology of the times and the services the 1,100 employee company offers its customers. Furthermore, by showcasing the technology with the state's highest profile event, GCI gets branding not available through any other sponsorship or advertising venue. There is only one Iditarod, and by dominating this category, GCI has a relevant story to take to the Alaskan marketplace. For many Alaskans, it might be their first exposure to the Internet. To have that first user experience happen in conjunction with the Iditarod provides GCI with a most memorable introduction.

Another externality is that it involves all facets of the company. GCI starts preparing months in advance for the actual execution of the event. As company spokesperson Dana Heidemann relates, "Everyone loves it. All levels of the company participate. We have one executive, Richard Dowling (Senior VP, Corporate Development) who is a pilot and he spends the time during the race flying people along the trail for the race organizers. Everyone likes the concept of pitching in."[9]

Heidemann points to a critical issue in sponsorship and product integration at a sporting event. The equipment needs to work, that is, be fully functional and reliable. It is one thing to supply Gatorade at a basketball game or golf balls at a golf tournament, but to set up remote Webcams, online stations, and other data lines, takes time, patience, and expertise. To do it in six feet of snow and minus-thirty-degree temperatures with a significant wind chill factor only increases the degree of difficulty. Having GCI's employees firmly behind the event only makes the product placement and operation that much more memorable to racers, administrators, and fans. Heidemann understands that the broad dimensions of the race also fit the breadth of GCI's needs. "At the end of the day," she says, "we know that we are getting great exposure to people who are our customers in a race that all Alaskans take pride in. We also get a chance to show our customers that we have valuable technology that they can use. As a company based in Anchorage, this shows the other parts of the state that we are an Alaskan presence and capable of serving their telecom needs."[10]

Product placement for the Iditarod has one set of needs. Other events present different challenges and opportunities. The USA Network, through Mark Burnett of *Survivor* fame, created the *Eco-Challenge*, a reality adventure race. It's first year (2002), the race hit the airwaves without one sponsor. The second year, all of its advertising was sold before the event aired. Coca-Cola, one of the main sponsors, even planned to use a part of the event in its campaign for the company's new Mad River brand (the competitive category response to Pepsi's SoBe brand). Additionally, returning sponsor General Motors will place its logo on the outfits and garments of competitors and supply vehicles that will be used on the show. Clearly, GM will feature its truck and SUV lines, not the Corvette. GM knows that its products can seamlessly fit into the presentation of the show and deliver great value for its money.

Eastman Kodak will also give a watersport camera to the competitors. Essentially, the show will only feature and promote brands financially tied to the event during the actual event. Just like Wilson provides footballs to the NFL, Eastman Kodak, General Motors, and other sponsors take advantage of the unique attributes of a show in order to communicate with their target markets. The lead time and preparation will only heighten the chances for success. The brands are happy, as they will not have missed out on any opportunities to access the competition and create valuable exposure, and the USA Network and Mark Burnett are extremely pleased, because they have the proper funds to put forth the best show possible.

ENDORSEMENTS

Another enduring form of sports sponsorship, endorsements, will exist as along as the games are played. Endorsements have provided some memorable moments, like Mean Joe Green chugging a Coke and then giving an admiring young fan his jersey. Athletes even develop personalities with products. Joe DiMaggio plugged Mr. Coffee for years and John Madden has helped Electronic Arts become one of the dominant forces in the video game industry by attaching his name to their excellent football game. More recently, George Foreman has helped create a new, half-billion-dollar-a-year product category, the indoor electric kitchen grill.

Michael Jordan has had an impact that clearly lifted Nike to its status as the number-one shoe and athletic apparel maker. Jordan became the first and only athlete to have a longstanding successful shoe. Alan Iverson might be the answer, literally and figuratively, for Reebok's bid to improve its industry position, but the market might allow for only one Michael Jordan. Another long-time endorsement heavyweight, Arnold Palmer, has made millions for himself and many more millions for the companies he has endorsed. For Arnie, it all got started with a $2,000-per-month deal with Wilson Sporting Goods in 1954. Palmer received a raise from Byron Nelson's day, when Nelson earned $200 and free cereal when he agreed to appear on the front of a Wheaties box during 1945, the year he won eighteen golf tournaments, including eleven straight.[11]

One aspect of endorsements in the current sports industry is that they help measure an athlete's popularity away from the action. Larry Brown, former coach of Iverson's Philadelphia 76ers, once commented, "Alan doesn't work for the 76ers. He works for Reebok." But the endorsement philosophy of associating a brand with the excitement and credibility of a personality will always be a tempting marketing strategy. Keys to success are picking the right match of product and personality, and maintaining the freshness of the relationship. Perhaps no other endorsement relationship, with the exception of Jordan and Nike, has been as persistently successful as the relationship between Richard Petty and STP.

STP is a brand that literally grew up with professional auto racing, primarily through its rock-solid relationship with automotive racing icon Richard Petty. Kids had STP stickers on their walls and were saying "The Racer's Edge!" before they could even ride a bike. Kyle Petty, Richard's son, fondly comments that he even had an STP bottle when he was a baby! Simply put, STP has what any brand wants: a highly visible image with a passionate following.

But to understand STP today, one should know a bit of its past. A quick study will help anyone appreciate the persistence and effort that has made it a blue chip brand in its field.

STP, or "Scientifically Treated Petroleum," started in a Missouri garage in 1954. The company had $3,000 in capital and three determined individuals (Doc Liggett, Jim Hill, and Robert Dehart) committed to making a supplement that helped motor oil resist thinning at high temperatures and pressures.

Originally selling the product out of their own cars, the troika built up a grassroots reputation and expanded their product line to include a gas treatment by 1960. In 1961, the company was bought by the Studebaker Packard Corporation. The corporate resources helped grow distribution and sales to $3 million by 1968. At that point, the company went public and enjoyed greater successful expansion, enhanced by its forays into racing sponsorships with both Richard Petty and Mario Andretti.

In 1978, the company was bought by Esmark, Inc. Six years later, the conglomerate Beatrice Companies purchased Esmark. The next year, Union Carbide bought STP. Then, through a leveraged buyout led by internal operatives at Union Carbide, the brand ultimately became the property of First Brands Corporation. In January 1999, The Clorox Company purchased First Brands and STP.

It might sound a bit confusing, but throughout all of the changes, one thing remained constant: Richard Petty. Despite the ownership turnover, the various management staffs all recognized the value of the Petty relationship. In many ways, the Petty-STP relationship is a microcosm for sports marketing, where both sides benefit. The buyer gets the marquee athlete to enhance the brand appeal, and the marquee athlete gets resources to enhance his image and business interests. For Richard Petty, the sponsorship originally helped him get the best car on the race track. Together, the STP-Petty team won over 200 races in more than 1,100 starts, including twenty-seven wins in one remarkable season.

STP, on the other hand, needed the relationship to increase exposure and usage of the product. And by 1982, less than thirty years after its creation, every car that started at the Daytona 500 used STP. Perhaps more important, millions of car owners have used STP products. It truly has been a symbiotic relationship from the very start.

Today, STP confronts a new set of challenges in marketing. Twenty-first century people are less inclined to work on their cars. As cars get more complicated technologically people simply do fewer of their own repairs. Jennifer Stansbury, associate marketing manager for the STP brand states, "Despite this trend, Clorox saw the opportunity to evolve the relationship with the Pettys to take STP to a new level of consumer understanding and use."[12]

First, STP streamlined the product line and focused its resources on a few core products. Next, it conceptualized a public relations campaign called "All 3, Every 3," a consumer education program that teaches the merits of maintaining fuel system cleanliness. The program reminds motorists of three critical maintenance issues:

- Change your oil.
- Clean your fuel system.
- Check your hoses, belts, and fluids.

STP knew that the oil change business did an excellent job of educating customers about the benefits of changing their oil every three thousand miles, so it leveraged this thinking to trigger the fuel maintenance behavior at the same interval.

Prior to their campaign, motorists had a haphazard approach to using fuel additives, almost treating it as an afterthought. The "All 3, Every 3" campaign represents a long-term commitment to educating car owners about their fuel systems. Central to the messaging and programs is the high-profile association with Richard and Kyle Petty. This endorsement makes the lofty goals of "All 3, Every 3" achievable.

All 3 Every 3 was so successful that Clorox has significantly deepened its involvement with both Kyle and Richard by featuring them in its integrated marketing platform, including advertising, public relations, and in-store programs. In January 2003, STP launched a new advertising campaign featuring Kyle specifically. The company supported this with a more than 70 percent increase over its previous year's advertising expenditure. The ads featured Richard and Kyle Petty in a campaign called "Dad's Advice." In it, the message of fuel system maintenance is cleverly interwoven into the relationship of father and son.

When it comes to automotive and engine maintenance, Richard

Petty sets the standard for authoritative expert. His advice has significant value. Known as "The King," Petty is a member of the Automotive Hall of Fame, and his name conjures thoughts of checkered flags. Petty is the most visible legacy to NASCAR's past, and through his son, the Petty name still shapes the competitive stock-car racing landscape.

The Pettys are icons in auto racing; STP was the first company to sponsor racing. After thirty years of working together, the relationship keeps expanding. The obvious link between the father and son, both on and off the track, only enhances the tie between STP and the Petty family. Kirsten Van Sickle, another associate marketing manager for STP sums it up best: "Our comprehensive relationship has evolved away from a straight endorsement to a more strategic fit. We are leveraging him in line with our brand strategy, which is educating users. Even though Richard Petty is retired he is as valuable as ever."[13]

The simple concept is that the athlete is an influencer. When he or she changes equipment or training supplements, the legions of admirers will notice and adopt the same behavior. Currently, Tiger Woods holds the distinction as the most coveted and influential endorser. Woods has high-profile deals with Nike, Buick, EA Sports, and American Express. He wins millions on the course and earns megamillions for himself and his affiliated companies off the course.

How good is Woods? Executive Vice President of International Marketing Partnerships and Sponsorship for Visa International, American Express's most significant competitor, Tom Shepard has this to say: "Tiger Woods is much, much more than just a spokesperson. He is a gateway to new places and new opportunities, and he will do things for American Express that no other individual athlete can. Would I like to have Tiger Woods in our arsenal? Absolutely."[14]

Woods, like Richard Petty before him, also has the advantage of a long career. Tiger Woods will be a viable personality and commercial presence for at least another forty years! Tom Shepard could not be more correct in assessing what he can mean for a partner today, tomorrow, and into perpetuity.

THE MULTIPLIER

Perhaps the most overlooked element in analyzing a sponsorship opportunity is how much it will cost to activate. When Coca-Cola buys its Olympic sponsorship, it buys privileges and merchandise opportunities. It does not buy marketing campaigns. Coke and other sponsors need to create the marketing programs, and the campaigns cost big money. In-store displays cost money to produce, print, and ship. They also take labor resources to install in the field. Furthermore, the planning takes coordination, phone calls, meetings, faxing, and discussion. All of those elements either cost money directly or have the indirect expense of time.

When Gatorade buys the "official sports beverage" rights and wants its jugs on the benches, dugouts, and sidelines of the games it sponsors, it has just made a serious commitment to more expense. Gatorade manufactures, ships, and administers products to all of the teams, leagues, and intermediaries necessary to execute the deal. It sends powder mix and cups and has people work on ensuring the delivery of the items. Similarly, every sponsorship comes with costs that will be paid by the company, not the property.

Not many sponsorships can be truly turnkey. They require investment support in order to succeed. That support costs money. It also employs people. There are separate companies that make billboards, scoreboards, and Bobbleheads. Supporting sponsorships has become a huge business. Like all of the other layers in the sports industry, it has grown over time to be a reliable and necessary mechanism in the final execution of sponsorships.

A CLOSER LOOK AT THE SPORTS PROPERTY SELLER

In short, almost everything is for sale. And if it is not, there is usually a sponsor relationship that the league, team, or event property owner is protecting. The sponsorship sales effort wants to index the opportunities associated with an event and try to make each one valuable, literally and figuratively. The seller will offer some, or all, of the following inventory items, in a variety of packages:

- Tickets
- Entitlement to a part, or all, of the facility
- Entitlement to a program run by the team ("Bud Light Super Fan")
- Premium promotions during the game, at half time, etc.
- Category exclusivity, e.g., "Official Airline Sponsor"
- Signage, banner space in the facility
- Pouring rights, food category, reseller concession privileges
- Ad space in all written communications
- Use of property logos, images, and/or trademarks
- Post-season access
- Access to players and private functions (golf tournaments, etc.)
- Access to other premium events (Q & A with executives or charity events)
- Media inventory: radio, TV, Internet
- On-site sampling opportunities
- On-site information distribution opportunities
- Mailing lists—exactly what is the New York Yankee season ticket list worth? It is priceless.
- The relationship

You don't need to be the fictional Artie Fufkin[15] in order to understand that investing your marketing dollars into a team or event vehicle is the most solid play in relationship marketing. This can allow access for unforeseen needs to the team, or an event, in the future. Perhaps you have a client who is a fan of a particular player, and you can get a meeting or autographed item from the individual. Maybe your business emphasis will shift from a consumer marketing strategy to a business-to-business objective. In that case, you will need to leverage your marketing investments to solidify your supply and channel relationships more than messaging to the end consumer. A good, need-based relationship will have the necessary flexibility to help the company accomplish their shifting aims through the sponsorship.

Today, many properties do not have set rates for clients. Instead, they craft specific packages based upon the needs of the company. A beer company will have different objectives than a bank, so why not build sponsorship agreements from the ground up with each client? It simply makes the most sense. The successful sponsorship sales representative will always be attuned to the customer's business and the ways they build their brand and meet their myriad objectives. Lee Trevino said, "[T]wo things don't survive. Dogs who chase cars and PGA players who putt for par." He could have added, "and sponsorship sales people who only want to cash checks." These days the competition for sponsorship dollars is so fierce and the relevant opportunities so prevalent, that a team, or event, that overlooks its duties to a sponsoring company will have to accept the fact that their relationship will be brief.

ONE EVENT'S SAMPLE INVENTORY

How many sponsors can a one-day event handle? How many different categories can it accommodate? A quick analysis of the Los Angeles Marathon sponsorship inventory will give anyone a good idea how events can cater to a variety of corporate interests.

At its core, a marathon is only a one-day event, but when a marathon organizing committee goes to sell the opportunity to partners, they offer much more than simple race-day exposure. And since marathons don't sell tickets they do not lead off with premium seats, exclusive access, or even high-end catering during the event.

They have race expositions, where runners, fans, family members, or anyone in the community can come and peer at sponsor products. They have "goodie bags" that include product samples for racers who notoriously research products and training aids. They have signage along the race itself and registration ads that appear in newspapers and appropriate running journals, all featuring the logo of corporate partners. Of course, the race also features significant product placements, especially water, sports drinks, energy bars, and energy gels. Not only are these lucrative categories, they are necessary for the health of the runners.

The L.A. Marathon is, arguably, one of America's top five marathons. It features over 22,000 runners, 80,000 visitors to its Expo, and is broadcast live on the NBC affiliate in Los Angeles. It also raised $2.5 million for fifty charities and nonprofits in 2002.

The event also attracts an impressive array of sponsors:

Company	Designation	Rights
American Airlines	Official airline	Exclusive
City of Angeles Medical Ctr	Official medical center	Exclusive
Gatorade	Official energy drink	Exclusive
Gatorade Energy Bar	Official energy bar	Exclusive
Honda Presenting	Official automobile	Exclusive
Robek's	Official juice	Exclusive
Salonpas	Official external analgesic	Exclusive
Saucony	Official running shoe & apparel	Exclusive
Sparkletts	Official Water	Exclusive

Uses, Applications, Rights, and Benefits

Use of marks & logos   Local TV broadcast
Category exclusivity   PA announcements
Official product/service status   Athlete/performer appearances
Tickets   Access to opportunity merchandise
Hospitality   ID in opportunity's media buy
On-site signage   Rent-free use of venue for
                                        sponsor functions
On-site sampling   Use of volunteers to
                                        implement promotions
On-site display rights   Title of proprietary component
On-site sales rights   Presence on opportunity Web site
Mailing lists
    program book ad   Nonprofit/cause overlay
ID in collateral material

Sponsor Packages and Prices

Official sponsor (category
    exclusivity) cost: $250,000
    Saucony, American Airlines, City of Angeles Medical Center,
    Sparklett's

Official supplier cost: $25,000–$50,000
    Gatorade, Robek's, Salonpas

Official product cost: $10,000–$25,000

Exhibitor cost: $1,000–$10,000

Goodie bag sampler
    (per product) cost: $1,000

To a marathon runner, the event is 26.2 grueling miles of physical application after several months of training. For the average sports fan, a
marathon might not offer that much from a spectator's point of view outside of a lot of sweaty, taxed people who desperately need a body massage.
A running fan, though, knows the sacrifice and hours of effort that go
into a marathon and enjoys the inspirational high that comes from the
event. Anyone who has seen the New York, Chicago, or Boston
marathon events has and witnessed the millions of people who exhort
the runners with passion and exuberance.

Sponsors see the opportunity to blend their product and their business into the race. For American Airlines, they knew that some runners
would need to fly to Los Angeles and that the average distance-running
enthusiast does travel a lot. Gatorade and Saucony were obvious choices,
since their products fit within the actual event. Honda felt that, with a
pace car, they could get valuable exposure to media coverage, and health-
conscious race fans. Honda also knows that when a news outlet reports
on a marathon, they show the lead runners, not the grind-it-outs who
struggle with each step.

Honda feels that it puts itself in prime space for residual media exposure.
What makes marathons, or regional races, interesting from a sponsorship
standpoint is that there are no premium incentives attached to the event.
Fans do not need tickets in order to watch. Little or no mass celebrity exists
among the elite runners. Sponsors will not want access to "experiences" like
running the first one hundred meters with the seeded competitors. In short,
the sponsorship for companies is the composition of the marathon runner
and the functional intuitive fit of their product with the race.

To the casual observer, a marathon might not seem to offer a lot in the way of marketing opportunities. In the final analysis, however, it is an event that has a very appealing demographic and proven methods to connect brands with consumers.

ANALYZING THE DEMOGRAPHICS OF A BUY

The Chicago White Sox have a great tradition of American League baseball on Chicago's South Side. Their sponsorships offer companies many of the same features as other teams. Any savvy marketer would be interested in hearing the Sox's pitch. They might want to leverage their access to sample products, reward/entertain employees, sell products, or simply create a fun internal sales promotion. For example, if a company wanted to be an official sponsor of the Sox and enjoy category exclusivity, it could cost up to $250,000. If the sponsor wanted to put their logo in, or around the ballpark, that has a different fee structure.

Premium Signage Items[17]
On field signage (8' x 16'):	$250,000 to $500,000
Signage behind home plate:	$100,000 to $250,000.
Dan Ryan Expressway/	
US Cellular Field sign:	$100,000

To make a decision, the marketing executive needs to know the demographics of a White Sox buy. They are as follows:[18]

Gender: male, 65%; female, 35%.

Age:
Young adults (ages 18–24)	20%
Adult (25–35)	22%
Mature Adult (36–50)	20%
Early Seniors (51–65)	18%
Seniors (66+)	7%
Teenagers (13–17)	6%
Children (8–12)	6%

Household Income

$0–$45,000	27%
$46,000–$75,000	40%
$76,000–$125,000	33%

Once the potential sponsor knows the audience composition, it can make an informed decision to assess the benefits of associating its product with the team, its logo, players, and audience. Next, the sponsorship buyer needs to determine what the team can offer. The opportunities are many, and the amount of expense will depend upon which combination is ultimately purchased.

At the end of the day, the seller needs to know what type of demographic it can deliver to a potential sponsor. The most important thing in any sponsor relationship with a property is to ensure that the company can achieve its objectives through the medium of the opportunity that it ultimately purchases.

WHEN SPONSORSHIP DRIES UP

In 2001, northern California golf fans could look forward to the Senior Transamerica event in Napa, Raley's Gold Rush in Sacramento, and the Siebel Classic in San Jose. By October 2002, none of those tournaments were on the 2003 schedule. They all expired due to sponsor exodus. The players lamented the loss of the Silverado site as one of their stops. Not only did spouses enjoy making the trip, but players liked staying at the Silverado resort and walking straight onto the range and course. Situated in California's wine country, Silverado had enough old-school charm and modern comfort to make it a very pleasant tournament.

Sports marketing giant IMG always helped bring an impressive field, including legends like Arnold Palmer, Gary Player, Raymond Floyd, and Lee Trevino, but their management savvy and the players' celebrity couldn't save the event! Tom Kite, winner of the U.S. Open in 1992, was just one of many great players to notice the problem: "All the guys have stepped up to help the Senior Tour. We've gone the extra mile, played the pro-ams, and everybody's trying to do everything they can to enhance the Senior Tour at a very difficult time. We need to step up and show our sponsors (that) we care about our product, and the product they're trying to sponsor."[19]

So what was the problem? As stated, it had nothing to do with IMG management, Silverado's hospitality, or the players' appeal. The problem was the northern California economy. After riding the high-tech "Dot Com" boom, the area staggered under its collapse. From 2000 to 2002, the Bay Area lost almost 200,000 jobs. In Santa Clara County, the heart of Silicon Valley and the Bay Area's high-tech engine, 85,000 people lost their jobs and over 9 percent of county-based jobs disappeared altogether. The unemployment rate went from 1.3 to 7.6 percent, which gave it the dubious distinction of being the highest jobless rate in the state for an urban county.[20] Unfortunately, the opportunities that sponsorship offer have very little to do with reversing regional or national job insecurity and securing long-term economic health for the general economy.

The sponsorship pyramid that supports events siphons off smaller events first and concentrates its available resources on the premier events. It does not spread its resources among all events to keep them afloat. Hence, a definite mortality factor exists. Furthermore, as corporate earnings go down, the first thing to be eliminated are sponsorships and marketing investments that are not considered core expenses to produce direct revenue. Since the tariff to get involved with sporting events continues to increase, and the multiplier expenses only drive up the cost of participation, companies find it easy to decline sponsorship opportunities when times get challenging.[21]

The dependence upon sponsorship is a hidden vulnerability to modern sports entertainment. Much like high blood pressure is referred to as "the silent killer," sponsor instability is the "silent killer" of events. The Transamerica, in its last year, was called the Napa Valley Classic, and it still paid the winner, Tom Kite, $195,000. The absence of Transamerica and Pacific Bell, the former presenting sponsor, did not mean that the winner's check went down to $25,000. As events scale up, they maintain their threshold, even if it seems that they should fluctuate as the economic climate dictates.

If the event diminished its prize money, then name attractions like

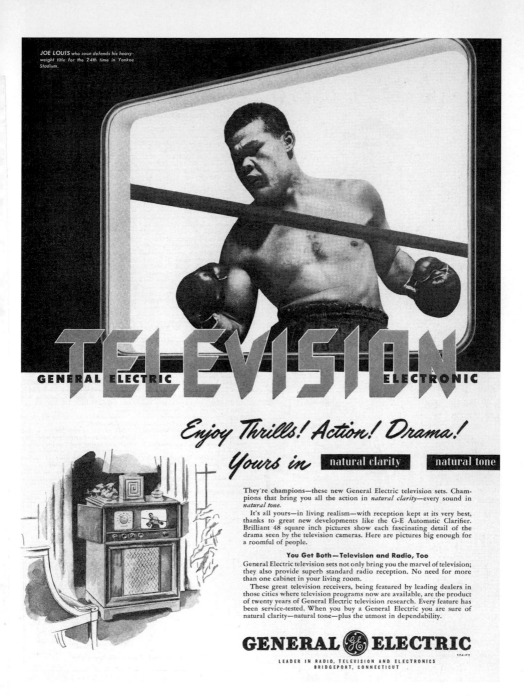

JOE LOUIS who soon defends his heavyweight title for the 24th time in Yankee Stadium.

TELEVISION
GENERAL ELECTRIC — ELECTRONIC

Enjoy Thrills! Action! Drama!
Yours in [natural clarity] [natural tone]

They're champions—these new General Electric television sets. Champions that bring you all the action in *natural clarity*—every sound in *natural tone*.

It's all yours—in living realism—with reception kept at its very best, thanks to great new developments like the G-E Automatic Clarifier. Brilliant 48 square inch pictures show each fascinating detail of the drama seen by the television cameras. Here are pictures big enough for a roomful of people.

You Get Both—Television and Radio, Too

General Electric television sets not only bring you the marvel of television; they also provide superb standard radio reception. No need for more than one cabinet in your living room.

These great television receivers, being featured by leading dealers in those cities where television programs now are available, are the product of twenty years of General Electric television research. Every feature has been service-tested. When you buy a General Electric you are sure of natural clarity—natural tone—plus the utmost in dependability.

GENERAL (GE) ELECTRIC
LEADER IN RADIO, TELEVISION AND ELECTRONICS
BRIDGEPORT, CONNECTICUT

Joe Louis's 1938 bout against Max Schmeling was one of the most important moments in sports history. No other event has had the sweeping financial, political, and social ramifications of that fight. Louis was also the first nationally accepted African American athlete, and the first African American to endorse products. A champion in the ring and a true patriot out of it, Louis will forever be in the most elite pantheon of sportsmen. (*Photo courtesy of GE, Joe Barrow Jr., and Tom Genova of tvhistory.tv.*)

Joe Namath on the *Ed Sullivan Show*. The NY Jets' signing of Namath in 1965 gave the AFL instant legitimacy, and ultimately led to the merger with the NFL. Not only did Namath become the face of the national sports scene, but his off-the-field activities drew just as much attention as his on-field prowess. He led the Jets to victory in Super Bowl III over the heavily favored Baltimore Colts and ultimately went on to become an actor, broadcaster, and ambassador for football. *(Photo courtesy of CBS Photo Archives.)*

The changing face of sports. This 1958 picture shows the Sports Illustrated Sportsmen of the Year getting feted on the *Ed Sullivan Show*. If the four top athletes were honored today, the athletes would represent far greater diversity. *(Photo courtesy of CBS Photo Archives.)*

Another changing face of sports: Super Bowl XVI. Before the first of four Joe Montana–led 49er championships, the Pontiac Silverdome preps for the game. Notice the complete absence of commercialization in the photo. The network, league, and advertisers all knew that over 130 million fans would be watching, but there is not one commercial billboard or corporate sign poised to take advantage of the opportunity! *(Photo courtesy of CBS Photo Archives.)*

The Opening Ceremonies for the 1960 Squaw Valley Games were simple by today's standards, but nonetheless spectacular. Brought to Lake Tahoe by the resourceful Alex Cushing, the 1960 Games changed the sports industry forever. They were the first televised Games and the first aided by IBM's computer technology. *(Photo courtesy of CBS Photo Archives.)*

Swedish-born LPGA star Annika Sorenstam played in the 2003 Bank of America Colonial PGA golf event and put the story in the headlines of news media outlets around the world. Bank of America, and Sorenstam's sponsors, got millions of dollars of unexpected exposure, showing that the platform of sports entertainment has incredible reach. (*AP Photo/Amy Conn-Gutierrez.*)

Omega Watches and Ernie Els help The First Tee provide the administrative and structural support to bring golf, and life skills, to inner-city communities. Each day, their successes help grow the sport of golf and, more importantly, stronger communities. The synthesis of sports entertainment and corporate support in community programs is one of the most important manifestations of sports' popularity. (*Photo courtesy of The Swatch Group Ltd.*)

Buick is, perhaps, the brand most committed to professional golf promotion. As the title sponsor to four PGA events in 2004, and the name that adorns Tiger Woods's bag, the auto manufacturer communicates with all sectors of golf fans. Buick also sponsors the world's largest amateur tournament, the Buick Scramble. (*AP Photo.*)

When Michael Jordan walked on a court, people would watch. By inserting its name into the action, Toyota reaches basketball fans via the NBA's proven promotional offerings. The assessment of the value and the subsequent pricing models associated with the opportunity are getting more sophisticated each year. *(Photo courtesy of the Memphis Grizzlies.)*

Fred Wagenhals and Dale Earnhardt teamed up to create one of the most successful collectible companies ever, Action Performance, Inc. Ringing the Opening Bell at the stock exchange is a privilege that shows NASCAR that Earnhardt and shrewd management is a winning combination with investors as well as racing fans. *(Photo courtesy of Action Performance Companies, Inc.)*

Wagenhals and Earnhardt, a duo who took Earnhardt's NASCAR success to the retail sector, relax at the track. The relationship formally began with Wagenhals selling his house to pay the required advance to secure Dale Earnhardt's exclusive rights. (*Photo courtesy of Action Performance Companies, Inc.*)

MAIN LOBBY | FedExForum

SOUTH ELEVATION | FedExForum

The FedEx Forum. Facility development has come a long way in the last one hundred years of sports. The focus is not just on the turnstiles, but on the cash register. Arenas, parks, and fields are designed to accommodate all categories of fans and sponsors in comfort and style. The idea of sponsors paying for entitlement, concession, and access privileges has contributed to the escalation in both services and revenue streams. (*Photos courtesy of the Memphis Grizzlies.*)

Tom Kite, Lee Trevino, and Gary Player might opt out and stay home. If that happens, then the Senior PGA Tour, or Champions Tour as it is now called, presents a diluted product and they can't risk that. It makes better business sense to cancel the event than to jeopardize its quality. If the entire brand is weakened, it will be more difficult to rebuild than to simply restart once the economy improves.

When events like this end, the concept of sponsorship has not necessarily failed, but forces that impact either the economy of the sponsor or the fan base have intervened. Enron, CMGI, Conseco, United Airlines, America West, Adelphia, and some other high-profile companies either battled bankruptcy, or total financial collapse, in the middle of high-profile sports sponsorships. Not only would properties that had long-term contracts be back on the market and open to new sponsors, but the notion that a high revenue stream could go away faster than you can say "Andersen Consulting" became a part of the sponsor-property relationship.

Kmart left its $20.25 million dollar NASCAR sponsorship after declaring bankruptcy. Kmart felt that high-profile auto racing sponsorships were an inappropriate allocation of precious resources. The Michigan retailer also had to exit a two-year Daytona 500 sponsorship (worth $685,000 in 2002, and $735,000 in 2003).[22] It was not easy for them to exit the agreements, either, incurring significant legal fees in the process of extrication.

The Astros actually had to pay Enron over $2 million to get out of their stadium deal with the tainted energy company. Since the Astros had not thought that their biggest sponsor, a local icon, might have to file Chapter 11 during the course of their thirty-year agreement, they had to seek legal help to terminate the contract. Enron, cunning and selfish to the end, figured that the entitlement contract on the Astros' ballpark was an asset worth keeping. Since they were current on all of their payments, the court ruled in favor of Enron, hence the $2.1 million payment. Shortly afterward, the Astros entered into a long-term agreement with Minute Maid for the naming rights of their ballpark. Minute Maid, a Coca-Cola Company, would appear to be as stable as any corporate entity. After the Enron fiasco, however, the unlikely occurrence of another Chapter 11 costing the team $2 million was most likely addressed by team attorneys in the new agreement.

KEY SPONSORSHIP CONCLUSIONS

As discussed earlier, the only significant revenue source in the first phase of the modern sports industry was from attendance, or the gate. Promoters and owners would sell tickets on the day of the game and that was their revenue stream. Some concession activity also contributed to their bottom line, but ticket sales drove the machine. The anxiety in the front office was about the individual customer and getting him to show up and buy a ticket and maybe some concessions.

Today, the primary concern for virtually all property rights holders is the corporate customer. Not only does the sponsor bring revenue to the bottom line, but the sponsor also markets the product through their promotional channels, including the electronic media. In-store displays sell Coke and Budweiser, but they also promote the NBA, NHL, NFL, and Major League Baseball. In short, teams always wanted to acquire more customers, especially ones with big budgets, but the discovery that teams, events, and sports properties could enhance a bank's business, or soda bottler's enterprise, has had a huge impact on the way sports is packaged, priced, and presented. The continuing evolution of the process by which sporting events and companies merge their interests further intertwines professional sports with the cultural fabric of a consumer society.

Sponsorship also helps spread the financial burden to multiple sources. The Montreal Expos would never have been able to exist solely on their modest ticket sales in the late twentieth century, but national broadcast dollars and licensing lessened the pain of their poor attendance. Since the Expos were guaranteed to receive monies from national sources, this allowed the franchise to avoid the crippling, massive losses that would have certainly folded it in the past. The entire underpinnings of the sports entertainment system relies upon Anheuser-Busch, IBM, Chevrolet, and the thousands of companies that invest billions into the games, events, and multiple platforms of sports. NBC bid several billion dollars for the rights to broadcast the Olympics well into the twenty-first century because it knows that it will be able to sell the ad inventory and various merchant opportunities to several companies.

Sponsorship has, in fact, become a platform for both the companies and the properties. By offering opportunities that nurture and support revenue streams, sports properties afford administration and expansion of their interests. At the same time, companies commit resources that turn into valuable marketing campaigns and generate valuable exposure and bottom-line revenues.

In NBC's Olympic broadcasting example, NBC made a straight profit from selling advertising and sponsorships at the Salt Lake Games of 2002, but it also promoted its entire programming schedule to the audience watching at home. Furthermore, it schmoozed its best customers and talent at the most prestigious venue in sports. In short, the platform of the Olympic partnership allowed NBC to create its own sales and marketing plans that benefited its image, coffers, viewers, and advertisers.

The symbiosis between the buyers and sellers is the ultimate manifestation of all sponsorship negotiations. The hard work that allows them to succeed is the overlooked "secret sauce" of savvy organizations. Companies like Visa, Coca-Cola, IBM, Anheuser-Busch, and Nike have dedicated staffs of capable people constantly searching for ways to make sponsorship relevant within their organization, and to resonate with customers who make brand decisions every day.

The key to sponsorship moving forward is to never forget two things. First, that the customer service component of the agreement is paramount. Since sponsorships are essentially need-based agreements, all parties must be oriented toward fulfilling the agreement to the fullest extent. Second, sponsorships succeed due to the efforts of many people, from ad sales representatives to art work specialists, printers, and photographers. The result is that fans get more sports images in even more places.

IN THEIR OWN WORDS:
VOICE OF A SPONSORSHIP GURU

Andy Dolich is to modern-day sports marketing what Copernicus was to the discovery of planetary motion. In the past thirty years, the Ohio University graduate has worked with properties like the Philadelphia 76ers, Oakland A's, Golden State Warriors, and AmericaOne, among others. Currently the team president of business operations for the Memphis Grizzlies, Dolich continues to develop his mastery of the modern sponsorship. The following excerpts capture his thoughts on the evolution of the sales side of professional sports organizations.[23]

The Start

"In 1971, I went to work for the Philadelphia 76ers when the sports industry was not as sophisticated an operation as it is today and the most important sales job belonged to the ticket manager. Front offices weren't oriented toward creative selling to companies, just selling game tickets on an individual, or season, basis.

"The ticket manager would give three sales reps a divided map of Philadelphia and they would go to companies in their territory and try to talk to corporate managers about buying season tickets before getting thrown out by security. You didn't have appointments held in conference rooms, or at expensive lunches. It was more haphazard than anything. And it was real selling. People needed to be persuaded to buy into sports. The mindset at the time didn't create the urgency to buy tickets like today. I still remember the first season ticket package I sold. It was to a nice guy named Walter Grove. He owned a company in Southern New Jersey who made tack for harness racing.

"In the 1970s, the traditional companies of the time were automobile, beer, cigarette, and soft-drink manufacturers. There was no telecom industry, no game companies, software, computer manufacturers, or even bottled water producers. You also didn't have the broadcast differentiation of cable, free TV, satellite packages, or multilingual radio. You were selling in a linear world, and only to a handful of categories.

"In the early 1980s, you could start selling the stadium, billboards, and game-day promotions along with ticket packages. The idea of larger corporate involvement became acceptable as some companies achieved measurable success through sponsorship. Sports is the ultimate 'follow the leader' industry, where if one automobile manufacturer sees his competitor gaining market share through sponsorship, the other car companies will want to respond with their own associations and programs. That certainly brought definition to our jobs in marketing the team, and we were able to attach costs to opportunities and talk about results the partners could expect.

"As the 1980s came to a close, stadiums ultimately brought in new types of inventory through suites, entitlement zones, PSLs, pouring rights, and premium seating. What we have discovered in sports is that there are many different ways to watch a game, and each one has its own fee structure. Luckily, as wealth generates through various sectors of the economy, some facet of a team's business fits into a part of a company's marketing strategy."

Sports Events as a Modern "Town Square"

"At the core of the sponsor/fan relationship is the fact that our time invested at a sporting event brings a feeling of community that very few activities in today's world can provide. The games involve family, friends, and business associates. Venues are a modern-day town square in a society that is losing those town squares. Sports entertainment is a medium that gives many generations the chance to communicate on the same plane. It used to be that the family gathered around the radio, television, or dinner table in their homes. Today, it is more than likely that everyone scatters. People retreat to their own worlds. Dad is on the computer, Mom gets on the phone, one child watches TV, and another kid is on his cell phone. But with sports, it pauses these separate lives and can bring people together.

"Fans buy tickets knowing that they are seeing the best that there is to offer on the face of the globe. And they are interacting in an environment which is getting more difficult to find; a place where the meaning of gathering is simple and well defined. Sponsors buy into sports because it offers an incredible opportunity to sell products, sample products, and it deliver people's eyeballs focused on your brand. The attendance and media ratings data shows that sports, from the amateur level to professional, has become a part of our cultural DNA.

"The Grizzlies operate in a one-team town. In a small market, the downside is that you have less target companies than in a large market. We have forty-nine corporate sponsors, and some we are bringing in who have never done something like this thing before. We don't do menu marketing. All of our programs are customized. Some of our sponsors are accustomed to working with the minor league baseball team in town, so the NBA is a whole new world for them, and there has been a small case of sticker shock for some of our partners.

"Our philosophy with the Grizzlies embraces 'need satisfaction selling.' We find out what kind of needs the customers might have instead of merely sending proposals with figures attached. There is no secret marketing equation—the sophisticated companies know as much, if not more than you do, about demographics and marketing program execution. The simple key to selling is communicating the value of our product and facilitating something that makes sense for our diverse sponsors.

"The NBA today is much more of a unified marketing engine from the league down through its teams. And we try to work with one another to grow our collective fan base and take advantage of the international appeal of the game. Just look at what Yao Ming has meant in the short time he has been in the NBA. In the coming years, the game will reach more and more people because fans know it is the place to watch the most gifted athletes perform at the highest level. It is a very simple equation, really."

Sponsoring the Grizz'

Operating in a smaller market, like Sacramento, Portland, Jacksonville, Vancouver, or South Bend (any team with a $9 million annual broadcast fee is a major league sport), the Memphis Grizzlies offer a little something for every type of corporate partner. Here are three partners that Andy discusses, representing the small, medium, and large partnerships that the Grizzlies currently have.

Small Partner

"Neeley's BBQ. In a super competitive local BBQ marketplace, Patrick Neeley is an independent operator. A classic example of the small business entrepreneur, Neeley operates three separate franchises in the Memphis metro area. From day one of the Grizzlies arrival in Memphis, Neeley made it clear that he wanted to be one of their partners and he did everything from introduce himself to bring over free lunches. He bought season tickets and kept a visible presence with the front office.

He ultimately made a deal at their current venue, The Pyramid, once Corky's vacated the BBQ category and he now sells BBQ at the forty-one home games plus other events. Neeley's has done everything in its power to make themselves a visible part of the Grizzlies experience. As Patrick Neeley extends his business in Memphis, he feels that identifying with the Grizzlies will help him develop a key identity with customers and the Memphis business community."

Medium Partner

"The Memphis area Toyota dealers contains three dealerships, and it is led by a guy named Kent Richey. In the past, they sponsored the AAA baseball team and the University of Memphis and SEC Football. Like many buyers—Kent was not necessarily a big NBA fan, but he knew that Toyota should be involved with Grizzlies . . . and became one of the first people to be a part of the Grizzlies. He aligned corporate forces, which is not always an easy thing to do, in order to get involved with signage, radio, and TV. Automotive is not an exclusive category for the Grizzlies but we forged a strong relationship that will probably get stronger. "

Large Partner

"They don't come any larger than FedEx. They are sponsoring our new facility, the FedEx Forum, and will be a part of every facet of sponsorship. FedEx is the largest company in the area and a high profile sponsor of many sports. We are honored and lucky to have them be such a visible and important partner. They are spending $90 million with us, and it is an example of their faith in the excitement of NBA basketball, the Memphis community, and the long-term value of the NBA that they made this commitment."

NOTES

1. George Raine, "Sponsors Look to cut through the Party clutter," *San Francisco Chronicle*, January 19, 2003, p. G6.

2. "By the Numbers 2003," *Sports Business Journal* (December 30, 2002):
150.

3. You will hear everything from political ads, to labor union commercials, as a part of a broadcast. They may not be selling products at the local Walgreen's, but they look to leverage the event for valuable publicity.

4. Prince and Wolf, "Bud Tries to Bowl Super Viewers Over," *Beverage World* (December 3, 2992): 3.

5. Michelle Hiskey, "Olympic Sponsor Scores," *Atlanta Constitution*, March 16, 1994, p. A1.

6. Mark Fainura-Wada and Ulysses Torassa, "Health Care Reform, Big League Style," *San Francisco Chronicle*, December 30, 2002, p. C7.

7. Automated external defibrillators are small, easy-to-use, portable devices that provide definitive treatment for sudden cardiac arrest. According to Catholic Healthcare West, sports arenas and facilities are one of the top five places where sudden cardiac arrest occurs.

8. Gary Bettman, speech to the Economic Club of Deteroit.

9. Dana Heidemann, personal interview, December 12, 2002.

10. Ibid.

11. "Byron Nelson Retrospect," CBS, May 18, 2003.

12. Jennifer Stansbury, personal interview, December 20, 2002.

13. Kirsten Van Sickle, personal interview, December 20, 2002.

14. Tom Shepard, personal interview, December 2002.

15. Fufkin, played by Paul Schaeffer, was the promotions representative of Polymer Records in *This Is Spinal Tap*, Rob Reiner's mockumentary on British heavy metal bands. He asks rhetorically in one scene, "What about the relationship? I thought we had a relationship here."

16. Previous names were: WTA Championships, Sunkist Championships, Murjani Championships, Lipton Championships, and Nutrasweet Championships.

17. IEG Sponsor Direct [online], www.iegsponsordirect.com [December 3, 2002].

18. Ibid.

19. Brian Murphy, "Kite Finds Right Salve, Longhorns Fan Takes Two-shot Lead at Silverado," *San Francisco Chronicle*, October 13, 2002, p. B8.

20. To make up for the flight of Senior Golf from northern California, the Charles Schwab Cup was moved to Sonoma County. The tournament features the top thirty-one money leaders from the season, and Sonoma County is near both the corporate headquarters of Charles Schwab, the sponsor, and the golf fans of Napa County's prior tournaments.

21. Stephanie Salter, "Down and Out in Silicon Valley," *San Francisco Chronicle*, October 13, 2002, p. D1.

22. "Kmart wants out of Daytona 500 deal," *Sportingnews* [online], www.sportingnews.com/nascar/articles/20020205/380239-p.html [February 5, 2002].

23. From a personal interview with the author, December 19, 2002.

CHAPTER 8

THE STADIUM GAME

*Gone is the emptiness of yesteryear's cold concrete shells. The new stadiums—
adult theme parks, really—create fresh revenue streams from sources such as
luxury suites, club seats, high-tech signage, restaurants and shops.*
                                        —Tom Lowry, *BusinessWeek*

When a prestigious magazine like *BusinessWeek* includes a discussion of club seats in a cover article, the average fan should
realize that facility development is not simply a sports spectator issue, but
an ownership, bottom-line business issue. To ownership, facility revenues
and stadium/arena planning are as critical to a franchise as the actual
competitive quality of the team on the field, court, or rink. Prior to
World War II, simply having a reliable place to play was enough for team
owners. Franchises had no leverage at all, with either city governments
or with the fans. They could not easily hold a city hostage by saying a
better deal awaited them in the Sun Belt, or that they really had to have
luxury suites in order to compete.

In the early twentieth century, francises did not sell personal seat
licenses and entitlement packages in anticipation of a team's arrival
because the public was not financially responsible for their survival. Rural
Americans did not take afternoons off from tending to chores in order to
catch a game. The teams had to establish a fan base with the more modern,
industrial worker and city dweller. Teams had one source of real income,
ticket sales. In order to make that revenue stream both viable and reliable,
the sports facilities needed to be in towns and accessible via public transportation or walking. As the car, the suburbs, and mobility became cultural

forces, the facilities would need to accommodate those interests, but that was not an ownership consideration until the late 1950s.

The sports teams and their owners had to work with city hall, not dictate to them. There simply was not enough appeal in professional sports to persuade a mayor, governor, or voting populace regarding a team's financial needs. The tide shifted once mass media and air travel became widespread. As soon as teams could afford to fly, they could have opponents anywhere a population could support them. This gave the owners their first taste of bargaining power: a potential suitor in another city, and the promise of a more eager fan base. It also gave the established leagues incentive to expand and migrate. They did not want rival leagues starting in cities that could sustain their team and then have another league threaten their dominance.

THE FIRST CRACK IN THE SYSTEM

The subtle shift in the balance of power between professional sports teams and cities began in the mid 1950s, when the Boston Braves relocated to Milwaukee in 1953, the St. Louis Browns became the Baltimore Orioles in 1954, and the Philadelphia Athletics moved to Kansas City in 1955. The tumult of the decade reached its crescendo when the Dodgers and Giants both left New York after the 1957 season. Though other teams had moved before them, the symbolic departure of two marquee New York teams for California had a lasting impact on both the business and culture of sports. The Dodgers meant more to Brooklyn than words could ever capture. Famed New York writer and Brooklyn native, Pete Hamill, wrote in *A Drinking Life*: "more important than the comics, I was reading the sports pages, where the columnists were Tommy Holmes and Harold C. Burr and where there was only one real story: the Brooklyn Dodgers."[1]

When the Dodgers left Brooklyn, it was the first high stakes "stadium game" relocation in professional sports. They had just won the World Series in 1955 and still fielded one of the best teams in baseball. The team was loved by its core fans and was profitable. Walter O'Malley, the owner, simply knew that Los Angeles would be a better market. He wouldn't have to compete with two other teams. Most important, he could get a better stadium.

Robert Moses, the controversial man who reconfigured New York

City to accommodate the car, had a different opinion on baseball stadiums than O'Malley.[2] "Nobody but the Government can really afford to
build a stadium these days, and the Government must be sure of getting
maximum use out of its land and facility," said Moses. "It would even be
criminal to build a stadium exclusively for baseball. Seventy-some days a
year isn't enough use, either, for public park land."[3]

Moses had the authority, cunning, and power to make or break
anyone's development plans in New York City. He truly was O'Malley's
gatekeeper, and the Dodgers owner knew the gatekeeper probably would
not budge from his stance.

"I never asked them to build me a new ballpark in Brooklyn. I said we
would build it on taxable land with our own money. We had a site where
. . . the subways intersected . . . in those days, I thought you could park
your car at any subway station and come to the ballpark for a dime. We had
a site and a sports authority set up to condemn the land we needed, but
Bob Moses blocked us. He had a site of his own, bounded on one side by
water, another by a cemetery, a third by a slum and on the fourth a parkway
. . . I couldn't see us drawing much from the water, or the cemetery . . . I
saw a future in empty seats. We had to come out here (Los Angeles)."[4]

O'Malley didn't want someone else to beat him to the L.A. market
and capitalize on the strong history of baseball out West. Its Pacific Coast
League had produced the DiMaggio brothers, Billy Martin, and many
other great Major Leaguers. O'Malley did not have a permanent stadium
deal in Los Angeles when he left Brooklyn, just a lease with the L.A.
Coliseum, a cavernous multipurpose stadium most prominently used for
the 1932 Summer Olympics.

O'Malley felt that in Brooklyn, there was no good open space left for
a new ballpark. And, worst of all, there was only one man to negotiate
with, Robert Moses. O'Malley also knew that Brooklyn was not going to
add landfill space, nor would Moses lose his intractable manner. On the
other hand, in Los Angeles, he would find plenty of open space and a
slew of people to negotiate with for a new stadium.

O'Malley's best move might have been convincing Horace
Stoneham, owner of the New York Giants, to move with him to California. Stoneham's circumstances made him an easy target. Despite featuring Willie Mays in center field, the team drew only 633,000 fans in
1956. He didn't particularly like his ballpark or the politics that governed

his situation. The thought of relocating to the burgeoning West made great sense. Stoneham's departure did not trouble his conscience, either. "I feel bad about the kids, but I haven't seen many of their fathers lately," he said about the move from New York.[5]

Once out West, both got their new facilities in a few short years. O'Malley persuaded a tough Los Angeles City Council to approve his stadium, but he had to finance it privately. Built for $22 million, Dodger Stadium in Chavez Ravine instantly became one of the best ballparks in all of Major League Baseball. Stoneham, in perhaps the most lopsided maneuver in the history of stadium deals, got the infamous Candlestick Park.

San Francisco Mayor George Christopher showed Stoneham the stadium site on Candlestick Point at the crack of dawn. As Christopher's luck would have it, it was a calm, peaceful morning. As the group surveyed the bay shimmering off the Point, the mayor bragged about all of the available parking, something Stoneham did not have at the Polo Grounds in NYC. Stoneham looked around at the serene scene and felt that the facility would be perfect for car-crazy Californians. Too bad Stoneham didn't ask anyone what happened to the weather later in the day. Candlestick Park became notorious for its wind and fog. The Giants would toil there until 2000, when they finally pulled a page out of the Dodger's playbook and built a privately financed ballpark that would instantly become one of the best in Major League Baseball.

The Dodgers-Giants departure from New York City to California has three distinct legacies. First, stadium-driven ambition could have culturally catastrophic consequences for the departed cities. Second, commercial air travel now became an absolute necessity in professional sports, and it would encourage expansion. One final footnote is that it was the last time a politician (George Christopher) would definitively outwit and out-negotiate a professional team (the Giants) in the "Stadium Game." As the 1960s approached, cities and teams now had to deal with one another, and they both sought the advantage.

THE FIRST WAVE

The Giants and Dodgers were ahead of the curve, or at least trying to anticipate the needs of the modern fan. They saw that populations started to spread out and that facilities did not need to be located in the middle of a city, but between the city and the suburban traffic arteries that people used for their commutes.

On the stadium-supply side, the prevailing feeling was uniformity and accommodation. Cities could build large structures that could house multiple tenants and thousands of automobiles. In the 1960s, construction projects on multipurpose, civic-run facilities began. Cities like Oakland, Houston, San Diego, New York, and Atlanta built big, unfriendly parks that maximized usage and minimized maintenance and other expenses. In order to attract teams, they felt that they needed significant capacity in both the stands and the parking lots adjacent to them.

The relationship was a variation on Robert Moses's old theme. The city owned, operated, and leased the facility to the team. The local Parks and Recreation Department would oversee the operation of the facility, the mayor would get his tickets, and a local concessionaire would sell hot dogs and soda. At the end of the season, they would all say goodbye until the following year.

First Wave of Stadiums	Year Opened	Cost (in millions)	City/Landlord	Capacity
Anaheim Stadium	1966	24	Anaheim	43,204*
Astrodome	1965	35	Houston	42,217†
Atlanta Fulton County	1965	18	Atlanta	50,893
Candlestick Park	1960	15	San Francisco	43,765
Jack Murphy Stadium	1967	27.75	San Diego	50,000
Oakland Alameda County	1966	25.5	Oakland-Alameda	50,000
Riverfront Stadium	1970	N/A	Cincinnati	52,952
Shea Stadium	1964	25.5	New York	55,601
Three Rivers Stadium	1970	55	Pittsburgh	47,971
Veterans Stadium	1971	50	Philadelphia	62,382

Source: Munsey & Suppes, "Multiple Team Pages," Ballparks [online], ballparks.com [December 31, 2002].

*In 1979, they exanded it to 64,593 to accommodate football, then contracted it to 45,050 in 1997.

†The Astrodome had another first: 53 luxury suites.

All of these facilities in the above table have much in common. The prevailing mentality among civic leaders and team owners prioritized selling tickets to the commuting fan. Franchises were thrilled that cities were building big places to play sports. That way, revenues truly could be maximized if the team attracted interest from all sectors of the metropolitan area. Most important, for a city with either a football or baseball team and seeking the other, the necessary infrastructure was in place.

Teams of that era did not envision the need for revenue-producing elements like advertising inventory, luxury suites, and prime concession areas. Franchises had no interest in owning or maintaining the venues, especially if they had to share them with another tenant. In 1960, even the Yankees wanted to sell Yankee Stadium back to the city of New York so that they could lease it out to the proposed, rival Continental League. Imagine that, encouraging the city to earn money by leasing their building to a rival!

The Yankees of that era did not want the added hassle of facility maintenance. The prevailing thought in sports was to minimize the extraneous details and stadium management was something to avoid, not demand. In one extreme case, Atlanta Fulton County Stadium did not even have a full-time groundskeeper until 1989. Major League games in Atlanta took place on fields groomed by the same people who did the rounds on other properties managed by the city.

In the wave of cookie cutter stadia, ticket sales were still the most important concept in team marketing.[6] Ballparks left the inner-city locations for the edges of the freeways as people moved to the suburbs. Cities saw the future as hosting multiple tenants while providing big parking lots. The cities even thought ahead in their architecture, building stadiums that could be expanded. Virtually all of the facilities listed in the previous table had seats added to them. By the time the San Francisco Giants left 3Com/Candlestick Park, it held over 63,000 seats for baseball and 70,207 for football.

THE SECOND WAVE OF THE FACILITY FRENZY

In 1991 the Chicago White Sox razed Old Comiskey Park and debuted New Comiskey Park, now called US Cellular Field. HOK, the Missouri

architecture firm that has since developed a famous reputation as the pre-
eminent sports facility developer, designed New Comiskey. They
upgraded all of the elements that needed improvement: concession areas,
fixtures, concourses, sight-lines, and luxury suites. The fans loved it and
turned out in record numbers to root for the Sox.

Stadium Transition Attendance Influence

1988	1,115,749	Old Comiskey
1989	1,045,651	Old Comiskey
1990	2,002,357	Old Comiskey
1991	2,934,154	New Comiskey
1992	2,681,156	New Comiskey
1993	2,581,091	New Comiskey

Source: http://www.baseball-almanac.com/teams/wsoxatte.shtml.

The White Sox experienced two stadium phenomena: the long goodbye
in 1990 to venerable "Old Comiskey," and the welcome addition of the
new facility the following year. In both cases, the team could exploit the
nostalgia of the past and the promise of the future.

New Comiskey was a hit with the fans, owners, and marketing partners. The only thing that HOK and the White Sox forgot to include in
their new park was charm. That became apparent when Oriole Park at
Camden Yards opened in 1992. It had the feel and look of a bygone era
and all of the amenities any fan could want. Most important, it had
luxury suites, appealing signage opportunities, and every single cash-
churning device that a modern sports facility could contain. Separated by
only one year on the chronological scale, and designed by the same firm,
New Comiskey and Camden Yards were separated by eons on the perception scale of baseball fans.

The ballpark was an instant hit and it drew rave reviews and coverage from all points of the baseball world. Presidents, dignitaries,
celebrities, and baseball fans of all ages went to see it and absorb its aura.
The Baltimore Orioles and HOK, their architects, changed the new
vision of modern facilities. Oriole Park at Camden Yards showed that
"retro" designs had significant value for fans, corporate customers, and
those interested in urban redevelopment. Camden Yards had another

effect: stadium envy. Every other team in every major league town wanted a copycat facility. They saw that the old and the new could blend to bring profits and people to city centers.

All of a sudden, a new formula existed for both teams and cities. For the cities, they could use a major league team as the anchor tenant to attract businesses to parts of town deemed old and undesirable. Cleveland and Denver became perfect case studies of how a successful team could energize a downtown area. In the short-term world of politics, building new ballparks would provide jobs, attract capital and give the press something positive to cover.

For the teams, the riches were far greater. The old-time park catalyzed interest with fans, corporate customers, and even players. In the wake of Camden Yards' success, construction on new or refurbished parks began in many other Major League Baseball cities.

Second Wave: New Parks after Camden Yards

Jacobs Field	Cleveland	1994
Ballpark in Arlington	Arlington	1994
Coors Field	Denver	1995
Turner Field	Atlanta	1997
Bank One Ballpark	Phoenix	1998
Safeco Field	Seattle	1999
Pacific Bell Park (SBC)	San Francisco	2000
Minute Maid Park	Houston	2000
Comerica Park	Detroit	2000
PNC Park	Pittsburgh	2001
Miller Park	Milwaukee	2001
Great American Ballpark	Cincinnati	2003
Citizens Bank Park	Philadelphia	2004
Petco Park	San Diego	2004

If one considers the fact that Sky Dome, Tropicana Field, and US Cellular Field are all considered new facilities, and that Edison Field was a complete overhaul, essentially making it a new facility, then it means that not too many teams were left behind in the second wave of new facilities.[7] Fenway, Wrigley, Yankee Stadium, and Dodger Stadium are virtually untouchable, even though most of their owners would like new or completely renovated parks. Only Minnesota, Florida (Miami), Oak-land, St. Louis, and New York (Shea Stadium) can realistically seek new ballparks. Montreal, a team in limbo as of this printing, will be relocated and get a new stadium in the process, but not in Montreal.[8]

All of the new stadiums leveraged the New Comiskey/US Cellular Field and Camden Yards examples as motivating factors. Once owners realized that municipalities could help raise funds through hotel, airport, and other taxes, they went to the ballot and asked the public for help. If they had to threaten a move, they did that. In short, there are few eth-ical, altruistic motivations or maneuvers that help a franchise win the "stadium game."

In the time since the Walter O'Malley-Robert Moses power struggle, the influence has completely shifted away from the municipalities that host teams, to the teams themselves. As owners and corporate interests increase the financial scale of professional sports, the political pressure to house, accommodate, and promote sports has grown dramatically in cities across North America. This condition has resulted in political forces losing negotiating power and virtually all leverage, despite the growing paucity of available suitor cities.

DIFFERENT SPORT, SAME STORY

Some teams barely pay rent, yet they retain majority control of all the rev-enue streams like advertising, signage, parking, and concessions. In San Diego, the municipality guarantees the Chargers a threshold of ticket sales. If the team fails to sell sixty thousand tickets to a game, then the city has to buy the difference until 2007. So far, the city has paid over $25 mil-lion to the team! The Chargers are not owned by the city of San Diego but by an individual, Alex Spanos. The team does not pay a financial div-idend to the taxpayers, either. It would be inconceivable to think that the city of Seattle would pay the Starbucks Corporation if their earnings did not meet certain projections, but that is essentially the agreement that San Diego has with its NFL team.

And as scary as it sounds, it might even be a deal that really does make sense for San Diego. As the closest professional football team to

Los Angeles, the second largest media market in the United States and the only major market without an NFL franchise, San Diego does not want to lose its Chargers to a community ninety miles north on the Interstate. San Diego knows that if this team leaves, the cost of getting another one can approach $500 million for a new stadium, plus usurious lease agreements for both practice and administrative facilities. In their cost analysis, guaranteeing 60,000 ticket sales to the present franchise makes the most sense.

The Chargers know that Houston, Cleveland, and Baltimore all lost NFL franchises. The city knows that they might not be able to afford to solicit a replacement team, much less find an interested owner with the necessary financial profile. Furthermore, the NFL might not even want to try to place a team so close to Los Angeles, believing that the culture of Southern California might not support two NFL franchises in this modern (read: expensive) era. Hence, the Chargers have 100 percent of the leverage.

The stakes are very high in San Diego. The football tradition that the Chargers represents certainly does not equal that of the Colts or Browns, two teams that left their cities and fans in the lurch. If the original franchises could leave Cleveland or Baltimore, no sense of loyalty could keep the Chargers in San Diego.

The Chargers' real trump card over the city is the Super Bowl. San Diego also benefits from being a part of the Super Bowl rotation, an informal dispersal of the game's host city. They do not want to jeopardize the millions of dollars the country's most prestigious sporting event brings its merchants and community every eight years. San Diego would probably not host the game without having a full-time NFL tenant. During the 2003 Super Bowl, for example, 348,000 people attended various game-related events and accounted for more than 168,000 hotel room nights. A study by the NFL and Marketing Information Masters, Inc. concluded that the game provided $367 million to the local economy, an increase of $72 million over the last Super Bowl played in San Diego in 1998. Lastly, the San Diego Padres, the Major League Baseball team, will leave Qualcomm Stadium for a new park, Petco Park, in 2004. If professional football fails, then the only remaining tenant for Quallcomm will be San Diego State University, something that the city would like to avoid.

Thus, San Diego finds itself boxed in by the circumstances of the times. The team and the league both wield tremendous influence because their property galvanizes people, generates revenue, and adds to civic pride. As Andy Dolich, ace executive of the Memphis Grizzlies, said; "there are very few 'town squares' in today's society. Sporting events offer people the chance to gather in that 'town square,' even if for a limited time."[9]

CONTRACTING A CASE OF "STADIUM NEGLECT"

Almost every team plays the stadium game. Each franchise wants the maximum revenue situation that their competitors have and nothing can stop the teams from pursuing their goal. One case stands out as particularly acrimonious. And although the franchise moved away, both the city and the team ultimately consider themselves victorious in the struggle.

The Charlotte Hornets played in a nice facility, the Coliseum, but one that did not have the revenue-friendly amenities that most other NBA teams enjoyed. Team officials approached the city of Charlotte and tried to get a new facility built, but without success. The local government did not have either the will or the inclination to make it happen for that particular ownership group. The irony, of course, is that at the time, the Hornets had the best attendance in the league.

The grumbling started only seven years after their first game in Charlotte. According to ownership, the twenty-three thousand–seat arena became outdated and obsolete in those years. It was structurally sound, and not dilapidated like the venerable, historic Boston Garden. It simply lacked the revenue-producing components and lease structure that would add millions to the Hornets' bottom line. Without club seats and rows of luxury suites, the Hornets felt they were losing money every time they tipped off. By the time they started publicly griping (1996), the Hornets knew that 21 out of 29 NBA teams were playing in newer or superior arenas.

To compound the problem, the Carolina Panthers, Charlotte's NFL franchise, had the gleaming new prototype stadium. The team came into town in 1995 and sold $150 million in personal seat licenses before the team had even played one down of football. The Hornets arrived first;

why couldn't they enjoy the riches, too? To Hornet ownership, the combination of the majority of NBA teams having better arenas and a newcomer in their own backyard poaching the sports dollars from the community put them over the top. The Hornet owners felt "stadium neglect."

This key issue of being the local priority is never lost upon the teams and the owners. To the politicians, the attention usually goes to the most vulnerable situation, not the largest brand of professional sports in town. But the "neglected" owners don't like that. Pat Bowlen, owner of the Denver Broncos, went through a period of stadium neglect in the 1990s where the Avalanche and Nuggets played at the new Pepsi Arena and the Rockies at spectacular Coors Field. "Without a new facility," he warned, "I'm afraid that the Broncos will not be able to compete in the National Football League." Bowlen ultimately got his new facility.

The Hornets, like the Broncos, did arrive first, and to a standing ovation. The team was a colossal success, selling out 364 consecutive games. They even averaged over 23,000 fans per game as recently as 1997–1998. But that was not good enough for Hornets management. Hornets executives felt that too many people were getting into the games on the cheap. Rather than being happy with the thousands of fans, they were irate that the revenue streams were not being maximized. Further complicating matters, the Hornets did not like the management lease. In the modern phase of professional sports, teams can get a little grumpy if the lease is not on their terms. At the Charlotte Coliseum, the Hornets split parking and concessions and the team received 75 percent of advertising signage. The Hornets felt that they could best sell Hornet basketball and that they should keep the profits. They needed to compete with the Blazers, Suns, Kings, Celtics, Pistons, 76ers, and other squads with revenue-friendly facilities. The facility managers and city believed the team simply wanted to rewrite the lease and get the maximum amount of revenue streams while the Hornets felt that facility operation is simply one task of an NBA team's management. Conflict ensued, fomented, and drove the two sides apart.

With the two sides in total disagreement, the ending was a slow, five-year dissolve that alienated the fans, players, and league. After listening to years of bickering over money, the fans that were originally bitten and smitten by the Hornets began to stay away. Attendance plummeted to

11,200 per game and finger pointing replaced high fives at the games. Subsequently, the Hornets, an exciting team, slipped out of town and went to New Orleans, where city officials were more than happy to accommodate them. They contractually promised to make $15 million in upgrades and renovations to the New Orleans Arena and to finance a new, state-of-the-art practice facility for the team.

New Orleans city officials bragged that adding the team would add $100 million of economic activity to the city. The commitment from the Hornets? Ten years, and they held two five-year options. No one really mentioned the fact that professional basketball had already failed in the Big Easy, but honeymoons aren't intended for such interjections of historical fact.

But the city of Charlotte had plenty of savvy in the stadium game. With the wonderful tradition of basketball in North Carolina and the proven success of the first years of the Hornets franchise, Charlotte and its citizens went to work. They passed legislation approving financing for a new arena and courted the NBA. The NBA, in turn, had no problem attracting interested bidders. The final choice: Robert Johnson, the billionaire owner of BET, the cable channel. Johnson, the first African American majority owner of any professional team, won't enjoy the sports marketplace by himself. He will be competing against the Panthers, the Wachovia PGA event in Charlotte, the NHL's Hurricanes (they play in Raleigh), and Lowe's Motor Speedway. But Johnson will have one thing the previous owners did not. He will have a beautiful $265-million facility with seventy luxury suites, three thousand club seats, and lots of signage to sell. Johnson feels that he can bring other events to the facility and a conciliatory approach to those customers who the Hornets' prior management alienated.

He will need it, because the facts are that the Panthers, the speedway, and the PGA event all have luxury-suite vacancies and open sponsorship categories that they could not sell in 2002. But Mr. Johnson has until 2004 to worry about the competitive marketplace. As founder and CEO of a major cable channel, he knows about competing for ad dollars in a tough market. It will be a fascinating return to Charlotte by the NBA, and all because the Hornets owners, George Shinn and Ray Wooldridge, had a severe case of stadium envy. In the end, the city rid themselves of a fractious ownership group that they did not trust and got a new one with more savvy. All it cost the city was a $265 million arena. In New Orleans, Shinn and Wooldridge get a second chance to make sure that they don't repeat their mistakes. In ten years, when the Hornets' New Orleans lease runs out, and the new Charlotte franchise has its franchise firmly entrenched in the NBA, it will be interesting to see if all parties, including the fans, are happy.

FACILITY MARKETING OPPORTUNITIES

Everyone has seen pictures of old stadiums with billboards and advertisements on the outfield walls. Fenway Park's famed Green Monster even had them in the early days of the franchise and recently saw them return. Local and national companies would seek stadium exposure on banners and signs. They would buy advertisements in the program and announcements by the stadium announcer. It was a very simple and inexpensive way to communicate with the home team. The relationships, though, were not negotiated by lawyers and for hundreds of thousand of dollars. Teams did not actively seek outside marketing opportunities via high-priced sales staffs. The advertising buying community had not seen the true opportunity that sports facilities could offer.

   In the second phase of the modern era, everything is for sale. The Oakland A's did such a great job in the 1980s of selling their team that they even had a sponsorship for their bathrooms. But it did not happen overnight. Getting corporate customers really started where the original fan relationship began: the simple ticket.[10] The individual game ticket turned into a season ticket and the season ticket turned into a luxury suite. The luxury suite was, in many ways, the catalyst to the corporate customer. Companies had been buying season tickets consistently since the 1970s. Since most of the prime locations, at midcourt, behind the plate, or on the fifty-yard line, were tied up with private owners, the luxury suite became a logical place for the corporate customer to upgrade his relationship with the team. Not only could individuals not afford a suite, it also became an opportunity for the company to get some regional bragging rights within their industry.

As soon as prime seats, or the idea of truly prime seats, took hold, the teams had an eager, receptive audience. Virtually every type of business could use tickets for business purposes. They could even be itemized as an expense! And though there was not much "luxury" in the early days of luxury suites, they still had an eager, receptive audience, providing that necessary measure of separation that the elite seek from the masses.

A luxury suite came equipped with its own TV, padded seats, and bar. You could order in your own food and feel like a big shot, even if you didn't get the immediacy of the crowd. Suites were different, exclusive, and became very fashionable. They also helped chum the waters for more corporate business with teams. Essentially, stadium operators, whether they were cities or teams, became convinced that the extra expense of constructing suites could be met by the actual demand for them. It was a big leap of faith for the sports property managers. It meant dedicating staff that would change its emphasis from the private individual to the individual representing a corporate entity. It also meant a lot more zeroes to the left of the decimal point.

Another feature of facility marketing arose at the same time as the luxury suite: naming rights. The fad started in Buffalo in the early 1970s, when Rich Foods paid $1.5 million for the rights to call the new football stadium of the Bills "Rich Stadium" for twenty-five years. In the 1980s, Dr. Jerry Buss, owner of the Lakers, integrated the name of the Fabulous Forum into a cable television advertising deal with Great Western Bank and that truly vaulted the concept into prominence.

Today it is no longer an experimental advertising concept, but an acutely important revenue stream. Naming rights agreements currently tie up more than $3.2 billion in marketing relationships. The practice is so universally accepted in the modern sports industry that companies pony up for buildings they haven't even seen. Pacific Bell, for example, committed $50 million for the San Francisco Giants' new ballpark before one shovel of dirt had been turned over. And Reliant Energy cut a thirty-year, $300 million deal with a team, the expansion Houston Texans, that hadn't even played a down of exhibition football!

What in the wide, wide world of sports is going on here?

FACILITY ENTITLEMENT CHART

NBA Only Facilities	Team	Years	Cost (in $millions)
American Airlines Arena	Heat	20	42
Arco Arena	Kings	10	7
Compaq Center	Rockets	6	5.4
Conseco Fieldhouse	Pacers	20	40
Delta Center	Jazz	20	25
Key Arena	Sonics	15	15
SBC Center	Spurs	20	41
Target Center	T-wolves	15	19
TD Waterhouse Centre	Magic	5	7.8

NBA + NHL	Team	Years	Cost (in $millions)
America West Arena	Coyotes/Suns	30	$26
American Air Center	Mavericks/Stars	30	195
Continental Airlines	Nets/Devils	12	29
First Union Center	76ers/Flyers	30	40
Fleet Center	Celtics/Bruins	15	30
MCI Center	Wizards/Capitols	13	44
Pepsi Center	Nuggets/Avalanche	20	68
Phillips Arena	Hawks/Thrashers	20	185
Staples Center	Clippers/Lakers/Kings	20	116
United Center	Bulls/Blackhawks	20	25

NHL Only	Team	Years	Cost (in $millions)
Arrowhead Pond	Ducks	13	19.5
Gaylord Ent. Center	Predators	20	80

HP Pavilion	Sharks	15	47
HSBC Arena	Sabres	30	24
Mellon Arena	Penguins	10	18
Nationwide Arena	Blue Jackets	TBD	135
Office Depot Center	Panthers	10	24
RBC* Center	Hurricanes	20	80
St. Pete Times Forum	Lightning	12	30
Savvis Center	Blues	20	70
Xcel Energy Center	Wild	25	75

Major League Baseball	Team	Years	Cost (in $millions)
Bank One Ballpark	Diamondbacks	30	66
Citizens Bank Park	Phillies	25	57.5
Comerica Park	Tigers	30	66
Coors Field	Rockies	TBD	15
Edison Field	Angels	20	50
Great American Ballpark	Reds	30	75
Miller Park	Brewers	20	41
Minute Maid Park	Astros	30	100
Pacific Bell Park/SBC	Giants	24	50
Petco Park	Padres	22	60
PNC Park	Pirates	20	30
Safeco Field	Mariners	20	40
Tropicana Field	Devil Rays	30	46

Baseball + NFL	Teams	Years	Cost (in $millions)
Network Associates	A's/Raiders	5	5.8
Pro Player Stadium	Marlins/ Dolphins	10	20

NFL Only Stadiums	Team	Years	Cost (in $millions)
AlltelStadium	Jaguars	10	6.2
Edward Jones Dome	Rams	12	31.8
Ericsson Stadium	Panthers	9	25
FedEx Field	Skins	27	205

Ford Field	Lions	40	40
Gillette Stadium	Patriots	15	100 (approx.)
Heinz Field	Steelers	20	57
Invesco Field at Mile High	Broncos	20	120
Lincoln Financial Field	Eagles	20	139
Qualcomm Stadium†	Chargers	20	18
Raymond James Stadium	Buccaneers	13	32.5
RCA Dome	Colts	10	10
Reliant Stadium	Texans	32	300

Source: P. Howard and D. Swangard, "Naming Rights," Advertising Age (October 28, 2002): 5–12.

*Royal Bank of Canada. There is some irony in a Canadian Bank sponsoring a hockey team in the South.

†The Padres are scheduled to leave in 2004, thus making it a single professional sports tenancy.

The average rights deal in 1995 was for approximately $1.3 million. Recent deals, like Reliant Energy's mammoth contract (almost $10 million annually) with the Texans, or the Lincoln Financial Group's deal ($7 million per year) with the Philadelphia Eagles show that both the NFL and the right property can mean huge dollars on the bottom line. Similarly, SBC's contract with the San Francisco Giants, $2 million annually, now looks like a bargain just six years after it was signed. With the Giants playing in the 2002 World Series, and Barry Bonds's home-run-record season in 2001, the Giants have given Pacific Bell/SBC way more exposure than they could have ever hoped to receive.

Even in distressed economic times, twenty-first-century prices are up over the 1995 market. Office Depot took over for National Car Rental Center (its parent company, ANC, filed for bankruptcy) and signed for nearly $2.5 million per year to be the building that hosts the Florida Panthers. Similarly, in Houston, where the ghost of Enron might chase every Texan for a generation, the Astros got more than double from their next stadium entitlement client, Minute Maid, at $6 million per year. Clearly, the market has increased for the right buyer.

Perhaps nothing indicates more clearly that naming rights have certifiable value than a recent deal the Montreal Canadiens secured through J.P. Morgan Chase. The Canadiens have used their naming rights as collateral to get a loan of fifty to seventy million Canadian dollars. Other teams have used their facilities as collateral, but included revenue streams like parking and concessions, luxury suite sales, and other inventory. The fact that a bank will accept the naming rights, exclusively, demonstrates the faith in the mechanism, and the strength of the marketplace.

DOWNSIDE

There is a downside, however. Some facilities are not "hot" properties, like the New Arena (NBA) in Oakland or the Ballpark in Arlington. In other cases, sometime the fans won't accept a change. For example, in Boston, it would be very hard to imagine a fan-friendly response to Fenway Field at John Hancock Park. Chicagoans might not accept Motorola Park at Wrigley Field, either. The double-edged sword of a loyal fan base might be that entitlement can go too far. The fans like the concept of the total experience, and for them, that can include the name of the facility. Invesco Field ran into a roadblock, losing support for the name from both the mayor and the city's major newspaper, the *Denver Post*. The *Post* did not originally refer to the stadium by name; definitely not the kind of publicity that Invesco had in mind when it decided to plunk down $6 million per year for the entitlement privileges. *Post* editor Glenn Guzzo at the time wrote:

> The *Denver Post* works hard—though never as hard as we could—to listen to our readers, to hear the language and understand the stake that citizens have in the problems that concern them most. This week's decision to label the new Broncos stadium Mile High stadium rather than Invesco Field at Mile High in the *Post*'s routine references is all of that—listening, hearing, understanding. And of giving the public its voice, as newspapers must do to deserve the First Amendment.
>
> As to the Pepsi Center, that facility was built with $150 million of private money, with the city contributing a relatively modest package of long-

term tax abatements and public infrastructure improvements. Because private investors provided the overwhelming share of the Pepsi Center's cost, the *Post* respects the right to call their arena anything they choose.

In contrast, taxpayers paid 75 percent of the new Mile High stadium's $400.8 million cost, with the Broncos paying 25 percent. Invesco bought the naming rights by merely dangling a little chump change before the unelected stadium district board—which blatantly ignored strong public sentiment to retain the Mile High name.[11]

Of course, as soon as Guzzo left, his successor, Gregory Moore, changed the policy. Moore's statement on the matter was simply, "We should call things what they're formally known as." Fortunately for Invesco, the real audience they want resides on the outside of a television screen, not reading a paper. Broadcasters are bound by the NFL to refer to facilities by corporate names, and they certainly understand the importance of entitlement and sponsors. But the Invesco precedent of potential civic controversy is now in play for other facilities and their corporate benefactors.

Another problem is conflict between the team and the landlord. When the naming rights deal to 3Com Park ran out after the 2001 football season, the 49ers and their landord found themselves embroiled in a disagreement. From a buyer's perspective, it may have been one of the top deals ever in naming rights history. For just less than $600,000 per year, an obscure technology company, 3Com, got valuable national exposure as the new name of Candlestick Park. When the deal expired, the 49ers wanted to bring in a new sponsor, but were rebuffed by the City of San Francisco's board of supervisors, and the name returned to Candlestick Park. The 49ers were a bit miffed at losing out on some easy money. Having delivered five Super Bowl trophies to the Bay Area in twenty years, they felt that they ought to have a little goodwill with their municipal landlord, but no such luck. The naming rights issue might be a bad omen for their own new stadium wishes, which have been on hold for several years.

Sometimes the real world of profits and losses can also wreak havoc on good intentions. Enron Field in Houston, CMGI Field in New England, PSINet Stadium in Baltimore, Adelphia Stadium in Tennessee, and United Center and the Conseco Fieldhouse in Indianapolis all represent deals that were either terminated or were jeopardized due to bankruptcy or severe cash flow issues. Furthermore, the September 11 tragedy has devastated the airline industry, already forcing United Airlines' bankruptcy, and certainly threatening the business of Continental, Delta, America West, and American Airlines, four prominent facility partners.[12] Not only do the teams lose the revenue, in many cases they become a photo opportunity for failure, the exact opposite message that these deals are supposed to bring between corporation, team, and community.

In North Carolina, the Carolina Panthers went from league darling (NFC title game appearance in its second season) to a middle-of-the-pack team struggling to find its playing identity on the field in 2002. The franchise also struggled with their stadium identity, Ericsson. When Ericcson signed the deal, their business model was business to consumer, so the high-visibility space of an NFL facility made great sense. Ericsson's focus shifted to business to business, which put their stadium deal in a lame-duck status. Coupled with the downturn in the economy, and especially in the telecommunications industry, Ericsson wanted out of the deal before its expiration date of 2004.

ENTITLEMENT PRIVILEGES

The process of facility entitlement no longer looks at a facility as if it were a big billboard with its corporate name inserted into its team's media. Companies now demand more from the sponsorship and they get it. Office Depot inked a ten-year deal with the Florida Panthers to name the facility The Office Depot Center and part of the agreement calls for an on-site retail effort. Moreover, the deal also includes player appearances over the length of the deal.

This can be very smart business for a savvy company with the necessary resources. If Office Depot wanted to contract players separately and individually to make appearances at their stores, it would be very expensive. Getting a player, in season, to take his valuable off-ice time for a mix-and-mingle opportunity is difficult to schedule and tough to promote. Furthermore, given the fact that the front-line players are probably too expensive, a second-tier player might not deliver the same value. Add to that the expense of producing promotional materials, getting permission to use a team photo (which they probably would not get without paying a premium), or producing an alternate promotional piece of art-work, and the total cost can be very prohibitive.

However, with a high-profile sponsorship, the Panthers will want to make this work for Office Depot. The brand is right there on the ice and in the arena. Getting a player to appear will not be difficult. Using the team's vast promotional resources will be a given. Office Depot will not have to pay to get access to photos and merchandise to make the appearance memorable. A successful relationship ensures that both parties have a lot at stake and much to gain from a successful venture. Perhaps more important, the small headaches that can appear will all be taken care of by the Panthers staff.

If Office Depot wants to be involved with Panther hockey, this is the best route to maximize the relationship. Trying to nickel and dime with their promotional efforts would probably be a feckless pursuit, but by integrating efforts at a high level, they can succeed with their mutual objectives. A company like Office Depot has the resources and needs of a large firm. If they were a local restaurant or a regional chain, then a high profile, maximum relationship might not make sense. However, their size, stature, and marketing needs warrant large participation, since small efforts would not make a perceived dent in their bottom line. Lastly, a large concern like Office Depot can then take the experiences with the Panthers and transfer them to other markets, whether it involves hockey or not.

In fact, if Office Depot decides to sponsor a NASCAR race, then they might be able to have drivers appear at their stores. They might be able to plug in the Panther program as a template and simply switch gears to NASCAR. Their PR people, art department, and media agencies will know the drill and be able to maximize the NASCAR involvement based upon their history with the Panthers. Also, they might be able to use the facility as a hub for other sports marketing programs. They can use it as a destination, meeting place, or facility to host events. And other new agreements reflect this type of relationship. When the Phillies sold the entitlement rights at their new ballpark to Citizens Bank for $57.5 million, they also sold $37.5 million worth of advertising, promotions, and hospitality to the bank, for a total deal value of $95 million.

In the 1970s, stadiums were simply shells built around the field of competition. The operating executives were interested in maximizing the facility, so they introduced maintenance-free Astroturf and multipurpose capacities to accommodate baseball and football, to the detriment of both.

By the 1990s, the number of sports fans making pilgrimages to Fenway Park, Wrigley Field, and the awesome reaction to Camden Yards demonstrated that the venue can be more than simply a place where people sit and watch games: it can be a place of business and entertainment. The venue became yet another medium for sports and advertisers.

Annually, global marketing groups rank the brand value of professional sports franchises. Consistently, the Dallas Cowboys and Washington Redskins rank in the top five. Dallas and Washington, D.C., are the seventh and eighth largest media markets in the United States, yet virtually all of the rankings place the Redskins and Cowboys in the same category as the Yankees, and ahead of the N.Y. Giants and Jets, their football peers.

Of course the rankings are arbitrary, but the stadium revenues that the Cowboys and Redskins generate vault them ahead of both New York football teams and those of other sports in larger media areas like Los Angeles, San Francisco, Chicago, and Philadelphia. It will be interesting to see what happens to those rankings once the new football facilities take root in Chicago and Philadelphia and the teams get more revenue from the same customer base.

CATCH-22 ECONOMICS

The irony of stadium economics is that sometimes logic does not apply. Venerable stadia like Wrigley Field and Fenway Park cost their tenants money, due to the deficiencies of their antiquated designs, yet they are industry beacons. The Cubs and Red Sox know that their fans love their parks, as outdated as they may appear to team management. In Illinois, the state government and the city of Chicago officials have particularly infuriated the Cubs. At some levels, they must almost feel as if it is a conspiracy. The Bears, White Sox, and Bulls/Blackhawks have all received a

form of facility subsidy. The White Sox have received it on two occa-
sions; once to commence construction on New Comiskey back in 1989,
and then twelve years later the state gave them $18 million to implement
some renovations. The Bears received $400 million to renovate Soldier
Field, and late in 2002, talks between state representatives and the St.
Louis Cardinals began. The discussion explored the Cardinals potentially
moving from Busch Stadium to a proposed one located in East St. Louis,
an Illinois/Missouri border town that could still serve the St. Louis fan
base. And the Cardinals are the Cubs' archival!

Furthermore, local neighbors in Wrigleyville have turned the Cubs
into a cottage industry beyond simple bar, restaurant, and area entertainment. Nearby buildings even sell space on the roofs to watch the
Cubs play. The Cubs want to build eight new rows of bleachers at the
team's expense, or at least obstruct the views for the roof-poaching community, but their own construction plans are being blocked by their prof-
iteering neighbors and the stadium is about to become a city landmark,
which will only further bureaucratize the process.

Ironically, the team is one of the best supported in terms of ticket
sales, so their unique situation, though frustrating, is not going to put the
team out of business any time soon. But it must infuriate their marketing
management that so many opportunities are going to poachers who do
not pay for the privilege of associating with the Cubs

The Red Sox are in a similar situation. To fans, Fenway Park is
looked at as an asset, and to those concerned with revenues, it is a lia-
bility. Former Red Sox CEO John Harrington once said, in reference to
renovating Fenway Park, that, "it would be easier to straighten the
Leaning Tower of Pisa."[13] Fenway Park could be the definitive symbol for
the stadium conflict in the modern sports industry. The oldest park in
Major League Baseball, it is much more than the home of the Boston Red
Sox. To millions of Red Sox fans, it is the temple of their team. To walk
inside, one can easily imagine Ted Williams and his magical 1941 season,
Roger Clemens striking out batters in bunches, and Carlton Fisk waving
a home run into fair territory in the sixth game of the 1975 World Series.
With its storied Green Monster in left field, a short fence in right, and
virtually no foul territory, it is the most intimate ballpark in Major
League Baseball.

Built on ten acres of land at a cost of $650,000, it opened in April of 1912. Critics claim that its seats are too small and bathrooms too scarce. But Red Sox fans love it. In fact, it is one of the top tourist attractions in Massachusetts.

New York Yankees & Boston Red Sox Attendance Comparison

Year	Red Sox Average per Game	Yankees Average per Game
1988	30,430	32,717
1989	30,988	26,963
1990	31,222	24,771
1991	31,635	23,009
1992	30,476	21,589
1993	29,901	29,839
1994	30,884	29,656
1995	30,061	23,521
1996	28,583	27,789
1997	27,483	31,856
1998	28,577	36,484
1999	30,201	40,662
2000	31,925	37,956
2001	32,412	40,807

Source: "New York Yankees, Boston Red Sox Attendance Analysis Page," Baseball Almanac [online], baseball-almanac.com [October 2, 2002].

In the fourteen-year comparison in attendance above, Boston outdrew the Yankees in eight of the years. The Yankees, in that time span, played in five World Series, winning four of them. The Red Sox have only played in four World Series since 1918, winning none! Also, the capacity at Fenway is just under 34,000, whereas Yankee Stadium accommodates 57,000, meaning the Red Sox are close to selling out each game, and in a much smaller market than New York. Clearly, they are a great draw. Fenway Park is one of the reasons and everyone associated with the BoSox knows it.

But its popularity did not matter to Red Sox ownership in the 1990s. They witnessed the professional sports facility construction boom over the decade and were wondering when it was going to be their turn to build a new, modern ballpark. Of course, they wanted to retain some of the Fenway charm but they really wanted to upgrade its premium seating options. They looked at revenue streams from other teams and felt that they needed to activate them, and the only thing that stood in their way was the ballpark itself. And if fans could develop loyalties to Fenway, they'd eventually feel the same way about a new park. They could not have been more wrong. To many Red Sox fans, Fenway Park is the identity of the team.

The idea of a "replacement park" is heresy to a town that truly loves the Red Sox with a passion. And in spite of their inability to win a World Series, the fans always turn out and swear by Fenway's charms. Luckily for Fenway fans, the Red Sox found a new owner, John Henry, who did not want to pursue Harrington's dream of another ballpark. Henry, who had owned the Florida Marlins, bought controlling interest, or 54 percent of the team, for $700 million.[14] Henry didn't see the dire circumstances that Harrington identified. He didn't feel that Fenway Park was a liability to the franchise.

Henry looked at the revenues and saw that the Red Sox earned over $176 million in operating revenue for 2001. He felt that the team, its tradition, loyal fan base, excellent regional TV cable network, and stadium were a good buy. Henry, a baseball fan and existing owner, knew that the things lacking during his tenure as owner in Miami existed in Boston. He did not want to ruin a good thing, like the Hornets' management did in Charlotte. Further complicating the matter is that Bob Kraft, owner of the Patriots, built a new stadium privately. The Red Sox solution is not through the taxpayer, or a new stadium located at a different site. It is to stay at Fenway and refurbish it respectfully. For the 2003 season, they added seats atop the Green Monster. Wildly popular, they bring in over $1.5 million to the team's bottom line.

Red Sox fans buy virtually every ticket to each game in spite of small seats, cramped bathrooms, and inaccessible concession stands. But that seems to make the fans like it even more. Henry knows that Fenway is a huge asset to the franchise and that the previous ownership tried to ignore that. Henry has tuned his ear to a different frequency and wants to renovate the park, to bring it up to more modern standards, yet retain the fierce loyalty and affection of his customers. It will only make the Red Sox more popular and more profitable.

WHO IS RIGHT?

The new stadium boom has meant $15 billion in new venue construction over the past twelve years, $10 billion of that in public funds. The stadium game is not as much a movement as it is a type of industrial policy. With so many teams getting new stadiums, arenas, and fields, two questions really remain:

1. So, are these good for municipalities, or not?
2. What about those left behind?

The first question has a very simple, two-word answer: "It depends." It depends on who you ask, by what criteria you judge the value, and how you analyze their answer.

The basic argument for the ballparks is that the construction and maintenance means jobs, and that the tax receipts from the economic activity are significant. Also, the games attract crowds and they fill up restaurants, bars, hotels, shops, and parking garages for businesses that pay city taxes. Studies show that events like spring training in Arizona mean an $80 million boost to the economy. One N.Y. Mets game means 850 game-day jobs and $62,000 in local taxes. The Olympics in Atlanta and Salt Lake City left behind over $1 billion in infrastructure and facilities. The Braves new ballpark, Turner Field, was paid for by the Atlanta Committee for the Olympic Games. Furthermore, the new facilities spur growth in areas needing urban redevelopment, and the new venues help attract both business and other events like concerts, truck pulls, and the circus.

Findings by Convention Sports and Leisure International show that the Tennessee Titans generate over $108 million for the area economy every year. Perhaps more important, 2,100 jobs can be traced to direct and indirect spending due to the team's presence. In Cleveland, the Jacobs Field/Gateway Project, which includes Gund Arena, has created over

6,000 jobs since 1994. Those jobs represent $6.5 million in payroll taxes and millions in direct and indirect spending. Those are impressive reasons for accommodating a pro sports team with the best facility possible.

The arguments against new facilities are fairly simple. The first argument usually mentions that there are other, better priorities for taxpayers' money: things like hospitals, education, raises for civil servants, infrastructure, and social welfare programs. Stadium opponents have no problem with taking offense at the notion that sports facilities represent an important public good. To them, a library is a public good, used by the entire public, and without a profit motive. For opponents, they see the facility as corporate welfare to already obscenely wealthy people for private enterprise.

Other people look at the financing of the parks and see how much they really cost a community when the debt is finally paid off. These analysts don't care about the honeymoon effect and extra hype a splashy new facility means for a city, its media, and fans. They are bean counters who think that if fans didn't spend fifty dollars to attend a Braves game, that they would spend the fifty dollars on another leisure activity, like attending an amusement park. To this group, the money a sports team attracts is really removing it from another sector of the same local economy. Most important, the antifacility sector wants to know who will pay for the inevitable cost overruns and how long it will take for the facility to be debt-free and off the books.

Often the small print does not receive too much attention and the pro-stadium voice beats the drum that promises the excitement of a new park, and brushes aside talk of the ultimate financial responsibility. Of course, the sports-friendly side usually has far greater resources in the campaign and that always counts in an election.

It comes down to priorities, and where sports rank for a city and its surrounding communities. And judging by the enormous investment into sports facilities over the past fifteen years, they clearly rank pretty high. Municipalities all over the country, from progressive urban areas to the Bible Belt, have all jumped on the sports bandwagon. The subtleties of the situation, though, are that the tax burden normally falls on the county that the facility city resides in. The San Francisco 49ers want a new, state-of-the-art stadium, and it will draw fans from Santa Clara County, San Mateo

County, Marin County, Alameda County, and Contra Costa County. The problem is that only San Francisco County will pay for it, unless it is in Santa Clara County, in which case San Francisco County will pay nothing. Since the municipalities usually do not distribute the burden fairly, that is where the difficulties of the "fine print" can begin.

The best facility for a community deals are those that have been privately financed, like the San Francisco Giants' Pacific Bell Park. Assuming that sports teams present no negative externalities, the fact that a city can host a team without paying for the privilege is a great deal. The NFL realized that the public's burden of facility expense might hurt the league's progress, so they issued bonds in the marketplace to help teams construct new facilities.[15] Gillette Field in Massachusetts and seven other facilities have benefited from the league's financial foresight.

But when facilities have a public money component, it makes judging their impact more difficult. Certainly, very few cities have surpluses from which they take funds to assist in facility construction, so to balance the opportunity cost of where the money would have gone, if not to a ballpark, is problematic. Certainly, the Dodgers vacating Brooklyn left a void in New York that is still lamented. Do people in Los Angeles reference the Rams' departure similarly? Absolutely not, but the team did have a core following of loyal fans and the team's presence stimulated valuable economic activity.

The Dodgers leaving Brooklyn or the Rams leaving Los Angeles should not be compared to General Motors closing down factories in Flint, Michigan. Thankfully, teams do not have that kind of community impact. What teams provide is that adrenaline rush and cultural adhesive that is so important to a community. Sports teams help define areas. Pittsburgh fans, for example, love the Steelers. The team struggled for many years but finally became an NFL powerhouse in the early 1970s. Drafting smart, the team built a core of Hall of Fame players around Mean Joe Green and won four Super Bowls in less than ten years. But the team did so much more than just win on the field. As the steel industry started to diminish in western Pennsylvania, the Steelers became one of the more refreshing developments in a region wracked by structural unemployment. Today, even though there is not one steel mill in the town of Pittsburgh, and the town has been completely revitalized around technology and banking, the football team remains a legacy to that crit-ical, blue-collar period. And the fans and the team rally around the idea of Pittsburgh being a town of hardened blue-collar workers.

That kind of emotion does have an impact on a city. The Steelers remain the most popular professional team by far in Pittsburgh, because the team did such an effective job of crafting its reputation out of the city's own image.

Just west of Pittsburgh, Jacobs Field became the hub of redevelop-ment in Cleveland in the 1990s. At the same time the new ballpark went up, the Rock and Roll Hall of Fame opened for business nearby. The combination of exciting downtown projects and the Indians' on-field success helped Cleveland experience a civic rebirth. The team's success meant more than just sellouts; it meant money for the city, and lots of it. The Cleveland Indians were one of the four marquee franchises in base-ball in the 1990s, not at all resembling the team featured in the movie, *Major League*. The Indians routinely made the playoffs and sold out 455 consecutive games, a Major League record.

They played an exciting brand of baseball and helped restore the downtown area in Cleveland as an important economic center. The Cleveland Convention and Visitors Bureau estimated that the team brought in $1.5 billion from 1996 to 2001, including all payroll taxes, related hotel expenditures, food, services, and entertainment. When cities push through stadium deals, they hope for the Cleveland experi-ence of the 1990s.

LEGISLATION AND FINANCING OPTIONS

Most public financing packages come through two sources: bond issuance or taxation, and sometimes both. Taxes usually mean either a sales tax in the community where the park is built, like Bank One Ballpark (half-cent increase in sales taxes in Maricopa County) and the Ballpark in Arlington (half-cent sales tax in the city of Arlington), or a hotel and/or car rental tax like they had in Houston, Chicago, Philadelphia, and other cities. The tax-increase mechanism can be the most straightforward, because county legislators can always put a new tax-increase bill on the ballot. Putting the tax increase on hotels and car rentals, that means that visitors pay, not the locals. In the stadium game, the citizens are just like the owners; they want the team, but they want to pass the expense!

Bonds can be issued by a city, county, state, or authority, but the states usually have a limit as to how much total debt they can assume. Most bond issues require voter approval and are either backed by specific revenue streams or financing sources, or the "full faith and credit of the city, county, or state." Bonds are not as straightforward as a tax, and present more confusing issues to the voting populace.

But often, the actual percentage of public commitment is lost in the general argument over the concept of public financing. The charts below demonstrate that actual percentages vary greatly.

Facility	Team	Cost	% Public Financing
Facilities Built with a High Percentage of Public Funds:			
Edward James Dome	St. Louis Rams	$299	96%
Ballpark at Arlington	Texas Rangers	$191	71%
Comiskey Park	Chicago White Sox	$167.8	100%
Camden Yards	Baltimore Orioles	$228	96%
Oakland Arena	Golden State Warriors	$225	100%
Georgia Dome	Atlanta Falcons	$210	100%
Minute Maid	Houston Astros	$250	68%
Facilities Built with a Medium to Low Percentage of Public Funds:			
America West Arena	Suns/Coyotes	$97.7	39%
Rose Garden	Portland Trail Blazers	$94	14%
Ericsson Stadium	Carolina Panthers	$247.7	20%
Delta Center	Utah Jazz	$168	12%
Ford Field	Detroit Lions	$430	51%
Comerica Park	Detroit Tigers	$300	38%
Citizens Bank Park	Philadelphia Phillies	$350	50%
Jacobs Field	Cleveland Indians	$175	48%
No Public Financing:			
FleetCenter	Celtics/Bruins	$160.0	0%
First Union Center	Flyers/76ers	$206.0	0%
Corel Centre	Ottawa Senators	$160	0%

FedEx Field	Washington Redskins	$185	0%
Ericsson Stadium	Carolina Panthers	$185	0%
Pacific Bell Park	San Francisco Giants	$255	0%

Source: Paul Munsey and Corey Suppes, *Ballparks* [online], www.ballparks.com.

In analyzing any facility financing structure, one needs to keep in mind the fact that several methods can come into play. Sometimes a bank will handle all of the construction financing, or a stadium authority will be established for that administrative purpose. Other times, multiple stadium development projects happen simultaneously. The city of Pittsburgh, for example, performed a sports facility bonanza, razing Three Rivers Stadium, and constructing Heinz Field and PNC Park. They also built out the Convention Center and took care of some other infrastructure needs under an $800 million program. The financing package had multiple sources of revenue.[16] They had the Regional Asset District contribute $13.4 million annually in order to finance $170 million in bonds. They put 5 percent surcharges on tickets to Pirates and Steelers games and levied a hotel tax in order to pay off other bond debt. They even put a 1 percent wage tax on players who didn't live in the city. Now that is sharing the burden!

The project also received $300 million in matching funds from the state, $28 million in federal infrastructure improvements, $11 million in parking revenue from the convention center, $36 million in interest earnings, $45 million from an investment capital fund, and $85 million from the Pirates and Steelers themselves. In short, everyone has something at stake in the commitment to sports along the North Shore of Pittsburgh. And it might pay off for the area. Plans for office buildings, hotels, parking structures, and the necessary restaurants and merchant businesses will try to set down roots around their new sports cathedrals. It might be a new way of prioritizing civic needs, but it has its believers.

With respect to the private financing of facilities, it does not mean that ownership writes a check; it means that they seek to place as much of the expense on their private and corporate customers as possible. Personal seat licenses (PSLs) changed the stadium game by introducing an unforeseen revenue stream from a familiar source, the season ticket holder. PSLs are essentially a surcharge for the privilege, or legal right, to buy season tickets for a team. First introduced on a mass scale by the Carolina Panthers in 1993, the team hoped that eager fans would embrace the program. And team management was proven correct when the Panthers sold 41,632 PSLs the very first day they went on sale!

Ultimately, the Panthers sold 62,000 PSLs to twenty-five thousand different customers without having played one down of football. The prices ranged from $600 to $5,400, and the program helped privately finance their stadium. The Panthers also created a model that every other team with a new facility would try to emulate in one form or another. Steve Andretich, a Chicago Bears PSL holder, sums up the phenomenon: "I had spent eleven years on the season ticket waiting list when the opportunity arose to buy a PSL to the new Soldier Field. Even though I had moved to California, I was still a rabid Bears fan and the decision was a no-brainer. . . . I bought it without hesitation."[17]

Additionally, the corporate customer pays in advance for everything from luxury suites to entitlement privileges and pouring rights. Because the stadium business model has matured, teams can seek and secure deals well in advance of the facility's construction.

In short, after aggregating as many financial commitments as possible, the team can then go to private lending institutions and get construction loans to build their own field of dreams. The NFL is the most progressive league, having developed its own Stadium Committee, which helps team secure their own stadium solutions. The New England Patriots won the Super Bowl in their last season at Foxboro Stadium, yet calculated they were losing up to $100 million a year in revenue by not playing in a modern stadium. They even lost their initial stadium sponsor, Internet conglomerate CMGI, to the economic downturn. But with the league's help, team owner Robert Kraft was able to build his fans a new stadium with private money. Kraft deserves applause for his stewardship in delivering a state-of-the-art facility to his fans. The stadium got some state assistance with respect to infrastructure around the facility, but Kraft agreed to pay $1 million a year in easement fees. Now they sell over six thousand club seats at premium prices and have McDonald's selling food in both end zones. The real high rollers get luxury suites, and the only enduring memory of Foxboro Stadium is not of the cold steel seats, but of Adam Vinatieri booting perhaps the most memorable field goal in NFL history. The last play in the history of the facility fittingly took place in a driving snow storm, when Vinatieri's kick put the Patriots in Super Bowl XXXVI. It was a great way for Patriots fans to say goodbye to an outdated facility.

WINNING AND LOSING CAN AFFECT THE STADIUM DEAL

As detailed earlier, the city of San Diego has a contractual obligation to buy tickets from the Chargers if certain sales figures are not met. Clearly, the team's performance will influence the amount the city has to pay. Another city where winning and losing might have stadium-financing ramifications is Cincinnati, where the Bengals football malaise could impact the lease between the team and the taxpayers of Hamilton County, where Paul Brown Stadium, the Bengals' $450-million facility, is located.

The lease between the team and the county cites that a 1996 half-cent sales tax increase intended to "keep competitive and viable major league football . . . in Cincinnati." The phrasing "competitive" has significant meaning in the debate. Hamilton County commissioner Todd Portune has a different definition of "competitive" than the team and feels that the Bengals' performance might invalidate the city's obligation.

During the campaign to levy the tax increase, team officials said that a new stadium was necessary in order to "remain competitive" within the NFL. The Bengals have the worst record in all of professional football since 1990. Comically referred to as "The Bungles," attendance and stadium revenues have suffered. Losing more than twice as many games than they have won since 1990, a good argument could be made that the team is not competitive at all.

Currently, the lease obligates the county taxpayers to pay the Bengals almost $30 million to play at Paul Brown Stadium in the final eleven years of the lease.[18] The team also keeps most of the concession, parking, and ad revenue, which does not help matters with city authorities. Also, the team has a technological upgrade clause in the agreement, which means that the county has to pay for upgrades to the facility if a certain amount of other NFL stadiums implement them.

Regardless of how the dispute evolves, the important development in the Cincinnati example is that acrimony can evolve between municipalities and franchises in the early phase of a new stadium arrangement. Consequently, the urgency that helps get deals done can haunt both parties. In the anticipation of a new stadium, or of a major league team coming to town, the lease can end up hurting the city. In cities like Chicago and Denver, for example, the White Sox and Rockies' rent is directly pegged by attendance figures. For those landlords, winning and losing does have meaning beyond simple fan satisfaction.

HALO EFFECT

There are three distinct pieces to the Halo Effect.

First, a new stadium for an old team can impact attendance greatly, but eventually it will taper back to previous levels. Teams move into new parks to modernize their revenue streams and enhance the game experience for all categories of their fans, not just the suite holders. Predictably, people want to see the new park, regardless of the quality of team on the field, and that initially leads to high attendance figures and big concession sales. However, a new park alone won't keep the fans coming back.

Year	Pirate Attendance	Astros Attendance	Tigers Attendance
1998	1,560,950	2,458,451	1,409,391
1999	1,638,023	2,706,017	2,026,491
2000	1,748,908	3,020,581–**Enron**	2,438,617–**Comerica**
2001	2,435,867–**PNC**	2,906,277	1,920,995
2002	1,784,988	2,517,357	1,503,623
2003	1,636,751	2,416,264	1,349,286

Source: "Detroit Tigers, Houston Astros Attendance Analysis Page," Baseball Almanac [online], baseball-almanac.com [October 13, 2002].

Both the Pirates and the Tigers, for example, struggled competitively in spite of a beautiful new ballpark. The Houston Astros, on the other hand, were a highly competitive perennial playoff contender. In all three cases, regardless of the competitive quality of the team, attendance spiked dramatically in the first year of the park, but then crept back to "old" facility levels.

Second, the Halo Effect of a new stadium attracts media attention. When the Detroit Lions wanted a new facility to replace the Pontiac Silverdome, they knew that anything would rate as an improvement. Old, ugly, and without any charm, the Silverdome had nothing but memories of Billy Sims, Barry Sanders, and quarterbacks named Hipple, Danielson, and Ware. But Ford Field, the beautiful new home stadium for the Lions, presented a new angle on the Lions' story when it opened in 2002. It might simply be a great place to watch bad football, but then again, it might be enough to attract some much-needed attention.

The Lions also drafted an exciting young quarterback named Joey Harrington for the 2002 season. Fox decided to air its national pregame show from Ford Field and it happened to be on the day when Harrington would make his first start as quarterback.

Joyce Julius Associates, a company that monitors media for sponsor mention, tabulated that Ford (and the companies' brands) had almost sixteen minutes of air time during the one-hour broadcast, and Ford was mentioned eighteen times. Julius calculated the value of that media to be worth $3.2 million. Seeing that Ford only pays $1 million per year in facility naming rights, they got a bargain.

If that game had been played at the Silverdome, Fox would have had to be paid $3.2 million to conduct its pregame show from the facility. But a swank new stadium, featuring one of the most tradition-laden rivalries in the NFL, and a team whose owner's (Bill Ford) company is one of the largest advertisers in America makes a lot of sense to a broadcaster, and Fox scheduled the event.

The third and most persuasive component of the Halo Effect speaks to the city's bottom line. The Phoenix Finance Department estimated that Bank One Ballpark's first year of operation (3.6 million fans) led to a 34.1 percent increase in city sales taxes. Restaurant and bar receipts went from $40 million to over $52 million, and the hotels within one mile of the stadium had almost a 3 percent increase in bookings over hotels in other parts of the city. In short, a new ballpark can help everyone; it's just not guaranteed to last.

Another way that new-facility influence can be peddled is through leagues awarding premier events to a city. Frequently, league commissioners will award prime events like All-Star games and Super Bowls to cities that build new facilities on the league's terms. Of the last six Major League Baseball All-Star Games, five have been played in stadiums that were built in the modern, post–Camden Yards era. All-Star Games used to be a nice, middle-of-the-season one-day exhibition, but now they are economic gold chips that cities and politicians covet. Hosting a game can mean tens of thousands of tourists and millions of dollars of activities for the local economy. The host city and Major League Baseball stage fan-friendly activities and exhibitions and truly make the town a desirable destination during the week of the game. Typical events include:

- The Futures Game: The best of baseball's rising stars play against each other in a United States versus the World format.
- The All-Star Gala: A black-tie party on the evening before the game.
- The Home Run Derby: This top event pits Major League stars from both leagues in an elimination Home Run Derby.
- FanFest: An interactive and educational exhibit. A great gathering spot for fans to enjoy autograph sessions, Baseball Hall of Fame exhibits, and memorabilia sales.

Basically, Major League Baseball and the host city devise good reasons for coming to the host city and staying a few days. The 1998 game in Denver meant an additional $40 million for the local economy according to Harris County-Houston Sports Authority. The 1999 game, played at the smallest and oldest ballpark in all of baseball, Fenway, generated $60 million in revenue via 100,000 visitors to the city.[19] And the city of Seattle estimated that it reaped approximately $50 million in benefit when it hosted the 2001 "Midseason Classic."

Cities get excited because past games have filled between 14,000 and 16,500 hotel rooms. The City of Houston will host both the Super Bowl and baseball's All-Star Game in 2004. The Harris County-Houston Sports Authority expects the combination to mean over $300 million in economic activity. In basketball, it is the same story. Atlanta hosted the 2003 NBA All-Star Game at the Phillips Arena, and the Atlanta Sports Council estimated that the three-day event was worth $25 million to the local economy. Special, marquee events only go to the premier destinations and facilities. When stadium financing deals stall during negotiations, an All-Star game can often be one of the deal points that makes it worthwhile.

HISTORICAL PERSPECTIVE ON ATTENDANCE

The core issue to all sports marketing principles has to do with the size and composition of the total audience. Beer companies continue to air commercials during football games because they know that their customers watch football. When it comes to facility analysis for sports teams, attendance will always be the lowest common denominator for the team. Today, more people attend professional sporting events than ever. More people watch, listen, and read about them. The extension of the modern facility as a marketing medium only promotes the interests of the sports industry. When people talk about the good old days of sports, it may be a slight misnomer. Remember, sports have never been more popular than now.

Year	Average Major League Attendance Per Team
1910	408,836
1920	635,538
1930	585,716
1940	679,224
1950	1,142,795
1960	1,153,316
1970	1,007,095
1980	1,563,575
1990	2,166,590
2000	2,262,557

Source: http://www.baseball-almanac.com.

Additionally, teams did not sell out their parks with rabid fans in the nascent days of sports. The chart below shows the years that teams first drew over one million fans.

Team	Year
New York Yankees	1920
Detroit Tigers	1924*
Chicago Cubs	1927
Brooklyn Dodgers	1930
New York Giants	1945
Boston Red Sox	1946
St. Louis Cardinals	1946
Philadelphia Phillies	1946
Cleveland Indians	1946
Pittsburgh Pirates	1947
Boston Braves	1947
Chicago White Sox	1951
Cincinnati Reds	1956

Source: http://www.baseball-almanac.com.

*The Tigers would not hit that mark again until 1935.

The table above is easily explained. Babe Ruth's arrival and his prodigious home runs clearly propelled the Yankees to the magic mark in 1920. Detroit cracking the barrier in 1924, in many ways, reflects the prosperity of the auto industry and the effect it had on the wealth of the city. The Cubs enjoyed several seasons of million-plus attendance in the 1920s because Chicago's North Side was a very prosperous place at the time. The New York Giants came close to one million fans several times— drawing over 900,000 fans in 1908, 1920, 1921, 1922, and 1928. They did not break the magic mark, though, until 1945, no doubt aided by the end of the War in Europe in May. The lone anomaly is Brooklyn's breakout season in 1930, during the earliest painful days of the Depression.

Clearly, the Depression and the population drain during World War II suppressed attendance throughout Major League Baseball. Similarly, postwar euphoria propelled Major League attendance to its highest levels ever (at that time). But teams didn't enjoy the type of fan support that franchises receive today. Sometimes, even the special milestone games didn't receive the support their historic dimensions would seem to indicate.

Milestone	Year	Attendance
Bobby Thomson "Shot heard 'round the world"	1951	34,320
Ted Williams's last game at Fenway	1960	10,454
Roger Maris's 61st home run	1961	23,154

Source: S. Miller, "It takes more than a new ballpark to draw fans," *Sportsline*, April 26, 2002.

Bobby Thomson's dramatic game winning Home Run off of Ralph Branca might be the most famous hit in Major League Baseball history. Called "The Shot Heard Round the World," or "The Miracle at Coogan's Bluff," Bobby Thomson hit a game-winning home run that got the Giants into the World Series. The radio call of announcer Russ Hodges has made the moment live on for baseball fans of every era: "There's a long drive, in center field I believe! The Giants win the pennant! The Giants win the pennant! The Giants win the pennant! The Giants win the pennant! Bobby Thomson hits into the lower deck of the left field stands. The Giants win the pennant, and they're going crazy, they're going crazy! OOOOHHHH!!!"

When Hodges said, "they're going crazy," he didn't mean the 20,000 empty seats at the Polo Grounds that day. A Giants-Dodgers playoff game in the twenty-first century could be staged in Albania and it wouldn't have 20,000 empty seats. The old days are great for nostalgia, but accuracy places them in the proper context.

Of course, baseball fans were not entirely immune to spectacle. Joe DiMaggio's fifty-seventh, and fateful, game during his fifty-six-game hitting streak in the summer of 1941 had 67,468 fans jammed into Cleveland's Municipal Stadium. DiMaggio had built up momentum throughout the streak, and since it occurred during the summer, kids could attend the games, which certainly helped attendance.

Today, by comparison, all milestone games are big draws. Whether it be Barry Bonds breaking Mark McGwire's record, Mark McGwire breaking Roger Maris's record, or Cal Ripken Jr. breaking Lou Gehrig's consecutive-game mark, the ballparks have been jammed, and the scalpers were charging premium prices.

NOTES

1. Pete Hamill, *A Drinking Life* (Boston: Little, Brown and Co., 1994).

2. Robert Moses was a New York State and municipal official whose public works projects transformed the urban landscape of New York City. He extended roads onto Long Island, and built bridges, tunnels, and causeways as a public official from 1924–1968, when Nelson Rockefeller ended his tenure.

3. *Sports Illustrated* (February 29, 1960): 39.

4. Roger Kahn, *A Season in the Sun* (New York: Harper & Row, 1977), pp. 49–50.

5. "1957: New York Reels over the loss of Two Teams," *San Francisco Giants History* [online], Sanfrancisco.giants.mlb.com/NASApp/mlb/sf/history/sf-history-timeline-article.jsp?article=22 [October 29, 2002].

6. By 1970, total NFL broadcast revenues (radio, local, and national TV) topped out at $49,435,000. MLB totaled 38,090,000, and the NBA $5,500,000. Ticket sales were still the primary revenue source for all leagues and teams.

7. Kansas City's Kauffman Stadium has undergone some renovations and can expect more. It still remains a beautiful, baseball-only facility.

8. It should be noted that the facility phenomenon relates to other leisure activities and attractions as well. New, gussied up abodes mean new business for all attractions. Los Angeles' new Museum of Contemporary Art hosted a twelve-week Andy Warhol exhibit and it was like hosting a NASCAR race. The twelve-week show goosed the Los Angeles economy by over $55 million, including $550,000 in hotel and revenue taxes from visitors and tourists specifically there to see the exhibit. The museum also scored big, reaping $5.4 million in donations, and generating $1.65 million in souvenir and concession sales receipts. The show had an increase in attendance by over 275 percent over the same time the prior year.

The museum used the same principle: mix excellent, revenue friendly venue with a highly desirable event and the crowds come, and they spend! The same thing could be said for the Olympics, Super Bowl, NCAA Final Four, or any marquee sporting event. Crowds equal money and sports entertainment is not the only thing that draws crowds!

9. Andy Dolich, personal interview, December 19, 2002.

10. In the NFL today, for example, $1.1 billion in revenue is via ticket sales, but $2.5 billion via broadcast contracts. Ticket sales are still very important, just not the primary source of revenue.

11. K. Dale, "The Name Game" [online], http://aspe.dallasnews.com/pdf/oct2001.pdf [August 8, 2003].

12. America West airlines had been facing financial difficulties prior to 9/11/01. The events of that day certainly only impacted their bottom line negatively as well.

13. Scott Greenberger, "New Fenway Push by Former Owners called into Question," *Boston Globe*, July 1, 2002.

14. Meg Vaillancourt, "It's Official: Henry Owns the Sox," *Boston Globe*, February 28, 2002, p. C1.

15. Tom Lowry, "The NFL Machine," *BusinessWeek* (January 27, 2003): 90.

16. Munsey & Suppes, "PNC Park," *Ballparks* [online], www.ballparks.com/baseball/national/pitbpk.htm [May 21, 2003].

17. Personal interview with the author.

18. B. Horstman, "The Fact Bengals Stink Could Mean New Lease," *Cincinnati Post* [online], www.cincypost.com [October 16, 2002].

19. Tom Haudricourt, "Milwaukee to Host 2002 All-Star Game," *Milwaukee Journal-Sentinel* [online], www.jsonline.com [October 1, 1999].

CHAPTER 9

LEVERAGING THE SPORTS PLATFORM IN THE MODERN ERA

I changed that night. It was now clear to me that my destiny would not be grim. Boxing may or may not have figured in; I couldn't see that far and anyway had no preference for boxing over anything else. I didn't know where I'd be going, only that I was going somewhere and I was going to be somebody. And that was all I ever fought for.

—George Foreman
By George

George Foreman went on to have a storied boxing career. Among Foreman's highlights are winning a gold medal in the 1968 Mexico City Olympic Games and knocking out the great Joe Frazier to win the heavyweight championship in 1973. An astonishing twenty-one years later, he won the title again, knocking out Michael Moorer with a big right hand in the tenth round of their bout. Amassing a 76-5 career record, Foreman is among the handful of greatest boxers who ever entered the ring. But Big George's legacy is far more than uppercuts and knockouts. Foreman has a true connection with people, and his ability to communicate has made him a successful preacher, author, actor, announcer, and consumer pitchman.

In fact, George Foreman is arguably the most successful product endorser of all time. His now-famous Lean Mean Fat Reducing Grilling Machine, manufactured by Salton, Inc., might be one of the single most popular electronic appliances of the last twenty years. The grill has swept through all channels of distribution, including retail, catalog, online, and even QVC, and spawned a whole legion of devotees while selling tens of millions of units.

It was an unlikely path. Reared on the mean streets of Houston, Foreman's life took a turn when he joined the Job Corps, a youth work program conceptualized during the Johnson Administration.[1] Foreman joined the Job Corps after he saw a public service announcement featuring Jim Brown and Johnny Unitas. The two football legends urged youths to give the program a chance if they felt their lives needed some direction. George Foreman happened to be one of those kids that needed direction. Once in the Job Corps, Foreman's aggression instantly became apparent. Doc Broadus, a Job Corps counselor, recommended that the brooding youth channel that energy into the boxing ring. In the ring, George Foreman found a necessary measure of purpose.

Foreman excelled like few others, and it culminated with his appearance at the 1968 Olympic Games in Mexico City. The improbable kid from Houston, Texas, won the gold medal in one of its most prestigious events. Foreman went from the most desperate edges of obscurity to an exalted international champion. He owed it all to the Job Corps, talent, and the sport of boxing. Foreman instantly became a professional, got some early pointers from Sonny Liston, and started pummeling opponents. When he became the heavyweight champion in 1973, it seemed like George had hit the big time. It just didn't last as long as the experts predicted. Foreman went from champ to ex-champ faster than anyone would have predicted. He successfully defended his title twice before losing to Muhammad Ali in Zaire in October 1974. Foreman fought for three more years before leaving the sport in order to devote his life to the ministry in 1977.[2]

Foreman then poured all of his energy and resources into preaching and his Youth Center in Houston. When he needed money to continue his pursuits, he reentered the ring in 1987. Some laughed at Foreman and many scoffed, but George did not listen to the skeptics. Instead, he fought intelligently and shrewdly. In 1994, when he won the heavyweight championship back, it was one of the greatest moments in boxing history.

Along the way, Salton, a home products company, had bought the rights to a two-sided indoor kitchen grill. It had not had much success selling as a stand alone product, so they decided to bring in a celebrity spokesman. Who better to preach the virtues of tasty meals than the large, loquacious Foreman? Neither side knew what to expect from the relationship, and Foreman accepted a straight royalty as compensation. With Foreman as the spokesman, the grill, under Salton's expert stewardship, became a sensation. Grill sales went from $5 million in 1996 to $400 million in 2002, and *Fortune* magazine has reported that Salton has grown over 46 percent a year since 1995.[3] Salton decided to stop paying George royalties and bought his name for the grill's perpetuity. It cost them $137 million in cash and stock, and it was money well invested. Not only had Foreman earned it with his past work, the franchise of the brand was still building. Salton developed new products around the Foreman name and line extensions on the existing grill. They also gave him a $9-million promotional contract in 2003 to further his global committments to marketing Salton's products through 2006. Credit for the product's success must be shared by Salton's visionary CEO Leon Dreimann, his team's ability to execute that vision, and Foreman's incomparable ability as a spokesman.

Foreman's athletic skill, charismatic personality, believability, and sense of timing helped him earn riches that few realize. If there were odds in Las Vegas for the largest endorsement deal ever, you would expect it to go to Michael Jordan or Tiger Woods, not a retired pugilist. The fact that Foreman had not fought in several years didn't matter, either. George Foreman was the American Dream meets Horatio Alger meets Andrew Carnegie meets P. T. Barnum.

Foreman really had two distinct careers. The first, in the 1970s, was of a superior athlete benefiting from the first layer of structure the industry supplied. He fought for money, and made money for promoters. In the 1990s, Foreman's disposition had changed, and so had the facets of his career. Now, after bouts, he talked about his grill, and how he ate meals off of it while training. He acted in his own sitcom, endorsed a wide variety of products from tortilla chips to mufflers, wrote books, and announced fights. George went from being a monodimensional athlete to a superior businessman using all layers of the professional sports platform. Foreman's athletic identity created a personality that the public wanted to see in other places and doing other things. Foreman happily obliged. He indeed enjoyed a professional renaissance, and Americans love seeing him to this day.

FAME AND THE SPORTS PLATFORM

There is a centrifugal force to fame, sensation, and spectacle; it trains a spotlight on a specific place, and especially on a specific person. The white-hot glare of the spotlight can be blinding.

Spectacle has long been the attraction of sports, whether it is Babe Ruth crashing home runs, or Muhammad Ali whipping up prefight interest by baiting his opponents with poems and publicity stunts. George Foreman saw the opportunities of celebrity and managed it expertly when he returned to boxing in 1987. His example shows that the sports platform can propel people to great achievements and distinctions in other disciplines. O. J. Simpson's demise demonstrates that the story can have a different outcome. The scale of spectacle grew toward the end of the twentieth century to improbable heights, where simple decisions can have dramatic consequences for a personality and a fan base.

Sports have become so much more than just the action of the game. Tiger Woods cannot simply drive into and out of a golf course. He can't walk into a movie theater without creating a stir. The same industry that allowed him to display his talents now confines him to a prism of awareness that few could ever understand, much less navigate.

As the business features of sports, like broadcast applications and sponsorship programs, have evolved over time, so have the stakes of publicity and hype. Sports have always provided a great setting for spectacle, and it keeps growing. Often personalities emerge from the center of the competition, or from the commercial interests of the game. At Super Bowl III, that was Joe Namath; during the 1977 World Series, Reggie Jackson. In the mid-1980s, Nike directed it through the clever marketing of incredible athletes like Michael Jordan and Bo Jackson. During the 1990s, Michael Jordan became bigger than Nike and maybe even bigger than the sport itself. The difference between the days of Dempsey, Jones, Ruth, and Gehrig versus Jordan, Gretzky, Woods, and Armstrong is that the marketing minds of companies today know how to capitalize on the celebrity of athletes for profit.

WINNING BUILDS A PLATFORM

There is nothing like winning or losing to affect your status with your customers. The unquestioned excellence of the Lakers and Celtics in the mid 1980s provides a good example. The two teams featured contrasting styles and traditions, which resulted in memorable championship climaxes. The respectful rivalry of the two teams, and their two marquee players, Magic Johnson and Larry Bird, energized the NBA. The teams, styles, personalities, and quality of play enabled the NBA to emerge from its 1970s malaise. For the Celtics and Lakers specifically, the teams restored their status as the benchmark franchises of the NBA. In turn, they maximized their profile and revenue streams. The Celtics even went public, sold stock in the franchise, and built a new facility, the Fleet Center. The Lakers, meanwhile, took the concept of "Showtime" and created a culture as much as a fan base. It became common to see celebrities like Jack Nicholson and Dyan Cannon courtside at Lakers games. It also helped attract marquee sponsors like Great Western Bank to groundbreaking advertising and marketing agreements. Currently, the anchor tenant of the Staples Center, the Lakers' most recent good fortune is due to shrewd management of on-court talent and leveraging the success of the team in their local marketplace. It didn't happen by accident!

The Celtics and Lakers weren't the only NBA teams to capitalize on their success. When Michael Jordan surfaced as the unquestioned greatest player in the game, the Bulls went on an impressive championship run during the 1990s. At the high point of their popularity, they decided to build a new arena, selling lucrative, long-term endorsement and ticket packages to eager Chicago fans. The Bulls knew that they had a window of opportunity. No one cared how much money Jordan, Scottie Pippen, or Phil Jackson made, or how much it cost to be on the joyride with them.

Management knew they had to build a new facility while the team was at its peak, and the United Center replaced Chicago Stadium to help the franchise realize its revenue potential. The team sold long-term deals that fans knew would expire well after Michael, Scottie, and the rest of the championship core took their last shots in Bulls uniforms. In spite of that, inevitably, fans and sponsors were willing to buy into the new arena in order to maintain their association with the championship era. Subsequently, after management dismantled the team, they still had a great season-ticket base and sponsorship agreements because they were all signed while the team was at its peak during the Jordan era. In other words, the success of the 1990s built a platform for the Bulls franchise to help maintain high revenues after Jordan's departure.

On the other end of the spectrum, losing can hurt a franchise's ability to succeed away from the field. The Cincinnati Bengals appeared in two Super Bowls in less than six years in the 1980s. Despite losing both times, the team was obviously a good one, and enjoyed excellent fan support. Unfortunately for the team and its management, not too many fans can live on the exhaust fumes of that success today. The team's decisions have mired the franchise in futility and the immediate future is dim.

The Bengals could use a new direction, or the promise of something great, and they might find it under the leadership of head coach Marvin Lewis. However, even the presence of Lewis cannot turn back the effects of ten years of losing and the loss of revenue. In short, the Bengals' modern sports platform has been weakened as they have lost their goodwill with their fans and sponsors. The problem for the Bengals will be leveraging the coverage and exposure to restore credibility with the people who pay money for their performance.

MAINTAINING THE BUZZ OF A NEW FACILITY

More than ever, with a competitive marketplace for both fans and sponsors, teams need to build a winner, capture fan support, and maximize revenue streams in order to remain competitive. When the San Francisco Giants moved into Pacific Bell Park in 2000, the facility instantly became one of the premier stadia in all of sports. The team on the field was also among the elite.

Led by then manager Dusty Baker, the Giants always seemed to be in the race despite never having the acknowledged best collection of talent.[4] Funding their park with private money, the Giants need to pay over $20 million annually on debt service, so winning and attracting fans has significant importance for the team. Given the team's cost structure of managing high-debt service, they need to spend prudently, ensuring that their payroll won't likely skyrocket into Major League Baseball's top five. In spite of these limitations, the team hit the new park with a winning attitude, won ninety-seven games, and advanced into the playoffs.

In 2001, the team didn't make the playoffs, but fell just short. Their star player, Barry Bonds, however, transcended the discussion of wins and losses by clubbing an eye-popping seventy-three home runs and winning the MVP Award. Bonds's record-breaking efforts not only kept the team in the playoff race until the last days of the season, but it also kept interest in the team high, and attendance at its maximum. It also occurred in the last year of his contract, which would have significant consequences.

The Giants had a serious decision to make with respect to their star left fielder. At the age of thirty-seven, did Bonds peak during his historic 2001 season? Certainly, hitting seventy-three home runs was a peak of some kind, but could they count on him to maintain the high level of performance that would justify a long-term contractual commitment? Furthermore, with the downturn in the economy, especially in the technology-rich San Francisco Bay Area, what were the next five years of revenues for the team going to look like? Also complicating the matter was the fact that big contracts to star players did not mean competitive success for the team. The Texas Rangers had signed Alex Rodriguez to a ten-year, $252 million contract, yet still floundered despite Rodriguez putting up great numbers. The Dodgers signed Kevin Brown to a $105 million contract, and he spent most of the early years of the deal injured. Tying up large percentages of payroll in one player has not been a wining formula for Major League teams. However, the question for the Giants was still this: if Kevin Brown and Alex Rodriguez were worth these amounts, what was Bonds worth on the open market?

Also in the mix was the fact that Bonds was approaching the 600 home run mark in 2002, with a very a realistic shot at 700 and beyond in the ensuing years. Would the Giants have to choose between guaranteeing his pursuit of the record in a Giants uniform, or pursuing multiple players with the certain cost of his contract? The team knew that if they dedicated 25 percent of the payroll to one player, that could have dangerous consequences. Their marketing people also knew that players who hit 700-plus home runs only come around so often. The Giants were in a situation that few teams had ever experienced.

The Giants felt that the market for Bonds was vastly different than the market for A-Rod. Teams felt the pinch of the economy and concern over yet another potential labor suspension. Perhaps most important, the Yankees had eyes for another left-handed slugging Bay Area product, Oakland A's star Jason Giambi. When the Yankees signed Giambi for approximately $20 million per year, the Giants knew that the market for Bonds would be similar. The next question the team had to answer was which strategy to pursue: divide the dollars Bonds would earn among three or four other players; or roll the dice by giving him a big contract, hope that he didn't get injured, and continue to build around him?

The team ultimately signed Bonds to a $90 million contract over five years, and the team made a great deal. Not only did Bonds follow up his 2001 season with another MVP season in 2002, but Bonds's bat led the Giants into the World Series, where they lost in seven games to the Anaheim Angels. The extra games at Pacific Bell Park and the bonus business they concluded with ticket holders and potential sponsors meant that the $90 million they dedicated to Bonds was getting significant return of investment.

Over the course of his career, Bonds has been notoriously uncooperative with various media personnel, team officials, teammates, and just about anyone who rubbed him the wrong way. He does not enjoy Michael Jordan–like reverence with fans, maybe not even Scottie Pippen status. He has a reputation for being detached, moody, and temperamental. But luckily for Giants fans, Bonds saves his worst moods for opposing teams, and he is the unquestioned best and most dangerous hitter in the game.

The Giants know that there is only one Home Run King, and that man could be the guy who currently plays left field for them. By retaining his rights through 2006, they know that no one else can capitalize on his pursuit.

In the absence of a pennant race over the course of the contract, the Giants will always have a great ticket draw. Perhaps Bonds was a marketing insurance policy. As he approaches more home run milestones, the Giants' record might be secondary to his quest. As the team experiments with variable ticket pricing, maybe they will price the projected games for Bonds's historic games accordingly. One thing is certain; by signing him after the 2001 season, the decision belongs to them alone.

To analyze what Barry Bonds means to his team and baseball today, one should think about what past home run hitters have meant during their time. In Babe Ruth's day, he was the first and only Home Run King. He hit more home runs by himself than entire teams could collect, and he was the catalyst to Yankee Stadium being built and the first million-person attendance mark for the team. When Mark McGwire and Sammy Sosa went after Roger Maris's single season record, it was a media circus for them and baseball's springboard to record attendance.

Home runs sell tickets. The single most important thing for the Giants franchise to do during the course of their high-debt obligation on Pacific Bell Park is sell tickets. They surely want to win, but they really need to sell tickets. Barry Bonds might not give the best interviews to local media, but he sells lots of tickets.

ENERGIZING THE FANS TO MAINTAIN THE PLATFORM

By signing Bonds, the Giants showed their fans, ticket holders, and sponsors that they were willing to spend top dollar to keep the best player in baseball. More important, they did not have to answer the question of why they let a guy who hit seventy-three home runs go to another team. Sometimes, the perception of what you are doing is just as important as winning to keep the faith of your constituents, the fans, and sponsors.

The Tampa Bay Buccaneers closed their 2001 season by losing to the Philadelphia Eagles in the first round of the playoffs. The Bucs had been to the playoffs in four out of five previous years, all under the direction of head coach Tony Dungy. During that time, they featured exciting players like Warren Sapp, Mike Alstott, Warrick Dunne, John Lynch, and Keyshawn Johnson. But despite the success, fans had started to grumble loudly about the team's shortcomings, and that was interpreted by ownership as a threat to attendance. Team owners had moved the team into a swank new stadium, Raymond James Stadium, in 1998, where they played before capacity crowds. Ownership knew that the goodwill that financed (via a half-cent sales tax) and filled the facility might not last through perceived disappointment. In short, the fans felt the Bucs should have gone deeper into the playoffs in their one and only run of success. After that 2001 playoff loss in Philadelphia, the team's management felt that they could not afford to be complacent; something had to be done in order to satiate their fan base.

The scapegoat became their one-time savior, Tony Dungy. Dungy was a long-time defensive assistant who came to Tampa Bay and turned around a terminally moribund franchise with an effective defense and shrewd play. But the lack of offense and persistent early exits from the playoffs became his downfall. They kept replacing coordinators, quarterbacks, and various personnel, but nothing worked. The talk shows crackled with disfavor. The newspapers questioned the once unassailable Dungy. The playoffs failure meant that Dungy's future was over, even after all the success.

It ultimately turned out to be a stroke of genius for Tampa Bay's owners, the Glazer family. The team knew it needed a big name and marketable identity and initial rumors focused on Bill Parcells, one of the best coaches in the history of the NFL. Parcells and the Bucs had been down this path before, but he was not destined to lead them. The Bucs then wanted Jon Gruden, the young wonder-coach who reversed the Raiders' fortunes. The first foray to secure Gruden failed and the team then set its sights on Steve Mariucci, then the head coach of the San Francisco 49ers. When the highly public talks with Mariucci broke down, the Bucs made one last run at Gruden, who still had a year left on his Raider contract. They made an offer that Al Davis, the Raiders' owner, couldn't refuse, and the Bucs had their man.

Gruden did not come cheaply. Tampa Bay sent Oakland first- and second-round picks in 2002, a first-round pick in 2003, and a second-round pick in 2004. But the Bucs didn't stop there. They also agreed to pay the Raiders $8 million over the first three years after the deal had been made. And then the team had to sign Gruden, which cost them $17 million over five years. In total, four draft picks and $25 million for one man who would never play a down. But given their predicament, this was a great move for the Bucs. The complete cycle of events related to the Tony Dungy era, whose quiet, dignified professionalism never wavered during his tenure, forced the Bucs to do something.

The personnel moves the team had made in recent years didn't get the Bucs into the Super Bowl. It was clear that the grumbling between the teams' two high-profile, high-priced stars, Warren Sapp and Keyshawn Johnson, was only going to escalate. It seemed, almost impossibly, that Dungy had run his course. The palpable fan unrest, even in spite of multiple winning seasons, threatened revenues. That is the one thing the Glazer family, the owners, found intolerable.

Year	Attendance	Record
2002	525,031	12–4
2001	**524,468**	**9–7**
2000	**524,775**	**10–6**
1999	**522,241**	**11–5**
1998	**518,047**	**8–8**
1997	**543,504**	**10–6**
1996	**333,350**	**6–10**
1995	473,587	7–9
1994	367,443	6–10
1993	377,498	5–11

Note: Dungy years in bold; 1993–1997 figures for Houlihan's Stadium; 1998–2002 for Raymond James Stadium

Source: Munsey & Suppes, "Raymond James Stadium," Ballparks.com [online], www.sfo.com/~mcsuppes/NFL/misc/index.htm?../TampaBayBucs/index.htm [June 5, 2000].

The Bucs were almost too good too fast under Dungy. He led them to respectability and sellouts in his second season! And respectability, for the Bucs, had been an eternally elusive thing. Prior to Dungy's arrival, the Buccaneers had only two winning seasons in their twenty-year history.[5] In fact, the combined record of his predecessors was 95–216, for a 30 percent winning percentage. Dungy should have been deified, but he was chased out of town. By bringing in the young and fiery Jon Gruden, a complete contrast to the placid Tony Dungy, the team remade itself in an instant. Dungy was a defensive mastermind, while Gruden had an offensive pedigree to compare with any NFL contemporary. Dungy's equanimity never wavered. Gruden was one of the most photographed coaches in all of sports as his expressive, demonstrative personality became a fan favorite.

Dungy's career mark, including the playoffs, was 56–46, for a 55 percent winning percentage. Gruden's record, also including playoff games, was not much different at 40–28, or 59 percent. But at the time of the coaching change, Gruden and Dungy were at polar opposites in the eyes of Tampa Bay. The hiring of Gruden, though it came at a steep price, energized the Bucs fan base. They were restless, impatient, and expectant of great things. Dungy, through no fault of his own, had no more goodwill left in Tampa Bay. By bringing in a new guy, supposedly "their guy," the Glazers bought themselves another five years with their customers, the season-ticket holders, suite owners, and sponsors.

The Glazers created a public relations bonanza. Gruden became the new face of the franchise, and he brought the idea of hope. The fans, instead of focusing on the playoff and offensive futility of the past few years, could now anticipate the new era under Gruden. Most important, the Bucs didn't need to wrestle with their salary cap and hope new playing personnel would gel. They put the onus on Jon Gruden. The Glazers, indeed, did all they could do to quell the developing mob-feeling of the fan base. And they did it with supreme efficiency, replacing only one key person. Now the phone calls weren't skeptical, pessimistic rants about near-misses and key losses; they were about optimistic outlooks on exactly the same team.

Tony Dungy deserved much better treatment than he received in Tampa Bay. He endured the ignominious questioning of his skills and leadership as the speculation about his job performance ran rampant. But that is the way it works in the sports industry. The platform the team wanted to maintain required image enhancement. Unfortunately for Dungy, it meant removing him from a job that he had performed quite capably. And as the dust settled on the 2002 NFL season, Tony Dungy's Colts lost in the first round of the playoffs, while Gruden's team won the Super Bowl over Gruden's former team, the Raiders. Warren Sapp, the loud defensive tackle, said it best, "Tony Dungy built this thing from the ground up. This place was nothing before he got here. He baked the cake. Jon Gruden has put the icing on the cake . . . you have to give Gruden the credit. He's really made the difference for us."[6]

The Gruden-Dungy Raiders-Bucs-Colts saga was part of a whole new wave in the NFL sweepstakes to vie for positive fan attention and to win the battle of the headlines. With so much at stake, owners know that they need to keep the masses happy. Employing players is extremely complicated. The really good ones are already with teams, and the way the labor agreements work, it is hard to sign free agents, or pry players from other rosters.

The salary cap rules are so complicated that trades and significant free-agent upgrades are difficult. In short, changing the top half of the roster or talent has gotten complex, bordering on the impossible, but changing the coaches and general managers has not. Furthermore, no expense ceilings exist for coaches or management. Therefore, the new, wide-open competition is not in the middle of a two-deep zone, but instead, for the best talent on the sidelines and in the observation booth. Coaches and front office personnel have no salary cap restraints, though they require significant compensation.[7]

The Washington Redskins hired college coaching whiz Steve Spurrier and forked out $25 million over five years, making him the highest paid coach in the league prior to 2002. The next best compensated coaches, at "only" $4 million per annum, were Mike Shanahan and Mike Holmgren. The two Mikes have more in common than their first names. They both have won Super Bowl trophies as head coach. Steve Spurrier hadn't even won one game and he got a 25 percent raise over their salaries.

But the Spurrier hiring had very little to do with a coaching pedigree and everything to do with energizing the Redskin fan base. The Redskins are truly one of the most storied franchises in the league and they had a tumultuous first few years of existence under the ownership of Daniel Snyder. Snyder paid handsomely for the club, almost $800 million and he had a right to see that things were done his way. He signed scores of players, fired and hired coaches and quarterbacks. He wanted a winner and was willing to do anything for it. When several head coaching positions became available after the 2001 season, Spurrier seemed to be the hottest property. Tampa Bay and Carolina were rumored as the front runners. Spurrier himself declared that he had done all that he could in the college game and that he wanted an NFL job. Snyder had hired Marty

Schottenheimer just before to the 2001 season. Would he let the esteemed Schottenheimer go after only one productive season? The answer was a resounding "yes" and Spurrier was inked to a five-year, $25-million deal. Snyder felt that Spurrier had more "upside" than Schottenheimer, and that his confident persona would be a catalyst both on the field and off.

A big personality can be good for business. When Bill Parcells took over a lackluster Jets team in 1997, it impacted all of the other revenue streams: retailers stocked more Jets merchandise; McDonald's bought signage at the stadium; and Toyota and Lexus signed up for local pregame broadcasts. Season-ticket holders who had stayed away in droves, started to show up in the stands. After signing Parcells to coach the team, less than two dozen season-ticket holders chose not to renew for the 1997 season.[8] And the Jets have 78,000 season-ticket holders! Parcells, at just over $2 million per year, was a bargain. Parcells, no doubt, leveraged that into his next job, with the Dallas Cowboys, who he agreed to coach in 2003. After spurning the Buccaneers one year earlier, he spent the 2002 season working for ESPN as a commentator. Before the season ended, Jerry Jones, the maverick owner of the Cowboys, knew that Parcells's championship resumé could bring discipline and performance on the field. Jones, who has rewritten the rules by which teams market themselves within the NFL, also knows that Parcells certifies the Cowboys' efforts with his ticket holders.

In fact, Jones fired Dave Campo and hired Bill Parcells just as many suite holders' six-year leases were up on their luxury boxes. Even though Parcells only signed for four years, most of those customers can be expected to renew for six. If his track record with the Jets' ticket holders provides any indication, Jones should be pleased with the results.

Bill Parcells has quite a record. Thirteenth on the NFL's all-time victories list, Parcells has 149 career victories, including eleven playoff games and two Super Bowls. He took New England to the Super Bowl and the Jets to the AFC Championship Game. Only Tom Landry, Chuck Noll, and Don Shula have more postseason wins than Bill Parcells.

Jones signed his new coach in the neighborhood of $17–18 million for four years. If the team reverses its on-field fortunes, then Jones will recoup that total investment in less than two years. If the team returns to championship form, Jones will have made his best deal since hiring Jimmy Johnson when he originally bought the team. In Detroit, the Lions pursued the same strategy when they invested $25 million in Michigan-native Steve Mariucci, in an effort to bring a positive identity to their team. Clearly, the trend or marquee coaches injecting vitality into a franchise is on the upswing. Management is now an integral part of a sport's team's platform.

WHEN THE PLATFORM ATTRACTS A DIFFERENT SPOTLIGHT

One fateful June day in 2002, Augusta National chairman Hootie Johnson opened up a letter from Martha Burk. Johnson probably gets a lot of mail, but this letter was a little different from the normal mail he receives. Burk did not write to say "I love the azaleas!" Nor did she ask, "Can I meet Jack Nicklaus?" She even avoided the obvious, "I'd do anything to play your golf course." No, Martha Burk wanted to know why Augusta National, a private golf club, did not have any female members. Johnson responded by saying that club membership is a closely held matter and that related matters would be determined by the club and its members. He had hoped that would clarify the issue. It only served to prolong it.

Augusta National is a private golf club that hosts a tournament, the Masters, which happens to be the most popular in all of professional golf. It is the perfect blend of tradition and competition. Jack Nicklaus, the greatest name from golf's past, won six separate Masters titles. Tiger Woods, the greatest player in golf's present, won his first professional Major at Augusta and has since added two more victories there to his record. The position, loosely, of Augusta National maintains that the club is a private golf club for fifty-one weeks every year, and it hosts an event for the public's enjoyment during the other week.

Without a doubt, this Dr. Alistar Mackenzie–designed course, started by the legendary Bobby Jones, is one of the top courses in all of the world. The week at the Masters is arguably the favorite one for touring professionals fortunate enough to qualify for the event. Undeniably, it is the favorite week for viewers, because it consistently gets the highest ratings in all of golf. CBS has been the exclusive broadcaster for the event's entire broadcast history and works well within Augusta's guidelines to present the least commercial tournament seen on TV.

Even though the club is steeped in history, it maintains its contemporary status as a true test of golf. The club even modernized the course before the 2002 tournament, adding three hundred yards to their famed track in order to test the titanium, along with the mettle, of their competitive field. No place conveys a sense of refinement, exclusivity, and civility quite like Augusta National—and that just describes the golf course!

But Martha Burk does not agree. Burk is a well-meaning, experienced activist who feels there is sex discrimination in Augusta's admissions policies. Sex discrimination in any form is certainly wrong, but it seems that Burk has taken it on herself to make this determination with respect to Augusta National. Women do play golf at Augusta National. In fact, women play over one thousand rounds per year at Augusta National. But Burk wants to have a woman admitted as a member—now.

Hall-of-Fame golfer Nancy Lopez told the *Albany Herald*, "I hate that that has come up because I have always respected the tradition at Augusta. And it was never a tradition of male or female to me; it was always just tradition. . . . I don't feel women have to go join Augusta because it's really not a man-woman issue. It's just understood," Lopez said. "I don't feel like there's discrimination there."

Lopez became a champion, and one of the greatest female players ever during the 1970s. She has won forty-eight tournaments, including three LPGA championships, in twenty-five years on the tour. She has also played Augusta twice. She has probably also felt the unfair sting of discrimination's cruelty more often than she cares to admit. Had Burk consulted with her and other professional golfers of both genders, and studied the situation of private clubs thoroughly, then she might have credibility. As it stands, one could argue that she is an opportunist making a name for herself. Burk even acknowledged in a *USA Today* article, "The Augusta problem isn't going to last forever. But it's brought attention to other issues. It's given us a chance to tell people about other things we work on."[9] Burk also said that the Masters could move, that it didn't have to be played at Augusta National. She might as well have said that the New York Yankees could play all of their home games at Fenway Park. It makes just as much sense.

Burk should be angry at discrimination or restricted access to opportunity. The Constitution, Bill of Rights, and federal courts attempt to uphold the ideals of equality and fairness. Augusta National certainly feels that it has the right to free association. Given the fact that women play the course, but they, as a group, have not expressed the sentiment that it is discriminatory, has merit.

It seems that Martha Burk likes the attention that the issue has brought and she brings her story to any outlet that will feature her and her cause. The incendiary matter has triggered a hail-storm of opinions and reactions. Burk said that she would go after the sponsors, so Augusta National cancelled all sponsorships and said that they would not allow any advertising during the broadcast. Burk then stated that she would pursue CBS, but the long-time broadcaster maintained its intent to broadcast the tournament in 2003.

CBS Sports President Sean McManus sent this reply to Burk: "I very much appreciate you sharing your position on CBS' broadcasts of the Masters tournaments. However, as a sports television programmer serving millions of men and women who eagerly anticipate and avidly watch the Masters network broadcast each year, CBS will cover the Masters as it has done for the past 46 years. To not do so would be a disservice to fans of this major championship."[10]

Burk then said she was going after the membership, and high-profile members were forced to respond to questions about the matter. The whole point is that every time Burk said anything, it was printed and carried nationally. Burk cleverly leveraged the platform and high profile of Augusta National to gain prominence.

Perhaps, Burk assessed the landscape and determined that she could get the most bang for her buck by targeting Augusta. Just like advertisers buy Super Bowl ads because it provides the largest potential audience, going after Augusta provides her with the biggest forum for her own profile. She has been on national media shows, done countless interviews, and become well known in the process.

It seems that Burke's ambition is to gain access to international media. Of all the issues concerning a woman's access to opportunity, compensation, and privilege, Augusta National is not the most relevant target. If she wants to apply her talents to a more useful cause, she could fight for Title IX privileges that are in serious jeopardy.

At the end of the day, Burk's problem is one of credibility, since she chose an issue where only two things were certain: the high profile of the target and her lack of preparation and research in pursing the matter.

PRESIDENTIAL CONNECTIONS

Dating back to accomplished hunter and horseman Teddy Roosevelt, sports and the Oval Office have had a very public relationship. Fittingly, the subject even goes back to our Founding Fathers. George Washington had been known as a superior athlete in his day, able to ride horses better and throw rocks farther than virtually all of his contemporaries. But not all patriots were created equal. The cerbral Thomas Jefferson once opined, "Games played with the ball are too violent for the body and stamp no character on the mind."

As the twentieth-century media age emerged, however, the presidential images came more sharply into focus. Dwight D. Eisenhower, a football player at West Point, loved golf and even practiced on the White House lawn. JFK had been an accomplished athlete at Harvard, and was a pretty fair golfer in spite of a debilitating back injury suffered in World War II. Richard Nixon was an unabashed baseball fan and even scripted football plays that he sent to noted coaches like Tom Landry. Gerald Ford played football at the University of Michigan and the first President Bush had a distinguished baseball career at Yale. Ronald Reagan announced Cubs games as a young man on the radio and President Carter even helped popularize the jogging craze during his presidential years. From first pitches to championship receptions, presidents of every era have enjoyed associating with athletes and teams.

The sports industry even gave us our forty-third president, George W. Bush. President Bush, a big sports fan, did not have the typical sports background. He migrated to sports ownership from the oil industry, and it ultimately paved the road to his career in politics. It is a remarkable chain of events that reveals the power of the sports industry and George W. Bush's public style.

In 1984, George W. Bush headed up a Texas oil company called Bush Exploration. The company struggled before being purchased by Spectrum 7 Energy Corporation. Spectrum displayed more proficiency for debt than profit and was bought by Harken Energy in 1986. George W. did not have a lot of luck in the oil business in the 1980s, but times were tough for the entire industry. In 1986, oil prices had dropped to near Depression-era levels. Bush needed a break. In 1988, he got a big one when his father was elected president. Having a dad as president does things for your profile, and in 1989, he used some Harken Energy Corporation shares as collateral to borrow $600,000 and joined the syndicate buying the Texas Rangers for $86 million.[11] He was installed as the managing partner, or front man of the organization, despite owning only 1.8 percent of the team and never having worked in the sports industry. Bush's oil career might not have distinguished him as a successful visionary or a rising sports executive but the ownership group felt that he would make the best front man for the team. Most important, they felt that he could help get a new stadium built for the Rangers.

Back at Harken, things were getting interesting. The small, teetering company had only drilled in Texas, Oklahoma, and Louisiana, but suddenly was awarded an offshore contract with the Emirate of Bahrain. Skeptics wondered why a middle eastern emirate would would want a struggling Texas oil company with no offshore drilling experience to extract its most precious resource. Well, George W. Bush was on Harken's exploration advisory board at the time. Although Bush vehemently denied that there was any opportunism behind the deal, his critics disagreed. It seemed, to his detractors, that Harken earned the multimillion-dollar contract because Bush's father was president of the United States.

Six months after the contract with Bahrain, Bush sold 212,140 shares of Harken and paid off the loan that he used to buy into the Rangers. He was now in the sports industry full time and his major priority was building a new ballpark in the city of Arlington. Central to the project was getting approval for a local sales tax increase. In January of 1991, legislation passed authorizing a half-cent increase in local sales taxes in order to fund the construction of the park. Bush had not sought, or suggested, a private sector alternative to financing the new ballpark project. He relied on taxation.[12]

Bush's nerve has its admirers. "I certainly give George credit for being able to pull it off with limited acrimony," said Jerry Reinsdorf, whose Chicago White Sox moved into a new, $137-million ballpark in 1991. "Our stadium was built with a hotel tax, so that people in Chicago wouldn't have to pay for it, and it *still* was a difficult issue."[13]

The Ballpark Authority also received eminent domain privileges, meaning that they could seize land deemed necessary to their project. While running for governor against Ann Richards, Bush made this statement about private land ownership: "I understand full well the value of private property and its importance not only in our state but in capitalism in general, and I will do everything I can to defend the power of private property and private property rights when I am the governor of this state."[14] Bush said this despite the fact that the Arlington Sports Facilities Development Authority, the entity formed by the city to condemn land for the new ballpark in Arlington, had seized private land for the new ballpark. And lots of it, too.

Bucky Fanning is one of the landowners who got squeezed in the facility development. "Anybody who was in their way, they just ran them over," says Fanning, a former landowner on the site. "I used to be a Rangers fan, but then they stole my property."[15] Fanning's grandparents had originally purchased the ten-acres of land in 1942 to raise Thoroughbreds. Today it is an infrequently used parking lot on one side of the ballpark.

The Arlington Sports Facilities Development Authority ultimately gave the Fannings $1.09 million for their property in 1991. Though a real estate company had offered $3.5 million three years earlier,[16] the Stadium Authority valued it at less than one-third the price. Fanning sued the Stadium Authority, claiming it had not given him a fair price for the ranch. Meanwhile, the IRS presented Fanning with a $1-million tax bill in 1992, saying the land was more valuable than the $1.09 million Fanning had been paid.[17]

The Rangers ultimately received control of 270 acres, an unusually large amount of land for a ballpark. Original plans called for a river walk, office buildings, amphitheater, housing, and a manmade lake to accom-

modate sailboats. The idea was that the area would be a tourist destination and pleasure center. Twelve years after the tax hike and land
seizures, there were no sailboats, no noticeable tourists, and none of the
ranches that used to extend far into that piece of Texas prairie. But Tom
Hicks, the team owner, did have to pay out many millions of dollars in
legal judgments to those who lost land during Bush's ownership tenure.

Why would the Rangers want so much land when the stadium didn't
require it? The reason is very simple: money. The added real estate made
the team more valuable. Land adjacent to Coors Field in Denver had once
been assessed at less than $2.00 per square foot prior to the ballpark's con-
struction. After Coors Field was built, the land sold for $27 per square
foot. Maybe this helps explain how the Rangers sold for $250 million in
1998. That small equity stake, which cost him only $600,000, yielded
almost $15 million to George W. Bush. Bush was very pragmatic and
honest about the sale. He told the Fort Worth Star-Telegram, "I think when
it is all said and done, I will have made more money than I ever dreamed
I would make."[18] The franchise had appreciated in value primarily due to
the new stadium and the development opportunities of the surrounding
acreage. In other words, Bush's moves to get a new ballpark and increase
the acreage of the ballpark area increased the value of the team.

The Rangers did more than make George W. Bush money; they
helped make him governor of Texas in 1994. The beautiful ballpark was
well received by the public. An affable man, he won the election touting
his vision for the state and his record as owner of the team. He specifically pointed to the new stadium as an example of his leadership skills. It
is hard to determine if George W. Bush would have become president of
the United States, or even governor of Texas, without his stint as the
Texas Rangers' owner. There is no doubt, however, that the job helped
his professional profile. As owner, Bush represented his partners well. A
team purchased for less than $90 million eventually sold for $250 million
twelve years later. However, his critics might point out that he was not
adroit at assessing the larger marketing needs of the game. Bush was the
only owner to vote against the expanded Wild Card playoff system. He
did not see the value of including more teams, cities, and fans in the pennant race or in the playoffs themselves.

The critics usually end their argument by saying that the Wild Card playoff system turned out to be one of the two best marketing decisions made by Major League Baseball in the 1990s. The Wild Card means that more teams play relevant games for a longer period of time. It increases attendance, viewership, broadcast contracts, stadium revenues, and overall interest in the game. These are things that all owners want, or at least, twenty-seven of the twenty-eight owners.

Those who defend Bush say that he did not want the "tradition" of the game to be diluted. But that rings hollow. The playoff system itself had been updated twice in the prior twenty-five years. In 1969, the American League and National League split into two divisions, and the two division champions competed for the pennant and the right to meet one another in the World Series. Originally the best of five games, they expanded to the best of seven games in 1985. When the National League finally balanced the leagues by adding two teams in 1993, the owners decided to split into three divisions and one Wild Card. This doubled the amount of teams in the playoffs from two to four in each league.

Expanding the playoffs to eight total teams in baseball makes sense on many levels. First of all, it prolongs teams' chances, which maintains fan interest, which sells tickets, hot dogs, and sponsorships. Since baseball had expansion plans at the time of the Wild Card vote, Bush knew that the league would grow by two teams, to a total of thirty, by 1998. Eight total playoff teams out of thirty is not that many, especially when you consider the other professional leagues. In the NFL, 12 teams out of 32 total franchises, or 37.5 percent, qualify for the playoffs. The NBA has an even more generous playoff system, where 16 of the 29, or 55 percent, teams get playoff berths. Baseball, meanwhile, at 26 percent, has the lowest percentage of playoff teams, even though the season is the longest. As for the argument that a Wild Card means poor quality of play, the two World Series teams in 2002, the Giants and Angels, were both Wild Card entries.

Furthermore, if Bush felt that modernization, in the form of a new, revenue-friendly facility, made sense for the Rangers, why couldn't he see that modernizing the playoff system meant more revenue, exposure, and promotion of the game on a national level? Obviously, the other owners disagreed. Why could Bush not be swayed by them?

At the end of the analysis, none of this makes George W. Bush a bad guy. In fact, no one within the game seems to speak pejoratively about him. But for someone who occupies an important job requiring well-thought-out, long-term strategies, some of his actions raise valid questions. A staunch Republican, he benefited from increased taxation and the seizure of private land. Once an owner, his decisions ultimately landed the team in court with the former landowners that his ownership group displaced. He also voted against an increase in one round of the playoffs, despite the obvious arguments from all of his fellow owners, broadcast partners, and sponsors. He made money for the ownership group he represented, but maybe he could have executed his duties without the contradictions in style, or to the citizenry of Arlington.

The irony of George W. Bush's public life is that baseball provided the perfect medium for his form of management and operation. He is not the first person to get ahead on his family's name. Certainly, the Kennedy family comes to mind. But no one coopted the public forum of sports' private interests quite like George W. Bush. Jesse Ventura, Bill Bradley, Steve Largent, Tom Osbourne, J. C. Watts, and Jim Bunning all pursued careers in politics after their athletic careers, but George W. Bush capitalized from the ownership end like none other.

President Bush had one more important moment in baseball. In office during the aftermath of the tragic circumstances of September 11, 2001, Bush took the mound at Yankee Stadium and threw out the ceremonial first pitch before the third game of the 2001 World Series.[19] Standing alone on the mound, Bush acknowledged the crowd and threw the ball to the plate.

It was a perfect strike.

TITLE IX: A PLATFORM AND CONSUMER GROUP

Title IX is a misunderstood, oft-cited piece of legislation that has had an enormous influence on the sports industry. It states, in part:

Title IX of the Education Amendments of 1972 protects people from discrimination based on sex in education programs or activities which receive Federal financial assistance. Title IX states that:

No person in the United States shall, on the basis of sex, be excluded from participation in, be denied the benefits of, or be subjected to discrimination under any program or activity receiving Federal financial assistance.

The United States Department of Education (ED) maintains an Office for Civil Rights, with 12 enforcement offices throughout the nation and a headquarters office in Washington, D.C., to enforce Title IX.

Education Programs and Activities Covered by Title IX:

Title IX covers state and local agencies that receive ED funds. These agencies include approximately 16,000 local school districts, 3,200 colleges and universities, and 5,000 for-profit schools as well as libraries and museums. Also included are vocational rehabilitation agencies and education agencies of 50 states, the District of Columbia, and territories and possessions of the United States.

Programs and activities which receive ED funds must operate in a nondiscriminatory manner. These programs and activities may include, but are not limited to: admissions, recruitment, financial aid, academic programs, student treatment and services, counseling and guidance, discipline, classroom assignment, grading, vocational education, recreation, physical education, athletics, housing and employment.[20]

Title IX covers a lot of ground, but the area where it has achieved its highest profile is through its impact upon sports programs for females. Women have long tried to gain equal footing in the sports entertainment industry, battling real discrimination and misperceptions along the way. Pioneers like Billie Jean King and Jo Anne Carner tirelessly promoted women's sports to gain exposure and fair compensation as far back as the 1960s. Women had the ambition to play individual and team sports and they deserved the opportunity. They needed one thing: a platform. Title IX became the foundation that helped create three important growth industries:

Female athletic participants.
Female spectators.
Female athletic consumers (and decision makers).

Title IX's intent was to give females a chance to play sports, especially if males were afforded the same opportunity. According to the U.S. Department of Education, in 1971 less than 300,000 high school girls played interscholastic sports. Twenty-five years later, that number grew to 2.4 million. The same study showed that in 1972, approximately 133,000 girls played high school basketball. By 1995, it had increased by more than 300 percent to almost 413,000 participants. At the collegiate level, limited budgets, no exposure, and no legislative support vexed women. With Title IX giving them some backing, sports have flourished at the collegiate level. Donna de Varona won two Olympic gold medals at the 1964 Olympic Games. But in spite of her international success, she could not receive a college scholarship in the United States for swimming, because sports scholarships for women did not exist at that time. The U.S. Department of Education estimates that 50,000 men received college and university athletic scholarships in 1974. That same year, about fifty women received them, a staggering disparity. Today women receive approximately 33 percent of all scholarship money.

Tension over the issue has erupted recently as schools cut men's athletic teams to equalize the funding distribution to men's and women's sports. Title IX was never intended to take away opportunity from anyone (the law states only that men and women must be provided an equitable *opportunity* to participate in sports, not that the actual numbers or funding need to be equal), yet the law consistently makes headlines, year after year. Normally, a lower-profile men's sport (wrestling or crew) at a major university will be cancelled due to budget cuts and Title IX will be cited as the reason.

Blaming Title IX is not fair. All athletic departments have strict budgets with tough choices for staffing, equipment, and simple existence. When only a few sports, namely football, men's basketball, and women's basketball, earn revenue, they garner a disproportionate amount of investment. When sports that require money, yet generate little or none, get cut, blame easily gravitates to Title IX. Since virtually no program can support itself, finger pointing and politicking take over, and the more established men's sports find it convenient to blame the women's sports. The problem lies in revenue generation and cost containment. If the various athletic departments could raise more money through donations and sponsorships, then Title IX would not have to be the scapegoat.

If anything, having more women compete in sports will only help the sports industry. Title IX has spurred growth for the global sports industry by creating new fans, customers, and sports decision makers. Back when the law was passed in 1972, the original women-only road race, the New York Women's Mini Marathon, was held. It was also the first year the Boston Marathon officially invited women runners, enabling Nina Kuscsik to become the first official women's champion of the race.

Since interest follows opportunity, women have taken to sports over the past thirty years with an enthusiasm best illustrated by their numbers. Between the 1971–1972 and 1999–2000 school years, girls' participation in high school athletics increased 800 percent.[21] At the collegiate level, the number of women in varsity sports increased from 33,000 to 163,000—quite impressive, considering that in 1972 they made up merely 7.4 percent of college jocks.[22] This increase in participation bodes well for women and girls across the board. It is well documented that high school girls who are on sports teams are less likely to become pregnant or get involved with drugs, and are more likely to graduate from high school. It appears that athletics also provide important training for future leaders as 80 percent of today's female managers of Fortune 500 companies have a sports background.

In addition to the obvious societal and moral obligations for letting women in on the game, there is an even more pragmatic argument for supporting Title IX: money. According to the Sporting Goods Manufacturers Association, women account for more than 80 percent of all sporting goods purchases.[23] Women are ardent spectators, too. Eighty-four percent of women polled by ESPN said they were sports fans. By contrast, 93 percent of men made the same claim, which means there is not a large disparity.[24] If sports marketing people attempt to chart the quantity of sports-related purchases over the past thirty years, this is not a customer segment that you would want to alienate or lose.

Perhaps the most telling sign is that advertisers have noted the shift and sought product endorsements from female athletes such as Marion Jones, Martina Navratilova, Dorothy Hamill, Mia Hamm, and the Williams sisters (Serena and Venus). According to the NPD Group, women's athletic apparel was a $15-billion business in 2001, while men's athletic apparel totaled $12 billion. Obviously, the boom in women's sports has been, and continues to be, good for business.

What Is the Future of Title IX?

Outside of controversy, the future can guarantee one certainty: debate. Despite continued demonstration of the benefits to women and girls who play sports, and despite the very real supporting data of female sporting-good consumption habits, Title IX is almost certain to be changed in some way. The Title IX Commission is considering proposals that could offer 78,000 fewer participation opportunities for high school girls and 1.4 million fewer opportunities for college women. Women could see a $188 million drop in college athletic scholarships.[25] Here is a clear case of a huge, continued-growth market that is fueled by the implications of Title IX. A market structure has developed through the empowerment of women. The bottom-line impacts of the proposed Title IX changes are impossible to ignore:

Fewer female athletes.
Lower self-esteem for high school girls.
Potential demise of a thriving market.

Furthermore, as more women become corporate decision makers, perhaps they will steer marketing dollars away from any sports activity due to estrangement. On the other hand, if the door remains open for women and girls to experience all that sports have to offer, they may then return the interest and support the industry.

The business side of the sports industry, specifically broadcasters and sponsors, need to nurture this huge demographic at this critical time. Not only do women represent over 50 percent of the population, they have significant purchasing power and influence over how children spend their time. Creative solutions must include women, not exclude them. They should participate in all facets of athletics.

ANNIKA-MANIA: WOMEN CAN PLAY!

Annika Sorenstam became the unquestioned best female golfer in the world in 2002 by winning thirteen LPGA events. Sorenstam was considered to be the Tiger Woods of the ladies' tour.

The Bank of America Colonial Tournament, the esteemed Texas PGA event closely associated with Ben Hogan, offered Sorenstam a sponsor's exemption for its 2003 tournament. Sorenstam considered the course, the conditions she would face, and her curiosity as to how she could compete against the great male players of professional golf and she accepted the invitation to play. She became the first woman since 1945, when Babe Didrikson Zaharias played in three PGA events, to play in a PGA tournament.

Sorenstam looked at her participation as a unique opportunity to test her skill against another field of competitors, but it was met with some resistance and ignorance. Vijay Singh, one of the world's top male golfers, even mentioned that he wouldn't play if paired with Sorenstam. He later retracted his statements in a hailstorm of criticism and ultimately withdrew from the tournament. But to golf fans, and people who didn't even play golf, Sorenstam was to be admired for her skill and determination. Perhaps ace CBS analyst David Feherty summed it up best when he stated, "If Tiger Woods had a place to play that was more difficult, more challenging, do you think he wouldn't want to go there?"

Her detractors were far outnumbered by those emboldened by Annika's talent and classy demeanor. Jack Nicklaus and Tiger Woods, the two greatest players in the history of the game, both endorsed Sorenstam. And the networks and related sponsors were overjoyed. Cable broadcaster USA planned to carry the full first two rounds, where Sorenstam was guaranteed to be in the field. The network enjoyed record ratings not seen since the first time Tiger Woods played in the Colonial in 1997.

CBS also knew how to run with a storyline. The network had no guarantee that Sorenstam would make the cut (determined after the first two rounds of play), and play during its telecasts on Saturday and Sunday, but it took more ad inventory to the marketplace just in case. Selling it on a "no-return" policy, CBS bumped up its thirty-second spots by approximately 10 percent to $70,000 per spot on Saturday and to $100,000 on Sunday.[26] Even though Sorenstam didn't make the cut and play on the weekend, CBS enjoyed a 4 percent increase in its ratings for the tournament, and the network had a newsworthy story to discuss as a backdrop to the actual competition.

And Bank of America became the luckiest brand in sports marketing since Terrell Owens decided to make the Sharpie a national story on *Monday Night Football*. The bank shelled out about $6 million for the sponsorship and had no idea that Annika Sorenstam would become the single biggest sports story of the year at their tournament. She took golf from the sports pages to the front pages and both inspired and entertained millions of people. In the process, Bank of America went with her story every step of the way. And all of the bank's guests at the tournament became a part of history, something not too many of its competitors could offer their key clients.

From a business perspective, 46 percent of new golfers in America are women. Callaway, Sorenstam's biggest sponsor, immediately capitalized on the opportunity to talk to female golfers about their own ambitions. How many more will pick up clubs and play remains to be seen. But Sorenstam's historic participation in the Bank of America Colonial will ripple through the sports industry for a long time. Not only is the novelty good for business for the industry, but it is good for any competitor who has heard whispers that she, or he, did not belong.

Ultimately, Sorenstam proved that she did belong. Her playing at Colonial will bring more people out to LPGA events, more sponsors to both tours, and more weekend players to courses and ranges. Critics complained that Sorenstam should stick with the ladies' tour, but they obviously did not know what the acronym PGA stands for: Professional Golf Association. Sorenstam is a true professional in every sense of the word. The added hype, publicity, entertainment, credibility, and class that her participation lent to the event is the exact thing that promoters, property rights holders, broadcasters, and sponsors in the sports entertainment industry have long aspired to achieve.

A VERY TIGHT NET

Not much gets through the dragnet of sports media. As the sports platform spreads and solidifies to include multiple outlets and all possible angles of preview and review, every possible permutation of the game and its participants receive coverage. Today, nothing goes unnoticed, unrecorded, and unreported. If you say it, someone will print it, photograph it, and dissect it. Much has been made of how the press protected figures like John F. Kennedy, Babe Ruth, and Franklin Delano Roosevelt in their times of high public profile. That would not happen today.

Through the 1940s, there were a few regular beat writers and maybe a few from smaller periodicals. As radio proliferated in the 1950s, radio shows and on-air interviews became a part of the game. TV, of course, added another dimension of reporting and cable made each game's broadcast a certainty. By the end of the twentieth century, the Internet added the newest level of reporting, and rounded out the journalistic endeavors associated with sporting events. Games receive multilingual coverage, for example, in Spanish, Japanese, Korean, and Chinese, which only adds to the total amount of media in attendance.

With increased coverage comes increased scrutiny and maximum exposure for all the nuances that surround a game. This can be both good and bad for a team or game. The Super Bowl's media day is the most famous day of press-related activity in America. Each player gets his own separate stage to conduct interviews. The coverage has grown so much that the league has strict dress rules for the players to ensure that products don't get free promotion. Max McGee never had to worry about that!

The Oakland A's won the AL West in 2002 to qualify for the playoffs for the third straight year. A small-market club with a payroll closer to the league's bottom than to the top, the A's benefited from shrewd direction in the front office by Billy Beane and great play by a core of talented young players. Their first round opponent, the Minnesota Twins, bore much in common to the A's: a scrappy team that spent less on its players than many clubs who didn't make the post season. The first-round Division Series was a seesaw affair that led to a fifth game in Oakland.

The A's had drawn over 2.6 million fans during the regular season to the Networks Associates County Coliseum, but did not sell out the cavernous multipurpose facility for the Division Series' fifth and final game. The final game between the Twins and A's went up against a 49ers football game at Candlestick Park and a Giants playoff game at Pacific Bell Park on the same day. Even ESPN noted the Bay Area's trifecta in their national telecast of *SportsCenter* that night.

One thing ESPN did not reveal was that the A's lowest priced ticket for the Division Series was $35. Whether it was the competition of other events, or the ticket prices, only 32,000 fans showed up to see the A's drop the last game to the Twins. Disappointed at losing the fifth game of a Division Series three years in a row, the A's had a lot to gripe about. Steve Schott, one of the co-owners, did some of the most-reported griping, especially when queried about tickets being priced so high.

"I have to laugh about the $35. Give me a break, if you really have loyal fans. . . ."[27] Schott was clearly not happy with the outcome of the game, or the size of the crowd.

Schott truly had a bad day from a professional point of view. His team got bounced and his season ended in front of a less-than-full facility, on a day when two of his area competitors enjoyed sellouts. His sentiments may not have been warranted, and could easily be criticized, but perhaps he blurted out something purely in the heat of the moment. Certainly, Schott's stated position is indefensible. To criticize his customers for exercising their rights as fans is no way to market his team. For Schott to dismiss, so callously, his constituents, made no business sense. But the quote does not capture his frustration with the loss, or helplessness to get his team beyond the first round.

After a week to think about it, Schott had a much more reasonable tone, "If I offended any of our fans in any way, shape, or form, I apologize." With respect to the ticket prices, Schott also had a different comment. "We were wrong, and we have to make sure that doesn't happen when we get into the playoffs next year."[28]

But the damage had been done. An agitated Mr. Schott, uttered a sentiment that might follow him around for the rest of his public life. Had he been a team owner just twenty years earlier, the comment might never have been recorded. Had he been an owner forty years earlier, the comment most certainly would have never seen print. Today, in the "every possible angle will be covered" style of the sports media, Schott had no chance that the comments would not be highlighted and ridiculed.

This points to a larger problem in the fan-owner-player relationship. The heightened stakes only act to fuel the emotions if one of the visible parties experiences a letdown. At virtually the same time Steve Schott made his remarks, Cleveland Browns quarterback Tim Couch had a highly publicized meltdown two thousand miles away. Couch had been booed heavily during a loss to the Baltimore Ravens, owned by infidel Art Modell, who had moved the original Browns franchise to Baltimore just a few years before. Couch suffered a concussion during the game and had been derisively cheered while he lay hurt on the ground.

In an emotional, postgame interview, Couch said, his face full of emotion, "I've been here four years now, and laid it on the line for this team and city. For them to turn on me and boo me in my home stadium is a joke. I got hit in the back of the head diving for the ball," Couch said. "And the next thing I know, the fans are cheering when I'm laying on the field hurt. I think it's crap, to be honest with you."

To Couch, getting hurt is a steep price to pay to entertain the fans, and to the fans, who pay a lot of money and expect to see a winner, they feel enfranchised to boo when they please, even when someone is hurt. The scale has increased to the point where the coverage, expense, and commitment from all the parties has driven up expectations and the need for some kind of release. In the case of Steve Schott, Tim Couch, and the Cleveland Browns' fans, it means frustration. And now that the ever-present media ensures the capture of every thought, reaction, and emotion, sports fans expect to be even more a part of the thrills of victory and the agonies of defeat.

What this means in terms of sports is that the cycle is immediate; we see the action, analyze it, and then react. In the old days, sports information slowly seeped out through limited channels and fans were left to dream about their heroes' next at bat, race, or fight. Today, with information available on television, radio, in print, on the Internet, or on your cell phone, the fan can stay connected everywhere he or she goes. If the peripatetic American thought that USA Today did a lot for the sports fan, the Internet is a never-ending smorgasbord.

But as Tim Couch's relationship with the Browns' fans and Steve Schott's off-the-cuff postgame comments indicate, relationships can fluctuate and cause frustration between the fans, athletes, and owners. The consequences result in soap operas and melodramas that take the attention away from the field and ultimately provide a different form of entertainment that is more gossip than competition.

The breathing room for those in the spotlight has disappeared. The financial commitment that teams require of fans makes the fans, in turn, expect more for their money, which might not be fair to those in the metaphorical arena. The phenomenon of change is that the lights are brightest on the field, but they don't dim once the athlete gets into the locker room, clubhouse, or even on the street. Before the 1980s, players had more freedoms away from the competition, but with the money and side industries that media coverage of athletics provides, there is significantly less separation between the competition and the players' lives away from the field. The ever-growing platform of sports entertainment provides profits from more access to athletes and events, but it comes at the price of anonymity and privacy.

IN THEIR OWN WORDS: A TIME OF TRANSITION FOR ATHLETES

It used to be that athletes would play their sport, get a job in the off-season, then report to some type of training camp, cut back on smoking and drinking (a bit), and don the togs of competition once again. Today, with agents, nutritionists, personal trainers, and the pressure of microscopic analysis, athletes compete and prepare in a different environment.

If you ever get a chance to talk with an athlete, perhaps their most blissful moments come during the competition as the off-field distractions and politics dilute the enjoyment of being a professional, or high-profile, athlete. Here are two athletes who transitioned from careers in sports at a time when sports transformed into a big-time industry.[29]

BEFORE THE MONEY

Pat Toomay played for the Dallas Cowboys, Buffalo Bills, Tampa Bay Buccaneers, and Oakland Raiders in a ten-year NFL career. He is the author of two books, The Crunch *and* On Any Given Sunday, *and has written numerous articles for prestigious outlets like ESPN.com and Salon.com.*

This section details an interview where Toomay was asked about the player's perspective on the business matters of football in the 1970s, when he played. Looking back today, it is easy to see that the 1970s connected the era of iconic 1960s personalities like Johnny Unitas, Dick Butkus, and Jim Brown with the big-money game that we know today.

Rookie

"I started my career (1970) . . . at the tail end of what people refer to as the good old days. The guys who played in the 1950s and 1960s, players like Y. A. Tittle and Jim Brown, were the game of football—truly men—not cogs in a larger conceptual machine. Offensive linemen would call blocking schemes—and tell the coaches what would work on the field, what match-ups were favorable. They made decisions and directed the flow of the game. They weren't specialists substituting on specific downs; they were football players.

"By the time I got into the game, that aspect was gone. Tom Landry, my coach with the Dallas Cowboys, wanted the players to be pieces of a game plan, not the determinants of the game plan. He wanted players to play off of repetition and drills, not athleticism and feel for the moment. Landry had coached with the New York Giants and been a colleague of Vince Lombardi. His demeanor was different than Lombardi, but his control was as absolute.

"Guys came in simply wanting to play football, and the financial part of it was more of a mystery than anything else. We all saw Joe Namath get the big dollars, and each time a rival league like the WFL or USFL came into existence, salaries would double, so we knew there was money in the game, we just weren't as focused on getting it. During my first season, we played an exhibition game in New Orleans at the Sugar Bowl and I remember looking around at the people in the stands and thinking, 'I am only getting $250 for this game. Somebody is making out here, but it's just not me.'"

Recognizing the Industry

"The whole concept of negotiating a contract was different. I didn't have an agent out of college. When I asked my college coaches about signing a contract, they said 'Tom Landry is a good man.' Gil Brandt told me to call D. D. Lewis, one of most respected guys on the team who was also from the SEC, and to ask him about their offer. It seemed that I had to sign. Landry had this image as an honorable Christian man and if other players felt the team was being fair, how could a rookie challenge that?

"Later, when the Player's Union started doing salary surveys, it turned out that D. D. Lewis was the lowest paid guy at his position in the league.

"In those days, players had very little leverage in the game. The Cowboys, despite their on-field success, were one of the lowest paying franchises in the league. They felt that the team would make the post-season and the players could count on earning postseason money, and that would make up the difference.

"It was the beginning of the business learning curve for the game. Once the owners figured out that the Super Bowl was a big deal, they took as many of the tickets as they could get and sold them to travel package groups and literally scalped them. They tried to blame the players for the scarcity of Super Bowl tickets and the secondary markets, but they nurtured it. The only commercial venture the players had going at the Super Bowl was with the shoe companies. There was no Nike in those days; the two companies were Adidas and Puma, and they were the first ones to understand what the Super Bowl meant in a business sense, that the exposure was valuable and that getting the players to wear their shoes meant something commercially.

"Puma gave away TVs to players in exhange for wearing their shoes. So I wore Pumas in pregame, and got my TV, and then wore Adidas shoes during the game and got whatever it was that they gave me. The shoe people would use retired players or people on the inside, who had access, so it was a cheap and easy way for them to get their products in the game. It would never happen today.

"In Dallas, I used to work out at an athletic club called the Aerobics Center where I met a group of businessmen who were interested in football. I later found out that they were huge gamblers and that the games, through gambling, put drama in their lives. They didn't appreciate the athleticism of the sport, but they wanted the adrenaline rush of wagering over the weekend. After playing a while, it seemed that the owners and their buddies were having all of the fun—they'd sit in

first class on the planes, drink, and laugh. Our work was their vaca-
tion. To them, the game was secondary to the party."

Just Win, Baby

"When I went to the Raiders, it was an entirely different mindset at the
ownership level. In Dallas, everything was about Tex Schramm's idea of
what a player should look like and act like, and they did everything possible to ensure that the players reflected the ideal they wanted to project. I once went and spoke to a boy's club while with the Cowboys. I
told all the kids the truth, that being twelve years old and running
around in the mud playing football was as good and as pure as the game
would ever get. The team never asked me to talk to another group of
kids again. I guess my version of football wasn't theirs.

"In Oakland, Al Davis could care less what you looked like or
what you said to anybody. He just wanted you to play hard on Sundays. In Oakland, comportment meant nothing; it was all about winning football games, a language that any player could understand.

"Davis was also a visionary and saw where the future was going.
When John Mackey won his suit over free agency, Davis knew the
party was over and that wealth would be the requirement for success in
the 1980s and beyond. And he knew he needed to get more revenue
out of his team. He paid players fairly and he felt that the Oakland
market wouldn't generate the necessary revenues, so he moved to LA."

Epilogue

"I recently went to a New York Giants game and just didn't get it. I
looked around and couldn't see the connection between the field and
the stands. The NFL ad where the guy wears the Eddie George jersey
and identifies with the image of a logo seems sad, as if there are disenfranchised males who don't find meaning in life outside of these
images. You go to a booster club meeting and meet people who want
to take pictures where the interaction is around the symbol rather
than something personal and meaningful. It is hard to know if we do
it to them, or if that is where they want us as personalities.

"Playing today is very different than just twenty years ago. I led the league in sacks in 1977, but didn't find out about it until 1999. The game was good in my day, but I don't think it has necessarily gotten any better."

NO MONEY AND LITTLE ALTERNATIVE

When discussions about great athletes arise, fans toss out many names like Michael Jordan, Jim Brown, Jim Thorpe, and Muhammad Ali. Someone will contribute a name that you rarely hear, but instantly recognize as deserving. Someone like Bob Hayes, for example. In the next breath, a person will nominate Bo Jackson, and then people will debate his greatness had injury not crept into his hip.

It might be one of the universally best sports discussions anyone can have. One name that might have been on the periphery of this discussion in the late 1970s and early 1980s is Renaldo Nehemiah. A superb hurdler, Nehemiah also played professional football in the 1980s for the San Francisco 49ers. Nehemiah missed the 1980 Olympic Games due to the United States' boycott, but managed to return to track and compete throughout the 1980s. Currently a representative with Octagon, one of the premier sports marketing firms in America, Nehemiah experienced the highs and lows of being a great athlete as the industry transitioned into the era of mass media.

Background

"As a teenager, it never dawned upon me to think about professional sports. My first and only incentive was to receive an athletic scholarship to college. Larry Thomas, my math teacher and high school track coach, told me that I could get one if I kept improving my times. So I tied my track career to my collegiate ambitions and the fact that I knew it would make my parents proud. Those were my original track dreams. I didn't think about the Olympics, or anything beyond college.

"My senior year in high school, I was the first man ever to break the thirteen-second barrier (in the 110-meter high hurdles). I ran 12.9

at the Eastern States meet. It was a huge deal, and I became a national, even international, story, because track had a big following in Europe. I felt that I was unbeatable when I got to college (University of Maryland), but I actually lost my first two races. After that, I told myself that if I didn't win my next race, then I would quit. My very next race, I set the world record.

"At that point, I became very newsworthy and I liked the attention. I liked the fact that track and field was now considered at the same level, even for a short period, at a school where football and basketball ruled everything from the headlines to the facilities. I used the attention as a motivational tool. I felt that as long as I was running at the elite level, I would continue to bring the same level of attention of track and field at Maryland."

Olympics

"In the late 1970s, winning a gold medal was the only way to make money through track. Bruce Jenner had won the decathlon in Montreal and we saw what happened to him. So I set my sights on the Gold and nothing else. And the table was set for me in the 1980 Games. I had a rival, Greg Foster, who was West Coast. I was East Coast. I was much smaller, he was bigger. The press seemed to like my personality and I was getting in the pipeline for all of the stories and hype as the Games were headed to Moscow. All I had to do was not get hurt, make the team, win the Gold, and get on the roller coaster.

"It seemed simple at the time. But then there was the boycott. We had been hopeful that there would be a resolution. President Carter had let the Winter Games go on in Lake Placid, and we had a false sense of hope of being like Mike Eruzione, and the 'do you believe in miracles' line. We all thought that we would get the same Olympic miracle, but it wasn't meant to be. President Carter used the Olympic team as a bargaining chip for peace, not as an example of our nation's strength and character.

"But the truth is that I was at my peak commercially. Everything was set. I was dominant in my field, had a lot to bring to the table. But as so many find out, things in life are simply a matter of timing, and I picked a bad time to be at my peak in the hurdles. It took me until about 1997 to get over my anger over not going and not being able to represent my country and compete. When athletes, especially in those days, had to compete as amateurs, that was all we had to look forward to. The day we could walk into an Olympic stadium as a member of the national team. A lot of athletes wanted their day in the sun, and I was one of them. To this day, people think of me as a past Olympian, but I have never walked into an Olympic venue as a competitor."

Decision to Play Football

"I was competing in the TV event, the *Superstars*, and doing well when Dwight Clark of the 49ers said he felt that I could play in the NFL. At the time, the world looked at me as an elite athlete, mingling and performing with other great athletes, but the reality was that I was just another college graduate who needed a paying job.

"Track and field, at the time, was governed by archaic rules. I had a $125,000 contract to wear Puma shoes, but I had to pay the Athletic Congress $50,000 of that in a fee and the remaining amount went into a trust account. I was earning money that I couldn't use. I worked in an industry where I excelled, yet couldn't receive any compensation, much less fair and reasonable compensation. It seems ludicrous, but that was the system in place just over twenty years ago.

"The $50,000 that I won competing in the *Superstars*, money that felt like winning the lottery, is supposed to go to a federation? When the people that I beat could take it home and deposit it in their bank accounts? It didn't make any sense at all and it forced athletes like myself to make tough decisions.

"I couldn't understand how the system could possibly help sustain athletics. I didn't feel it represented anything relevant to the contemporary athlete. So when Dwight Clark was pumping me up to play football, it started to sound pretty good. And my analytical side told me that moving to another sport made sense. I had won everything in my event, was a world-record holder. The only place for me to go was down, in track. So why not go and play America's most popular game with America's best team? Bill Walsh, coach of the team, liked speed, so I felt that it was a good match.

"The irony in my timing is that once I got into football, the I.A.A.F. established events where track athletes would get paid. One would think that they would have mentioned it to one of their top attractions, but no one said anything to me. The fact that the I.A.A.F. never said anything about their future plans infuriated me. There was no reason for secrecy, but they felt otherwise. So I fought them in court, and have the Nehemiah Rule as a legacy where an amateur can be a professional in another sport."

The State of Track and Field

"Athletes can be selfish. The sport comes to life through the athletes and that makes the athlete a god, so it is a deadly combination. Factor in that track is largely an individual sport, and the system breeds selfishness. Carl Lewis could have helped catapult the sport, but he was not the guy to do it. He either didn't want to, or was simply concerned with his own career, not the sport itself.

"Where is the sport today? Where are the big events? Track markets just the stars and not the sport. They are like the shoe companies, who control everything about the way a star presents himself, or herself, publicly. It is understandable that Nike is only concerned about its brand through its athletes, but track does not promote the competition through its stars. It simply promotes the stars. Track needs to make every competitor feel that they matter. The sport was a lot more popular in my day because the events were great, not just a few athletes.

"Today, the star system in track is just too powerful. Until it is more inclusive of its members beyond the top three performers, then the brand will continue to suffer. The NFL and the NBA are powerful brands because they promote the sport and competition as much as the stars.

"The system is inherently flawed. The most powerful entities are the shoe companies. They control the athlete's image and life. The runner can't wear a PowerBar hat or shirt if they are a Nike athlete. It has to be Nike head to toe. In my day, the shoe company money had to get divided up with the federation. Now the shoe company is the federation, but only for a few individual stars. Track needs to get back to promoting the competition from the grass roots level on up. Only then can the sport truly reach its potential."

The Present

"I was a licensed financial planner, and as a way to stay around sports, I targeted athletes. I felt that I could help make athletes more empowered, more educated on the matters of their career, and I got involved in gold medal management. I would go to big meets and do seminars and the athletes told me that I should pursue this field, so I went from being a financial planner to an agent. I am now with Octagon and I hope to help my clients understand things like sportsmanship and integrity along with the business principles that govern their careers."

NOTES

1. When Foreman met LBJ, he said to the president, "This is to thank you for making the Job Corps possible, giving young Americans like me a chance for hope and dignity."

2. After losing to Jimmy Young in 1977, Foreman had a religious experience in his dressing room. He stopped fighting and started preaching after that bout.

3. J. Sloane, "Gorgeous George," *Fortune* [online], www.fortune.com/fortune/smallbusiness/marketing/articles/Ø,15114, 453574-1,ØØ.html [May 27, 2003].

4. Dusty Baker was a three-time Manager of the Year during his tenure with the Giants from 1993–2002. He left the Giants after the 2002 World Series to manage the Chicago Cubs. He was one of the most popular figures ever associated with the franchise.

5. They also finished 5–4 in the strike-shortened 1982 season, but that is not considered one of their winning seasons.

6. Mark Maske, "Gruden Bucs the Trend," *Washington Post*, January 18, 2003, p. B1.

7. Bill Parcells, Dick Vermeil, Bill Bellichik, and Mike Holmgren were all exchanged, in essence, for draft picks, prior to Jon Gruden.

In 1986, oil prices had dropped to near Depression-era levels.

8. P. Lentz, "Parcells' impact means ticket price hikes, more TV ads, big deals with retailers," *Crain's New York Business* (August 25, 1997): 34.

9. Harry Blauvelt, "Burk Not Afraid to Take on Status Quo," *USA Today* [online], http://www.usatoday.com/sports/golf/masters/2002-10-09-burk_x.htm [September 15, 2003].

10. Letter from McManus to Burk, September 19, 2002 [online], http://www.womensorganizations.org/news/augusta_CBS_response.pdf [September 15, 2003].

11. M. Kranish and B. Healy, "Board was told of risks before Bush stock sale," *Boston Globe*, October 30, 2002, p. A1.

12. By contrast, in San Francisco, one of the most liberal cities in the world, the Giants' ownership built a ballpark entirely through private funding. Giants' ownership is not tied to a political legacy, but they managed to do, through the private sector, what the private sector's future leading advocate could not.

13. T. Farrey, "Man builds ballpark, ballpark makes man," *ESPN* [online], espn.com [November 9, 2000].

14. R. Bryce, "Governor Deadbeat," *Austin Chronicle.* [online], http://www.austinchronicle.com/issues/vol17/issue19/pols.bush.html [December 1, 2002].

15. "Broken promises plague parks Owners, mayor are Texas two-faced," *NY Daily News*, October 12, 2002.

16. Ibid.

17. Ibid.

18. Robert Bryce, "Bush Makes a Killing While Arlington Stuck with Fee," *Austin Chronicle* [online], http://www.austinchronicle.com/issues/vol17/issue19/pols.bush.html [September 15, 2003].

19. Bush became the fifth president to throw out the first pitch at the World Series. The others were: 1915, Woodrow Wilson; 1924 Calvin Coolidge; 1932 and 1936, Franklin Roosevelt; 1956, Dwight Eisenhower.

20. Title IX and Sex Discrimination," *U.S. Department of Education* [online], www.ed.gov.offices/ocr/docs/tix_dis.html [November 7, 2002].

21. R. Finn and E. Seifert, "Pioneers of women's running are saluted by the New York Road Runners . . . ," *Women's Sports Foundation* [online], womenssportsfoundation.org [October 30, 2002].

22. Shelley Burns, "Share the Sandbox," *College Sports* [online], collegesports.com [October 29, 2002].

23. Stu Watson, "The Dollar Dribble in Women's Sports," *My Prime Time* [online], www.myprimetime.com/misc/bae_wsport/index.shtml [October 30, 2002].

24. Stu Watson, "A New Age of Women's Sports," *My Prime Time* [online], www.myprimetime.com/misc/bae_wsport/index2.shtml [November 1, 2002].

25. M. Stefan, "Women's Sports in Jeopardy: Commission Seeks to Weaken Title IX," *Women's Sports Foundation* [online], http://wfsgi.org/_wfsgi/women_title9.html [November 1, 2002].

26. M. McCarthy, "'Huge Public Interest' Drives Sorenstam Ads," *USA Today* [online], www.usatoday.com/money/advertising/2003-05-21-annika_x.htm [May 22, 2003].

27. David Steele, "Owner's Crack on A's Fan Nothing but Cheap Schott," *San Francisco Chronicle*, October 9, 2002, p. C1.

28. Philip Matier and Andrew Ross, "Fund Raising Photo Fumble Was Part of Long Simon Drive," *San Francisco Chronicle*, October 13, 2002, p. A21.

29. Based on personal interviews with the author.

CHAPTER 10

GOIN' GLOBAL

We are the most international of the four major professional sports. Our players come from nearly two dozen countries. Our games are viewed in more than 170 countries, and more than 30% of the visits to NHL.com come from outside North America.

—Gary Bettman, NHL Commissioner

For a long time, hockey's diversity along the European lines hurt the game's North American marketability. Now, looking into the future, it is an unbelievable asset. The NFL, NBA, and Major League Baseball are making every attempt to play meaningful games abroad. They schedule exhibitions, season openers, and clinics. The NFL even established a league, its off-season development league, in Europe. The various commissioners talk about internationally based franchises (in addition to those based in Canada) and worldwide sponsorships. They know that there are sports fans there, and just like Coke, McDonald's, and Microsoft, sports properties want to export their product and cultivate significant financial patronage in overseas markets. Furthermore, they see the Olympics and the World Cup moving about the globe, pulling in fans and raking in sponsorship fees from heavyweight sponsors. The major sports leagues feel that now is the time to start growing their businesses similarly.

Since most of the NHL's players come from abroad, the league already has lucrative foreign markets. Historically, the NHL has worried about taking a foreign product and making it palatable and profitable for the American market. Essentially the NHL has grown over the past twenty years through two critical events. First, the U.S. hockey team's "Miracle on Ice" at the 1980 Olympic Games was soon followed by the greatest career on ice. Wayne Gretzky became the face of professional hockey, and the NHL leveraged his skill, charisma, and classy demeanor to promote their product on the entire North American continent.

Once Gretzky left Edmonton to play in Los Angeles, the NHL expanded its reach into a whole new geographic realm. The NHL spread to markets like Anaheim, Phoenix, Tampa Bay, Miami, and North Carolina. The 1980 Olympic hockey team captured the American sports consciousness and Gretzky's inimitable talents built upon that to spread the game to places once considered impregnable.

Today a predominantly American league is stocked with Europeans and Canadians. With the advent of universal broadcast access and the Internet, foreign players continue to bond with fans in their native countries. Jaromir Jagr has played in the NHL for many years, but to the people of the Czech Republic, he is a native son who has played for their colors in the Olympics and represents them on the most competitive ice in the world. The Internet allows fans to follow him in Washington, D.C., and, of course, to still keep tabs on his old teammate Mario Lemieux, in Pittsburgh.

Media Metrics, the Internet marketing analyst, once rated the NHL as the eighth most popular Web site. More important, netScore, a Web-advertising analyst group, once rated the NHL's Internet audience with a buying power index of 233, more than twice the normal rate for other Web sites. The league might be struggling to keep franchises afloat in Buffalo and Ottawa, but its Web site shows that its hockey content has an avid following.

Gary Bettman's philosophy is "develop the global network voice and penetrate locally." That objective pervades all of professional sports. Player and brand mobility is at an all-time high. When Ichiro Suzuki came to Major League Baseball, he did not leave his Japanese fans behind. They can watch his games on television and follow his progress on the Internet. They can even vote for him in the All-Star Game. Ichiro's following in Japan has been compared to Elvis Presley's American audience in the 1950s. Due to technology and the mass media, players, teams, and events can be followed dynamically.

The confluence of media, telecommunications, and general moder-
nity means that the marketplace for an athlete's skill is global. Furthermore, as more athletes like David Beckham, Yao Ming, Hideki Matsui,
and Ernie Els reap the rewards of international careers, the number of
athletes crossing borders will increase. For fans, it means that they get to
see the best possible competitors, even if the competition doesn't take
place in their hemisphere. It seems staggering that professional sports will
aggregate more wealth, but it is true. As teams and leagues successfully
establish their brands in foreign markets, their resources will increase and
that will only put more pressure on the system to deliver the adrenaline
rush of championship-caliber excitement.

OPPORTUNITIES AND OBSTACLES

The sports entertainment industry has been international ever since the
Olympic Games were reinstated by Pierre de Coubertin in 1896. And as
immigrants traveled in the early twentieth century for work or pleasure,
they brought sports, mainly soccer, with them.

In the twenty-first century, the global sports industry is poised to
explode. As cultural barriers diminish, players' mobility allows them to
gravitate where the financial rewards and competitive quality is greatest.
Most important, eager markets await the action, the merchandise, and the
sponsors' call to action. It might have been difficult selling tickets for international soccer competitions held in conjunction with the Olympic
Games in Sweden in 1912, but in Japan and Korea during the 2002 World
Cup, demand was borderline riotous. Soccer players roam the globe playing
for teams in England, Korea, Germany, Japan, Italy, Brazil, Spain, and the
United States. American sports such as baseball and basketball now feature
Europeans, Asians, and Latinos as premiere players, and competitive base-
ball and basketball leagues thrive in Europe, Asia, and Latin America.

Properties, promoters, and agents know that the infrastructure is in
place. In the early part of the twentieth century, Jack Johnson had to
travel to another continent in order to fight for the heavyweight championship. Segregation forced him outside of his own borders. When Mike
Tyson lost to Buster Douglas in Tokyo in 1991, it was money that had

attracted him to Japan, not social freedoms. The popularity of championship soccer, boxing, or basketball has been proven over many decades of spirited play. Athletics today can clearly sell as a form of entertainment in person, or over an airwave.

One hundred years ago, sporting events and teams attempted to establish themselves in any market, not foreign markets. Major companies struggled to implement simple structures of payments and inventory. Foreign trade was in its nascent form. In 1916, for example, U.S. commercial trade set a record with domestic commerce at $45 billion, and exports accounting for $8 billion. Today, those numbers could apply to some multinationals.

In the current sports landscape, the struggle is to convert foreign sports markets into revenue streams. For American sports interests, professional sports almost mirrors the fast-food industry. Saturated in terms of domestic revenues in the early 1990s, the industry started expanding abroad. McDonald's opens about five new restaurants a day. Eighty percent are on foreign soil. In 1992, McDonald's had about three thousand restaurants outside the United States. Today, there are more than seventeen thousand in over 120 countries.

Teams, leagues, and the sports promoters know that there are only so many places where franchises and events can thrive via attendance and sponsor support in North American markets. Given that the four major sports leagues and college sports enjoy widespread broadcast support and timely scheduling, the rights holders realize that the limits might be reached in the near term in the United States and Canada.

So, like the fast food industry, powerful sports properties look abroad. The NBA, NHL, NFL, and major European soccer leagues might not be capable of replicating McDonald's international retail outlet construction but they can lay the groundwork for foreign enterprise. This explains the small amounts of exhibitions and more widespread broadcast efforts. More important, the exposure helps them slowly enter the retail segments, supplying merchandise, or even establishing their own locations. The most expensive thing is to play a game overseas. The costs associated with staging the event are significant. Broadcasting, on the other hand, costs very little, since each game is televised anyway.

Professional sports are clearly exploring ways to link their brands globally to fans. The NBA might seem to be lackluster in the current domestic marketplace, but it is booming abroad. They broadcast the 2002 All-Star game in forty-one languages to 210 countries and an aggregate audience of 2.5 billion people. The whole league has experienced recent problems drawing fans in some American markets like Cleveland, Denver, Oakland, Milwaukee, and Atlanta, but foreign players like Dirk Nowitizki (Germany), Pau Gasol (Spain), Yao Ming (China), and eastern Europeans such as Vlade Divac, Pedrag Stojakovic, Predrad Drobnjak are helping the brand grow around the world.

The NBA's overall business plan also includes the women's game, the WNBA. By 1999, their games were broadcast in 125 countries in seventeen languages. The NBA's brand is so strong that they can nurture women's basketball in order to dominate that market as well. The NBA knows that marketing partnerships for women athletes is a huge growth industry internationally. The best way to attract long-term sponsors and the financial security of the arrangement is to have a persuasive product. The NBA can implement their WNBA strategy alongside the parent league both domestically and abroad. Luckily, the NBA controls the Olympic roster, which means they can continue to promote their players and product through someone else's event. Since the men's game enjoys such great international appeal, the women's game has no pressure to evolve ahead of schedule.

Major League Baseball features the most foreign-born players. In 2002, 222 out of 849 Major League roster players were born outside the United States. That 26.1 percent of the roster will certainly grow, since 49.6 percent, or 2,865 out of 5,781 minor leaguers are foreign born. The 2002 All-Star Game might have only been watched by 100 million fans globally, but it was broadcast in more than two hundred countries.

Major League Baseball is quietly making a name for itself in foreign markets. They opened the 1999 season in Monterrey, Mexico, with the Colorado Rockies playing the San Diego Padres and in 2001 when the Texas Rangers and Toronto Blue Jays squared off in their season opener in San Juan, Puerto Rico. Additionally, in 2003, the erstwhile Montreal Expos played twenty-two of their "home" games in San Juan as well. Major League Baseball might one day expand to play more official games in places like San Juan, Mexico City, and even Cuba.

CONSIDERING HAVANA, CUBA

Cuba might sound improbable for 2004, but maybe not by 2014. Cuba has long been a place of great baseball tradition, supplying players to major league rosters throughout the twentieth century. If the political climate changes, it might make perfect sense to expand there with a Major League Baseball team one day. Havana's 1994 population was estimated at 2,175,995. Furthermore, the island population exceeds 11 million, which should provide ample broadcast area for advertisers via radio and television. Havana could easily support a baseball team in terms of enthusiasm and market size, even if the luxury suites might not have a long list of prospective clients in the early days.

With a city population of almost 2.2 million and another million located close by, Havana would be the twenty-second largest market of any Major League city. Furthermore, they would not have to worry about an NFL, NBA, or NHL team coming to the city to compete with it at any moment. The chart on the next page shows twenty-five metro area populations and the number of the major sports leagues (NBA, NFL, NHL, Major League Soccer, Major League Baseball) who have a franchise based there.

The fascinating questions to consider are how fast could the market support a team and how long would it take for the nation's infrastructure (transportation, security) and overall economic stability to rise to the Major League level. An utterly improbable thought will one day be very possible. The Dodgers, after all, once had an entire spring training on the island. The Baltimore Orioles even recently played an exhibition there. It won't be too long before a curious glance gets cast in its direction again. And it would be a triumphant turn of events for the island nation that cherishes the sport.

Rank	Metro Area	Population	# of Teams
1	New York-Northern New Jersey-Long Island, NY-NJ-CT-PA	20,124,377	10
2	Los Angeles-Riverside-Orange County, CA	15,781,273	7
3	Chicago-Gary-Kenosha, IL-IN-WI CMSA	8,809,846	6
4	Washington-Baltimore, DC-MD-VA-WV CMSA	7,285,206	6
5	San Francisco-Oakland-San Jose, CA CMSA	6,816,047	7
6	Philadelphia-Wilmington-Atlantic City, PA-NJ-DE-MD	5,988,348	4
7	Boston-Worcester-Lawrence, MA-NH-ME-CT	5,633,060	5
8	Detroit-Ann Arbor-Flint, MI	5,457,583	4
9	Dallas-Fort Worth, TX CMSA	4,802,463	5
10	Houston-Galveston-Brazoria, TX	4,407,579	3
11	Atlanta, GA	3,746,059	4
12	Miami-Fort Lauderdale, FL	3,655,844	4
13	Seattle-Tacoma-Bremerton, WA	3,424,361	3
14	Phoenix-Mesa, AZ	2,931,004	4
15	Cleveland-Akron, OH	2,911,683	3
16	Minneapolis-St. Paul, MN-WI	2,831,234	4
17	San Diego, CA	2,780,592	2
18	St. Louis, MO-IL	2,563,801	3
19	Denver-Boulder-Greeley, CO	2,365,345	5
20	Pittsburgh, PA MSA	2,346,153	3
21	Tampa-St. Petersburg-Clearwater, FL	2,256,559	3
22	Portland-Salem, OR-WA	2,149,056	1
23	Cincinnati-Hamilton, OH-KY-IN	1,948,264	2
24	Kansas City, MO-KS	1,737,025	3
25	Sacramento-Yolo, CA	1,685,812	1

Source: http:geography.about.com/library/weekly/aa122099b.htm.

The 11 million people who live on Cuba will one day be bombarded by the same marketing tactics seen in the rest of the Western world. It is merely a matter of time before the Internet, satellite TV, and the global village seep into its borders. Sports, a longtime cultural passion, will likely be a place where companies can make traction in the marketplace. Coke, Nike, Budweiser, and the other high-profile sports brands will certainly lead the charge into the sports-friendly nation once the opportunity is available. The likely scenario is that exhibitions will take place, perhaps even extended periods of play, before a team would ever consider calling it home.

The important thing for Major League Baseball is to have a plan targeting potential destinations, partners, and revenue streams. As of this book's writing, they are entertaining the notion of their own broadcast network and are building up the Internet broadcasting component. Most likely, behind closed doors, they look to Mexico, Puerto Rico, and maybe Cuba and/or the Dominican Republic as either destinations for exhibitions, opponents in a World Cup–type tournament, or even some type of expansion. They already look to these nations as baseball-hungry places where they currently develop players and coaches. And they also look at these places as revenue sources. The trick will be discovering and implementing the most efficient way to earn money.

Baseball needs to work wisely with foreign markets, governments, and the Player's Association to ensure that everyone agrees in the expansionary efforts. Since the regular season is so long, the logistics of getting the various players to participate against one another in a world-tournament format and not disrupt the season, or even spring training, is difficult. But the idea of Pedro Martinez, Miguel Tejada, Bartolo Colon, and their Dominican brethren going against Hideo Nomo, Ichiro Suzuki, Tsuyoshi Shinjo, Hideki Matsui, and the other great Japanese ballplayers teases the imagination. Maybe Major League Baseball knows the demand exists for their product, and they need to determine the satisfactory delivery mechanism. Perhaps the new Labor Agreement might provide a working platform for the pursuit of foreign markets through actual game competition.

The NFL hasn't been left behind, either. They have been playing games abroad for the past decade, and even started another league, NFL Europe. So far, the league has not really caught on, but the broadcast component has. Super Bowl XXXVI was broadcast to 166 countries in twenty-six languages, to a total of 800 million people. You might not be able to find Budweiser in all of these places, but you can find the Super Bowl. The NFL hopes that one day all of these countries will have Super Bowl parties where all of their sponsors products get consumed and commercials get watched, discussed, and analyzed. It might not catch on to that extent, but the ease of transmission ensures that all of the sports properties will make their events available to the widest possible audiences.

In short, leagues and properties of mass scale realize that promotion and partnership can bring them exposure and toe-holds in markets outside of their own countries. Just like kids in South Dakota can buy a Red Sox baseball hat, kids in Kanazawa, Japan, can buy a Yankees or Rams T-shirt, trinkets, cards, or memorabilia, and be just as passionate in their loyalties.

The difference between today and the first ninety-plus years of the sports industry is that George Steinbrenner can do two things to make the marketing opportunities possible. One, he can lure a talent like Hideki Matsui and/or other foreign players to cement the connection with a distant market, and then allow the satellite broadcasting and Internet communication mechanisms develop a fan base for merchandise and any other retail or advertising opportunities.

Essentially, by taking talent out of a market, the team brands can create foreign pockets of loyalty in the absence of the player. Ironically, Matsui's departure means that millions of his fans will now follow him with the Yankees. This will surely result in more merchandise and broadcast patronage in Japan of the Yankees brand. It used to be that fans would get mad if a player defected for the money. But today, many loyalists take pride in their best players excelling against the top competition, even if it means leaving the country to do it.

George Steinbrenner has learned much in his thirty years as owner. He may have gotten a reputation as impatient for hiring and firing Billy Martin during his first years of ownership, but he has maximized the considerable assets of the Yankees. More important, he has spared no expense in acquiring talent and assembling a team. And he knows that the hype of being a Yankee only makes his team more appealing to worldwide talent. After the team invested over $50 million in signing both Matsui and Cuban defector Jose Contreras, prior to the 2003 season, Steinbrenner said the obvious, "Each of these young men came out and said, 'I want to be a Yankee.' It's global and worldwide. That's good for baseball." Of course, the Kansas City Royals, Minnesota Twins, and Pittsburgh Pirates probably do not agree. These teams know that they cannot even begin to think about the benefits of foreign marketing, or importing foreign stars, but they can let the Yankees build the model and perhaps one day follow it.

In fact, to most properties in every sport, the foreign market is still elusive and unattainable. The potential exists, but some very practical obstacles exist to the actual mining of foreign markets. Mainly:

- Geography
- Competition from existing events
- Perception
- Patience
- The talent

The biggest problem facing globalization of sports leagues is simple geography. Japanese and European teams could never link up to play full-time in American Leagues, or vice versa. Further, since leagues are so entrenched in those areas at the moment, it would be difficult to carve out the necessary time to form competitions, and create tradition and value. Given that the Olympics, the World Cup, track and field, swimming, skiing, and many other sports currently enjoy their own form of world championships, it would be difficult to add another layer to the mix.

American broadcasters and companies have attempted for years to get an elimination tournament for college football and have failed. If they cannot succeed on their own turf, within the framework of the existing sports economy in the host country, then integrating a larger competitive structure is unrealistic. Also, the public already has emotional bonds with certain events that give them the satisfaction of international competition. Golf, for example, has the Ryder Cup every two years. The other efforts, whether it be the Dunhill Cup, or Presidents Cup, just do not seem to capture the imagination of the fans, sponsors, or players, at least not yet. The Ryder Cup augments a very international game whose major tournaments (Masters, U.S. Open, British

Open, and PGA) all feature the best international fields. Greg Norman talked of starting a World Tour in 1994, and the PGA soon quashed it, but it would be difficult to add more international competition that would have significant meaning to the fans and broadcasters.

Galvanizing a cohesive effort in the current climate of competitive events might be prohibitive. Since all of the major sports properties, or promoters, compete for the fans and sponsors, they do not coordinate efforts. Baseball, football, basketball, the Olympics, World Cup, and Don King all compete for the attention of the fan and the commitment of his or her dollars. Even in the same sport, no one wants to give up their own benefit so that another organizer can reap the rewards. At that point, the issue becomes one of compromise and revenue sharing. If a deal can be made, then the event has a chance.

The Olympics and the NHL worked out a scheduling arrangement by which NHL players could play in the 2002 Olympics. The Games had the best talent on ice and the fans got to see the best possible hockey. The NHL enjoyed the exposure and the ability to cross-promote its league and its international players. If the NHL could get its players featured on global television for a fortnight, without having to leave the North American continent, then it made sense to contribute to the event. If the global forces of baseball wish to determine the truly best international team, then maybe they could do something similar. However, the Boston Red Sox might not want to loan Pedro Martinez to the Dominican National Team in September of any year to pitch for the gold medal when they are vying with the Yankees for their own postseason berth.

Perception will play a large role in the globalization of sporting events. Since expanding operations essentially implies that an entity wants to enhance its enterprise, the organization that increases its investment into the new marketplace bears risk. In sports entertainment, properties diffuse risk by bringing in sponsors, or paying broadcasters, or by having cities help them build facilities. When Don King staged the Ali-Foreman fight in Zaire, he got Zaire's dictator to put up the purse for the boxers. King did not empty his bank account. The rival leagues that ultimately failed, the USFL, XFL, or ABA, all lost their broadcast agreements due to poor ratings or did not have one at all. Without a revenue stream and the exposure of sponsors and promotional partners, staging sporting events simply gets too expensive. Also, without a link to a broadcaster and several sponsors, it gives the impression that the product doesn't have paying corporate customers because there is no audience. Business relationships help pay for events and legitimize them. The perception that a scarcity of partners exists can doom a property. Therefore, extending into global markets is an interdependent process between the properties and their partners.

What really makes foreign expansion a difficult proposition is that sports owners and event properties are notorious for a lack of patience. The reason so many coaches get fired and players get benched is that ownership wants to win today, not tomorrow. The flip side, however, is that oftentimes the only definitive requirement to building a financially stable franchise is patience. Unfortunately, that does not come easily for those paying the bills in the sports entertainment industry. Pulling off a large-scale international competition in a league format remains highly unlikely.

Lastly, successful expansion will require cooperation from the actual players. If a team locates in Mexico City, will it appeal to all cultures that now comprise a Major League roster? Could they count on signing free agents and retaining the necessary talent in order to compete? Also, will the athletes want to cooperate with management to build new markets? Any team that did try to play ball in a foreign location would likely have to stock it with players native to that region in order to get fan turnout. The current climate of ownership might not be patient enough for that process.

BIGGEST GLOBAL BRAND

To Americans, any argument over the richest franchise probably starts in New York. Most people would logically assume that the Yankees are the globe's most valuable team. Given the size of the market, history of the team, its time-honored traditions, timeless logo, and on-field success, the Yankees seem like the safe bet. Others might argue that the Dallas Cowboys and their rich heritage as "America's Team" makes them number one. But both of these are wrong. To the surprise of no European, the most valuable team in global sports is located in an industrial town in England.

Manchester United (MU) is a publicly held soccer team that has expected annual revenues in excess of $200 million. Billionaire Rupert Murdoch bid $900 million for it in 1998, and it was deemed too low. If soccer, or football, is the world's sport, then Manchester United could arguably be called the World's Team. The World's Team has approximately 200 fan clubs: 151 in the United Kingdom, 25 in Ireland, and 24 scattered around the rest of the globe. In total, the team has a reported 50 million fans worldwide.

Manchester United might play in a gray and drizzly town, but they reap rewards around the globe. MU has a diverse mix of revenue, including lucrative sponsorships, its own TV station, merchandise sales, ticket sales, and it even rents its facilities to companies for conferences and meetings. It is determined to increase merchandise sales and expand its telecast revenues in new, soccer-hungry areas like Asia. The team provides content via cell phones and barnstorms in Asia and North America. Manchester United also has plans to open dedicated merchandising stores in Singapore, Kuala Lumpur, and Bangkok, and all of it makes perfect sense. In short, MU is a global brand that will only get bigger. Part sports team, part rock band, the team is all business. Everything it does has revenue in mind.

MU's formula is pretty simple. They sign the best players and spread the product wherever they can, whenever they can. In a statistic that must infuriate the American team owners, MU has achieved all of this success and only spent 33 percent of its revenue on labor.[1] By contrast, the average NFL team spends 60 percent of its revenue on its players. Second, MU maximizes its reach through media and partnerships. Essentially, by being the first one to enter foreign markets and capitalize on relationships, resources, and revenue streams, it feels that its brand will retain its luster. Most important, by keeping the team relevant, in the news, and performing at the elite level, it holds up the entire structure of MU worldwide.

The team is relentless. It has a subscription TV station and a Chinese language Web site. It has a direct betting link on its own site, so that passionate fans can move on their emotions. It has a deal with the Yankees, as much for mind-share as for actual profits. But by aligning its image with the most valuable brand in America, MU goes to the top of the list, not fighting its way up from the bottom.

In the old days, when the Globetrotters, or even the Bustin' Babes went out on the road, they played for a piece of the gate for the scheduled event. They didn't have sponsors foot the bill. MU is different. Courts, a furniture retailer, is on the Manchester United bandwagon. Courts spent almost $1 million to be the title sponsor of Manchester United's 2002 Asian tour. Now, Manchester United brings its team and leaves a store and cable subscriptions while minimizing its financial risk in the venture. This means that the money can still flow swiftly to the parent club, even in the absence of the team. These are elements that their barnstorming forefathers probably never imagined. The team is so powerful as a brand that it can even sell its biggest star, David Beckham, and still not suffer a loss in popularity with its fans and sponsors.

WORLD SPORT TIMELINE

Soccer, or football, has come a long way since the nineteenth century. In looking at the accomplishments of the soccer industry, one should know that it took years of grassroots interest and refinement before achieving its status. Originating in Great Britain, the sport randomly followed the Empire and its travelers around the globe, settling into the fabric of its new communities and manifesting the personality of the locals. Currently a $5-billion European industry, soccer is culturally and economically one of Europe's primary points of global identification.[2]

1855: First soccer club: Sheffield Football Club.
1860s: British industrialists introduce soccer to the Argentineans.
1872: First international game (England vs. Scotland: 0–0). The game is introduced to France and the size of ball becomes standardized.
1875: Oxford University tours Germany and some German universities take up the game.
1876: Game is introduced to Canadians.
1880: Clubs charge for admission. Players are paid lost wages and expenses.
1882: Uruguay starts playing.
1887: British introduce "football" to Russia.

1890: Goal nets are used for the first time and Brazilians start to play.

1891: Penalty kicks are introduced. Argentina becomes the first country outside Britain to have a national champion.

1893: First club formed in Italy.

1898: Spain begins play and the official rules governing the game reach seventeen, the current number.

1899: Austria and Iceland begin playing.

1904: FIFA formed with Belgium, Denmark, France, Netherlands, Spain, Sweden, and Switzerland.

1914: Twenty-four nations are now associated with FIFA.

1908: International soccer competition is associated with the Olympics in England.

1912: International competition in conjunction with the Swedish Olympics.

1927: First league match is broadcast on radio.

1930: First World Cup (Uruguay)—Uruguay beat Argentina 4–2 in the final.
      Forty-one members in FIFA.

1938: First live TV transmission of FA Cup Final.

1950: Seventy-three nations are FIFA members.

FIFA is, perhaps, the best barometer of soccer's health. Trailing only the IOC in membership as a sporting association, FIFA is also within hailing distance of the United Nations. As the organizing body of the World Cup, it truly captures the passion of the competing nations unlike any other. The World Cup literally means that the identity of a nation can rest in the feet of a few men running around a grass field. The cultural implications for the victorious nation are enormous.

Perhaps the biggest question among U.S. soccer fans centers around the concept of a true American contender. In fact, Major League Soccer (MLS) roots are in the 1994 World Cup, staged in the United States. The World Cup came to the United States on the condition that it would set up a Division I soccer league and the MLS has delivered a true big-league product.

But U.S. soccer will be on fragile ground as long as the National team struggles in World Cup competition. When the U.S. team got blown out of the 1998 World Cup in France, Alan Rothenberg, president of the U.S. Soccer Federation said, "At the end of the day, when you're in a World Cup, it's results that count. Based on that, we're obviously disappointed with the '98 World Cup. At the same time, we've been very, very realistic about U.S. soccer. We think a great deal of progress has been made. . . . We're inching forward as a soccer nation. We're not leaping forward. It's a long, hard struggle to the top."[3]

And four years later, U.S. soccer inched forward some more as the U.S. World Cup team had a strong showing. Led by Landon Donovan, the team's energetic, aggressive style of play helped position the sport as something other than an activity that overprotective parents let their kids play before taking them back to the suburbs in SUVs. Donovan ended up making the cover of Sports Illustrated and the U.S. team got some much-needed exposure. The media figures bore out the fact that international success translated into interest. ESPN's ratings in 2002 were up by 19 percent over the 1998 figures, and total households went up by 37 percent. Winning breeds success, and ratings!

The performance also helped spur some patriotism. Landon Donovan ultimately spurned a German team to play in San Jose with his MLS franchise, the Earthquakes, one of the league's best teams. Donovan took less money to play in California for the 2003 season, and it provided American soccer and the MLS with a valuable public relations coup. Donovan's desire to stay validated the competitive quality of the league. The MLS will succeed because soccer has a great base of fans, expanded interest among the casual spectator, and emerging stars that will one day vault the United States even higher in international circles. Most important, the league has quality franchises, excellent sponsors, and administers its business for long-term stability.

The MLS has pockets of great fans, from the families of the kids in soccer leagues, to the Latin and European transplants. The MLS and sponsors interested in the Latin markets know that soccer enjoys high priority among the Spanish-speaking community. A fascinating case will be to see if the MLS can attract and retain the Latin demographic. The Latin market is alluring because the 2002 World Cup Final game (between Brazil and Germany) drew 66 percent of Hispanic television households. More incredibly, the Univision (Spanish language) stations in the Chicago, Dallas, Houston, Los Angeles, Miami, Phoenix, and San

Antonio markets outdrew the ABC affiliates (official broadcaster) in the same towns. The 2002 World Cup Final was seen by more Hispanic viewers than the most recent NBA Finals, World Series, or any of the last five Olympic broadcasts. It drew almost 2.9 million Hispanic households and it aired in the early morning!

Univision even outdrew ESPN during the tournament at key points. The apex for Univision came during the U.S.-Mexico game, when 4.2 million viewers tuned in, 42 percent more than on ESPN's broadcast. The MLS's goal is to convert these passionate soccer fans into MLS fans. It is also incumbent upon the advertisers and companies looking to court the Latin market to think of the role that both Univision and the MLS can play in communicating with millions of potential customers.

THE BIGGEST TARGET

The most important athlete in the world might just be a guy who hails from Shanghai, China. The seven-foot-five-inch Yao Ming arrived in America as a twenty-two-year-old rookie who carried the twin burdens of expectation and relentless curiosity. Yao also had to assume the mantle of representing the nation of China to the West while acclimating to the rigors of the NBA. Much like Elvis Presley was the first face of rock and roll, or Charles Lindbergh was the first icon of daredevil international aviation, Yao is the first high-profile, nonpolitical Chinese personality under the scrutiny of the Western media, and basketball is his main mechanism for expression.

Yao didn't ask for the role, but he will forever be identified with helping to build a new commercial China as it emerges from the shadows of twentieth-century Communism. The bridge that he might help build between the Chinese and the American sports fans could potentially be as impressive as the Three Gorges Dam currently being constructed on mainland China.

China accounts for over 20 percent of the world's population. Walled behind political ideology for as long as the mass consumer society has existed, the country's billion-plus market has long been coveted by virtually any company that has ever manufactured, boxed, shipped, or shelved anything. Many felt that China would be prime for mass marketing by the 2008

Beijing Olympics, but that might be too conservative an estimate. As things stand in early 2003, China has already assimilated, accepted, and implemented many Western marketing philosophies, brands, and tactics. Most important, it had delivered profits to the blue chip firms doing business there:

- Eastman-Kodak's second biggest film market is China.
- Procter & Gamble said that it already has invested over $1 billion into China and has already seen profits.[4]
- KFC, still brandishing Colonel Sanders's image, opens up a new store every other day in China, and all expansion is based on realized profits made in the Chinese market!

Big Names and Big Profits

Company	Capacity	Revenue (billions)	Profitable?
Coca-Cola	31 Bottling Plants, 20K employees	1.1	Yes
Kodak	5 plants, 8K outlets, 5K employees	1.2	Yes
Motorola	2 plants, 12K employees	3.4	Yes
P & G	5 plants, 4K employees	1.0	Yes
Siemens	40 separate companies, 21K employees	.610	Yes
Yum Brands	800 KFC, 100 Pizza Huts 45K employees	.400	Yes*

Source: L. Chang and P. Wonacott, "Cracking China's Market," Wall Street Journal, January 9, 2003, p. B1.

*China expected to account for 29 percent of international profits in 2002. The employee estimate varies from forty thousand to fifty thousand.

The possibilities are staggering. Doing the math on the Chinese market is like taking the U.S. market, multiplying it by four, and then still needing to do some addition. Coca-Cola reaches more than 600 million Chinese consumers already, and that's not even half the market!

In many ways, China is the last great consumer frontier. Furthermore, an eager populace awaits commercialization and yearns to compete economically with the developed world's economic superpowers. As the Olympics approach, companies like Coke, Visa, and the other top-notch Olympic sponsors will look to blend their brands with the understandable national pride in hosting the games and the warp-speed consumerism sweeping its cities.

And by 2008, Yao Ming, barring injury, will certainly be the most important athlete of those Games. Not only is he a top-flight player, but he will have been acclimated to the NBA and to global multinationals. Perhaps most important, he will likely play for the Chinese National Team, and be the first recognized Chinese global superstar to compete on sports' largest stage. Only one person will be the first high-profile Chinese Olympian, and the companies that identify with Yao will have an historic opportunity. If Olga Korbut or Nadia Comaneci felt the overnight bright lights of Olympic fame, Yao will have had a five-year high-profile buildup to accentuate the euphoric impact of the Games.

Yao's NBA exploits are currently big news back in China. His first professional game, for example, was available in 287 million households in China.[5] The NBA knows a good thing when it sees it, and the league broadcasted 170 games in China, including thirty featuring the Rockets,[6] during his first season. By the time the Beijing Olympics start, Yao will have had five full years of NBA competition.

Furthermore, the Chinese-language NBA Web site will have had many years to promote Yao to the Chinese masses. Smart companies will lock him up now and hope that his career develops as his early play indicates. By the time Yao goes back to China for those Summer Games, he could literally make a brand overnight with his endorsement.

The hype will likely exceed the original 1992 U.S. Dream Team featuring Michael Jordan, Magic Johnson, Larry Bird, Patrick Ewing, Chris Mullin, Clyde Drexler, John Stockton, Charles Barkley, and others in what is widely considered to be the best basketball team ever assembled. The only thing that team lacked was a worthy adversary. By 2008, there will be plenty of legitimate teams vying for the gold medal and the host country hopes that their squad is one of them.

All of this bodes well for the NBA. The activation of the largest consumer market and the simultaneous ascendancy of basketball will have significant effects in sports marketing, and marketing programs in China specifically. It will also mean a lot for the sport's sponsors. No one is saying anything right now, but there hasn't been this much attention on Houston since the old Apollo moon shot days. The early returns to the franchise have been good as well. Yao's first game a Rocket drew 16,285 fans (capacity). The prior two seasons' home openers attracted 9,500 and 11,327 respectively. For the season, the Rockets averaged two thousand more fans per game. The team enjoys enthusiastic support on the road and Yao even won the All-Star balloting for the center position, beating out Shaquille O'Neal, one of the most dominating players in the history of the game.

In the San Francisco Bay area, which has a large Chinese population, the Rockets' arrival meant special preparations. The team made in-game announcements in both English and Chinese, and when the Warriors played an announcement taped by Yao, people cheered! The Warriors, long struggling with fan apathy, even devised miniticket plans featuring games against the Rockets. But Yao's influence most impacts his own team. As the Rockets themselves have declared: "The Time is Yao!" The team will ultimately cash in his presence in ways that no professional sports team has ever realized. Not only did Yao immediately help spur ticket sales and increase buzz around the team, but he will bring in sponsors like no individual player since Michael Jordan's heyday.

Currently, even Chinese companies are looking into ways to sponsor the Rockets, and Chinese fans purchase large blocks of tickets. As soon as Nike, Coca-Cola, Kodak, and other companies figure out that Yao might be the single biggest influence in China since a guy named Mao, they will make great strides to further their brand in the marketplace.

Pretty good for a young rookie just looking to fit in. Yao has already signed a few endorsement deals. Sifting through the myriad offers and inquiries, Yao chose carefully and signed deals with blue chip companies like Visa, Apple, and Sorrent Entertainment, an emerging wireless video game company that recognizes the opportunity with the biggest star in the world's largest marketplace.

Most important, Yao is a true gentleman athlete, deftly adjusting to the cultural shock of America and complete exhaustion of the media scrutiny that follows his every move. On misunderstandings he encounters with NBA players and fans, Yao said, "There are a lot of difficulties in two different cultures understanding each other. Especially two very large countries. The world is getting smaller and I think it's important to have a greater understanding of other cultures." When asked his favorite English expression, he calmly answered: "Last question."[7]

Yao is one of those rare personalities who define an era, or a place in time. Jackie Robinson will always be the icon for baseball's integration. Joe Namath was the poster boy for the AFL-NFL merger. Babe Ruth personified the Roaring 20s, the New York Yankees' dominance, and the home run. Frank Sinatra and Bruce Springsteen are the faces of two different eras of New Jersey music. Yao happens to be the person bursting onto the global stage at the precise time when China is opening its doors to the West in virtually all forms of capitalism and consumerism. The extraordinary circumstances around the simultaneous investment of billions of Western dollars, the popularity of basketball, and Yao's status as China's most important public persona merging toward an Olympic stage will make him the face that represents China to the world, and the personality that delivers a world of products to China.

Oh, and he can really play, too.

SAME REGION: HAVING A WEAPON

Companies contemplating the possibilities of working with Yao Ming might want to consider the excellent work that Visa International pulled off with the 1988 Summer Games in Seoul.

Prior to those Games, Visa had ideas about using the Games to increase business throughout Asia. At that time in Japan, for example, Visa ranked third in the marketplace. The company felt that the Seoul Olympics offered an excellent opportunity to do something about their position in Japan. Visa's management proceeded to craft, present, and implement programs with client banks. The goal, simply, was to increase business in the region. It turned out that their member institutions, customers, and people within their channels had a tremendous amount of excitement over the Games. Furthermore, the region was doing very well economically, so the timing of the programs could not have been better.

The partnerships and programs yielded tremendous results. By 1990, Visa hurdled the competition and became the number one credit card in Japan. Visa had the perfect mix of product, strategy, support, and execution. Visa's efforts paid off when it leapfrogged its two main competitors in Japan.

The Olympics gave Visa the tools to deploy their assets in a focused, symbiotic manner. That is the real key to the mechanism of sponsorship. Sponsorship is not necessarily a "turnkey" investment for the buyer. Often, sponsorship simply empowers companies to create opportunities for themselves and their customers. The smart companies, like Visa, optimize the relationship.

Whether it be an upcoming Olympic sponsorship, or an endorsement with a 7'5" basketball player, companies will be looking for ways to increase their presence and leverage within the Chinese marketplace in the very near future. Sports might be a place that helps create opportunities for sponsors, properties, and end-user consumers.

IN THEIR OWN WORDS: MANAGING A GLOBAL SPORTS SPONSORSHIP

Visa is the world's leading payment brand. Visa-branded cards generate more than $2.3 trillion in annual volume and are accepted at more than twenty-nine million physical locations globally. Visa is also one of the most successful international sports sponsors. The brand has a fifteen-year high-profile history with the Olympic community and has done landmark work in leveraging the sponsorship over the course of their relationship.

Visa has committed to the Olympics through 2012 and will surely create many memorable and successful campaigns in association with those upcoming Games. To understand the breadth and the responsibility of the task, Tom Shepard, VP International Marketing Partnerships and Sponsorships of Visa International, discusses developing sponsorships from the negotiating table through the organization and into effective marketing programs.[8]

Global Perspective, Global Reach

"Visa is owned by 21K financial institutions in six global regions. We give them access to a marketing platform such as the Olympics and they, in turn, make it relevant in their community. We want to create brand advocacy. It takes a lot of patience and commitment to go from the idea stage and then filter it down through the organization to the customer, but when it works it is a very gratifying thing.

"One program of note was the Visa Gold Medal Athlete Program. Visa wanted to find a way to connect cardholders with the games, its traditions and personalities; to get people to support the products that support the athletes.

"Visa saw that America had a great tradition in the Decathlon. Names like Bob Mathias, Milt Campbell, Bill Toomey, Rafer Johnson, and Bruce Jenner are all heroes in sports history. These are people that defined the event. After Jenner, though, there was a huge fall-off, a void. Where had all of the great U.S. decathletes gone?

"We saw this as huge opportunity to revitalize the present day decathlon team and back its past success through our resources. So Visa sponsored clinics and, over a period of time, it evolved into a program that included coaches, experts, clinicians, advisors on biometrics, sports science, and past medalists to talk about being a champion.

"The magic number in the decathlon is 8,000 points—and the U.S. had no 8,000-point decathletes when we started the program. Within two years, every member of the team had achieved the 8,000-point level. This wasn't accomplished through the sports scientists, or stipends we provided, it was more about the recognition that they got. Once the athletes knew that they didn't have to work three jobs or train at odd hours and were being watched by fans, their focus, resolve, and results soon followed.

"Visa, with the direction of people like Harry Marra and Fred Samara, helped develop Champions like Dave Johnson, Dan O'Brien, and Kip Janvrin and Chris Huffins. All of those guys won medals, set records, and embodied the ideal of a national champion. Once we got involved, the athletes knew that the media was watching and that the track and field community was watching. When you, as a sponsoring organization, communicate to your partners and customers that they are responsible for developing champions, it validates the process. Using a Visa card became a tangible vehicle for showcasing direct athlete contribution on the part of the cardholder, and meaningful activity for the brand within the Olympic movement through the Visa Gold Medal Athlete Program."

Olympic Origins—Starting the "Top" Program

"Prior to Visa getting involved with the Olympic Games, there was an incumbent (American Express) who passed on retaining their category. Visa, at the time, had a couple of real visionaries who understood the opportunity and the timing of the moment, Jan Soderström and John Bennett. Because of them, we became the first worldwide partner that helped to launch the TOP program.

"Visa signed on in '86 and our first games were in '88 in Seoul and Calgary. The Olympics came alive in conjunction with a new campaign created by BBDO on behalf of Visa—'Visa. It's Everywhere you want to be.' We angled the exclusivity platform by saying in our messaging 'When you go to the Olympics, take your Visa card, because at the Olympics, they don't take American Express.' The true rationale of the program was to separate Visa from Mastercard and it was a brilliant strategy where American Express became the foil.

"And in 1988, that was the use of the platform; to highlight merchant business that didn't take American Express. By 1992, '94, and '96, we got richer in our applications and understanding of the platform. Today, everyone talks about integrated marketing where you have, at the high end, brand advertising—but you really have all of these different channels that you address with programs developed from the platform. The evolution of all event marketing is that you figure out ways to accomplish more objectives as time goes on. If you don't, then you aren't doing your job.

"We search for ways to drive card usage, acquisition and issuance. We need to help the merchant community understand our broader goals and make a strong case that demonstrates ROI on the platform investment. I imagine that McDonald's does the same thing with their franchises."

Behind the Scenes Work

"At headquarters, we are twice removed. We have banks and a regional structure that needs to control the program and communicate with their banks. A question we ask ourselves is, 'how do we get the message through in a way that can be distilled where people feel enfranchised in the overall platform?'

"We have retail bankers and subcategories that need to feel a commonality in our goals. And when you talk about a sports program, certain people along the way will say it is frivolous, that it is not mainstream and they don't want to use it.

"People see evidence of sponsorship and they think things happen overnight, the marketing programs, the advertisements, the hospitality, merchandise. It does not happen easily, or come off without some resistance from your own team. Part of the process is proving the value to our network of member financial institutions. Sometime the most difficult task is on the internal educational side."

The IOC

"We have a lot of history with IOC and we continually build on it and refine what we have done. Our negotiations are friendly, as evidenced by our commitment to be a partner through 2012. Relationship management is a key component. With something as big as the Olympics, there will be category crossover, so escalating emotions and yelling won't accomplish anything. Screaming about rights means very little. At the heart of a dispute, it will come down to what the contract says. If someone watched our negotiations, you would see a lot of resident knowledge. Stan Koppel wrote our first contract and he is still on our negotiating team. You can't replace what his experience represents to our position. We currently have seven contracts to write: an IOC bridge agreement, USOC definitive agreement, IOC definitive agreement and then separate contracts with the four OCOGs [Organizing Committees of the Olympic Games].

"The OCOGs change and we need to educate the OCOGs on our rights as a sponsor, how we work with our members, and what the pass-through rights are with various merchants. The IOC, after years of negotiations and relationship interchange, understands the nuances of our category, but that doesn't always mean the OCOG will.

"The sponsor rights are the price of entry and broadcast rights are layered on top. That poses difficult questions to a partner. The ramifications are 'do we buy the broadcast exclusivity? or don't we?' These can be expensive questions—where you need to project out and see where your priorities exist within the marketplace.

"Today, the property should be able to offer the partner the ability to retain rights in the broadest sense, or at least ask them where they need the coverage. The property should be able to price out in the new model what pieces you consider essential to the platform. The IOC is looking into getting a better handle on everything, especially the broadcast piece. It is the biggest piece of the puzzle that is missing. Once you buy your partnership, then you go out and talk to the broadcaster. An improvement would be to get our agency and our experts involved with the IOC and broadcasters from the beginning so that we can shape a better relationship. It makes little sense in today's world not to have discussion among those three entities at the earliest part of the planning stages. It is too big a decision to tell the sponsor: 'Here, pay us and now go talk to them if you want TV advertising, and by the way, you are very exposed.'"

What, Exactly, Is "Carpaccio Marketing"?

"Carpaccio marketing, as I define it, is not a feeling, it is a reality. Where there was once one category, there are now five as the I.O.C. has thinly sliced one broader category into five. Properties are beginning to realize that they can make more money out of categories and subcategories. When Visa started out, the credit card category covered banks and products. Now what used to be just the credit card category has become payment systems, retail banking, and financial consultancy. And the insurance categories and Telcos are not too far away.

Telcos are very interested in how people pay for their products and the systems by which they will do it. Swatch already utilizes their watches to pay for services. We brush up with almost everything in the retail banking category, so we need to be very careful as to how the property manages and crafts the spaces where we operate.

"It would be a daunting task, I would think, to negotiate at that level without having done it before. If someone new came in and wanted to be a global partner, they might not understand how to sell it through to their organization. Maybe they might not know how to best deal with the OCOG or interpret their rights, because if someone can encroach on their rights, they will—other companies will take advantage of the inexperience."

Rules to Sponsor By

"One size never fits all. Even the Olympics, the most robust property of them all, doesn't touch everything. The World Cup is a great event, but it is still only one sport that engenders certain demographics and results. The future is about segmented media, segmented attention spans, and the need to be more customized in approaching. At Visa, we need to be involved in the global dimensions of cross-cultural experiences. The shrinking world has meaning where sponsorship here can affect sponsorship there, and the point of origin is irrelevant.

"Shikira has meaning in many places to many groups who aren't sports fans. The Yankees and Yomiuri Giants pursuing a partnership is a thing of beauty because they share common goals and bring great resources to companies. We get almost 10,000 proposals annually, involving all forms of media and all forms of entertainment. We want to do a few things very well and take advantage of our relationships with powerful entertainment properties like the Olympics and Disney."

NOTES

1. Richard Heller, "Big Kick," *Forbes* [online], forbes.com [July 8, 2002]. In addition to those based in Canada.

2. Kate Carlisle, "For Italian Football, La Dolce Vita May Be Over," *Business Week* (September 16, 2002).

3. Paul Obejuerge, "U.S. Exits World Cup with Modicum of Respect," *Soccer Times* [online], http://www.soccertimes.com/worldcup/1998/games/jun25.htm [September 15, 2003].

4. Leslie Chang and Peter Wonacott, "Cracking China's Market," *Wall Street Journal*, January 9, 2003, p. B1.

5. By comparison, 106 million households have TVs in the United States.

6. Tom Fowler, "Apple ad leads a bevy of Yao-endorsed products," *Houston Chronicle* [online], www.chron.com [January 8, 2003].

7. Adam Schefter, "Yao Ming," *Denver Post*, April 13, 2003, p. C4

8. Personal interview with the author, December 2002.

CHAPTER 11

SELL, SELL, SELL

If you're not in sales, or engineering, you're overhead.
—An unnamed greedy technologist

T he above sentiment has its application in the sports industry, essentially a massive industry of selling. Teams sell tickets, broadcast rights, the backs of the chairs players sit on, virtual space, air space, billboard space, the names of buildings, kid zones, and anything that might have value to a company outside the event. Any area of entity, in or around a sporting event, can be bought. The Super Bowl half-time show had been maligned for many years, but now it is a big windfall.[1] AT&T Wireless paid a reported $6.6 million to be a part of a halftime spectacular featuring Shania Twain at Super Bowl XXXVII. Team and event representatives sell their properties' inventory 365 days a year. They make presentations, pitches, and alliances to a variety of partners, all in the name of profit!

There are the direct sellers of the actual entertainment, employees or agents directly representing teams, leagues, event promoters, and tournament directors. And then are the vast groups of resellers, like the television and radio broadcasters who have paid for the broadcast privileges. Another large group of resellers are companies that have purchased the privilege of using the logo or likeness of a team, personality, or sports brand: the licensees. Ironically, licensees pay for the privilege of building even more equity into sports brands over the long term in order to further the immediate sales objectives of their own brands in the short term.

If the basic mechanism for sports subsidy is sponsorship, then one of the fundamental premises of sports sales is licensing. At one time, the only licensed sports product was a trading card. The major properties, the NFL and Major League Baseball, initiated licensing divisions in the 1960s as the concept of replicating, or using, the images and logos of players and teams became viable. By the mid 1990s, the NFL had agreements with over 350 manufacturers on 2,500 products producing $3-billion worth of merchandise sales.

Licensing has emerged as one of the major revenue streams in the sports industry and one of the key components of sponsorship and the sports properties' sales strategies. Simply put, licensing is the reproduction of an image, or portion thereof, of a team, personality, league, company, or any copyrighted property for a fee to the rights holder of the said property, trademark, or copyright for a specific time period and placement of the licensed image in association with the licensing organization. Every key chain, T-shirt, hat, sweatshirt, rug, credit card, trading card, Bobblehead, poster, or trinket that features a logo or likeness of any athlete or team, or is associated with a team, league, or property (such as an event like Wimbledon, Boston Marathon, Olympics, World Cup, Rose Bowl, etc.) has contractually agreed to a fee for the right to use the image.

When you see an image of a well-known player, but his hat, jersey, helmet, or other identifying team characteristics are obscured, then the personality has been compensated, but his or her affiliation has not. The brands of sports teams are protected like Colonel Sanders's secret recipe.

Total merchandise for the major sports leagues, NASCAR, and college sports approaches $20 billion in annual sales, a figure greater than the movie industry and the video game industry combined! With figures like that at stake, the protection of the images, manufacturing, and profits is extremely important to all parties involved. Leagues send out special teams of undercover investigators to find bogus merchandise. The protection of the marks and images that have taken decades to build now represent a full-time investment of labor resources.

IT'S IN THE GAME

One application of licensing revenue not anticipated in the 1960s is video game entertainment. In 2001, according to the Interactive Digital Software Association, total video game industry sales were $6.35 billion on 225.1 million units (consoles, CDs, and cartridges) sold. Additionally, 22 percent of all games sold come from the sports genre. If racing is included as a part of the "sports genre," then the figure approaches 40 percent.

More important, sports is a big piece across all categories of the video game culture. Established sports like football, soccer, hockey, golf, and basketball enjoy widespread popularity, while new extreme sports like skateboarding appeal to their own demographics. Furthermore, as technology improves the user experience and the environment of the game for the player, its appeal continues to grow.

Top 10 Video Titles of 2001

Grand Theft Auto	Take 2
Madden NFL 2002	Electronic Arts
Pokemon Crystal	Nintendo
Metal Gear Solid 2	Konami
Gran Turismo 3: A Spec	Sony
Super Mario Advance	Nintendo
Tony Hawk's Pro Skater 3	Activision
Tony Hawk's Pro Skater2	Activision
Pokemon Silver	Nintendo
Driver 2	Infogrames (now called Atari)

Source: NPD Group

The video game industry exceeds the movie industry in terms of sales. And the talent assemblage, necessary licensing, and associated production costs are much cheaper. A top flight sports video title might cost between $5 and $6 million in development costs, while a major movie release frequently tops $40 million. Furthermore, Tiger Woods, Michael Jordan, and the many players associated with the games earn far less in the video game business than Arnold Schwarzenegger, Julia Roberts, and their elite brethren receive in remuneration for their acting efforts.

For the leagues and athletes, licensing income has become a very important revenue stream. For the video game publishers, it is a necessary expense. The licensing fees, for example, associated with a game like EA Sports's John Madden Football reflects licenses purchased from both the Player's Association and the National Football League itself.

Since both licenses are nonexclusive—meaning that multiple game publishers can buy the licenses, and do so—it probably costs Electronic Arts in the neighborhood of $500,000 for each. Of course, they also need to pay John Madden for the rights to use his name and likeness. The licensing royalty rate (on sales revenues) to both the league and the Player's Association will be around 5–6 percent. The key for the NFL, or any licensor, is that the burden of risk, and development, and any infrastructure, rests entirely with the licensee. The licensor simply negotiates the license and waits for the checks. In the case of nonexclusive licenses, where multiple developers can purchase the rights to use the names, images, and logos of the specific athletes and teams, the licensing property spreads the risk among many. When a property awards an exclusive license to a developer, or manufacturer, then the licensee pays a premium for the privilege.

If John Madden Football sells three million units across all platforms to retailers such as Toys R US, Wal-Mart, Kmart, Target, and "boutique" stores like GameStop and EB (Electronics Boutique), they will probably charge a wholesale price of $40 per unit, accruing $120 million in revenue. This results in approximately $6 million to the NFL and the Players Association.

Madden Football, in the sports category, is a unique product. The only game that compares to Madden Football, FIFA Soccer, needs an international audience in order to reach comparable sales figures. EA has an exclusive license with FIFA, but not with the NFL or the NFL Players Association. In John Madden Football, though, EA Sports has the single best sports video game franchise ever.[2]

The industry has some rigid structures. The publishers need to develop for the existing three game platforms (Sony, Microsoft XBox, and Nintendo) and for play on the personal computer. Clearly, a big piece of the future for gaming will be in the online and wireless environments. The Interactive Digital Software Association estimates that 31 percent of the most frequent game players played games online in 2002. This represents a 7 percent increase over the 2001 figures. Numbers like that are impossible to ignore. Since PCs continue to get more powerful and integrate greater development capacity, the future of the PC monitor in the gaming environment could impact the PlayStation, XBox, and Game Cube markets. And as the global wireless revolution continues, publishers are rushing to enter that market as well.

Video Game Demographics

Gender
Male:	62%
Female:	38%

Ages
Under 18:	34%
18–35:	26%
36+:	40%

Buyers
Gender (PC Games)
Male:	45%
Female:	55%

Console Systems
Male:	54%
Female:	46%

Source: NPD Group

The video game business is an extension of both the entertainment industry and the sports industry. It also has significant consequences for the economy. The U.S. government estimated that, at the peak of the economic boom in 2000, the sales in the software game category grew at 14.9 percent while the U.S. economy grew at a 7.4 percent. Furthermore, the computer and video game industry employs 220,000 people and generates $9 billion in wages and tax revenues.[3]

Total Industry Sales (Video Games + Computer Games + Edutainment)

Year	Millions of Units Sold
2001	225
2000	219
1999	215
1998	181
1997	133
1996	105

Source: NPD Fun World (TM) & NPD TechWorld (TM)

One analyst group, Bear Sterns, estimated in 2001 that "growth in the game software market is likely to outpace that of the Internet (advertising), television, radio, motion pictures, music, and newspapers." Whether or not those bold predictions materialize, the permanence of the video game market as an important revenue stream for the sports industry cannot be questioned.

GENERAL LICENSING

Sales Figures of the Major Properties

NFL	$2.5 billion
MLB	$2.3 billion
NBA	$1.0 billion
NHL	$900 million
College	$2.5 billion
NASCAR	$1.2 billion

Source: Sporting Goods Manufacturers Association's Licensing White Paper

Licensing, as improbable as it might have seemed fifty years ago, is now a multibillion-dollar industry. Fans like their personal identity to be integrated into the colors of a team and licensing allows them to display their loyalties. Pittsburgh fans enjoy the blue-collar association with the steel industry. People still refer to Pittsburgh as "Steel Town" even though steel is nothing but a memory. Similarly, Raider fans revel in their renegade image, and enjoy deriding 49er fans as the "wine and cheese crowd." Fans like to stay current, too, and they respond by snapping up the latest in color schemes and retro-marketing gimmicks that harken back to a team's past. The "retro-wear" fad was the NFL's idea to honor its seventy-fifth anniversary. Teams wore their original jerseys five times during the 1994 season, and sold $40 million of the replica wear.[4] The throwback attire has been a staple in all professional sports ever since.

Perhaps no other sports fans identify with the image of its competitors like NASCAR. NASCAR might be the single most successful sports marketing property in the last twenty years. Capitalizing on iconic drivers, the sport works tirelessly with sponsors and fans to promote its product, keep it accessible, and sell anything and everything associated with it. Its merchandise sales figures keep growing as the popularity of the sport spreads. With the sport getting a national broadcast contract with Fox and expansion to tracks in more major markets, it continues to be a growth industry.

INDUSTRY CONTEXT:
SELLING GETS MORE SPECIALIZED

Back in chapter 3, one table showed the front office of the 1959 Chicago Cubs and another one listed the front office personnel of the 1961 Los Angeles Dodgers. The Cubs had eleven employees, including one ticket manager. The Dodgers listed fourteen people, including two types of ticket salesmen, one of whom was the basic manager, and the other one in charge of group sales. In 2000, the Los Angeles Dodgers media guide listed the following categories of employees:

Category	Number of Positions Listed
Executive Office	9
Administration	8
Advertising & Special Events	5
Baseball Operations	18

Broadcasting, Publications and New Media	6
Client Services	3
Community Affairs	7
Dodgertown	8
Finance and Accounting	9
Human Resources	5
Legal	2
Management Info. Systems	6
Media Relations & Publicity	5
Medical Staff	4
Merchandising	7
Stadium Operations	15
Ticketing	14
Ticket Marketing	11
Game Day Personnel	4

Note that this chart merely states "positions listed." In many cases, the team employs several people under one heading. In ticket-related activities, many tasks have specific job titles, including everything from "Manager, Youth Marketing" to "Service Assistant, Premium Seating." In the forty-one years between media guides, twenty-three new positions were added to the Dodgers' ticketing staff. The 1961 team drew 1.8 million fans in their last year of playing at the L.A. Coliseum. In 2000, the team drew almost 2.9 million fans. The extra employees all have one basic job: to sell the team.

All in all, the Dodgers' front office went from 14 positions to 146, while the average ticket price rose from $2.04 to 15.44. While the 1961 media guide probably skimped on adding a few names, and the twenty-first century addition might have given out the maximum amount of acknowledgement, the point is that the scale of the team's business grew dramatically and so did the staffing requirements. Essentially, the team created many more categories to sell, even if the game on the field changed very little. Selling tickets expanded from single-game ducats to season packages, premium seating, and corporate deals. More important, the buyer's expectation of service escalated. The ticket buyer of the twenty-first century, especially at the higher price levels, expects a more sophisticated sales relationship than buying them through a window.

Today, teams want to sell everything and anything. Daniel Snyder, owner of the Redskins, has sold tickets to fans attending training camp. The Houston Texans sell tailgate tickets for pregame parties, grossing $1.5 million from their first-year, tailgate-ticket sales. The Texans figured that people want to eat and drink before the game, and that they might as well be the ones to profit from the activity. They constructed twenty-six tents that could host over one thousand people and they were in business. Revenue from special tailgate areas never would have been a consideration for a franchise in the early days of sports, but as the platform grows, everything has a price attached to it. If the concept really takes off, the tents will become permanent pavillions, and companies like Kingsford Charcoal and other barbecue-related sponsors will emerge as part of the pregame fun.

The 2001 sports industry was a $194 billion industry. Money comes and goes in and around all aspects of the competition. From gambling to equipment and medical expenses, billions of dollars change hands via the platform of sports entertainment. From the competition at the core of every sports event, these powerful and profitable interests manifest via long-term sponsorships and sales rights.

WHERE THE MONEY IS SPENT

Huge purchaes of sports entertainment and its marketing opportunities means that a lot of good old-fashioned selling goes on.

PURCHASES	AMOUNT SPENT (Annually)
On-site Spending	$26,100,000,000
Tickets, Parking, Concessions, Seating Preferences	
Advertising	$27,400,000,000
Facility Signage, All TV, Radio, Print	
Sporting Goods	$25,600,000,000
Equipment, Footwear	

Operating, Admin. Expenses	$22,900,000,000
Players, payrolls, (excludes travel)	
Gambling	$18,900,000,000
Horses, Internet, Sports Books	
Travel	$16,000,000,000
Fans for all forms of events	
Professional Services	$15,200,000,000
Facility, Marketing, legal, insurance	
Medical Spending	$12,600,000,000
Total Injury Costs	
Licensed Merchandise	$10,500,000,000
Pro, College	
Broadcast Rights	$6,990,000,000
Pro, College	
Sponsorships	$6,400,000,000
Includes teams, events, leagues, media	
Facility Construction	$2,480,000,000
Stadiums, facilities, speedway	
Multimedia	$2,100,000,000
Magazines, Videos, Books,	
Endorsements	$900,000,000
All categories of players (estimated)	
Internet	$239,100,000

Source: "By the Numbers 2003," Sports Business Journal, December 30, 2002, pp. 150–51.

All of this economic activity means that sellers and buyers work furiously to do deals. Furthermore, a lot of these deals go between all of the groups, keeping the wealth within the sports circle. When Gatorade signs an athlete to endorse the product, they promote the athlete within sports environments, or as a part of a sports broadcast. Hence, the industry helps perpetuate itself. In the past one hundred years, the layers of specialization on the business side have evolved like the layers of specialization within the sports themselves. From sponsorship sales organizations to broadcast to public relations firms, specialists make a difference for the event, its sponsors, and fans.

The New York City Marathon, for example, employed three outside public relations companies and has their own internal one. The mission for the agencies is to promote the event, the host organization (The New York Road Runners), and its sponsors. The thirty thousand–person race has a host of sponsors and a need to promote itself within the running community and the New York metro area as well.

The science of executing an ambitious event like the New York City Marathon means that an international strategy has to be conceived and executed. The marathon, run on the first Sunday in November, takes place in all five boroughs and attracts 2.5 million spectators. The PR blitz typically works fabulously. Segments routinely appear on national media outlets, including CNN, ESPN, *Good Morning America*, and *The Late Show with David Letterman*. Even international outlets like the BBC and Telemundo have picked up pieces of the event and broadcast it. The total global numbers have been 244 million viewers in 125 countries.[5] Adding to the enormous reach, print coverage in domestic and foreign markets has increased awareness of the event. Lastly, New York City generated $140 million in economic activity via the world class event.

SELLING SYNDROME

Events need to be packaged to fans, partners (primarily TV and radio broadcasters), licensees, and sponsors.

This syndrome spreads the sports umbrella and creates more opportunities for the properties to sell to sponsors, and more opportunities for the sponsors to sell products to the fans. Coca-Cola entered into an eleven-year, $500-million deal with the NCAA to become the exclusive partner in the soft drink, water, and isotonic beverage categories. Coca-Cola knows it has a highly desirable target market in the collegiate marketplace and that this agreement can give it a great platform to create several promotions and sales efforts over the course of the agreement. Coca-Cola wants to sell product in these three categories at colleges and universities everywhere. High schools and grammar schools are beginning to prohibit the sale of soda and other high-sugar products on their campuses, so Coca-Cola needs to cement agreements where its products can be distributed and sold.

The move to the college sponsorship program makes sense for Coke and its bottlers. They know that they are a target in the current debate over childhood obesity. It is convenient to target Coke, Pepsi, and the vending business done at these campuses as record numbers of teenagers and preteens develop diabetes, and other complications associated with obesity. In the 1980s and 1990s, the soft drink and food-vending business targeted primary and secondary schools in many of their business development deals aimed at expanding their sales figures. Often they would enter sponsorships to school districts, or leagues, for cash and the privilege to place their vending machines around the various campuses. The arrangement helped the schools raise money for all sorts of programs, including sports programs, and it gave the companies direct, exclusive access to a prime market.

Because the "selling syndrome" had evolved to include the needs of the sponsor and manufacturer, implementation was swift and simple. Coca-Cola may lose at the high school level in the soda category, but might be able to reposition some of their juice and water products in the existing soda machines for the school districts that want to restrict actual soda sales.

The selling syndrome means that every possible sales channel gets explored. Boxers have worn temporary tattoos into the ring. High-school basketball phenom LeBron James played some of his final high school games on Pay-Per-View and on ESPN.[6] The word of mouth on James created so much interest that ESPN, after the first James game, had one of its three highest basketball game ratings ever. The curiosity over LeBron James was only surpassed by two previous Duke–North Carolina contests, a storied rivalry. James, an amateur, made no money directly from the experience. Instead, the exposure increased his legend. Once he made it to the NBA, his first deal with Nike was worth $90 million and his replica jersey sold like hotcakes. Before playing a single professional game, James became an integral part of the NBA's selling cycle.

The selling of sports has made an impact on all the athletes, too. PGA Tour purses grew by 272 percent from 1992 to 2002. Over that same time span, NBA salaries increased by 200 percent, the NFL's 65 percent, and Major League Baseball players enjoyed a 109 percent increase.[7]

DEPLOYING A DIFFERENT TYPE OF SALESMAN

At the beginning of the twenty-first century, Michael Jordan was still playing basketball, still promoting products and still driving the engine of the NBA. But there was another Mike on the horizon, and this one plays with a different ball. Michael Vick, in his second season, ascended to the role of starting quarterback and franchise savior of the Atlanta Falcons. The Falcons have been in the NFL for well over thirty years and have had some memorable players like Tommy Nobis, Steve Bartkowski, and Jamaal Anderson. They even played in a Super Bowl in 1998. But they never had anyone like Vick. Trading with San Diego for the rights to draft Vick, the Falcons gambled that this multifaceted QB could lead the team from the doldrums, both competitively and perceptually.

Atlanta had become a tough sports town. With so many transplants and transient white-collar business interests moving there, the core constituency of fans has been difficult to galvanize. All of the teams play in premium facilities and one of them, the Braves, has epitomized success for over ten years. But for reasons that are tough to pinpoint, though evident in the empty seats, Atlanta sports teams, including the Falcons, do not enjoy rabid, unconditional support. Vick might be the guy to change that. The early behavior of the fans would seem to indicate it. In his first season as starter, the team not only sold out every home game, but they sold twenty-two private suites, twelve more than they had privately hoped to sell. They also sold nine hundred club seats, approximately twice as many as they sold during their Super Bowl season of 1998.[8] In his rookie year, Vick made a lot of appearances and assumed some off-field obligations. In his second year, he scaled back to concentrate on football, and the franchise and its fans became the beneficiaries.

He even tape recorded a message the team's marketing department sent out to season ticket holders: "Hi, this is Mike Vick, quarterback of your Atlanta Falcons. As I'm sure you know, we've got a big game this Sunday against the New Orleans Saints. We already beat them once in their house, and I'm sure my cousin (New Orleans quarterback) Aaron Brooks is going to be looking for revenge. That's why we need the 12th man out there making some noise at the Georgia Dome, cheering us on."

After the team won the game, Vick called again to thank everyone for showing up. Judging by the fans' response, Vick brings that degree of electricity to the stadium that few players have. Jordan, Gretzky, Montana, Bird, and Shaq are all players that helped define their teams' images, enthused a fan base, and elevated the profile and value of a franchise. If Michael Vick can maintain his health, he has a chance to bring the Falcon franchise to that rare space in modern sports history.

FORE! SELLING ATTITUDE AND IMAGE IN GOLF

Perhaps no space or demographic appeals to manufacturers quite like the golfing demographic. Tens of millions of Americans say that they are golfers and they all share one important attribute, they love to buy lots of golf-related products. Most important, they have the money to spend on golf equipment. That makes golf marketing an exciting place for observation. The two most prevalent areas for purchases and change, in terms of technology and marketing muscle, come in the golf-ball market and the driver club market.

Many balls and clubs perform capably. One of the most fun activities for golfers of all levels is to experiment with new equipment. The golf ball industry had clear lines until the late 1980s when Titleist, Top Flite, and Wilson dominated the marketplace. Today, the landscape has many more players. Peruse the shelves in any pro shop and the aforementioned brands compete with Pinnacle, Maxfli, Precept, Strata, Hogan, Callaway, and the new kid on the block, Nike. And they all have several different types of balls. Some claim to spin more, to go straighter, to roll better, to not cut or disfigure. The one thing they all can agree on is that they make the ball that goes the farthest. The bad news for these companies is that they all make great products and the field is highly competitive. The good news is that players use approximately 4.5 balls per round and always search for a way to hit it farther and longer. Hence, eager buyers can always be found.

Wilson thinks that the average golfer is far more interested in having a good time with his buddies and relaxing than really thinking about the flight dynamics of various construction techniques. Wilson feels that performance attributes are too abstract and, instead, wants to go after personality. Hence, its product team has developed the "Jack" ball. The name does not refer to golfing great Jack Nicklaus, but the phrase "You don't know Jack!" Wilson's Jack ball has no intention of ever finding its way out onto the PGA Tour, but they want to be at the Harrington Golf and Country Club in Harrington, Washington, and all of the other outposts that support the game for the players who comprise the largest majority of golfers, the weekend hackers and duffers. Wilson will put an initial $3 million into a campaign that approaches the recreational golfer in nontraditional forms of male media: Maxim Magazine or ESPN *SportsCenter* instead of the strict golf media.

Wilson's gamble is a smart one. The manufacturers might deliver superior designs, but the end user has no bandwidth for the details. They want to tee up a ball, swing hard, and not worry if it rolls out of bounds. Wilson knows that the National Golf Foundation has conducted extensive research indicating that the greatest opportunity for growth in the game comes from those who currently play less than twenty-five rounds per year, and those that consider themselves former golfers. These are players who do not care about losing a ball. They care more about swinging hard and laughing hardest. This large and attractive group of potential players just needs a little nudge. By appealing to their sense of humor, Wilson hopes to lure them out to the links for the fun aspect first and for playing pleasure second. Wilson knows that those who derive pleasure from playing are the customers who have an interest in the ball specifics and will want to test a variety of designs and manufacturers to get the best fit for their game. For that customer, Wilson markets the "True" ball. But for the more casual golfer, Wilson thinks the new "Jack" might find a loyal and profitable niche.

Wilson's main concern has very little to do with its ability to develop, manufacture, and market products. Wilson is more concerned with what its competitors do in the marketplace. And no competitor can do what Nike is doing, because no competitor has a marquee personality like Tiger Woods.

The Tiger Factor

When Nike signed Tiger Woods in 1996, they won the golf lottery. When they renegotiated his contract in 2000, a sportswriter named Michael Bamberger referred to the $100-million deal as the "deal of the century."

In sports marketing terms, Bamberger might have underestimated the magnitude of the Nike-Woods alliance. This contract was the deal of any century. Tiger Woods's name, likeness, greatness, and focus cannot be accurately appraised. If he never hits another golf ball, it is likely he will still be considered the greatest player of all time. In fact, the only reason people don't mention that in every descriptive breath is that they need to leave some suspense in his life. He's not even near the age of thirty and he might not have peaked as a player.

Prior to his arrival, Nike Golf was a few spiked shoes, a Curtis Strange endorsement, and some apparel that didn't really register with the golfing community. Tiger's name alone increased sales by 100 percent in the first year. Now with a few years of working experience, Nike is poised to take advantage of Woods's status as the world's number on player and most influential global presence.

Before the Ryder Cup matches in 2002, Woods switched to new Nike irons, leaving the Titleist irons that had helped him win eight Majors and tens of millions of dollars, in the closet. "Any time we get him to switch, it adds credibility to our products and shows people we're serious. It doesn't just help this product. It helps the whole product line," said Kel Devlin, the global sports-marketing director for Nike.[9] And that might even underestimate the impact of Woods's playing decision.

Not only is Woods the best-compensated spokesman in the industry, he is also the single most exciting individual in sports. Tiger delivers for the golf fan and the industry. Since he has come on tour, ratings have increased, and so have the tournament purses. Tiger's success has brought more people and more money into the professional golf world. And he might be the one guy to have verifiable "trickle down" influence. Nike, one of his original endorsers, moved into the serious end of the golf manufacturing business by producing balls and then clubs. After approximately two years in the serious golf business (balls and clubs in addition to shoes and apparel), Nike Golf generated $450 million for the company. Riding Tiger's success, Nike Golf not only positioned itself as a major player, it literally became one.

Nike persuaded Tiger to switch golf balls in the late spring of 2000. After ninety-eight tournaments with Titleist, he tried a Nike ball in Germany. But even overseas, what Tiger does is news. The press seized on it and publicized Woods's switch. He had the clause in his contract with then-sponsor Titleist that he could try other balls and equipment. When he made the change, he put a rocket under Nike Golf, starting with the ball. The ball is the perfect way to sample the brand. Golf balls, by design, need to be replaced.[10] Nike makes it easy for finicky, brand-loyal players try one of its products with minimal investment. As Tiger kept on winning and adding to his legend, the balls sales kept soaring as well.

Nike had 1.3 percent of the $1.5-billion golf-ball market in May 2000. After Woods won the U.S. Open and British Open with the Nike ball, its share of the market rose one full percentage point to 2.3 percent. As Woods keeps winning, the percentage of share goes with him. Tiger Woods sells, and he does it convincingly. It should be noted that Nike Golf has also taken advantage of associations with other great players, such as David Duval, the winner of the 2001 British Open, but it is Tiger who receives the emphasis of their campaigns. And Nike should be applauded for nurturing the relationship with Woods. Nike signed Tiger in 1996, and he won his first Major, the Masters, in 1997. He started playing the Nike ball in 2000 and Nike irons in late 2002. He has also used the Nike driver and won two Majors with it, but rotated another driver into his bag. All golfers experiment and rotate equipment. The difference is, when Tiger Woods does it, people notice. Nike, which owns almost 4 percent of the driver market, knows it'd own closer to zero without Tiger.

Tiger Woods is the largest single attraction in the history of golf. And he has only been a professional for six years! His victory at Augusta in 2002 resulted in a 9.9 Sunday rating for CBS, the broadcaster. This audience represents a 40 percent increase in ratings over the previous three Majors when he wasn't in contention on Sunday. The three highest Saturday/Sunday afternoon ratings in the forty-seven years of airing the event also correspond to Woods's three victories. It is not a coincidence. The public likes Tiger and they really like it when he wins. And in the six short years that he has worked with Nike, his success has completely reconfigured Nike's Golf business. Simply put, Tiger sells.

Nike Golf, still in fledgling mode in 2003, has over three hundred dedicated employees to its golf business, selling, marketing, manufacturing, and designing balls, shoes, clubs, drivers, and wedges. Nike learned how to leverage megastars like Bo Jackson and Michael Jordan, but Nike was limited to primarily shoes and apparel in its golf business. With Tiger Woods as its lightning rod, Nike Golf can now effectively brand anything found in a player's bag as well as on his body.

Nike's motivation is not to merely barge in and claim market share. Nike knows that the golfer is as close to a recession-proof customer as it can find. And not only do the customers have money, they have a longer lifetime playing the sport. Not too many people play basketball, football, or the "sweat while chasing a ball sports" for more than twenty years. Will a fifty-year-old man buy a pair of Air Jordans? He might, but he is more apt, as a golfer, to need a new driver every few years, or several sleeves of balls, maybe some clubs and apparel, in addition to shoes. People play golf for forty or more years, and there are higher margins on golf equipment, so it is a shrewd move by Nike to leverage its best promotional spokesperson, Tiger Woods, to the fullest.

Nike's best move is its deliberate pace. Starting with the ball in the 1990s and then later moving into the driver, wedge, and irons market, Nike is being patient with the golf consumer. Nike knows better than to think it can just swoosh its way to the top; it needs to earn its place with the discerning golf customer. Winning over Tiger Woods is the highest standard.

Cobra: A Star Brand Selling a Driver without a Star Vehicle

Golfers may lose an average of 4.5 balls per round, but they pull out their drivers an average of ten times per round as well. It is the single most important swing, in the mind of the golfers, on any hole. Jeff Harmet, general manager of Cobra Golf, which manufactures the driver that Tiger Woods first used when he exploded on to the PGA Tour in 1996, states the manufacturer's philosophy behind promoting the driver: "The driver is the point of entry with the customer. It creates excitement. A great performing driver can generate strong 'word of mouth.' When golfers go into the office on Monday; they talk about bombing drives past their buddies, not finessing iron shots. It is much easier to pull people into your irons in the wake of the driver, but it is harder to go the other way. And it is easier to get people talking passionately about a quality driver than a high-performance sand wedge."[11] Harmet knows that big drives mean much more to the golfer's ego than those short, four-foot putts, even though they count the same on the score card. Putting and iron shots are moments of precision, of getting a ball near a target. On the other hand, hitting a driver just plain feels good. And the thought of success off the tee moves products from the retailer to the golf bag.

As Cobra Golf's top strategist, Harmet knows his customer. "We want to tap into the excitement and promise of hitting a great tee shot. It is the one shot most golfers want to master. Golfers control everything on their tee shot. We want them to feel if they hit our driver, they will have better control over the hole, and more enjoyment from their game."[12]

Selling a driver goes after the customer's emotion. With so many manufacturers like Ping, Taylor Made, Titleist, and Nike putting out great products and substantial marketing support behind them, the marketplace is very competitive. Manufacturers need to develop products that work and get the customers to try them.

In the case of Cobra, it has a great tradition of quality club-making and excellent visibility. For a long period, the company had the best player in the first half of the 1990s, Greg Norman, as the company's spokesman. With the charismatic and bold Norman as a frontman, the company rode his popularity, and early innovation (in the early 1990s, Cobra brought the first oversize iron to the market), to early marketing successes. Cobra wants to get back its customer base by bringing back quality products and getting golfers to test them at demonstration days at courses and ranges around the United States.

Harmet does not want to go the tour-player way of marketing. Instead, he wants to develop superior products and talk about their performance features in targeted marketing communications. "Our print support is unique and breaks through the clutter," says Harmet. "For example, most driver print ads that you see today are fairly standard: heavy in copy and they say the same thing . . . greater distance and forgiveness, a bigger sweet spot via a thinner, hotter face. At Cobra, we talk about the sweet spot in a unique way. We promote nine points on the face of the driver where the ball return speed is optimal. We market our nine-point sweet spot as the element that differentiates our driver product line. Discussing a sweet zone is more intuitive than talking about a "thin" face."[13]

Cobra knows that it cannot take on the task of signing up marquee players. A part of the Acushnet Company (Titleist, FootJoy), Cobra will fulfill a niche not dominated by names like Woods, Mickelson, and Els. "If you market through the PGA Tour, you have to take one of two primary strategies. One is that you get a top player (or players), a star like Cobra had in Greg Norman. Option two is that you go to a numbers game, where you get a deep Tour staff promoting the credibility of your product. While it is great to have Tour players validate your product, it is a costly game. The real problem lies in determining ROI. Yes, the validation of a Tour player means a lot. But, will they offer the best return on investment at retail?"[14] For Cobra to sell into its channels, it will not rely upon the name of a single celebrity, or even a passel of them. Harmet and his staff are going the old-fashioned route: direct communication with the trade sales interests and the customers.

Harmet states: "Our rebirth story at Cobra calls for a more direct impact strategy over the short-term. We are maximizing the 'hands-on' trial opportunity. If we can accomplish that, we have confidence that will compel a purchase decision. If we focus on demonstration days at local courses and on optimizing performance/price ratios at retail, we will increase our market share if the product performs. As part of the Acushnet Company, we have a lot of advantages. One is that we share the Titleist sales force, and it is the strongest sales force in the industry. We do have some separate Cobra Sales people at the national level, but we rely on the Titleist channel for regional selling. However, we maintain our own separate research and development team that really shapes our identity through our product development, so there is no ambiguity to our respective images."[15]

In the high-stakes game of golf marketing, companies like Cobra simply need to develop great products. Harmet concurs. "Product performance is everything! And we want to promote as long a life cycle as we can. It used to be that manufacturers could expect a three- to four-year life cycle out of a new product. Now, there is so much pressure to hit numbers that it is driving product development faster than ever. Coupled with the advent of new technologies, materials, and construction, the temptation to develop new products is a strong one. But it is a double-edged sword. Some companies develop on a 'planned closeout' mentality, where, for example, they plan to introduce a new product at price A for eight months, and then discount it to price B for four months before introducing a new product in the thirteenth month. And they schedule production accordingly. That puts them, and their sales channel, out on a slippery slope."[16]

IN THEIR OWN WORDS: A TRUE SALESMAN

Fred Wagenhals, CEO and founder of Action Performance Companies, Inc., parlayed a lifelong interest in motorsports into a half-billion-dollar-a-year business. His company produces the industry standard in racing collectables. Their brands include Action Racing Collectables, the Racing Collectables Club of America, Revell Collection, Winner's Circle, and Chase Authentics. Sold at the racetrack, on QVC, though mass-market retailers like Wal-Mart and Kmart, and over ten thousand "mom and pop" stores around the United States, Action Performance continues to set a standard for quality and value in racing collectables. Wagenhals's key move was signing Dale Earnhardt to an exclusive arrangement with Action Performance in early 1994. The combination of Wagenhals's marketing savvy and Earnhardt's charisma proved to be a winning formula as Earnhardt became, next to Michael Jordan, the most valuable license in all of sports. More important, Wagenhals's story, like that of so many other sports marketing visionaries, demonstrates that perseverance and patience can lead to success.[17]

Getting Started

"I was interested in motor sports since I was fifteen; playing with hot rods and getting involved with drag racing. It was the James Dean influence. Drag racing started to become famous, especially where I came from in Ohio, when *Rebel Without a Cause* came out. That movie fueled a fire among kids like myself and gave us the urge to get involved in racing.

"I went to Daytona and saw the 500 for the first time in 1959. My first thought was 'who in the hell is going to watch people run around in a circle?' I really felt that stock car racing would never catch on. Drag racing was loud, fast, and fun. I loved it, the motors and the speed. It was as much fun as a kid could have, and I won a lot of races and trophies, but no money. My dad told me, 'go down to the store and try to buy some food with those drag racing trophies you have.' He made his point, but I couldn't completely stay away from motors and speed.

"I became involved in a snowmobile business and go-carts and anything that had a motor attached to it. By the 1980s, I saw an article that said the baseball card industry was worth a half billion a year, so I thought that building a stock car replicate and putting a card with it would make for a great package.

"I became a founder in a company that is now my competitor, Racing Champions. My idea was to enter the collector market, and the other people felt that the company needed to stay in mass retail. In 1992, we split up and I formed Action Performance.

"I knew that my concept of a high-end collectable market could succeed if I could get the Michael Jordan of motorsports, Dale Earnhardt, to sign an exclusive deal with us. That was the key component, getting exclusivity. Only with that element could the Earnhardt name and image be managed properly so that the company could grow with the popularity of NASCAR."

An Important Phone Call

"Neil Bonnet set up the clinching conversation with Dale Earnhardt. I had been trying to track him down for months, and enlisted Neil to help me out. They were hunting when Neil called me. We ended up making the deal over the phone. Dale wanted a guarantee of $300,000 up front. I sold my house and gave him the money. That meant that I owned nothing except the chance to take the Earnhardt name and market a unique product to a passionate group of fans. But I knew that it was all that I needed.

"In those days, the stick-and-ball sports had some rough times. It seemed like players were either going on strike or getting into trouble with the law. Motorsports, and especially NASCAR, offered a refreshing alternative. NASCAR was clean-cut American drivers who drove American cars. And the fans had a unique sense of community at the races. The drivers were average guys, very accessible, and it made for a great fit. I originally thought that the racing collectible business was a $50 million industry, but I was wrong. We are aiming to do $500 million in 2003.

"The best idea I had, next to the exclusive licenses, was to build distinct distribution channels and produce sales figures that the public could believe in. So I needed two products: one for collectors and another for mass retail. I knew if we could control the distribution component, then we could expect to grow over time.

"We have three distinct channels. The first is the Racing Collectables Club of America, and we manufacture products exclusively for these collectors. It is the most discriminating and passionate group that we cater to, and they buy over $30 million worth of products every year.

"Our Action Racing Collectables sells through seventeen distributors to over 10,000 hobby and specialty stores in the U.S. Our third line, Winner's Circle, sells in Kmart and Wal-Mart. Our goal is to keep the distribution strong and deliver great products into the channel."

February 18, 2001

"I had dinner and drinks with Dale on his boat the Wednesday before he died. I told him that he had laid the foundation for a company that was getting ready to explode. His last words to me were, 'one of these days, I might put a roof on the company.'

"That Sunday, on Fox's first Daytona 500 broadcast, Dale died. The coverage of the race and the magnitude of the moment took everything to the next level. In the wake of the tragedy, the Earnhardt phenomenon just grew. Our sales went from $250 million to $407 million. Everyone in the racing community lost so much when Dale died. He had a way about him that made others feel important. When he talked, people listened. And when he raced, everyone rooted for him. His influence will never leave the sport and his kind will never be seen again."

Looking Ahead

"There's an old saying: 'Win on Sundays, sell on Mondays.' We need to position ourselves as being a reliable way to make money, because the new drivers are a different breed. You won't see guys like Earnhardt and Petty and Waltrip, who drove for twenty years. Guys will drive for six to ten years and leave the business. Dale once told me that he discovered the next Dale Earnhardt, and that his name was Dale Earnhardt, his son. Dale couldn't have known how much success any of us would have, but he could tell that his son was a great driver and personality. And he was right about his son. He is becoming the biggest name in NASCAR and the most important active driver for us.

"We have the Earnhardt name through 2013, and we are the ones to market it tastefully and appropriately. We will constantly search for the next new guy and maintain our standards so that we will be the best option in the market. We do special marketing programs, or premium promotions, with big brand companies and that will be a business worth over $25 million next year. The simple concept of licensing has many outlets, and it is our job to explore the markets that make sense. We manufacture an NFL towel line, but we wouldn't want to do hats or T-shirts and compete with four other licensees in the category. We have learned that the key to our success comes with exclusivity with the personality.

"NASCAR is almost like a cult. I have had Daniel Snyder and Jerry Jones come and spend time with us. They wanted to see how we made money, and they are amazed at the loyalty and passion of our fans. I think the fans know how hard it is for these drivers to make it. They know that nothing came easy and that they earn their pay every Sunday.

"In 1959, at that first Daytona 500 I saw, there might have been 30,000 people. Back then, it was a bunch of white and blue shirts, no souvenirs. Now it is a sea of energetic people all dressed in the shirt and hat of their favorite driver. As the money grows and the big companies come in, more major cities, like Denver and Seattle, will start building racetracks. NASCAR is now one of the big boys. Sponsoring a racing team costs $18 million a year, and you offer a sponsor a big billboard that criss-crosses the nation. It comes down to the corporate person buying that hood of a car, or a swoosh on a wristband. Which will be a better marketing tool? The fans will decide.

"We will keep doing what we do well and develop new programs that make sense for our company, customers and drivers. We have made special cars featuring Elvis Presley and James Dean images. We plan on working with other iconic figures, such as Marilyn Monroe, in 2003. I figured that there are 545,000 people in Elvis fan clubs, maybe they'd like a car even if they aren't NASCAR fans.

"I look back at my life, and I am a fortunate guy. If you never give up, it is tough to beat you. Working the hardest doesn't mean you'll always be successful. You need breaks and can't quit. I never wake up and think I've got it made. We work hard every day to maintain our success and show the new generation of drivers that we will work just as hard for them as we did for our original guys. People look at me and think I'm a huge success. Well, instant success took me twenty-five years."

NOTES

1. Who can forget "Up With People," an oft-mentioned, eminently forgettable halftime show? Number of halftime appearances by the musical group Up With People in the first 20 Super Bowls: 4. Number of halftime appearances by Up With People in the past 17 Super Bowls: 0.

2. During the 2002 NFL season, Sega wanted to dent the dominating Madden Football franchise which had ruled the football video game category for thirteen years. To make in-roads, Sega put $15 million into promoting its game, but it was to no avail. Madden Football ended up outselling the Sega NFL 2K3 game by a ten-to-one margin.

3. From a 2000 study by Natahn and Associates on the U.S. economy. "Essential Facts about the Computer and Video Game Industry" [online], http://www.theesa.com/IDSABooklet.pdf [September 15, 2003].

4. Michael Heistand, "Check out these items . . . ," USA Today, November 22, 1994, p. 3C.

5. Wayne Henninger, "NYC Marathon divided PR . . . ," Sports Business Journal (January 12, 2003): 9.

6. Fourteen counties in northeast Ohio will offer games on PPV, or about 600,000 homes, for about $4 to $7 a game. Additionally, most home games will be played at the 6,000-seat University of Akron arena. The venture will be a partnership between Time Warner and James's school.

7. Ron Sirak, "Peddling Harder," *Golf Digest* (February 2003): 75.

8. Ira Miller, "MVP Candidate," *San Francisco Chronicle*, November 22, 2002, p. C4.

9. "Tiger Switches to Nike Irons," MSNBC [online], www.msnbc.com/news/809513.asp [January 11, 2003].

10. According to Callaway research, golfers lose 4.5 balls per 18-hole round.

11. Jeff Harmet, personal interview, November 25, 2002.

12. Ibid.

13. Ibid.

14. Ibid.

15. Ibid.

16. Ibid.

17. From a personal interview with the author.

CHAPTER 12

THE FUTURE
OWNING AND SHAPING THE SPORTS INDUSTRY

We don't sell basketball, we sell fun experiences in a group environment, and technology tends to make things individual. So you won't see us do anything technological while the game is going on.
—Mark Cuban, Owner of the Dallas Mavericks

Would Peter O'Malley, Tom Yawkey, Harry Frazee, Charlie Finley, or even Bill Veeck have spoken like Mark Cuban? Probably not. Ownership and stewardship of a sports brand in the twenty-first century is a much more complicated task than it was at any point in the past. Yet it is in their hands that so much will be determined. Will the leagues, events, and athletes truly be marketed globally, or will the emphasis remain on the local markets and the reliable revenue streams of today? Many owners, leagues, and agents of sport look to the Internet as the Holy Grail of their financial future. It used to be that we could only get NFL highlights during halftime of *Monday Night Football*. Now you can get virtually any sports highlight or news item 24/7 from multiple sources. The key question today is: "How do we make all of our content profitable?"

Mark Cuban represents both parts of sports' future direction. He is both a technologist (he sold Broadcast.com to Yahoo! for $5 billion) and a sports fan. He fell in love with NBA entertainment as a fan and knows that the competition is the true magic of sports entertainment. More important, the secret to success is still placing an exciting, winning team in front of eager fans.

THE FUTURE STARTS AT THE TOP

Ownership determines the direction of sports management as it presents itself for public viewing and patronage. Since owners control the supply chain of the sports property, they will have the most to say about the partnerships and direction of their respective sports. Cuban specifically bears watching because he wants to win for all of the right reasons, not just to build the brand of Mavericks basketball and cash out down the road.

Contrast Cuban to Carl Pohlad, owner of the Minnesota Twins. Pohlad might be the modern-day Ebeneezer Scrooge. One of the one hundred richest Americans, Pohlad owns one of baseball's best young teams. In spite of his on-field fortune, Pohlad has hesitated to put his significant resources into the team. Instead, he has had great baseball people assemble him the best team that cheapness can buy. His current gripe is a familiar one, a poor stadium.

Due to his unhappiness over this, Pohlad openly courted contraction for the Twins after the 2001 World Series, hoping to get Major League Baseball to buy him out for $150 million. Pohlad could sell the team, but then would risk someone coming in and running a fan-friendly organization that would really sully his legacy. He could invest some of his fortune in signing more of his stars to long-term contracts to motivate his fan base to support his product. But Pohlad does not consistently appear to want to pursue any reasonable solution for the public good of the franchise. He wants to cut corners and get the state to build him a new, cash-machine ballpark. He peers out at the baseball landscape and cannot believe that his team has been left behind in the stadium frenzy.

He also looks at the unruly politics of his state that let the Minnesota North Stars move to Dallas over a stadium dispute only to grovel back at the feet of the NHL to get another franchise. Pohlad is very tight with Commissioner Selig and a success in virtually every business endeavor that he has ever attempted. But, for some reason, he cannot succeed in leveraging the Twins against the municipal/state government and the citizens of Minneapolis.

Pohlad needs to go to "Camp Cuban." Mark Cuban would show Pohlad that he needs to care about the fan experience and that he can connect with their desire to have an entertaining winner. Cuban would look at the Twins and see nothing but good fortune. Cuban knows that, as an owner, you cannot be arrogant with your customers. Furthermore, fans are both educated and inundated with choices. As a team owner, one cannot be the least bit duplicitous in charting the course of the fans' team. Pohlad should realize that backroom shenanigans only irritates the fans, and makes them view him with great suspicion.

Pohlad should look within his own division for an example of how to act. In the early 1990s, the Cleveland Indians had a nucleus of great players with tremendous star quality, like Charlie Nagy, Jim Thome, and Omar Vizquel. The team signed them to long-term contracts early in their careers and made them cornerstones in the community. General Manager John Hart shrewdly assessed that they would form the competitive base for a championship run in the American League. And they performed. Nagy was a three-time all-star for the Indians and one of only two pitchers to win fifteen or more games in a row for five straight years in the mid-1990s. (Greg Maddux was the other.) Thome became the franchise leader in home runs and Vizquel crafted a reputation as the best fielding shortstop in baseball history. As the team moved into Jacobs Field in 1994, the teams revenues soared and Hart then brought in valuable free agents like Chuck Finley and Pat Borders while trading for standout players like Matt Williams, Marquis Grissom, David Justice, Ellis Burks, and Steve Reed. These players and key management personnel like Bud Black helped the Indians become perennial playoff contenders in the mid- to late-1990s.

Three things made this possible. Hart persuaded owner Dick Jacobs to commit to the young nucleus. The new stadium bolstered their cash supply, and they went out and invested it in talented ballplayers to perpetuate their window of winning. By the time the decade ended, the Indians had enjoyed one of the best stretches in recent Major League history, including 455 consecutive sell-outs at Jacobs Field.

Given Pohlad's situation—great players and no new stadium—his best chance at getting the stadium is to sign the players, build support within the political channels, and appear to be an agent for positive change, not the Grinch of the Twin Cities. The Twins turned out to be the surprise team of 2002, winning their division and advancing in the playoffs by beating the Oakland A's. That off-season, they signed Torii

Hunter, their star player, to a four year contract extension worth more than $30 million. They also made the playoffs in 2003. Maybe Pohlad learned his lesson. Time will tell. For Twins fans, one hopes that Pohlad will move his ownership style into contemporary times.

Owners are the caretakers of the sports. They largely determine the rules by which fans get to consume the entertainment. Owners also make the deals to leverage their brands across different mediums and package the personalities who will be influencers for new generations of fans and sports enthusiasts. As sports branches off into its many financial permutations and continues its evolution, the winners will be the ones who prioritize the fan's experience and perception of interaction. The minute the trust between fans and team breaks, then you have a fan willing to recalibrate his compass on another team, passion, obsession.

WHY PEOPLE WANT TO OWN TEAMS

League	2002 Revenues
NFL	$4.8 billion
MLB	$3.5 billion
NBA	$3.0 billion
NHL	$2 billion

Source: T. Lowry, "The NFL Machine," *BusinessWeek*, January 27, 2003, p. 90.

With revenues like this, and the allure of free publicity so great, professional franchise ownership remains appealing to many individuals.

Public Corporate Ownership as a Growth Industry?

As the ownership profile changed from old-school rich guy to high-profile rich guy, corporate America got involved in some of the sports action. Ted Turner bought the Atlanta Braves because it gave his SuperStation three hours of programming 162 days a year. It ultimately helped him forge a cable television dynasty that merged with AOL to become one of the largest and most diverse media companies in the world. The Tribune Company had the same strategy when it purchased the Cubs. It made great sense to own these broadcast properties outright and not pay a premium for the rights to broadcast the team, build a fan base, and only enhance the value of the club for the next round of broadcast rights negotiations.

Media companies clearly became the future of professional sports ownership in the late twentieth century. They could absorb the costs and profit the most as they leveraged the team against their media assets. But media companies in the early twenty-first century are looking to sell their teams. Why?

Simply put, media companies heavily involved in sports were getting hammered on Wall Street. AOL, Cablevision, Disney, and Comcast had lost billions as their stocks diminished in investors' eyes. When the stock price is depressed, then companies look to sell off assets. Assets like sports teams bring in lots of cash. In economic periods of booming, the power of synergy between broadcast networks and entertainment content is easily seen and, in some cases, realized. But when the tables turn, cash is hard to come by, and sports teams are perceived as luxuries, not sources of ROI.

As sports owners, media companies think that they will sell advertising to one sponsor across all platforms. There will be online, offline, new media, old media, rich media, and cross promotions across multiple platforms! These concepts, theoretically, can work, but as soon as there is a hint of a recession, the first thing that gets cut is unnecessary ad spending. And all of that ad synergy turns into unmovable inventory.

For a publicly held media company, selling a sports team does bring in millions. Shareholders also appreciate getting out of an industry with spiraling talent costs, labor uncertainty, and maxed-out income streams. Wise shareholders know that sports revenue creation areas are limited by national deals, contracts, and commitments. The reality is that public ownership of a sports franchise has very little upside on Wall Street. The basic product, athletic competition, can't readily expand into new markets, can't be spun off, franchised, or developed into an asset that has a higher ceiling than the predictable cash flows of ticket sales, broadcast contracts, licensing, sponsorship, and stadium-generated revenues. The only upside for a stockholder could be new areas of business, such as branded restaurants and retail outlets, or the elusive championship season, and more revenue via more games. But revenues are not likely to increase dramatically, or predictably enough to enhance shareholder value.

The Yankees were once owned by CBS. At the time of the sale (1973), it was one of the three most important media companies in North America. The network had landmark achievements in sports television like broadcasting the first Winter Olympics and crafting some of the first multimillion-dollar deals with the NFL. CBS was the home of Cronkite, Gleason, innovation, and tradition, but it didn't see the long-term opportunities with the Yankees. CBS sold the team for $10 million and left sports ownership.

They certainly regret selling the team for $10 million, and Disney might one day rue its 2003 sale of the Anaheim Angels, but ownership is better suited for the private sector, not necessarily rich companies that operate publicly. The best future owner is a lot like the old owner: very wealthy, egotistical, and interested in building a winner.

Senators and Sabres—Aberration or Indication?

The Ottawa Senators closed out the 2001–2002 NHL season as one of the top hockey teams in the NHL. Playing in a small media market and without a deep-pockets ownership group, the Senators still fielded an incredibly effective and entertaining team.

The only thing wrong with the team was its SCFP, or Statement of Changes in Financial Position. If any accounting professor showed the Senators' balance sheet to his or her students, it would have shown a negative cash flow. The team had to file for bankruptcy during the 2002–2003 season.

The same thing happened in Buffalo. All of a sudden, the NHL had two franchises teetering on the brink of financial collapse. The Senators owed $160 million to creditors and the Sabres had more than $206 million of debt. Compounding the problem, the league faced an almost certain labor problem on the horizon in 2004. Looming labor squabbles do not help sell professional sports teams. Healthy sports teams need labor security and a healthy TV contract. Who, exactly, would buy these teams?

No easy solution really exists. Hockey is the national sport of Canada. Furthermore, Ottawa is the capital of Canada. The sport needs to succeed there for the national purpose as well as the 1.05 million people who live there. In Buffalo, a border town to Canada, hockey is just as important. Unfortunately, it is a market barely larger than Ottawa, and with the Bills and Bisons (AAA baseball) being solid draws, the Sabres have a tough time attracting the large corporate dollars necessary to survive.

Neither team was an attractive financial target to purchase during the 2002–2003 season. Since the upside in their current locations is limited, that means potentially moving the franchises. Two problems exist with moving either team. First and foremost, both teams have nice followings and important heritage in their current places. Ottawa is the fourth largest city in Canada (behind Toronto, Montreal, and Vancouver) and the NHL needs to succeed in all of its Canadian cities. Leaving Canada cannot even be an option. Buffalo once lost an NBA team, the Braves, to San Diego in the late 1970s, and they desperately want to keep the Sabres. Not only was the team just in a Stanley Cup Final in 1999, but they also have some of the best fans in the game.

The teams had a debt load that made them poisonous to a buyer. Furthermore, the financial context of maintaining a competitive franchise meant that the new owners could not drastically cut labor costs in the short term in order to recoup revenue.

The biggest problem for fans of these and other small-market/low-revenue teams is living with the nagging lack of confidence in their ability to compete. Even as both teams get new owners, can they realistically compete in the long run? Following a team requires many resources of the fans, largely time and money. Simply put, owners want people spending their time and money to follow their franchises. The sports industry can only maintain itself as long as its credibility remains intact. Small-market teams are vulnerable and live in a constant state of financial insecurity. Leagues need to address this situation and implement sensible checks and balances in order to make the system work for all teams and their fans. The Sabres were ultimately bought by billionaire Tom Golisano, founder of the payroll company Paychex, and the Senators by Canadian billionaire Eugene Melnik. The teams need men of these resources, but their presence raises the question: how many billionaires can come to the rescue of future small-market franchises?

Labor

The other side of the management equation will always be the labor side, or athletes. They will always be the reason fans buy tickets and companies buy sponsorships. Fans don't buy tickets or watch the games on TV to see who is sitting in the owner's box, they want to see the action of the game.

The players earn the vast majority of the revenues the games produce, as they rightly should. The NFL, for example, pays out 63 percent of its revenues to the players and they have the lowest annual average salary of the major sports! Owners grumble about rising player costs, yet they are the ones agreeing to the contractual demands of the agents. The conflict inherent to the owner is that other owners want to win just as badly as they do and so there is usually another bidder on the market for a player's services.

In the first phase of the modern sports era, players did not know how much teams were making. In most cases, they didn't even know how much their teammates were making! They did not organize and share contract information. The laws inhibited freedom of employment and the owners held every advantage in negotiation. Today, the athletes have made tremendous strides in their efforts to gain a larger share of the revenues their skills help generate. And they have access to information on how much their peers earn, how much the networks pay for broadcast rights, and how much revenue teams make from their venues and select licensing agreements. The confluence of savvy representation, collective bargaining, and exploding revenues have helped the professional athlete make great strides in the field of compensation.

Salary comparison

League	Year	Average Salary
MLB	1990	$597,537
MLB	2001	$2,138,896
NBA	1990–91	$823,000
NBA	2000–2001	$4,200,000
NFL	1990	$430,000
NFL	2000	$1,116,000
NHL	1990–91	$271,000
NHL	2000–2001	$1,642,590

Sources: 1990, 1991 salaries: "Average Salaries by Sport," SLAM! Baseball [online], www.canoe.ca/BaseballMoneyMatters/Salaries-by-Sport.html [June 3, 2003]; 2001 (MLB): Major League Baseball Players' Association; 2001–2002 (NBA): "Salary Cap Information," The Red Zone [online], www.theredzone.org/capinfo.asp [June 3, 2003]; 2000 (NFL): NFL Players' Association; 2000–2001 (NHL): NHL Players' Association.

It is a great job if you can get it. Clearly, salaries have risen dramatically as more money flows into the sports industry. And no one really trusts the owners when they say that they are broke. They want cities to make concessions in order to get the best possible facility, and they want players to take "home town" discounts and not seek the highest compensation on the open marketplace. The dance between labor and management in the early twenty-first century is over revenue division. Owners claim that they lose money, yet they do not seem willing to provide the most accurate accounting of their businesses. The players, in turn, tend not to trust the information that the owners present.

The flow of information goes both ways, though. Baseball owners, for example, know that no team since 1985 has won a World Series paying one player more than 15 percent of its payroll. The data gets even more refined: only 7.7 percent of the teams allocating that 15 percent to one player have ever made the playoffs, and only two teams ('87 Cardinals with Ozzie Smith and the '02 Giants with Barry Bonds) have made it to the World Series.[1]

SPONSORSHIP IS A GROWTH INDUSTRY

In 1969, 53 percent of all advertising expenses went to ABC, CBS, NBC, and the print magazine sector.[2] Sponsorship as we know it today did not really exist. Integrated marketing campaigns where companies and sports properties weave their brands together had not been invented, much less perfected. By 1994, sponsorship had evolved and developed context. And it was big business, totaling $4.25 billion in investment.

Eight years later, total ad expenditures exceeded $249 billion and sports sponsorship alone accounted for over $6.4 billion in expenditures. The sponsorship industry keeps growing.

The big spenders like Anheuser-Busch, Coca-Cola, Nike, Pepsi, General Motors, Ford, and other long-time stalwarts keep pumping millions into opportunities. But sponsorship isn't only for the blue chippers. It has evolved to include a diverse portfolio of brands, and that has helped the industry grow.

Sports as a Logical Promotional Mechanism for Many Brands

Sports exposure, in terms of developing sponsorships, is not a precise science. Teams and athletes do not wear lab coats and perform formulaic procedures with beakers, Bunsen burners, and microscopes. Sports marketing still has a nebulous area where the exposure and consumer activities are closely related, but not necessarily 100 percent causal. Of course, smart brand managers and intuitive salesmen know that the thrill of athletic competition and the proper associations can do wonders for a brand. And they negotiate for the opportunities which provide the best fit in terms of their target markets and overall brand needs.

One of the best developments in the modern era of sports marketing has been the realization that sports can effectively market a diverse number of products and services. In the olden days, it used to be simply cars, soda, beer, and tobacco. After World War II, the oil companies and television came into the marketing mix. But by the 1990s, sports attracted diverse technology companies, banking firms, the insurance industry, and virtually every type of commercial enterprise around the globe.

Even indelible felt markers.

One of the unsung prerequisite pieces of equipment for every major sports team is the quality felt marker, or Sharpie. Like the white athletic tape used to tape ankles, or shiny silver whistles that dangle around coaches' necks, the Sharpie is ubiquitus in the entire athletic community's clubhouses, pit areas, training, and equipment rooms. Rob Grady, Director of Promotions and Public Relations, Sanford (Sharpie's parent company) sums it up best, "When someone asks for a Sharpie, they do not want an imitation product. You may ask for a Kleenex, but will really accept any facial tissue. . . . But when people say that they want a Sharpie, they want a Sharpie, not some other type of marker."[3]

Grady is right. When people want an adhesive strip for a cut, or scratch, they will ask for a Band-Aid, and gladly accept a Curad, or private label brand, as a substitute. But when it comes to indelible markers, only one product will suffice for anyone in the sports community: a Sharpie.

Sharpie, a brand of Sanford, has long been associated with celebrities, along with many other uses. Jack Paar, the former host of *The Tonight Show*, was one of the first noteworthy people to use it. Over time, the Sharpie slowly spread to athletes and entertainers for signing autographs. The practice has almost a ritual status. Mike Finn, a Sharpie spokesman, expands on the significance of celebrity moments. "Fans seek the connection to fame, and especially to their heroes. When fans walk away with an autograph, they want it to last forever. People know when they walk away with a Sharpie autograph that it will last. When people have been waiting many years to meet a celebrity, the autograph really does mean something. The Sharpie becomes an important part of the experience."[4]

Sharpies have that unique combination of name, user experience, and most important, quality. When equipment managers mark the tags of shirts and pants and need to read them six months into the season, the Sharpie makes that possible. If a fan gets a glossy autographed, he or she will want it done with a Sharpie. If a NASCAR pit crew chief wants to mark the hood of a car, he will use a Sharpie. When a golfer marks her golf ball for tournament play identification, she uses a Sharpie. Simply put, everything about the Sharpie works perfectly. Its usefulness keeps it near the teams, players and the action.

In October 2002, Sharpie got a surprise boost, when it truly became part of the game. Terrell Owens, star receiver of the San Francisco 49ers, scored a touchdown on *Monday Night Football* against the Seahawks in Seattle. Instead of the usual end-zone dance and display of emotion, he pulled a Sharpie out of his sock, autographed the ball and handed it to a friend in the stands. The incident generated nationwide publicity, a cover story on *ESPN the Magazine*, and endless talk show debate. Sharpie got millions of dollars worth of exposure through the incident. Many public relations analysts like to discuss how the incident put Sharpie onto the front pages of newspapers and on the tips of talk show hosts' tongues. But they fail to mention one thing: the universal presence of the Sharpie in the sports industry in the first place.

Like the kicking tee, the clipboard, or resin bag, the Sharpie has long held a rightful spot in sports. Had Owens pulled out a Kodak disposable camera and taken a picture of himself, the press would have reported that he pulled out a disposable camera. Kodak would surely have been dropped from the story. But that was not the case with Owens's fateful Sharpie. The brand name stayed as an integral part of the story. Ultimately, the legacy of "Sharpie-Gate," as some people in the press referred to it, will be Owens's burst of individualism and the legitimacy of the Sharpie as the product he put in his sock. Sharpie even capitalized on the moment and filmed a humorous advertisement that they ran during football games; they also decided to use Owens in later campaigns. The incident's cycle of influence will only help further elevate the brand in terms of recognition within all sectors of the sports community.

But the Sharpie has not all of a sudden emerged as a sports marketing force. It has an evolving history in the formal sports marketing scene. Its recent forays include a college bowl sponsorship (Sanford Independence Bowl) and a high-profile sponsorship with NASCAR, including its own race, The Sharpie 500.

NASCAR welcomed Sharpie with open arms as a sponsor. Rob Grady relates, "People at NASCAR felt great about Sharpie coming on board. Everyone associated with the event from NASCAR said, 'This is a no brainer!' They knew that convincing their people to integrate Sharpie into the NASCAR family had been done informally years prior. By extending it into race entitlement, it was a logical extension of an existing relationship."[5]

Sharpie's feedback supports its strategy of working both behind-the-scenes and on the front lines with sports properties. Sharpie sales grew by 24 percent in 2002. And the partnership has been quite profitable for NASCAR as well. The involvement between NASCAR and Sharpie helped NewellRubbermaid, the parent company, buy into the Kurt Busch #97 driving team. This enhances the Sharpie brand's reach into the NASCAR community even further.

Having a star driver like Kurt Busch traveling the NASCAR circuit further ties Sharpie to the consciousness of the NASCAR community, and gives Sharpie and Rubbermaid an enhanced opportunity to leverage the whole NASCAR season, not just The Sharpie 500 at Bristol, Tennessee.

Synergies abound between both properties as Busch helps promotes one of Sharpie's biggest marketing programs, a million-dollar giveaway. The million-dollar giveaway is featured on packaging at retailers, on the race car and as an identifier of the continuous loop between Sharpie, NASCAR, NewellRubbermaid, its retail partners, and customers.

Sharpie shows that the sports entertainment platform accommodates products and services that might not have received consideration in the past. And Sharpie knows how to leverage the experience. "We constantly integrate the things that we learn in working with the sports community to our overall brand strategy," says Grady. "From TV, to our store presence, sports helps us feature our products in ways the customer both understands and appreciates. We will always evaluate new opportunities to see if they makes sense for our sales objectives."[6]

The important thing that the experience of Sharpie, Sanford, and NewellRubbermaid demonstrates is that sports entertainment furthers their internal and external business objectives. If the combination of shrewd brand management, stock-car racing, and football can help increase felt pen sales by 24 percent in one year, think what that tells all buyers and sellers of sports marketing opportunities. It indicates that sports marketing works, and that other products that might not have a visibly logical place in the sports-marketing universe simply haven't tried.

OPPORTUNITIES

One last wrinkle of the sports marketing phenomenon, besides the effective promotion and placement of brands, is the innovation of products and solutions. Just as Sharpie has capitalized on its pen being used by athletes, teams, and exuberant wide receivers, many companies have looked to the sports industry as a place to develop and market new products.

Sporting events create industries and products. The memorabilia industry is one such entity. Auction houses like Sotheby's and online destinations like eBay specialize in offering rare and valuable merchandise to the eager faithful. In addition to carrying, merchandising, and perpetuating the business, they also help create a stable pricing structure. This act of perpetuating a price for an athlete's autograph, or image, helps keep the athlete in the afterglow of the sport and add to the layers around the sports entertainment industry.

On the product side, the competition identifies a need for products that have consumer crossover into the mainstream world. Gatorade and PowerBar are two brands that quickly come to mind. These are products that were developed for athletes and have become staples of the athletic experience.

Gatorade is the famous work of a group of University of Florida researchers in the mid-1960s. The Florida heat enervated the football team and they would tire in the second half of their games. Researchers developed the now-famous mixture that allows athletes to better manage their fluid and mineral retention levels. Whether the results were mental or physical, the 1965 Gators steamrolled through the season and into the Orange Bowl, crediting the product. Today it is a two-billion-dollar brand and undisputed market leader. It has rock-solid agreements with the NFL, NBA, NASCAR, the PGA, and Michael Jordan. The sports beverage is as much a part of athletics as a jockstrap.

PowerBar presents an even more interesting case. Invented by Brian Maxwell, a track and field coach from the University of California at Berkeley, PowerBar created an entirely new category of athletic energy products and forced its way into supermarket aisles around the globe, which is no easy feat. PowerBar first squeezed into bike shops and out-door outlets and then slowly, inexorably found its way into the main-stream. The product accomplished this by addressing a need for athletes of all skill levels: a healthy food source for physical activity. In 2003 the entire category will sell over $700 million in products, and it grows by 20 percent annually.[7]

PowerBar and Gatorade became so successful that they were bought out by food giants Nestle and Pepsi, respectively. From humble origins to the rarified air of Wall Street conglomerates, those two products and the billions of dollars of activity their brands and categories generate annu-ally can be directly attributed to the sports industry.

Cultural fads, likewise, find a place in the sports industry. Skate-boarding, snow-boarding, and off-road biking were once obscure hobbies. Today they are the hubs of a multibillion-dollar extreme sports industry.

Skateboarding and surf brands like Billabong, Quiksilver, and Ocean Pacific now are part of a $2.5 billion catagory.[8] Perhaps more important, many impressionable teens and grammar school kids are as likely to emulate skateboard sensation Colt Cannon as Hoops star Kevin Granett. And savvy companies, such as Element Skateboards, are there to capitalize on the opportunity that athletes like Cannon provide.

So the cycle is perpetuated. ESPN and other influential networks and content creators pour resources into building extreme sports franchises, such as the X Games. At that point, manufacturers like Quiksilver and Element Skateboards have a platform to conduct business. And personalities like Colt Cannon have a profitable place to display their talents.

Today, the infrastructure is in place in terms of venues, television producers, sales agents, talent agents, and PR people. All that trends, products, and personalities need to do is plug into the equation. Once a committed following emerges, advertisers assign it a designation like "Gen X," or "thirty-somethings" and align advertisers with it to provide the necessary subsidy to maintain the sports organism. The formula is entertainment, excitement, and suspense. If that can reliably occur, then the sponsors and broadcasters will follow the fans.

FORECASTING NEW TRENDS

In 1962, Sam Walton opened his first Wal-Mart. Eight years later, he had eight total stores and sales of $44 million. At that point, Walton took his enterprise public. Today, each Wal-Mart store does about $46 million in sales and the chain has $159 billion in annual revenues. In addition to Wal-Mart stores, there are now Sam's Clubs and inside Wal-Marts, you can eat fast food and shop for the freshest produce. Walton's humble beginnings now stretch to geographical places and financial dimensions that were not forseen in the early 1960s.

The point is that Walton built his empire slowly, surely, and by applying the lessons from regional markets and retailing on a larger scale. The same principles apply to sports entertainment. The NFL used to be a fourteen-week season, followed by the playoffs, the Super Bowl, and a long off-season. Now, it is a year-round business. A week after the Super

Bowl is the Pro Bowl, then the jockeying for free agents and the draft in April. The scouting combine precedes the actual draft and then mini-camps start up and before you know it, the teams are back at training camp and ESPN starts their review and preview of each team. The NFL is a 365-day business on a global level.

No one in the 1920s and 1930s could have predicted that the NFL would be the most popular sport in America, much less a year-round busi-ness. Similarly, prognosticating the next business trends is never easy, but one can see significant developments taking shape. One characteristic is certain. Precedents are difficult to set; but once proven, they are loyally followed.

FOUR TRENDS WORTH FOLLOWING

Preferred Pricing

Location, Location, Location: comes to a facility nearest you. Everyone knows the real estate mantra. The same theory holds true for ticket holders. Prime seats and marquee matchups on the schedule always get fans salivating. And they always will. When a new team moves into a new ballpark, franchises want to handle the coveted seats nearest the action with the utmost care. Closer and more exclusive has always been a premium item. Courtside at Madison Square Garden, behind home plate at Pac Bell Park, the fifty-yard line at Lambeau Field, or ringside at the MGM are highly desired items. It used to be that teams charged the same price for the same category of seat for each game. Now preferred pricing is attached to two obvious factors, appeal of matchup, and quality of the weather.

Perfected by the Rockies, preferred pricing brings different levels of pricing to a team's games. For example, a weekend date in the middle of the summer against a top competitor costs more than a Monday game against a weak rival. The New York Mets, San Francisco Giants, and sev-eral other teams adopted the concept after it became apparent that fans would tolerate the change. The Chicago Cubs, after a 2002 season where they lost ninety-five games, even instituted the program. Frankly, it makes sense for teams. Scalpers on the open market charge more for marquee matchups. A team has just as much of a right to leverage the legitimate demand for superior inventory as those on the secondary markets. The move could mean an additional several million dollars to a team's coffers.

A Different Kind of Facility Development

Local progressives in Ottawa have on the drawing board a concept for a massive soccer park on the outskirts of Ottawa called the Ottawa Sports Park (OSP). The concept is to develop a totally "green" (environmentally sustainable development) soccer complex to serve the community and attract national youth tournaments. They hope to lease land from the neighboring airport and extend a special light-rail line out to the park to serve the city. So far, the concept has overcome safety, environmental, commercial, bureaucratic, and political obstacles to become a leading example of potential sustainable development in North America.

Traditionally, sports and government pursue commercial development ambitions like building Olympic facilities or downtown stadiums, without regard to objectives like long-term environmental responsibility.[9] In the case of the OSP, the driving forces behind the project want government, sports, and athletics to merge their interests in order to build a long-term sustainable athletic center that will truly have no negative externalities within the community. Project leaders have had to overcome obscure issues like potential bird strikes with the neighboring air traffic in addition to the tangible concerns of federal and local transportation agencies.

The OSP knows that large soccer developments have served both community and sponsor needs elsewhere. Soccerplex, in Maryland, has over nineteen fields with plans for five more. It has also attracted several high-priced sponsors like Discovery, Pepsi, and Adventist Health Care, whose associated fees total in the millions for the development. Soccerplex hosts over 250,000 visitors each year, and has an indoor multisport facility called the Discovery Sports Center. In short, the soccer complex as a regional destination is a great idea for local residents and regional sponsors.

The Ottawa developers hope to create a similar success story in their nation's capital and add responsible environmental integration as an identifying attribute. What makes the ambition of the OSP so remarkable is that they plan to integrate advertising and marketing with the airport and rail transit authorities, even having plans for visible corporate markers for landing and departing planes, which truly opens up a whole new category of captive audience demographics! Their goal is to build thirty separate fields, an indoor sports complex, cross-country skiing trails, ice hockey rinks, and other facilities to serve local, national, and international enthusiasts. The scope means that sponsorship will make sense for companies.

In short, the OSP will be innovative from both a developmental aspect and a marketing aspect. As the first aerial billboard related to an athletic facility, the residual publicity could be worth millions to a participating company. Furthermore, as a proponent of the "green" movement, sponsors could activate the network for those seeking better environmental records for all projects. The OSP is a great idea for both the community and potential sponsors. Its timely development will only inspire more progressive, environmentally friendly facilities and unique marketing features for corporate partnerships.

Insurance Policies on Nonprofessional Athletes

With professional millions awaiting them, how do college, and even high school, stars protect themselves? Insurance, naturally. For $10,000–$13,000, a top college player can take out a $1 million policy protecting himself or herself against injury. Not too many players seek this, but top football and basketball players frequently do take out policies in order to protect their future earnings. The basic policy insures up to 65 percent of the estimated after-tax earnings of the first three years of the policy holder's professional career. Furthermore, as agents and parents smell the money, and as more teams demonstrate a willingness to invest in project players, the external industry of insurance makes sense. Young athletes have gone from playing multiple sports to specializing in one. Since they are developing themselves as precious assets, it only makes sense that they seek insurance. People have pushed teens out into the sports of tennis, golf, skating, and gymnastics for years. Team sports have merely accepted a trend over twenty years in the making.

A Different Kind of Expansion

One hundred and twenty teams of the NHL, MLB, NBA, and NFL reside in thirty-eight of the top forty-eight cities. There are some oddities, like Milwaukee having two teams, three if you count the Green Bay Packers, and Portland and Sacramento only having one each.

Perhaps the strangest data point is the fact that Jacksonville, Florida, has an NFL team and Los Angeles does not. One look at their relative market size, number 45 versus number 2, and you realize that revenue sharing does indeed work!

With respect to expansion/relocation, Los Angeles will get a football team and Washington, D.C., will most likely receive a baseball team. Whether they will be relocations of existing franchises, or brand-new expansion franchises, one would have to ask a Vegas bookie. Which brings up another point about expansion: Las Vegas. New Orleans, Salt Lake City, Nashville, Buffalo, Memphis, Raleigh, and Jacksonville all have something in common. Besides the fact that these seven cities host a total of ten professional sports teams between them, they all have smaller populations than Las Vegas, Nevada.

As professional sports looks to expand, they need to gauge their capacity to bring in sustainable business. League and team operatives already consider Mexico City a potential expansion site. The question is: Who will be the first to go there and put down roots? Sports owners must be thinking the same thing about Las Vegas. Bugsy Malone's "Sin City" has pleasantly reinvented itself as a family destination and might be poised to be home to a professional sports franchise. What makes Las Vegas such a compelling place is that the political and business climate would welcome a team with an open checkbook.

In fact, a Las Vegas team could become one of the more lucrative franchises in any sport. As a town completely reliant upon the hospitality industry, virtually every significant business would pay handsomely to have privileged access to the team. Furthermore, the town needs to legitimize and diversify its offerings to take away from the notion that gambling is the only pastime.

A simple look at the map shows that the West has concentrations of sports teams in Northern California, Southern California, Seattle, and

Denver, with a couple of outposts in Portland and Sacramento. Entire states have been left out of the professional sports franchise mix (only twenty-five states have professional franchises). But nobody does events like Las Vegas. Its tourism and convention business buoys the entire state and a professional team, especially a baseball team, would be a tremendous asset to the city's image and population. When states lobby for teams and dangle facility-friendly terms in front of contemplative owners, no one could make a case quite like Las Vegas. Not only would the state of the art facility host a team, it could also be the venue for one of its many prize fights and other major events.

The NFL is highly unlikely to have a team in Las Vegas. They won't even let the town advertise on its Super Bowl broadcast. The Las Vegas Convention and Visitor's Authority tried to be one of the sixty-one Super Bowl XXXVII advertisers at $2.2 million a spot and were denied by the league. Gambling and football might go together like peanut butter and jelly, but not with the league's public blessing. The NHL might be too risky a venture, as there is a scarcity of hockey fans in Las Vegas. The league has too much to lose by relocating to the southern tip of Nevada at this point. The NBA is on the periphery. One of its WNBA teams, the Connecticut Sun, plays on a gaming facility's property, at the Mohegan Sun Arena. The NBA also has the most progressive commissioner in David Stern. It is still a long shot.

The best fit is baseball. Not only are there a few teams (Devil Rays, Expos, Marlins) who could use a change of scenery, but Las Vegas could use the summer attraction. In a city famous for fabulous, alluring attractions, the only one it does not have is major league team sports. But the city does have a track record with professional sports. NASCAR has hosted 137,000 fans at the Las Vegas Speedway, and the PGA has been there for twenty years. It's time to make Vegas an official big-league town.

The argument that legalized gambling is too toxic for a big-league franchise has little or no merit. Not only do towns near major league cities have reservation gambling, but Atlantic City is situated near the New York–area teams. In all of the years that games have been played within driving distance of those big-league towns there has not been one problem with a player gambling. In fact, the only real gambling problem in Major League Baseball came with the Pete Rose suspension in 1989, where Rose proved you can make bad gambling decisions in nongambling towns. The problem was with Rose, not with Cincinnati. Last, many more serious problems, including drugs, alcohol, murder charges, and spousal abuse, have arisen with professional athletes in the last ten years that make gambling seem trivial.

The basic argument is that being close to gambling might make athletes and coaches susceptible to bribes, and compromise the integrity of the games. That argument is poor, at best. People can get in trouble no matter where they are. The original point-shaving scandal of college basketball happened in New York; the Black Sox scandal, of course, originated in Chicago. It is time for the NBA, NFL, NHL, and Major League Baseball to drop their bias. Pro sports should place a team in Las Vegas and give the locals a professional identity and a chance to see the best in modern athletics. They already play exhibitions there and schedule off-season events like made-for-TV home run contests. It is time to rectify the situation and let a team open up shop in Clark County and expand professional sports entertainment to a deserving community.

THE FINAL FRONTIER—THE INTERNET

The Internet began, quietly, as a military application. It was first conceived in the mid-1960s under the Department of Defense's Advanced Research Project Agency (ARPA) as a way to connect supercomputers on a network, called ARPANET. In 1969, ARPANET went live between scientists at UCLA, UC Santa Barbara, the University of Utah, and Stanford. The connection between the four academic institutions started the wiring of the world.

Much like when Guglielmo Marconi successfully transmitted the first intercontinental wireless message in 1903, the Internet would change the way the world communicated and information was processed.[10] By 1971, e-mail quickly became the most popular use of the Internet. In 1976, the queen of England sent the first royal e-mail. In 1993, a young engineer named Marc Andreesen led the development of Mosaic, the first graphical browser, the tool that allowed Internet "surfing" as we know it today.

In 1994, Andreesen started Netscape Communications, a company that would go public one year later in the most historic initial public offering of the late twentieth century. By 1996, forty million people around the globe were on the World Wide Web and over $1 billion in commerce took place in the medium. The Internet quickly became the biggest story and the acknowledged "next big thing" in virtually every industry, including sports.

Almost overnight, sports Web sites became some of the top destinations on the Web. IBM, the company that introduced sports to technology all the way back at the 1960 Winter Olympics, also built the first Olympics Web site in 1996. It was a huge success and received over 200 million hits, a staggering amount at the time. ESPN, the NBA, and the NFL all licensed their brands to Starwave and promoted their sites on national telecasts. Site traffic went through the roof as fans realized that they could follow their teams, fantasy leagues, and players via their computers. On the evolutionary scale, the Internet is still a fairly recent development, so it is impossible to gauge its true potential. One thing is certain: usage is growing. Online sales were $1 billion in 1996. According to Forrester Research, that figure toped $76 billion in 2002. Furthermore, aggregate advertising exceeded $4 billion in 2002, after being only a skimpy $1 million in 1994. Clearly the medium, as a place where people aggregate and act, is growing.

And the Internet does loom in the minds of broadcasters. CBS recently bought the NCAA basketball championship rights for $6 billion over eleven years, a 250 percent increase over the last contract with the NCAA. But this contract also gives them the radio and Internet rights as well, so CBS will be able to deliver the NCAA tournament in all of its electronic formats over the period of the contract. By the end of the deal, CBS will either have made the best deal ever, by locking up Internet rights that prove to be lucrative, or they will have simply entered into an agreement that was ambitious in scope, but did not mature in the lifetime of the contract. With the popularity of the tournament ranking behind only the Super Bowl, CBS knows that creating franchises with its TV, Infinity Radio, and CBS Sportsline (Internet) brands make a lot of sense conceptually and financially.

The World Wide Web is so alluring, because it can aggregate viewers, and activate purchases from their audience instantly. The switch from passive viewing to active consuming is one that attracts significant attention and why so many brands and properties look to develop the Internet component of their business wherever possible. As more forms of media converge online, the investment and returns from the medium will continue to increase.

Online Marketplace: The Leader and Undisputed Champ

Out of all the hype emanating from Silicon Valley's technology companies in the 1990s, perhaps no other company delivered on its promise like eBay. Founded in 1995, eBay got an early taste of the power of the sports industry as it built a part of its core community through the impassioned world of memorabilia sales.

eBay's seamless service of online auction sales helps tie people to the Internet trinity of content, community, and commerce. Today, over one million items are up for auction at eBay Sports each day, and a sports related transaction takes place every second! In short, eBay is an unbelievable marketplace for both buyers and sellers. In the average week in 2002, these items were bought or sold:

- 20,000 autographed sports items.
- 60,000 pieces of memorabilia.
- 200,000 trading cards.
- $1,442,307.60 worth of tickets.[11]

eBay is such a flexible platform that it even featured the Dartmouth Men's and Women's Swimming and Diving team in an auction. An enterprising student dating a Dartmouth team member wanted to see his girlfriend's team stay afloat rather than fall victim to the announced budget cuts. He looked to the public marketplace for a solution, but did not find it through the *Wall Street Journal* or a fancy consultancy. He went to eBay, and he received bids, too! The auction attracted a bid for $212,000 before university officials had it removed.

Greg Fant, eBay sports director, sums it up best. "We empower individuals and businesses to sell. Our 'secret sauce' is that we rely upon

others to do what they do best, and we merely provide the tools."[12]
Secret sauce indeed. eBay had more than sixty-two million registered
users as of January 2003, and boasts one of the "stickiest" sites on the
entire Web (sticky refers to the length of time browsers tend to spend
while in the domain).

Rank	Site	Unique Users	Hours
1	AOL/Time Warner	50,807,000	2:03:31
2	Microsoft	43,835,000	0:35:55
3	Yahoo!	38,110,000	0:43:59
4	Google	13,180,000	0:07:29
5	**eBay**	**12,207,000**	**0:50:58**
6	Amazon	10,496,000	0:13:18
7	RealNetworks	8,355,000	0:12:22
8	Terra Lycos	8,348,000	0:10:18
9	About-Primedia	7,749,000	0:09:11
10	Sharman Networks	7,551,000	0:56:18
11	United States Government	6,900,000	0:10:16

Source: Nielsen NetRatings, December 1, 2002.

The above statistic applies to all of eBay, not just eBay Sports. The gaudy
figures, though, help explain the success of the entire eBay community.
eBay not only attracts users, but its content retains them with far greater
success than its competitors.

"Just a few short years ago," Fant relates, "companies had to consider
the Internet as a necessary function of their brand. Now eBay is here to
help broaden their market and help increase their profits."[13] eBay Sports
is simply a logical extension of the larger eBay community. It came about
as the total dollar value of transactions approached one billion for the
category (remember, total global online commerce for 1996 was one billion). Fans clearly gravitate toward their favorite teams and players, so it
makes sense that eBay, the ultimate aggregation of online merchants,
would start its own sports brand.

And eBay Sports offers unique opportunities. For sports fans, they
can bid on premium experiences like a round of golf with Tiger Woods,

or take a special ride with Lance Armstrong. Prior to eBay, you had to be the president of the United States or a rock star if you wanted a chance to do anything like that. But the world's largest marketplace can create unique opportunities.

It can also create a whole new complementary sales channel that can help a manufacturer. One such program is called Callaway Pre-Owned.[14] Callaway retailers are authorized to give consumers coupons to buy new clubs when they trade in their old clubs. Callaway then puts the used clubs through an exhaustive, ten-step refurbishment process to ensure the clubs meet their standards. The certified, refurbished clubs are sold on eBay. In the example of the Callaway pre-owned clubs, the tool of the Internet merges with the passion of the golfer and the quality-driven concerns of the manufacturer all through the personal exchange of the retailer-customer relationship. You don't need to be a motivational speaker to know that is a win-win situation.

Another "win-win" involved the 2002 Salt Lake City Winter Games. As Fant explains, "Mitt Romney [executive director of the Games] is a visionary who decided to take the top sixty events, sell the best tickets on eBay, and give all the money to the Paralympics. By selling the tickets on the eBay platform, the Paralympics received an average of eight times the face value of the ticket. We did a big push on eBay itself and placed ads in the USA Today to promote the venture."[15] This kind of opportunity did not exist prior to eBay galvanizing the sports fan around its auctions. Maintaining the interest of a diverse, passionate community is its greatest trait and the key to enduring success.

eBay Sports keeps itself relevant because its community believes in it as a medium. If you collect cards, there are over three hundred thousand new listings each week. In the same week, over fifty thousand auto-graphed items and hundreds of thousands of sporting goods are made available to the entire world. The diversity of goods, reliability of the community and service, and the enjoyment of the experience add up to make eBay a great place for sports fans. Again, the industry data says it all:

Online Activity at Work			vs.	Online Activity at Home		
Rank	Site	Unique Audience	# Hours	Site	Unique Audience	# Hours
1.	eBay	5,730,590	157	eBay	9,128,831	126
2.	Datek	623,912	120	Pogo	701,730	70
3.	Yahoo!	21,516,955	106	E Trade	1,951,736	69
4.	MSN	17,893,880	88	Rivals.com	600,598	67
5.	Schwab	904,626	86	Yahoo!	43,247,006	61

Source: Nielsen, Media Research and NetRatings, January 2000.

Regardless of the user being at home, or on the job, the fascination with eBay is undeniable.

The next frontier for eBay might be in terms of promotional part-nerships. Even though the company has been around for eight years and completely dominates the online auction and commerce space, it is still in its developmental stage.

In reality, eBay Sports is an emerging media property. It has more than sixty million registered users, and over one million items that, as the "sticky" statistics show, rhapsodizes its audience. It can now go out and leverage its reach and audience composition with both properties and sponsors. As sports merges with the online world, expect eBay to play a vital and useful role.

Now, to Make It Profitable

Old-time fans used to consume sports simply by going to the games, while the majority of the current crop of sports fans prefers to watch sports the new old-fashioned way, on TV. Online companies currently bet that fans will pay via subscriptions. Yahoo!, the leading portal service, had a $19.95 service for the 2002 World Cup that allowed fans to catch high-lights via their site.

Major League Baseball has also entered the online Webcast business. MLB.com Webcast a game without charge in August of 2002 and fol-lowed up with a subscription service offer of $9.95 per month, or $4.95 per game. Customers couldn't get every game, but were offered a diverse mix, plus archival access. The video portion of Webcasting presents larger problems than the audio version, for which Major League Baseball already has 150,000. Regardless of the various technological challenges, baseball knows the medium will soon be a significant place for the baseball fan to follow his favorite team.

As broadband and high-speed data transfer becomes better distributed, the battle between the online viewer model and traditional television broadcasting formula will begin. Given the fact that billions of dollars are at stake, feedback from the customer in the first decade of the twenty-first century will determine how sports entertainment is priced, packaged, and delivered to homes and fans around the globe soon. And as soon as the advertising industry specializes to qualify the online component of an audience, then the advertising revenues and rates will determine realistic profits of the medium.

Major League Baseball recently licensed its Web radio rights to Real-Networks (Microsoft's main competitor) for $20 million over three years. That is a small figure by normal broadcast standards, but it represents brand new dollars in a category that did not exist five years ago. The fact that it matured this quickly shows that there is potential for it to explode. As the online content providers convert their audiences to meaningful subscriptions and pay-for-viewing privileges, the value of the online medium will keep climbing. And at that point, it will time to write another book and detail how technology has transformed the cash flows of sports yet again. Until then, be assured that sports entertainment will continue to gravitate to the place where profit potential exists.

IN THEIR OWN WORDS: THE REACH OF SPORTS: JOE BARROW JR.

Much is made of role models and athletics. People attach enhanced significance to athletes because of their marvelous skills. Naturally, the hope is that their integrity, character, and conviction equals their speed, agility, and competitive zeal. Perhaps the fault lies in the fan, who invests so much in the relationship and immerses his or her identity into the image of the player, team, or sport.

In the debate over role models and hero worship, one fact goes unquestioned: participating in sports teaches youths about life, discipline, and making healthy choices. One such program, The First Tee, teaches life skills and golf skill in communities across America. Run by executive director, Joe Louis Barrow Jr., the son of ex-heavyweight champion, Joe Louis, the program goes about changing the lives of kids without the hype, flash, and glitter of TV, entourages, and materialistic trappings. Barrow discusses the goals and objectives of the organization, and how The First Tee will reach youths across America through golf.[16]

Background

"The First Tee set numeric objectives at its outset. Specifically, we wanted to reach 500,000 kids by 2005. Additionally, we also wanted to have 500 affiliate relationships and 250 dedicated facilities, where a 'dedicated' facility is defined as one that is a financially independent, free-standing place.

"The First Tee brings two things to a community. First and foremost, we improve the asset of the land. After we identify a site and build a facility, it raises the value of public resources with private capital, from one to two million each facility. Prior to The First Tee, a community might have a large tract of land performing no service, or providing any function to the community. But, if we can find the right space and the right terms, we can build a beautiful asset that enhances the city and its resources. The second point is that the priorities for the site utilization is for use by kids. This is not just a golfing destination. We emphasize helping kids through golf with lessons in learning life skills.

"We have 5 Regional Development Directors who go out and work with individuals and organizations that want to bring The First Tee into their communities. They form a Board of Directors and work with public officials to get the actual space that we need. And getting land speaks to the 'Tiger effect,' as city officials see that golf can make a difference and that kids can now identify with an activity that used to be the exclusive domain of adult males.

"While The First Tee teaches grip, stance, and posture, we also help kids set goals, feel self-confident, and make decisions that they will be proud of. Golf serves as a great introduction to life skills since it is a sport that requires patience, persistence, honesty, and integrity. If you can reinforce those attributes via a sport, then teaching life skills becomes transferable. Through learning golf, the kids have a representative, tangible example that they can reference in other educational or work pursuits.

"We just had our fifth anniversary, and we estimate that the financial impact of The First Tee has resulted in $115 million in capital investments, excluding the value of land. Our programs have $29 million in annual operating expenses, over 1,000 employees and 1,200 volunteers. We can't get complacent as we still have a long way to go before we can begin to feel satisfied.

"To build such an ambitious program over so much territory, we put program benchmarks into place. Over time, we developed the necessary experience to estimate what it will cost to turn 50 acres into a facility. But our focus reinforces the guidelines and disciplines that go into our youth instruction. These come through a program developed with outside consultants and representatives from the PGA and LPGA. We have modules that help kids learn about discipline and self-assessment. To make sure that things don't deviate, we teach both instructors and kids the life-skills curriculum.

"Our modules are called Par, Birdie, and Eagle. Our hope is to bring a kid into this and ultimately turn that child into a role model or mentor. We have helped kids get into college and even provided scholarships. Three words are essential to our network's mission: 'educate, cooperate, and communicate.' If we can maintain consistency in our program and remain true to the goals of the program, we can continue to develop mentors and help people realize their dreams through education and good choices."

Success Leads to Sponsorship

"When we approach a potential site partner, we seek 15- to 20-year lease agreements. We shy away from anything less than this because we need time to make our goals come to fruition. We plan to be around for a long time and we won't put ourselves in a situation where we fail because we did not have enough time in the community. One of the byproducts of having roots in multiple communities is that it gives us the necessary scale in order to seek corporate support. Price Waterhouse Coopers, eBay, and Coca-Cola are all involved with us. Price Waterhouse has recently run some television ads in addition to furnishing services for us.

"Companies are beginning to look at us because we provide a national dimension that they can relate to. There are great junior golf programs around the country, but The First Tee is different in its scope. And we have hit all of our goals, actually exceeding them. This impresses businesses, and it means that we are relevant to their marketing people because we represent so many places. Golf has impacted these execs so we don't have to explain 'why golf.' They already appreciate the game of golf. Our goal is to get them to assist us in implementing our program nationally.

"Furthermore, business leaders also know the organizations that support us: The PGA, LPGA, USGA, and Augusta National. We offer many things, mainly a chance to impact, partner and develop programs that will influence youths for the rest of their lives. And that means that The First Tee is not just a charity. By teaching both life skills and the game of golf, we are helping develop people who will one day work for these companies, buy their products, invest in them through the stock market. The game of golf is the carrot we dangle, but the kids want to learn about life, too."

Future

"Looking into future, we want to provide scholarships for some kids. We already have $1.2 million in scholarships committed to our program, and that will allow us to fulfill greater expectations of those who go through our program. We are just about to name a scholarship advisory committee, and that means The First Tee works and that our strategy to build deliberately and with standards makes sense for communities and kids. It is a lot of work that demands a significant commitment from everyone involved. By having guidelines, standards, and capable teachers, we can accomplish our objectives.

"Our challenge is to manage the opportunities without getting diverted. Every chapter is independent, a franchise-type situation. Given that, our major challenge is looking to the consistency of the experience. With 115 facilities, we need the experiences to be consistent and have the discipline so that the new 30 are run well.

"If there is an evolution gap, our challenge is to make sure that they are up to speed from the start and that everyone knows that our mission is to teach life skills in a fun and healthy environment. By staying focused on our goals, The First Tee will make a difference in all of its communities."

NOTES

1. Peter Gammons, "Schuerholz Says Braves Will Rebuild, Not Reload," ESPN [online], espn.com [January 10, 2002].

2. Phil Schaaf, *Sports Marketing: It's Not Just a Game Anymore* (Amherst, N.Y.: Prometheus Books, 1995), p. 19.

3. Rob Grady, personal interview, January 10, 2003.

4. Mike Finn, personal interview, January 10, 2003.

5. Rob Grady, personal interview, January 10, 2003.

6. Ibid.

7. Carolyn Said, "The Battle of the Bars," *Chronicle*, April 27, 2003, pp. 14–16.

8. Tiffany Montgomery, "Surfing Brands Enjoy a Swell in Popularity," *Orange County Register*, November 21, 2002.

9. This is not to suggest that all, or any, sports developments are environmentally irresponsible, but they do not pursue the lofty standards that the OSP developers set for themselves.

10. In January 1903, the first wireless message was transmitted directly from the United States to England. Marconi ultimately won the Nobel Prize in 1909 for his work. Contemporary scientists had once doubted Marconi, an Italian engineer, for his belief that wireless transmission could take place. His invention ultimately revolutionized the world's communication systems.

11. A total of $75 million in sports ticket sales were sold between June 2001 and June 2002. The 41.4 million figure represents the fifty-two week average.

12. Greg Fant, personal interview, December 10, 2002.

13. Ibid.

14. Callaway Golf Pre-Owned is an agreement between Callaway Golf Sales Company and Tadpole Golf Corp. "Callaway Golf Pre-Owned" is officially endorsed by Callaway Golf Company, but Tadpole Golf Corp. is not related to Callaway Golf and is not acting as an agent or a representative.

15. A total of $75 million in sports ticket sales were sold between June 2001 and June 2002. The 41.4 million figure represents the fifty-two week average.

16. Personal interview with the author, November 7, 2002.

JUST WHERE CAN I WATCH THE SUPERBOWL?

News wire services frequently report the number of countries where a game will be broadcast, or how many nations are represented at the Olympics. However, they never actually list the places. Here is a list of the places Super Bowl XXXVI aired. The reach means that the NFL has a relevant market, or promotional objective, in each country. Remarkable!

Countries broadcasting Super Bowl XXXVI

Abu Dhabi	Bahamas	
Algeria	Bahrain	Brazil
Andorra	Bangladesh	British Virgin Islands
Anguilla	Barbados	Brunei
Antigua & Barbuda	Basse-Terre	Bulgaria
Argentina	Belarus	Cambodia
Armenia	Belgium	Canada
Aruba	Belize	Cayenne
Australia	Bhutan	Cayman Islands
Austria	Bolivia	Chad
Azerbaijan	Bosnia	Chile
China	Dubai	Germany
Colombia	Ecuador	Greece
Costa Rica	Egypt	Grenada
Croatia	El Salvador	Guadeloupe

Cyprus	Estonia	Guatemala
Czech Republic	Fort de France	Guyana
Denmark	France	Haiti
Djibouti	French Guiana	Honduras
Dominica	French Polynesia	Hong Kong
Dominican Republic	Georgia	Hungary
Iceland	Korea	Macau
India	Kuwait	Macedonia
Indonesia	Kyrgystan	Malaysia
Ireland	Laos	Maldives
Israel	Latvia	Malta
Italy	Lebanon	Martinique
Jamaica	Libya	Mata-Ut
Japan	Liechtenstein	Mauritania
Jordan	Lithuania	Mauritius
Kazakhstan	Luxembourg	Mayotte
Mexico	Netherlands Antilles	Papeete
Moldova	Nevis	Papua New Guinea
Monaco	New Caledonia	Paraguay
Mongolia	New Zealand	Peru
Montenegro	Nicaragua	Philippines
Montserrat	Nouvelle de Ledonie	Poland
Morocco	Oman	Portugal
Myanmar	Pakistan	Puerto Rico
Nepal	Palestine	Qatar
Netherlands	Panama	Reunion
Romania	South Korea	St. Vincent & the Grenadines
Russia	Spain	Sudan
Saint Denis	Sri Lanka	Suriname
San Marino	St. Barthelemy	Sweden
Saudi Arabia	St. Christopher	Switzerland
Serbia	St. Kitts	Syria

Singapore	St. Lucia	Tahiti
Slovakia	St. Maarten	Taiwan
Slovenia	St. Pierre	Thailand
Somalia	St. Pierre et Miquelon	Trinidad & Tobago

Tunisia   Venezuela
Turkey   Vietnam
Turks & Caicos   Yemen
UK
Ukraine
United Arab Emirates
United States
Uruguay
Uzbekistan
Vatican City

Source: Sportsline.com, January 31, 2002

APPENDIX B

ONE FINAL LIST

There are so many lists in sports of the greatest everything that even the list of all those lists is too long. You can find the list of the greatest players, best teams, and most memorable moments, but not too many lists like this one. Here, in alphabetical order, is an arbitrary list of ten indispensable figures from the business of sports since 1896.

ROONE ARLEDGE

Roone Arledge realized earlier than most that TV and sports were destined to be a tremendous match. Not only did he foresee the development, he was instrumental in making it happen. The brain behind *Monday Night Football*, his legacy still touches sports programming today. Arledge pioneered the use of slow motion, the replay, and the whole concept of sports as a prime-time pastime. He had an eye for the business angle as well, making events enjoyable for those at home and profitable for the networks. One of his ideas was to hold back advertising spots during the 1976 Olympics and use them to promote ABC programming. ABC soon after became the number one network. A visionary who had the nerve to get things done, Arledge is one of those individuals who was the right person at the right time—and we still benefit from his work today. Sadly, Arledge passed on in 2002, but his legacy lives on in each and every sports broadcast.

GUSSIE BUSCH

For anyone that has ever attended or watched a sporting event, you have likely seen very visible evidence of Gussie's company, Anheuser-Busch. Busch owned the St. Louis Cardinals and helped navigate a Missouri beer company to the top position in two industries: beer manufacturing and sports marketing. Busch not only worked the back channels of baseball to feature Budweiser in every possible major league facility, but he created an environment within his company that looked at sports as an opportunity to promote Anheuser-Busch and its family of products. The company, year after year, consistently invests more money into the sports industry than any other company and consistently gets the best results. There is not one team, one event, or one sales person who does not try to do business with Anheuser-Busch. And there are few places where the beer giant hasn't sponsored an event. Their commitment to sports began with Gussie and his vision of using sports to enhance brand exposure and, more important, actual sales.

GEORGE HALAS

The NFL today is a juggernaut that rules the airwaves and the public's consciousness on Sundays in the fall and winter. The Super Bowl is the biggest television event annually, and the third largest eating day of the year, too. During all of those extravagant halftime shows and endless analysis shows, it is hard to remember that the NFL really got its start in a car showroom in 1922. And George Halas was there.

The NFL is the ultimate "rags to riches" story in every sense of the word. Football had many obstacles in its early days, from inclement weather to demanding logistics. But the league met its early challenges and persisted. Patient, smart men gave the sport a chance through innovative management and effective leadership. George Halas was a man like that. He had the smarts to move his team from Decatur to Chicago, sign the hottest property, Red Grange, and immediately take him on a national barnstorming tour to spread the popularity of football. Halas's work built the framework for a league in what eventually became the most popular sport in America. He was at the NFL's first organizational meeting, coached the Bears for forty years, and literally created the prototype administration. He was the MVP in the 1919 Rose Bowl, too.

JEAN CLAUDE KILLY

Americans tend to overlook the international scene when it comes to compiling lists, but Jean Claude Killy is no token addition. He is a sports marketing tour de force, and has been a tremendous influence to the business of sports. Killy is the role model for the athlete turned businessman. He won three gold medals at the 1968 Grenoble Games and instantly became a national hero in France. Killy had a keen eye, though, for more than the bumps and turns. He became an accomplished entrepreneur, running his own clothing empire and ultimately shepherding the 1992 Olympics to Albertville. Killy chairs the Amaury Sport Organization, the supervising organization for both the Tour de France and the Paris-Dakar motor race. He is also a member of the IOC. A success on the slopes and in international boardrooms, he has had an inspiring business career in disciplines ranging from management to marketing. His athletic career is surpassed by few competitors. In business, the same sentiment holds true.

JOE LOUIS

Louis had a huge impact on the business of sports and the integration of athletics. Here is a short list of his accomplishments:

He was the first African American athlete successfully marketed to the mass market in the United States.

He was a national hero who galvanized the nation's pride in a period of great doubt when he fought Max Schmeling.

He was the first African American athlete to endorse products nationally and be a marquee performer.

He was one of the first athletes to be featured on sponsored television and radio performances (the very first featured on an international radio broadcast).

He was a war hero who raised hundreds of thousands of dollars via
exhibitions for the Allied war effort.
He walked easily among presidents, dignitaries, and common men.

Joe Louis's first professional fight was against Jack Kracken on
Chicago's South Side on July 4, 1934. The fight lasted less than two minutes and Louis made fifty-nine dollars. At the age of twenty, after his first
pro fight, Louis earned more than he had in the best week when he
worked for the Ford Motor Company in Detroit. For his 1938 rematch
with Max Schmeling, Louis earned $351,622, a nice raise.

Louis had become the biggest draw in boxing, despite being a
minority in a time of segregation and pandemic injustice for people of
color in the United States. People say it was Louis's quiet, humble
demeanor that allowed him to be embraced by white America. Others
cite the fact that the United States, wallowing in the Great Depression
and on the brink of war, needed a hero and were willing to accept Louis.
There might very well be truth to both of those arguments, but the fact
is that Joe Louis Barrow, the man who fought as simply Joe Louis, made
it because of his athletic greatness and mental toughness. If he couldn't
have mastered the sweet science, he would have been forced to live by
the cruel boundaries of segregation that doggedly pursued all African
Americans of his time. And he would have certainly done it in obscurity.

People have different definitions for the same words. Misunder-
standing about words like role model, hero, and accountability blur mass
culture. People get nostalgic for the old days when hero worship seemed
to be more simple, but the reality is that the "good old days" had plenty
of flaws.

The times may have never been more convoluted than in Depression-era America. The financial hangover from the indulgent 1920s crip-
pled the nation and the cultural compass was fixed on simple survival.
Racism and segregation were not issues to be debated; they were simply
a way of life. Into this mix came Joe Louis. Not only did he rise above his
modest background, he put the nation on his back and became its first
true hero.

In a November 7, 2002, interview with the author, Joe Louis Barrow
Jr., son of Joe Louis, had this to say about heroism in his father's time: "A

hero is someone who can challenge society and force people to think about things differently. Joe Louis challenged the consciousness of the nation. How could he represent the nation in the boxing ring, yet live in a segregated society? When he fought Schmeling, people had to deal with a black man standing up for the freedoms and democracy without enjoying those very freedoms in his own life. . . . Consequently, the political significance of fascism versus democracy, of Schmeling versus Louis, brought the troubling issues of our own society into focus."

Born in Alabama and raised in Detroit, Joe Louis succeeded as a black in the middle of the Great Depression. His son summed it up well: "Times were tough for everyone, and for Joe Louis to rise from obscurity and challenge Americans to think about their society, and to help it transition into a better one makes him an important hero." Well said.

MARK MCCORMACK

Before Jerry Maguire, there was Mark McCormack. He didn't need to tell potential sponsors, "show me the money!" because they had already handed it over to him. From a macro and micro perspective, his firm, IMG, grew to be the biggest and best event management and athlete representation group in the world. At the time of his passing in 2003, IMG had moved beyond strictly sports marketing to include many forms of entertainment and enterprise.

McCormack might not have been the first person to recognize that sports, fans, and companies were on a collision course, but he was the first person to really do something about it. A college golfer, he went after Arnold Palmer and convinced him that he should be his agent in 1960, with only a handshake agreement. The rest, as they say, is history. McCormack also secured Jack Nicklaus and Gary Player. Together they were known as "The Big Three" and they helped McCormack become the most significant sports marketing business figure of modern times.

McCormack took the notion that executives, their minions, and end user customers would all like to identify with athletes and the competition. Not only was he right, but IMG made the process of endorsements, entitlement, merchandising, broadcasting, and long-term collaboration an endogenous part of all athletic competition. Like Galileo following Copernicus, no one negotiates a deal, sells a ticket, or prospects for a sponsor without doing something that Mark McCormack did first.

MARVIN MILLER

Marvin Miller might be the most influential person in the baseball industry who never had a jersey and locker. Hired in 1966 to lead the Player's Association, Miller galvanized the union behind him and won for them the rights that they had been denied by their employers and the federal government. His tenure did involve several work stoppages, but he neutered the grip of the Reserve Clause, created an effective form of free agency, implemented an effective pension plan, and enfranchised the players in their careers.

Miller had everything against him, but still won virtually every reasonable right for his membership. Some say that the results of his work helped manifest the greatest spurt in baseball's growth in terms of fan interest and attendance. The players loved him and the owners . . . well, they didn't agree with the players. But Miller undeniably set the standard for union leadership in the sports industry. When Miller took the job in 1966, the average major league salary was $19,000 annually and there was no mobility. In 2002 players, through the right of mobility, earned an average of $2.295 million.

BRANCH RICKEY/JACKIE ROBINSON

Jackie Robinson walked perhaps the toughest path of any athlete in the history of the world. Branch Rickey navigated the troubling waters of prejudice to help Robinson integrate baseball. They will be forever linked together, and deservedly so.

Much has been written about Robinson and Rickey, but none of it could truly capture the feeling of the times. Think back to what it must have been like to be so bold in the face of such ignorance. The easiest thing would have been to wait for the other guy to do it, and quietly say that "it just isn't done."

Yes, there have been many other athletes who have been subjected to the senseless ignorance of racism, like Larry Doby, Hank Greenberg, Jack Johnson, Jesse Owens, Hank Aaron, and others. But no one bore the burden that Robinson managed.

Jackie Robinson became the symbol for integration, the painful attempts at equality in the anachronism of American society. And he did it while having to keep his mouth shut. Try playing with that as a backdrop to your at bats, attempted steals, and put outs.

Today, Robinson would earn well over $10 million per year and have shoe contracts and endorsements galore. And his team could market his accomplishments as a ballplayer, not hope that his race wouldn't keep fans away from the park. Lost in the mix of politics, social change, and symbolism is the fact the he was a great player as well; a truly special talent who played the game as well as anyone of his era. Robinson proved he belonged and he paved the way for other minorities to follow.

And it all started with Branch Rickey. As general manager of the Dodger's, he gave Jackie Robinson his chance and he did not do it for symbolism, either. Rickey quickly recruited other African Americans like Don Newcombe and Roy Campanella to help his team win. In the end, Rickey showed that he was a great judge of talent and character.

PETE ROZELLE

Pete Rozelle was a Los Angeles Rams public relations executive when he got the NFL's top job as commissioner. He was not groomed for the position, nor significantly popular when elected. At the time, professional football had just established itself as a stable major sport. By the time Rozelle stepped down from the top post, it had risen to the unquestioned pinnacle of America's sports ladder, where it remains today.

Rozelle manned the ship through the merger with the AFL, the birth of the Super Bowl, and the long-term marriage with television through his work on Congress's Sports Broadcast Bill in 1961. He also helped start the Properties Division and laid out the road map that the league follows to this day. Maybe most telling, he represented his employers, the team owners, quite well. The value of the Dallas Cowboys in 1960, his first year as commissioner, was $1 million. Some say the franchise might be worth close to $1 billion today if sold on the open market. Rozelle's work laid the foundation for league revenues that top $4 billion annually.

BILL VEECK

Whenever people refer to Bill Veeck, they feel compelled to describe him as a maverick or promoter extraordinaire. Veeck was all of that and much more. He had more in common with the people in the stands than he did with his fellow owners. His famous promotions, like employing midget Eddie Gaedel, will forever put him in the annals of baseball lore. But from a business standpoint, he knew that fans were precious customers and he wanted the emphasis to be on entertainment. He would never tolerate aloofness from his players or staff. He was a risk taker within the confines of the sport for the fans' amusement and he left the game a much better place.

Veeck was not afraid to be a great American, either, even if it meant choosing sides. He never viewed himself as one of the elite. He also believed passionately in civil rights, and was a proud war veteran. Veeck never lost sight of the importance of an employee or the value of a customer, a business philosophy that will never go out of style.

A LEAGUE OF HIS OWN: MUHAMMAD ALI

He blended politics, religion, civil rights, humor, promotion, business, and global popularity unlike any other person in the history of sports. A man without peer, he is an extraordinary list unto himself.

INDEX